Advanced BASIC and Beyond
for the IBM PC

Larry Joel Goldstein, PhD
University of Maryland
College Park, MD

Robert J. Brady Co.
A Prentice-Hall Publishing and Communications Company
Bowie, MD 20715

Executive Editor: David Culverwell
Production Editor: Paula Huber
Text Designer: Michael Rogers
Art Director/Cover Design: Don Sellers
Assistant Art Director: Bernard Vervin
Photography: George Dodson

Typesetter: Alexander Typesetting, Indianapolis, IN
Printer: R. R. Donnelley and Sons Company, Harrisonburg, VA
Typefaces: Palatino (text), Folio (display), OCR-B (programs)

Advanced BASIC and Beyond: Techniques for the IBM PC

Library of Congress Cataloging in Publication Data

Goldstein, Larry Joel.
    Advanced BASIC and beyond for the IBM PC.

    Includes index.
    1. IBM Personal Computer—Programming. 2. Basic
(Computer program language) I. Title.
QA76.8.I2594G637   1983   001.64'2   83-15725
ISBN   0-89303-324-3

Prentice-Hall International, Inc., London
Prentice-Hall Canada, Inc., Scarborough, Ontario
Prentice-Hall of Australia, Pty., Ltd., Sydney
Prentice-Hall of India Private Limited, New Delhi
Prentice-Hall of Japan, Inc., Tokyo
Prentice-Hall of Southeast Asia Pte. Ltd., Singapore
Whitehall Books, Limited, Petone, New Zealand
Editora Prentice-Hall Do Brasil LTDA., Rio de Janeiro

Printed in the United States of America

84 85 86 87 88 89 90 91 92 93   10 9 8 7 6 5 4 3 2

Contents

1. **Introduction**   **1**

    1.1   The Purpose of This Book   1
    1.2   An Overview of This Book   1
    1.3   Prerequisites   2

2. **Planning and Developing Large Programs**   **5**

    2.1   Planning THE BAR CHART GENERATOR   5

3. **Introduction to Graphics and Sound on the PC**   **9**

    3.1   Line Graphics   9
    3.2   Drawing Bar Charts in Text Mode (For All PC Owners)   18
    3.3   Colors and Graphics Modes   24
    3.4   Lines, Rectangles, and Circles   30
    3.5   Computer Art   41
    3.6   Drawing Pie Charts   44
    3.7   PAINT and DRAW   47
    3.8   Saving and Recalling Graphics Images   58
    3.9   VIEW and WINDOW   62
    3.10   Bar Charts—A Case Study, I   67
    3.11   Sound and Music on the PC   71

4. **Input the Professional Way**   **77**

    4.1   Why You Need an Input Routine   77
    4.2   The INKEY$ Variable   78
    4.3   The Function Keys and Event Trapping   80
    4.4   Extended ASCII Codes   86
    4.5   Inputting Characters   91
    4.6   Inputting Strings and Numbers   96
    4.7   Bar Charts—A Case Study, II   103

5. **Your Computer As A File Cabinet**   **111**

    5.1   What Are Files?   111
    5.2   Sequential Files   112
    5.3   More About Sequential Files   120
    5.4   Random Access Files   124
    5.5   An Application of Random Access Files   131
    5.6   Sorting Techniques   138
    5.7   BASIC File Commands   145

6.   Memory Management on the PC   **149**

    6.1   Binary and Hexadecimal Numbers   149
    6.2   Bits, Bytes, and Memory   155
    6.3   How is Data Stored in Memory?   162
    6.4   Operations on Bytes   166
    6.5   Some Applications of Byte Operations   170
    6.6   Further Graphics Tricks (BASIC 2.00 Only)   180
    6.7   Plotting Characters in Graphics Mode   183
    6.8   Bar Charts—A Case Study, III   186
    6.9   Extending the PC's Character Set   191

    Appendix A—Some Useful Memory Locations   192
    Appendix B—How BASIC Stores Single- and
      Double-Precision Numbers   192

7.   The BAR CHART GENERATOR—A Case Study   **199**

    7.1   The Initialization and Control Routines   199
    7.2   Error Trapping   203
    7.3   The BAR CHART GENERATOR   205
    7.4   Further Tips for Planning Large Programs   224

8.   The IBM/EPSON Printer   **227**

    8.1   Printer Fundamentals   227
    8.2   Printer Command Sequences   232
    8.3   Printer Graphics   236
    8.4   A Graphics Screen Dump   243
    8.5   Back to Our Case Study   247

9.   Computer Communications   **249**

    9.1   Fundamentals of Computer Communications   249
    9.2   Communications Files   253
    9.3   Trapping Communications   263

10. Using Your PC with Other Devices   **267**

    10.1 Using a Light Pen   267
    10.2 Using a Joystick   271
    10.3 Using a Plotter   277

11. The BASIC Compiler   **281**

    11.1 Why Compile Programs?   281
    11.2 Compiling a Program   282
    11.3 Compiler Parameters   294
    11.4 Differences Between the Compiler and the Interpreter   295

11.5 Compilation Errors   296
11.6 Back to the Case Study Once Again   297

12. Assembly Language Subroutines in BASIC   299

12.1 The 8088 Microprocessor   299
12.2 Why Use Assembly Language Subroutines?   301
12.3 Calling a Machine Language Subroutine   303
12.4 Writing a Machine Language Subroutine   305
12.5 Using the Assembler   308
12.6 Placing Your Subroutine into Memory   311
12.7 Some Final Observations   316

13. Some Features of DOS 2.00   317

13.1 Paths, Directories, and Subdirectories   317
13.2 A Survey of Changes in DOS 2.00   324
13.3 New Commands in DOS 2.00   328
13.4 Enhanced Batch File Capability   334
13.5 Redirecting Input and Output   341
13.6 BASIC 2.00   343

Answers to Selected Exercises   345

Index   353

Documentation for Optional Program Diskette   359

Note to Authors

Do you have a manuscript or a software program related to personal computers? Do you have an idea for developing such a project? If so, we would like to hear from you. The Brady Co. produces a complete range of books and applications software for the personal computer market. We invite you to write to David Culverwell, Editor-in-Chief, Robert J. Brady Co., Bowie, Maryland 20715.

Preface

If you are already familiar with the elementary portions of IBM PC BASIC and wish to learn about its "advanced features," then this book is for you. In this book, we bridge the gap between elementary books on BASIC and the advanced books on, say, communications or assembly language programming. By the end of this book, you will be in command of all aspects of PC BASIC.

A unique feature of this book is its case study. We guide you through the construction of a large case-study program, which incorporates graphics, man-machine interface, data input and verification, and file usage. Discussion of this program is interwoven throughout the book, beginning with a discussion of program planning in Chapter 2. You will see how to build programs that go beyond textbook exercises. Moreover, we suggest various extensions of our case study for you to try.

Here are the topics we discuss: planning large programs, graphics, professional input routines, files, binary and hexadecimal arithmetic, memory management, custom character sets, printer graphics, communications, joysticks, light pens, the BASIC compiler, machine language subroutines in BASIC, BASIC 2.00, and DOS 2.00.

The book contains many interesting and useful programs. Especially useful are the professional style input subroutines that you may use in your own programs.

To make this book a genuine teaching tool, Test Your Understanding questions are included at strategic points in the discussion. Answers to these questions are at the end of each section.

I wish to thank the reviewers for their many valuable suggestions over several drafts. Thanks to the staff of the Robert J. Brady Company for the fine way in which they produce and distribute my computer books. Special thanks to Paula Huber for the efficient and accurate job of manuscript editing and to my friends Harry Gaines, President, and David Culverwell, Editor in Chief, for favors too numerous to mention.

Larry Joel Goldstein
October 5, 1983

1

Introduction

1.1 The Purpose of This Book

Many of my friends, family members, and students have learned BASIC programming on the IBM PC, using one of the numerous fine texts for novices.

After completing such a text, they usually ask me: What do I read next? How can I learn more about BASIC programming on the IBM PC? I understand their problem. BASIC on the IBM PC is an incredibly rich langauge. It is unreasonable to expect a single book to cover all that there is to know. After all, PC BASIC contains more than 150 commands, statements and functions! The books available seem to concentrate on the more elementary half of BASIC. So there wasn't a source I could recommend.

After thinking about the gaps in the literature for more than a year, I decided to write this book. My intention is to discuss all of the "advanced" aspects of BASIC programming, as well as some of the tricks you can use to make BASIC do clever things.

In talking with my friends and students, I gradually came to realize that all the various elementary books on BASIC had an additional serious gap: they were devoted almost exclusively to the syntax of the various BASIC statements and commands. However, they included almost no discussion of planning and developing reasonably complex programs. Accordingly, I decided to make the subject of program planning and development one of the major themes of this book.

There is no substitute for "hands-on" experience. So I decided to teach program planning and development using a case study, in which we will build a program called THE BAR CHART GENERATOR. This program is long, reasonably complex, and will motivate us to develop a number of routines that you will find useful in your programming.

1.2 An Overview of This Book

In Chapter 2, we develop the requirements for THE BAR CHART GENERATOR and identify the major routines required. Then we turn to our study of "advanced BASIC". In the course of our discussions, we develop ideas that

1

are useful for THE BAR CHART GENERATOR. As we encounter these ideas, we build the various required routines. By the time we reach Chapter 7, we are ready to assemble the routines into a program.

The case study is a theme that is interwoven throughout the book. However, not every section relates to the case study. For example, Chapter 3 is a self-contained discussion of graphics and sound on the PC. However, it is not until the end of the chapter that the case study comes into play.

Chapter 4 is a detailed discussion of professional style input. We'll learn how professional programmers perform input in a "bullet-proof" way. We'll even build professional style input routines that you may use in your own programs.

Most programs make use of the file capabilities of the PC. So in Chapter 5, we discuss files, both sequential and random access. We will build a list manager as an application and discuss several sorting algorithms.

In order to build THE BAR CHART GENERATOR, we will need to know something about binary and hexadecimal arithmetic. We'll learn what we need to know in Chapter 6. We will then discuss the internal organization of RAM, memory addresses, designing alternate character sets, and many other interesting topics.

In Chapter 7, we collect the various program fragments of the BAR CHART GENERATOR and assemble them into a working program. Chapter 8 discusses the fine points of the IBM/EPSON printers. We apply our knowledge of binary numbers and the printer graphics commands to program a graphics screen print subroutine.

In Chapter 9, we learn to use the RS232-C interface to effect computer communications. To illustrate these commands, we will build a communications program to allow two IBM Personal Computers to communicate with one another.

Chapter 10 is devoted to a discussion of joysticks, light pens and plotters, as used with PC BASIC.

In Chapter 11, you'll meet the BASIC Compiler. If you are going to get serious about BASIC, you will eventually want to compile your programs to achieve the additional speed afforded by machine language.

In Chapter 12 we show how to use machine language subroutines in BASIC. This chapter provides a springboard for you to start studying assembly language programming.

Throughout the book, the enhancements to BASIC afforded by version 2.00 are discussed, especially the changes in LINE and PAINT, and the new statements VIEW and WINDOW. However, we avoid DOS 2.00 until Chapter 13, where we give a full-blown treatment.

My goal for this book plus its predecessor has been to tell the whole story of BASIC on the IBM PC. I think that it's an exciting tale to tell and hope you will agree.

1.3   Prerequisites

I assume that you are already acquainted with the rudiments of programming in IBM PC BASIC, as covered, say, in the book *IBM PC—Programming and Applications* by Larry Joel Goldstein and Martin Goldstein, Robert Brady Company, 1982.

In what follows, we will cite this book as [GG].

More specifically, I assume that you know about DOS (version 1.1) and elementary BASIC (version 1.1) on the IBM PC, including the following:

DOS 1.1 Commands

CHKDSK	ERASE
COMP	FORMAT
COPY	MODE
DATE	RENAME
DIR	SYS
DISKCOMP	TIME
DISKCOPY	TYPE

BASIC 1.1 Statements, Functions, and Commands

ABS	INSTR	REM
ASC	INT	RENUM
ATN	KILL	RESTORE
AUTO	LEFT$	RIGHT$
CHAIN	LEN	RND
CHR$	LET	RUN
CLEAR	LINE INPUT	SAVE
CLOSE	LIST	SGN
CLS	LLIST	SIN
CONT	LOAD	SPACE$
COS	LOCATE	SPC
DATA	LOG	SQR
DATE$	LPRINT	STOP
DEF FN	LPRINT USING	STR$
DEFtype	MERGE	SWAP
DELETE	MID$	SYSTEM
DIM	NAME	TAB
EDIT	NEW	TAN
END	ON...GOSUB	TIME$
EXP	ON...GOTO	TRON
FIX	OPTION BASE	TROFF
FOR...NEXT	PRINT	VAL
GOSUB...RETURN	PRINT USING	WHILE...WEND
GOTO	RANDOMIZE	WIDTH
IF	READ	WRITE
INPUT		

If you have forgotten (or never knew) about some of these statements, consult the appropriate IBM manual (*DOS* or *BASIC REFERENCE MANUAL*) or an elementary book on PC BASIC, such as [GG].

2

Planning and Developing Large Programs

In elementary books on BASIC programming, you learn the syntax of the most rudimentary BASIC statements and how to combine such statements into programs. However, the illustrative programs in such books are usually short and their logic fairly simple. In this book, however, one of our main goals is to provide some tips on building larger programs. So before we discuss any BASIC statements at all, let's highlight this goal with an overview of THE BAR CHART GENERATOR, the case study to which we will return many times.

2.1 Planning THE BAR CHART GENERATOR

In developing a large scale program, careful attention to program design is essential. You must have a clear idea of what you want your program to do: What outputs will it produce? From what inputs?

One of the principal defects in BASIC is that it allows you to sit down and start writing a program without much thought or planning. (And I'll bet many of you thought that was an advantage!) You may be able to get away without planning if you are writing a small program. But as soon as the program requires the interplay of a number of different subroutines, producing differing outputs and affecting various program variables, program planning becomes a necessity.

Let's outline the planning process for THE BAR CHART GENERATOR.

Examine the graph in Figure 2.1. It is a typical bar chart. You should note the following features of the graph. The chart graphically depicts three sets of data, with one set of bars corresponding to each set of data. We distinguish among the different data sets by the shading of the bars.

The bars are set in a **coordinate system**, a rectangular box whose edges are labeled with information necessary to read the chart. The bottom horizontal edge of the coordinate system is called the **x-axis**. Just below this axis are labels that describe the various bars.

The vertical, left edge of the coordinate system is called the **y-axis** . Along the y-axis is a numerical scale which allows you to determine the numerical heights of the bars.

The x-axis and y-axis are labeled with titles, as is the entire graph. Note that the y-axis title is arranged vertically to the left of the scale, centered vertically on the coordinate system. The x-axis title is centered under the coordinate system, just below the x-axis labels. The chart title is centered above the coordinate system.

Each of the three sets of data has a title, displayed to the right of the coordinate system. To the left of each title is a square containing a sample of the shading type corresponding to the particular data set.

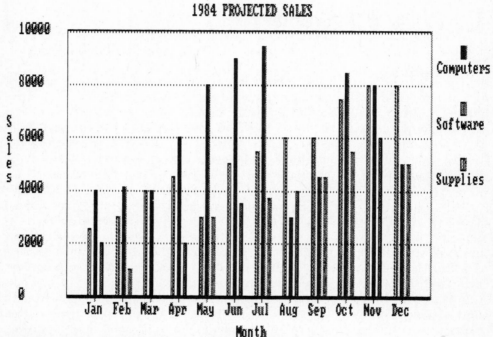

Figure 2.1. A Typical Bar Chart.

We have just taken a quick tour of a bar chart. Now we can state:
GOAL: Construct a program, called THE BAR CHART GENERATOR, which displays bar charts corresponding to user-supplied data.

Before we can achieve our goal, we will need to learn a great deal about programming. However, let's proceed with the first step in program development: Program Planning.

To plan our program, we begin by making a list of the specific functions that the program is to perform. This is our list of **program requirements**:

R1.   Draw bar charts on the screen.

R2.   Save on diskette the data corresponding to a bar chart so that it may be reproduced at a later date.

R3.   Recall bar chart data from diskette.

R4.   Read numerical data items from a diskette data file.

R5.   Edit bar chart data to make changes and corrections.

Once we have drawn up the above list of requirements, let's see what inputs our program will need. Examine Figure 2.1. Each visual element of the chart corresponds to an input:

I1.   Chart title

I2.   x- and y-axis titles

I3.   x- and y-axis labels

I4.   Bars

    a.   Provision for several sets of bars, reflecting different data series.

    b.   Bars of different data series need to be distinguished by different shading.

    c.   Each set of bars needs an identifying title.

In examining the above list, we ask: How many sets of bars should we allow? How many bars should we allow? Let's allow up to 3 sets of bars, with at most 20 bars per set. Using these numbers we can display all the data on a single screen. This will make the data entry portion of the program easier. In any case, these numbers are too generous. There is no way to fit 3 x 20 = 60 bars on the screen at once. The bars will overlap. However, there are applications where you want to display, say, 20 bars of a single series or 12 bars each of a set of 3 data series. And our numbers are large enough to accomodate these choices.

Now that we know what the program is to do and what inputs are required, let's think of how the program will work. And I don't mean that you should sit and start to code at this point. Rather, you should ask yourself how the user will use this program. Actually picture the user sitting down at the computer and ask yourself: What does he or she do to use this program? When I thought about this question, I pictured the user choosing from a menu of various actions, as displayed on a function key display. This leads us to define a sequence of actions that correspond to the function keys.

F1—Define bar chart parameters

F2—Enter x-axis labels and numerical data

F3—Draw the chart based on current data

F4—Save chart

F5—Recall chart

F6—Enter data from a data file

F7—Exit

At this point, we start to see the structure of the program emerging. There must be seven main routines, one corresponding to each of the seven function keys. Note that the requirement R5 (Editing capability) does not appear as a routine. As we'll see, it's easiest to build the editing directly into data entry routines, F1 and F2.

In addition to the seven basic routines, we will need a **control routine**, which allows us to choose from among the various functions by pressing the appropriate function key. Our program will need a number of arrays and many of the variables will require particular initial values. It is convenient to have a particular part of the program, called the **initialization**, handle all such definitions.

Based on our discussion, we may now sketch out our program:

```
100 'Initialization
900 'Control Routine
1000 'Define Bar Chart Parameters
2000 'Input Data
3000 'Draw Chart
4000 'Save Chart
5000 'Recall Chart
6000 'Read Data File
7000 'Exit
```

Well, there's the program plan! We've left plenty of room to fill in the various program lines. And, as we'll see, there are several other routines that are required by the seven fundamental routines. However, the above sketch will be our guide.

Let's now learn enough BASIC to construct the various routines called for in our plan.

3

Introduction to Graphics and Sound on the PC

To build THE BAR CHART GENERATOR, it will be necessary for us to study (among other things) the graphics and sound statements of PC BASIC. That's the purpose of this chapter.

3.1 Line Graphics

When you first start BASIC, the screen is in **text mode**. In text mode, the video display of the IBM Personal Computer is capable of displaying 25 rows of either 40 or 80 characters each. This gives us up to 25 X 80 or 2000 possible character positions. These various character positions divide the screen into small rectangles. Figure 3.1 shows the subdivision of the screen corresponding to an 80-character line width.

The rectangles into which we have divided the screen are arranged in rows and columns. We number the rows from 1 to 25, with row 1 at the top of the screen and row 25 at the bottom. The columns are numbered from 1 to 80, with column 1 at the extreme left and column 80 at the extreme right. Each rectangle on the screen is identified by a pair of numbers, indicating the row and column. For example, we have indicated the rectangle in the 12th row and 16th column in Figure 3.2.

We may print characters on the screen using the PRINT and PRINT USING instructions. For graphics purposes, it is important to be able to precisely position characters on the screen. This may be done using the **LOCATE** instruction. Remember that printing always occurs at the current cursor location. To locate the cursor at row x and column y, we use the instruction

```
100 LOCATE x,y
```

EXAMPLE 1.   Write a set of BASIC instructions to print the words "IBM Personal Computer" beginning at row 20, column 10.

9

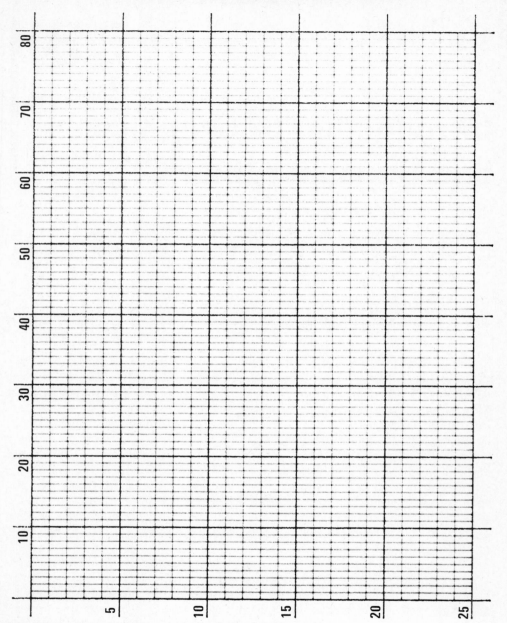

Figure 3.1. Screen Layout for Text Mode (80-character width).

SOLUTION.

```
10 LOCATE 20,10
20 PRINT "IBM Personal Computer"
```

Till now, we have printed only characters such as those found on a type-writer keyboard (letters, numbers, and punctuation marks). Actually, the IBM

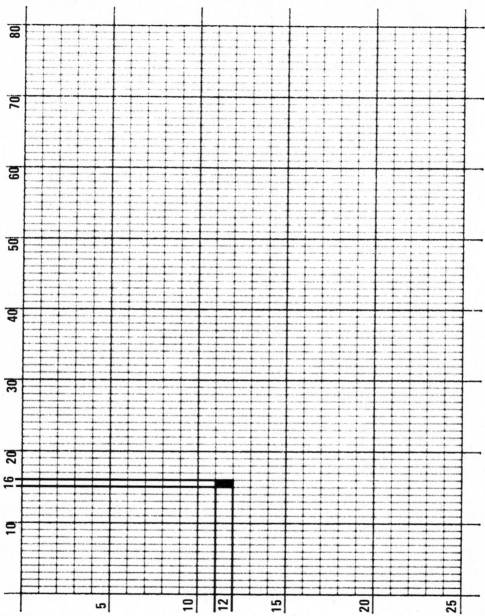

Figure 3.2.

Personal Computer has a very extensive set of characters, including a collection of graphics characters, as shown in Figure 3.3. Note that each graphics character is identified by a number. For example, character 179 is a vertical line. To place this character at the current cursor position, we use the instruction

```
30 PRINT CHR$(179)
```

ASCII Value	Character	ASCII Value	Character	ASCII Value	Character	ASCII Value	Character
128	Ç	166	ª	204	╠	242	≥
129	ü	167	º	205	═	243	≤
130	é	168	¿	206	╬	244	⌠
131	â	169	⌐	207	╧	245	⌡
132	ä	170	¬	208	╨	246	÷
133	à	171	½	209	╤	247	≈
134	å	172	¼	210	╥	248	°
135	ç	173	¡	211	╙	249	•
136	ê	174	«	212	╘	250	·
137	ë	175	»	213	╒	251	√
138	è	176	░	214	╓	252	ⁿ
139	ï	177	▒	215	╫	253	²
140	î	178	▓	216	╪	254	∎
141	ì	179	│	217	┘	255	(blank 'FF')
142	Ä	180	┤	218	┌		
143	Å	181	╡	219	█		
144	É	182	╢	220	▄		
145	æ	183	╖	221	▌		
146	Æ	184	╕	222	▐		
147	ô	185	╣	223	▀		
148	ö	186	║	224	α		
149	ò	187	╗	225	β		
150	û	188	╝	226	Γ		
151	ù	189	╜	227	π		
152	ÿ	190	╛	228	Σ		
153	Ö	191	┐	229	σ		
154	Ü	192	└	230	μ		
155	¢	193	┴	231	τ		
156	£	194	┬	232	Φ		
157	¥	195	├	233	θ		
158	Pt	196	─	234	Ω		
159	ƒ	197	┼	235	δ		
160	á	198	╞	236	∞		
161	í	199	╟	237	Ø		
162	ó	200	╚	238	ϵ		
163	ú	201	╔	239	∩		
164	ñ	202	╩	240	≡		
165	Ñ	203	╦	241	±		

Figure 3.3. IBM Personal Computer Graphics and Special Characters.

You may insert a graphics character into a program line by holding down the ALT key and entering the character number on the numeric keypad. This has the advantage that in a PRINT statement, you can see the character to be printed. For example, the above statement line would appear on the screen as

```
30 PRINT |
```

where the symbol | is entered from the keyboard by holding down ALT and typing 179. In what follows, we will use the CHR$ notation to make clear the code numbers of the various characters. However, in you own work, you should use the ALT key to indicate graphics characters.

TEST YOUR UNDERSTANDING 1 (answer on page 17)

Write a set of instructions to print graphics character 179 in row 18, column 22.

TEST YOUR UNDERSTANDING 2 (answer on pages 17, 18)

Write a program to display all 128 graphics characters on the screen.

We may use the graphics characters to build up various images on the screen, as the next example shows.

EXAMPLE 2.   Write a program that draws a horizontal line across row 10 of the screen. (Assume you have an 80-column screen.)

SOLUTION.   Just in case the screen contains some unrelated characters, begin by clearing the screen using the **CLS** instruction. Then print character 196 (a horizontal line) across row 10 of the screen. Here is the program.

```
10 CLS
20 LOCATE 10,1
30 FOR J=1 TO 80
40    PRINT CHR$(196);
50 NEXT J
60 END
```

Note that the semicolon in the **PRINT** statement causes the characters to be printed in consecutive positions. Lines 30-60 may be abbreviated using the STRING$ function. The function value STRING$(80,196) equals a string consisting of 80 copies of character 196. So lines 30-60 could be written more simply:

```
30 PRINT STRING$(80,196);
```

EXAMPLE 3.   Write a program that draws a vertical line in column 25 from row 5 to row 15. The program should blink the line 50 times.

SOLUTION.   The blinking effect may be achieved by repeatedly clearing the screen. Here is our program.

```
10 CLS
20 FOR K=1 TO 50:'K CONTROLS BLINKING
30    FOR J=5 TO 15
40          LOCATE J,25
50          PRINT CHR$(179);
60    NEXT J
70    CLS
80 NEXT K
```

TEST YOUR UNDERSTANDING 3 (answer on page 18)

Write a program to draw a vertical line from row 2 to row 20 in column 8.

EXAMPLE 4.   Draw a pair of x- and y- axes as shown in Figure 3.4. Label the vertical axis with the word 'Profit' and the horizontal axis with the word "Month." (Assume you have an 80-column screen.)

Profit

Month

Figure 3.4.

SOLUTION.   The program must draw two lines and print two words. The only real problem is to determine the positioning. The word "Profit" has six letters. Let's start the vertical line in the position corresponding to the seventh character column. We'll run the vertical line from the top of the screen (row 1) to within two character rows from the bottom. (On the next-to-last row, we will place the word "Month." We won't print in the last row, as this will cause some of the material printed above to scroll off the screen!) Here is our program to generate the display.

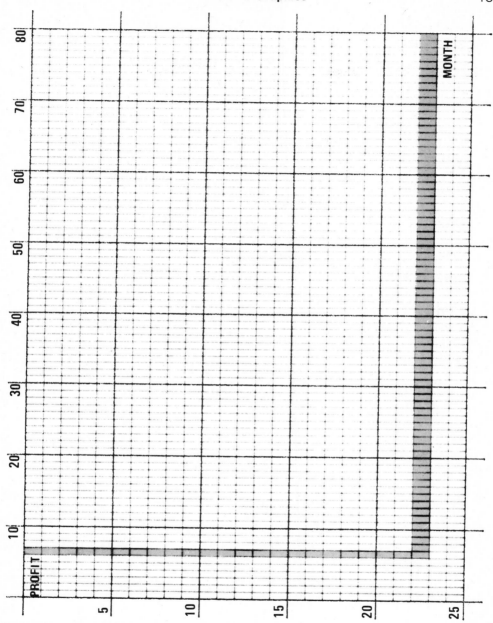

Figure 3.5. Display Layout for Chart of Figure 3.4.

```
10 CLS
20 LOCATE 1,1
25 PRINT "Profit"
30 LOCATE 23,75
35 PRINT "Month"
40 FOR J=1 TO 23
```

```
50  LOCATE J,7: PRINT CHR$(179);
60 NEXT J
65 LOCATE 22,7: PRINT CHR$(192);
70 FOR J=8 TO 80
80  LOCATE 22,J: PRINT CHR$(196);
90 NEXT J
100 GOTO 100
```

Note the infinite loop in line 100. This loop will keep the display on the screen indefinitely while the computer spins its wheels. To stop the program, press **Ctrl-Break**. To see the reason for the infinite loop, try running the program after deleting line 100. Note how the **Ok** interferes with the graphics. The infinite loop prevents the BASIC prompt from appearing on the screen.

Exercises (answers on page 345)

Draw the following straight lines.

1.   A horizontal line completely across the screen in row 18.

2.   A vertical line completely up and down the screen in column 17.

3.   A pair of straight lines that divide the screen into four equal squares.

4.   Horizontal and vertical lines that convert the screen into a tic-tac-toe board.

5.   A vertical line of double thickness from rows 1 to 24 in column 30.

6.   A diagonal line going through the character positions (1,1), (2,2), . . . (24,24).

7.   A horizontal line with "tick marks" as follows:

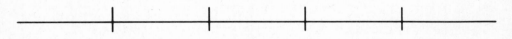

(Hint: Look for a graphics character that will form the tick marks.)

8.   A vertical line with tick marks as follows:

9. Display your name in a box formed with asterisks:

```
*****************
*    Your Name    *
*****************
```

10. Display a number axis as follows:

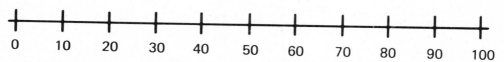

```
0   10   20   30   40   50   60   70   80   90   100
```

11. Write a program to display a graphics character that you specify in an **INPUT** statement.

12. Create a display of the following form:

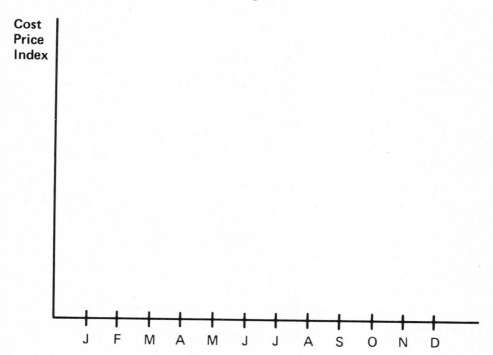

Cost
Price
Index

J F M A M J J A S O N D

ANSWERS TO TEST YOUR UNDERSTANDING

```
1:  10 LOCATE 18,22
    20 PRINT CHR$(179)

2:  10 FOR J=176 TO 223
    20    PRINT CHR$(J); " "; :' ONE SPACE BETWEEN CHARS
```

```
    30 NEXT J
    40 END
3:  10 CLS
    20 FOR J=2 TO 20
    30    LOCATE J,8: PRINT CHR$(179);
    40 NEXT J
    50 END
```

3.2 Drawing Bar Charts in Text Mode (For All PC Owners)

Consider the chart of Figure 3.6. It illustrates the monthly profits of a business. Each month's profits are represented by a vertical bar. The height of the bar is determined by the amount of profit for the month. Such a chart is called a **bar chart**. It is common to construct bar charts in business reports to illustrate trends in various statistics. In this section, we will show you how to use the IBM Personal Computer to construct bar charts from given data.

In the preceding section, we showed you how to construct the horizontal and vertical axes of a bar chart. Let us now construct the bars. In order to be specific, let's draw the bar chart given in Figure 3.6. In the following analysis, we will proceed manually for most of the computations. In the exercises, we'll enhance our program by letting the computer do most of the calculations.

The bar chart of Figure 3.6 has 12 bars corresponding to the 12 months of the year. Let's make each bar one column thick. The screen is 80 columns wide. Let's reserve the first 8 columns on the left for the word "Profit," the vertical axis, and the tick marks. Leave 12 columns on the right as a border. This leaves 60 columns for the bars. (Note that 60 is a multiple of 12. This is good planning!) Each bar should be centered in a field of 5 columns. After a moment's calculation, we see that the first bar should be in column 13. The next bar should be in column 18, the next in column 23, and so forth.

TEST YOUR UNDERSTANDING 1 (answer on page 24)

Suppose that the bar chart above contained only 8 bars and that the axes are to be positioned as above. In what column would the first bar appear?

For the vertical spacing, let's place the horizontal axis in row 22. This leaves us some space for month indicators. The bars will go immediately above the line, beginning in row 21. The chart in Figure 3.6 indicates profits from $100,000 to $1,000,000 on the scale of the vertical axis. There are 10 tick marks on the vertical axis, so let's make each tick mark correspond to

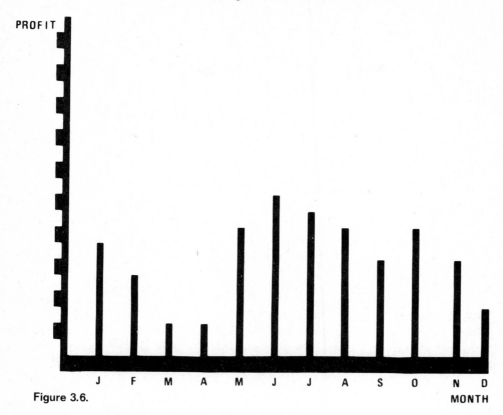

Figure 3.6.

two vertical graphics blocks. The tick marks will be placed in rows 20 (=$100,000), 18 (=$200,000), . . . , 2 (=$1,000,000). Our display design is indicated on the video display worksheet in Figure 3.7.

Let's now design a program to create the display. Our program will consist of three parts: draw the axes; display the text; and draw the bars. First, let's concentrate on drawing the bars.

To indicate a profit of J hundred thousand dollars, we draw a bar from row 22 to row 22-2*J. For example, a profit of $200,000 corresponds to J=2 and to a bar from row 22 to row 22— 2*2 = 18. Here is a program that draws the bar corresponding to January, which recorded a profit of $350,000.

```
100 P=350000
110 J=350000/100000
120 FOR K=22 TO 22-2*J STEP -1
130    LOCATE K,13
140    PRINT CHR$(219);
150 NEXT K
```

Store the monthly profits in a **DATA** statement. The first part of the program will read the monthly profits into an array A(K) (K=1,2,...,12). Next, the program will draw the bar for each month, using a program like the one

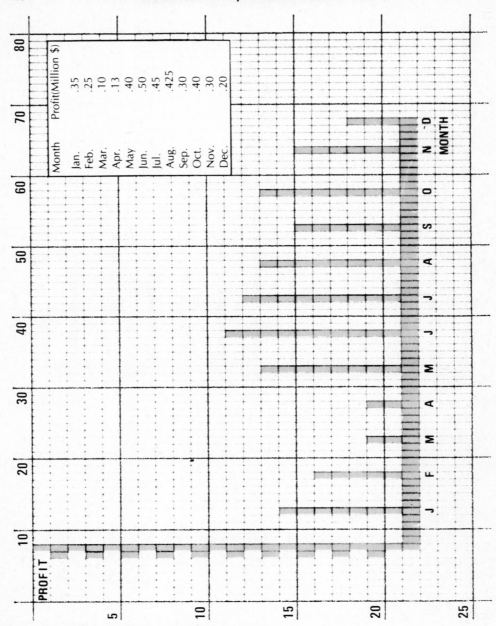

Figure 3.7. Video Display Worksheet For Figure 3.6.

above. The only new point is that the bars for month M (M = 1, 2, ... , 12) are located in columns 13 + (M-1)*5. This positioning is correct for M = 1 (column 13) and as M is increased by 1, the columns increase by 5. Thus, the initial part of our program, up to and including drawing the bars, is as follows:

```
10 DIM A(12)
20 DATA 350000, 250000, 100000, 130000, 400000, 500000
30 DATA 450000, 425000, 300000, 400000, 300000, 200000
40 FOR M=1 TO 12
50    READ A(M)
60 NEXT M
1000 FOR M=1 TO 12
1010     J=A(M)/100000
1020     FOR K=22 TO 22-2*J STEP -1
1030        LOCATE K,13+(M-1)*5:
                PRINT CHR$(219); :'BARS
1050     NEXT K
1060 NEXT M
```

Recall that we reserved the first 8 columns for the word "Profit," the vertical axis and the tick marks. Let's put the word "Profit" beginning at row 1, column 1, the vertical axis in column 8, and the tick marks in column 7 at rows 2, 4, 6, . . . , 20. The horizontal axis will run along row 22 from columns 8 to 78. Finally, we will put letters under the bars. Referring to Figure 3.7, we see that the letters of the months go in row 23, columns 13, 18, 23, . . . , 68. Here is a program to create this part of the display.

```
100 DIM B$(12)
110 DATA J,F,M,A,M,J,J,A,S,O
120 DATA N,D
130 FOR J=1 TO 12
140   READ B$(J)
150 NEXT J
160 FOR J=1 TO 12
165   LOCATE 23, 13+(J-1)*5
170   PRINT  B$(J);:'MONTH LABELS
180 NEXT J
185 LOCATE 1,1
190 PRINT   "Profit"
200 FOR J=1 TO 22
210   LOCATE J,8: PRINT CHR$(179);:'VERTICAL AXIS
220 NEXT J
230 FOR J=2 TO 20 STEP 2
240   LOCATE J,7: PRINT CHR$(196);: ' TICK MARKS
250 NEXT J
260 FOR J=8 TO 68
```

```
270   LOCATE 22,J: PRINT CHR$(196);: ' HORIZONTAL AXIS
280 NEXT J
290 LOCATE 22,8: PRINT CHR$(192);: 'CORNER
```

We may now put all the program parts together with an initial clearing of the screen and a loop to keep the display on the screen. We obtain our final result:

```
5 KEY OFF:CLS
10 DIM A(12)
20 DATA 350000, 250000, 100000, 130000, 400000, 500000
30 DATA 450000, 425000, 300000, 400000, 300000, 200000
40 FOR M=1 TO 12
50    READ A(M)
60 NEXT M
100 DIM B$(12)
110 DATA J,F,M,A,M,J,J,A,S,O
120 DATA N,D
130 FOR J=1 TO 12
140   READ B$(J)
150 NEXT J
160 FOR J=1 TO 12
165   LOCATE 23, 13 + (J-1)*5
170   PRINT  B$(J); :'MONTH LABELS
180 NEXT J
185 LOCATE 1,1
190 PRINT   "Profit"
200 FOR J=1 TO 22
210   LOCATE J,8: PRINT CHR$(179);:'VERTICAL AXIS
220 NEXT J
230 FOR J=2 TO 20 STEP 2
240   LOCATE J,7: PRINT CHR$(196);: ' TICK MARKS
250 NEXT J
260 FOR J=8 TO 68
270   LOCATE 22,J: PRINT CHR$(196);: ' HORIZONTAL AXIS
280 NEXT J
290 LOCATE 22,8: PRINT CHR$(192);: 'CORNER
1000 FOR M=1 TO 12
```

```
1010          LET J=A(M)/100000
1020          FOR K=22 TO 22-2*J STEP -1
1030              LOCATE K,13+(M-1)*5:
                      PRINT CHR$(219);:'BARS
1050          NEXT K
1055          LOCATE 22,13+(M-1)*5:PRINT CHR$(223);
1060 NEXT M
1100 GOTO 1100
1200 END
```

You may have wondered if all of the above effort is really worth it. After all, we have just managed to produce a single bar graph! Well, I think it is. I am a firm believer in "learning by pain." This tedious exercise gave you lots of practice in placing text on the screen (even the graphics was really text). And this is an indispensible part of graphics work. I don't mean for you to take the above bar chart program seriously as a graphics program. We'll develop a real bar chart program over the next few chapters. But this section provides useful practice toward that end. Trust me!

Exercises (answers on page 347)

Exercises 1-6 refer to the bar chart program developed in the above example.

1. Key in and RUN the bar chart program of the program above.

2. Modify your program so that, instead of DATA statements, the program asks for the monthly profits via an INPUT statement.

3. Use the program of Exercise 2 to make a bar chart for the following set of data:

   Jan. $175,238   Jul. $312,964
   Feb. $ 35,275   Aug. $345,782
   Mar. $240,367   Sep. $126,763
   Apr. $675,980   Oct. $324,509
   May $390,612   Nov. $561,420
   Jun. $609,876   Dec. $798,154

4. Modify the program of Exercise 2 to include the label "Mil. $" on the left of the vertical axis under the word "Profit". Moreover, add calibrations .1, .2, .3, .4, . . . , 1.0 by the tick marks on the vertical axis.

5. Modify the program of Exercise 2 so that it asks for the labels to be placed on the vertical axis. This is a first step in developing a program to draw bar charts for any set of data. You should limit your labels to 2 lines of 6 characters or less, so that you may use the same position for the axes. Modify the program so that it asks you for the number to be placed beside the first vertical tick mark, and the interval between

consecutive tick mark labels. For example, you might wish to label the tick marks .3, .7, 1.1, . . . , 3.0. In this case, you would INPUT the number .3 as the first tick mark label and .4 as the interval between consecutive labels. You program should generate the desired tick mark labels. Moreover, your program should ask for the "scale factor." This is the number corresponding to $100,000 in the program and is the amount represented by the length of each interval on the vertical axis. To put it another way, the scale factor is the number you must divide each data item by to get the height of the appropriate bar in terms of intervals (tick marks) on the vertical axis.

6. Enhance the program of Exercise 5 so that it asks for the labels on the horizontal axis (the month labels in the program). Your program should allow for a variable number of bars, up to the 12 bars of the program. (Just omit the bars and labels on the right if you have fewer than 12 pieces of data.)

7. Use the program of Exercise 6 to produce a bar chart corresponding to the following data.

Income	Percentage of Population
Under $10,000	15.8
10,000–20,000	25.7
20,000–30,000	27.4
30,000–40,000	11.1
Over 40,000	20.0

ANSWER TO TEST YOUR UNDERSTANDING

1: Column 15

3.3 Colors and Graphics Modes

There are three display modes on the PC—**text mode**, **medium-resolution graphics mode**, and **high-resolution graphics mode**. The text mode is the one you have been using up to this point to display characters (including graphics characters) on the screen. Text mode may be used on any IBM PC. However, the two graphics modes require a special circuit board, called the **color/graphics interface** (also called the **color/graphics adapter**). Medium resolution graphics mode lets you draw figures in color or black and white. High resolution allows you to draw very detailed figures, but only in black and white. In this section, we will be concerned mainly with these two graphics modes, so we will assume throughout that your computer is equipped with the color/graphics interface, even though it may not have a color monitor.

You may select between the various display modes by using the **SCREEN** command.

SCREEN 0 = text mode

SCREEN 1 = medium-resolution graphics mode

SCREEN 2 = high-resolution graphics mode

When BASIC is started, the display is automatically in text mode. The above commands may be used to switch from one display mode to another, either within a program or via a keyboard command. Note, however, that the SCREEN command automatically clears the screen.

Pixels and Colors in Graphics Mode

In the medium-resolution graphics mode, the screen is divided into 320 positions across and 200 down. To give you some idea of how fine this subdivision is, refer to Figure 3.8. Here we have drawn a grid which is 160 across and 100 down. (The actual grid is too fine to print. It would look almost totally black!)

Each of the small rectangles (more properly, dots) is called a **pixel** ("picture element"). You have individual control over every pixel. In medium resolution, you may color a pixel in any of four available colors.

In the high-resolution graphics mode, the screen is divided into 640 positions across and 200 positions down. Each pixel is individually controllable. However, there are only two colors: a pixel is either ON (white) or OFF (black).

Graphics Coordinates

Each pixel is specified by a pair of coordinates (x,y), where x is the column number and y is the row number. Note the following important facts:

1. **Rows and columns are numbered beginning with 0** (not 1 as in text mode). In the medium-resolution graphics mode, the rows are numbered from 0 to 199 and the columns from 0 to 319. In high-resolution graphics mode, the rows are numbered from 0 to 199 and the columns from 0 to 639.

2. Coordinates in graphics mode are specified with the column (x-coordinate) first. **This is the opposite of the coordinates in text mode.** (For example, the LOCATE statement requires the row first.)

Relative Coordinates in Graphics Mode

In graphics mode, the cursor is not visible. Instead, the computer keeps track of the **last point referenced**. This is the point whose coordinates were most recently used in a graphics statement. You may specify the position of new points by giving coordinates relative to the last point referenced. Such coordinates are called **relative coordinates**. Relative coordinates are always preceded by the word STEP. For example, suppose that the last point referenced is (100,75). Then here is a point specified by relative coordinates

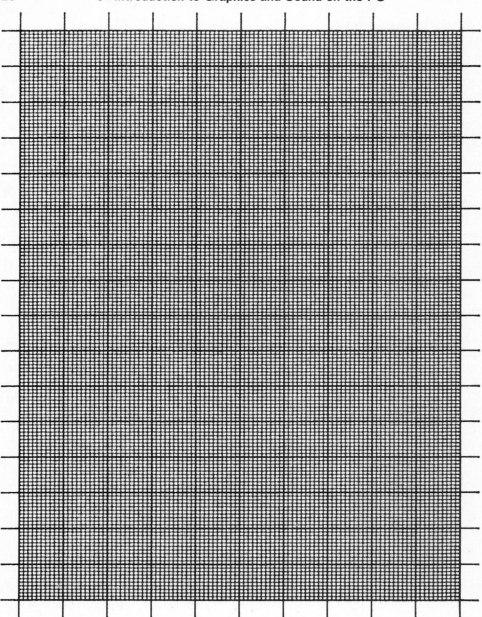

Figure 3.8. Video Display Worksheet for Medium-resolution Mode.

STEP (20,30)

This is the point that is 20 units to the right and 30 units down from the last referenced point. This is the point with coordinates (120,105). Similarly, consider the point specified by the relative coordinates

```
STEP (-10,-40)
```

This is the point that is 10 units to the left and 40 units up from the point (120,105), that is, the point (90,35).

TEST YOUR UNDERSTANDING 1 (answer on page 30)

Suppose that the last referenced point is (50,80). Determine the coordinates of the following points:

(a)	STEP (50,50)	(b)	STEP (-20,10)
(c)	STEP (10,-40)	(d)	STEP (-20,-50)

Color in Graphics Mode

Medium-resolution graphics lets us use color on the screen. High resolution, however, allows displays only in black and white. To use color in your display, you must first enable color with the SCREEN statement

SCREEN 1,0   (means medium-resolution graphics, color ON)

You may disable color with the statement

SCREEN 1,1   (means medium-resolution graphics, color OFF)

Once color has been enabled, you may choose both background and foreground colors. A pixel is considered part of the **background** (at a particular moment) unless its color has been explicitly set by a graphics statement. When you execute CLS, all pixels are set equal to the background color. A non-background pixel is said to belong to the **foreground**.

Here are the possible background colors, numbered 0-15.

0—black	8—gray
1—blue	9—light blue
2—green	10—light green
3—cyan	11—light cyan
4—red	12—light red
5—magenta	13—light magenta
6—brown	14—yellow
7—white	15—high intensity white

Foreground colors may be selected from one of two palettes:

Palette 0	**Palette 1**
1—green	1—cyan
2—red	2—magenta
3—brown	3—white

Background and foreground colors are set using the **COLOR** statement. You may select the background color and the palette using a statement like

```
100 COLOR 12,0
```

This statement sets the background color as light red (color 12) and the palette as 0. These choices remain in effect until they are changed with another **COLOR** statement.

TEST YOUR UNDERSTANDING 2 (answer on page 30)

Write BASIC statements that select the medium-resolution graphics mode, set the background color to high-intensity white, and the palette to 1.

Illuminating Pixels

The **PSET** statement is used to illuminate a pixel. For example, the statement

```
200 PSET (100,150),1
```

will illuminate the pixel at (100,150) in color 1 of the currently chosen palette. Similarly, to turn off this pixel we use the statement

```
300 PRESET (100,150)
```

Actually, this last instruction turns on pixel (100,150) in the background color. This is equivalent to turning it off. In using the **PSET** and **PRESET** statements, you may specify the pixel in **relative form**. For example, the statement

```
400 PSET STEP (100,-150), 2
```

will turn on color 2 at the pixel that is 100 blocks to the right and 150 blocks up from the current cursor position.

A Word About Monitors

There has been much confusion about monitors and display adapters. Here is an attempt to clear the fog.

1. **Monochrome display interface and IBM monochrome display**: No medium- or high-resolution graphics are possible with this configuration. In addition, character size is limited to the small characters (80-character lines). If you select a 40-character width you will confine your display to the left side of the screen.

2. **Color graphics interface and a black and white monitor (not the IBM monochrome display)**: Black and white graphics in both medium and high resolution are possible. In addition, both character widths are allowed. However, if you run a program that uses COLOR commands, the gray tones corresponding to the various colors may lead to illegi-

ble displays. In this configuration, you should stick to a black background and white characters.

3. **Color graphics interface and a television set**: Medium-resolution graphics and text mode will work just fine. However, you cannot get the high-resolution graphics mode.

4. **Color graphics interface and a high-resolution color monitor (a so-called RGB monitor)**: In this configuration, you have it all—text, medium-resolution, and high-resolution, with the first two possible modes in color. However, it should be noted that some game type programs that make clever use of color capabilities actually work better on television sets, because they are designed to take advantage of TV color characteristics.

Many PC owners equip their computers with both the monochrome display interface and the color/graphics interface. It is possible to address only one of these boards at a time. Moreover, BASIC will intially go to the monochrome display. In order to use the color/graphics interface, it is necessary to turn off the monochrome display and turn on the color/graphics interface. You may do this by inserting the following instruction lines at the beginning of your program

```
10 WIDTH 80
20 DEF SEG=0
30 A=PEEK(&H410)
40 B=(A AND &HCF) OR &H20
50 POKE &H410,B
60 WIDTH 40
70 SCREEN 0
80 LOCATE ,,1,6,7
```

Suppose you switch display interfaces. To successfully return to DOS, it is first necessary to turn off the color/graphics interface and turn the monochrome display interface back on. This may be done by terminating your program with the following statement lines:

```
10 WIDTH 40
20 DEF SEG=0
30 A=PEEK(&H410)
40 POKE &H410, A OR &H30
50 WIDTH 80
60 LOCATE ,,1,12,13
```

(Don't worry about how these programs work.)

Exercises (answers on page 347)

Write BASIC instructions that do the following:

1. Select the background color magenta and the foreground color from palette 1.

2. Select the background color light red and the foreground color from palette 0.

3. Turn on pixel (200,80) with color 1 of the current palette.

4. Turn on pixel (100,100) in red with background color cyan.

5. Set the pixel that is 200 blocks to the left and 100 blocks above the last referenced point. Use color 3.

6. Turn on the pixel that is 100 units to the right of the last referenced point.

ANSWERS TO TEST YOUR UNDERSTANDING

1: (a) (100,130)   (b) (30,90)   (c) (60,40)   (d) (30,30)

2: `10 SCREEN 1,0`
    `20 COLOR 15,1`

3.4   Lines, Rectangles, and Circles

Straight Lines

You may use the **PSET** and **PRESET** statements to design color graphics displays. However, BASIC has a rich repertoire of instructions that greatly simplify the task. Consider the task of drawing straight lines. If you have the color/graphics interface card, you may use the **LINE** statement. For example, to draw a line connecting the pixels (20,50) and (80,199), we use the statement

```
10 LINE (20,50)-(80,199)
```

To draw a line from the last referenced point to (100,90), use the statement

```
20 LINE -(100,90)
```

To draw a line from the last referenced point to the point 80 units to the right and 100 units above, use the statement

```
30 LINE -STEP(80,-100)
```

You may also specify the color of a line. For example, if you wish to draw the line in statement 10 in color 1 of the current palette, use the statement

```
40 LINE (20,50)-(80,199),1
```

This line is drawn in Figure 3.9.

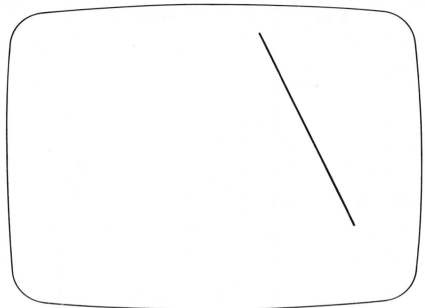

Figure 3.9.

If no color is specified in a LINE statement, then color 3 of the current palette is used.

Note that there are lines the computer cannot draw perfectly. Lines on a diagonal are displayed as a series of visible "steps." This is as close as the computer can get to a straight line within the limited resolution provided by the graphics modes. The higher the resolution (that is, the more pixels on the screen), the better your straight lines will look.

TEST YOUR UNDERSTANDING 1 (answer on page 41)

(a)   Draw a line connecting (0,100) to (50,75) in color 2.
(b)   Draw the triangle with vertices at (0,0), (50,50), (100,30).

BASIC version 2.00 allows you to specify the "style" of a line. For example, you can specify that your line is to consist of 5 dots followed by 5 blanks. This makes a dashed line with wide spaces between the dashes. Using this style feature requires a knowledge of binary arithmetic and is discussed in Chapter 6.

Rectangles

The **LINE** statement has several very sophisticated variations. To draw a rectangle you need to specify a pair of opposite corners in a **LINE** statement and add the code B (for BOX) at the end of the statement. For example, to draw a rectangle, two of whose corners are at (50,100) and (90,175), use the statement

    50 LINE (50,100)-(90,175),1,B

This statement will draw the desired rectangle with the sides in color 1 of the current palette. (See Figure 3.10a.) The inside of the rectangle will be in the background color. You may paint the inside of the rectangle in the same color as the sides by changing the B to BF (B=Box, BF=Box Filled). (See Figure 3.10a.) These instructions greatly simplify drawing complex line displays.

TEST YOUR UNDERSTANDING 2 (answer on page 41)

(a)   Draw a rectangle with corners at (10,10), (10,100), (50,100), (50,10).
(b)   Draw the rectangle of (a) and color it and its interior with color 2.

Mixing Text and Graphics

You may include text together with your graphics. Use either PRINT or PRINT USING exactly as if you were in text mode. You may use LOCATE to position the cursor at a particular (text) line and column. Note the following points, however:

1.   In medium-resolution graphics mode, you may use only a 40-character line width. This corresponds to the "large" characters. In high-resolution graphics, you may use only an 80-character line width. This corresponds to "small" characters.

2.   Text will print in color 3 of the current palette.

3.   In the graphics modes, you may use only the text characters with ASCII codes less than 128. ASCII codes 128 through 255 will be displayed as random garbage. (You may, however, make ASCII codes 128 through 255 correspond to custom-designed characters. See Chapter 6 for details.)

In planning text displays to go along with your graphics, note that all letters (regardless of line width) are 8 pixels wide and 8 pixels high. Thus, for example, the character at the top left corner of the screen occupies pixels (x,y), where x and y both range between 0 and 7.

EXAMPLE 1.   Write a command to erase text line 1 of the screen in medium-resolution mode.

SOLUTION.   Our scheme for erasing a line will be to draw a rectangle over the line, with color equal to the background color (color 0). The first text line of the screen occupies pixel (x,y), where x ranges from 0 to 319 (x equals

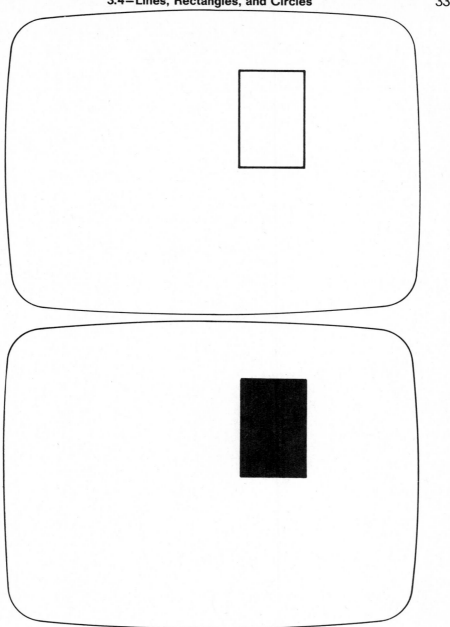

Figure 3.10(a). The B Option (top); (b). The BF Option (bottom).

the column number) and y ranges from 0 to 7 (y equals the row number).
Here is the desired statement.

```
LINE (0,0)-(319,7),0,BF
```

BASICA

All of the commands described so far are included in Disk BASIC. (This is the BASIC you get by responding to the DOS prompt with BASIC.) However, there is an enhanced version of BASIC, called BASICA (=BASIC Advanced), which includes all the commands of Disk BASIC as well as many other advanced commands. A copy of Advanced BASIC is on the DOS diskette you purchased with your diskette drive. To use BASICA, first obtain the DOS prompt A>, then type:

```
BASICA
```

and press ENTER. You will obtain the prompt Ok. From here on, you may use any of the BASIC commands you have learned until now. In addition, you may use the CIRCLE command discussed below.

Circles

BASICA has the facility for drawing circles and circular arcs. To draw a circle, you must specify the center and the radius, and, optionally, the color. For example, here is the command to draw a circle at center (100,100) and radius 50:

```
CIRCLE (100,100),50
```

Since no color has been specified, the circle will be drawn in color 3. (See Figure 3.11.)
To draw the same circle in color 1, we would use the command

```
CIRCLE (100,100),50,1
```

Note that the circles on the screen are not smooth, but have a "ragged" appearance. This is due to the limited resolution of the screen. If you use high-resolution mode, you will notice that the appearance of your circles improves greatly.
Circular arcs are somewhat more complicated to draw since their description is based on the radian system of angle measurement. Let's take a few moments to describe radian measurement.
Recall the number pi from high school geometry. Pi is a number, denoted by the Greek letter π, which is approximately equal to 3.1415926 . . . (the decimal expansion goes on forever). Ordinarily, angles are measured in degrees, with 360 degrees comprising one complete revolution. In radian measurement, there are 2*pi radians in a revolution. That is,

2*pi radians = 360 degrees

1 radian = 360/(2*pi) degrees

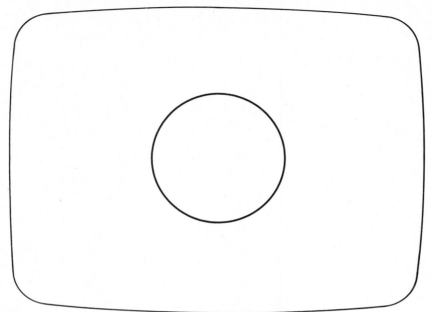

Figure 3.11.

If you use the value of pi and carry out the arithmetic, you find that 1 radian is approximately 57 degrees. When describing angles to the computer, you must always use radians.

To draw a circular arc, you use the following variation of the CIRCLE command

```
CIRCLE (xcenter,ycenter),radius,color,startangle, endangle
```

where startangle and endangle are measured in radians. For example, to draw a circular arc for the above circle, corresponding to an angle of 1.4 radians, beginning at angle .1 radians, we may use the command

```
CIRCLE (100,100),50,1,.1,1.5
```

The resulting angle is pictured in Figure 3.12.

Note that Figure 3.12 does not include the sides of the sector. To include a side on a circular arc, put a minus sign on the corresponding angle. (You can't use -0, however. See below.) For example, to include both sides in Figure 3.12, we may use the command

```
CIRCLE (100,100),50,1,-.1,-1.5
```

The resulting arc will look like the one in Figure 3.13.

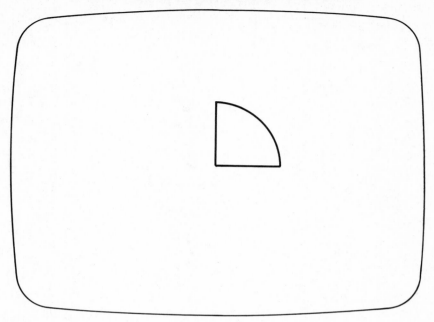

Figure 3.12.

TEST YOUR UNDERSTANDING 3 (answer on page 41)

(a) Draw a circular arc with radius 60, center (125,75) and going from
     a starting angle of .25 radians to an ending angle of .75 radians.
(b) Draw the same circular arc as in (a), but with sides included.

If you have an angle 0 and wish to include a side, just note that the angle 0
and the angle 2*pi are the same. So just replace 0 by 2*pi = 6.28 . . . , and
put your minus sign on this new angle!

Aspect Ratio

The CIRCLE statement has an added complication we haven't yet mentioned, namely the **aspect ratio**. Usually, when you plot circles on graph
paper, you use the same scale on the x-axis as the y-axis. If, for example, a
unit on the x-axis is larger than a unit on the y-axis, your circle will appear as
an ellipse, stretched out in the x-direction. Similarly, if the unit on the y-axis
is larger than the unit on the x-axis, the circle will appear as an ellipse
stretched out in the y-direction. So, like it or not, the geometry of circles is
intimately bound up with that of ellipses. And on the PC, the CIRCLE statement may also be used to draw ellipses.

Consider the following example in high-resolution graphics mode:

```
CIRCLE (300,100),100,,,,.5
```

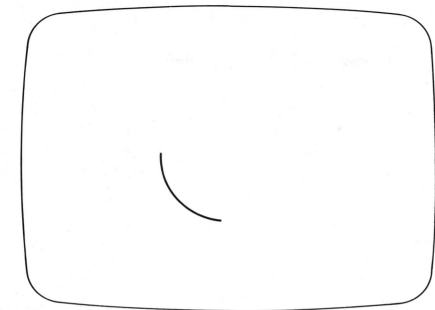

Figure 3.13.

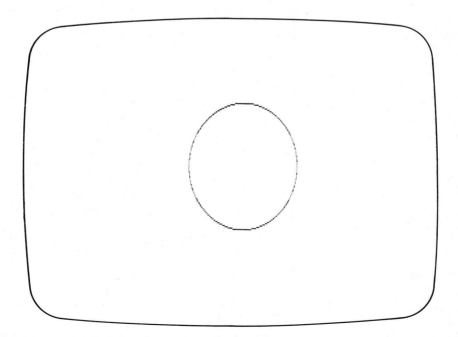

Figure 3.14. The Ellipse CIRCLE (300,100),100,,,,.5.

This statement plots an ellipse with center (300,100). The x-radius is 100. The number .5 is called the **aspect ratio**. It tells us that the y-radius is .5 times the x-radius, or 50.

Similarly, consider the statement

```
CIRCLE (300,100),100,,,,1.5
```

Here the aspect ratio is 1.5, which is larger than 1. In this case, BASIC assumes that the radius 100 is the y-radius. The x-radius is 1.5 times the y-radius, or 45. The corresponding ellipse is show in Figure 3.15.

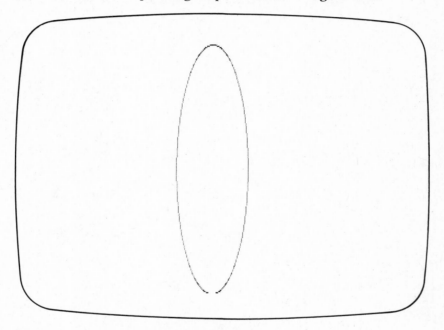

Figure 3.15. The Ellipse CIRCLE (300,100),100,,,,1.5.

What is the aspect ratio for a circle? Well, that's a tricky question. On first glimpse, you would probably guess that the aspect ratio is 1. And indeed it is if you are looking for a mathematical circle. However, if you draw a circle with an aspect ratio of 1, you will get an ellipse. The reason is that the scales on the x- and y- axes are different. Let's consider high-resolution graphics mode. The screen is 640 x 200 pixels. The ratio of width to height is 200/640 = 5/16. So to achieve a circle, you would expect to have to multiply the x-radius by 5/16 to get the proper y-radius. That is, an aspect ratio of 5/16. Well, not quite! TV screens are not square. The ratio of width to height is 4/3. So in order to achieve an ellipse that is visually a circle, we must multiply by 5/16 **and** by 4/3. That is, the aspect ratio is

$$(5/16) * (4/3) = 5/12$$

Strange, but true. In medium-resolution mode, the aspect ratio giving a visual circle is 5/6. If you use the CIRCLE statement without any aspect ratio, then BASIC assumes an aspect ratio of 5/6 in medium-resolution mode and 5/12 in high-resolution mode. With these aspect ratios circles look like circles. However, the y-radius is quite different from the x-radius!

You can get even finer-grained control over circles and ellipses if you apply some mathematics. Suppose that an ellipse (or circle) has center at the point with coordinates (x0,y0). Suppose that the horizontal half-axis has length A and vertical half-axis has length B. Then a typical point (x,y) on the ellipse is of the form:

$$x = x0 + A*\cos(t)$$

$$y = y0 + B*\sin(t)$$

where t is an angle between 0 and 2*pi radians. The geometric meaning of the angle t is shown in Figure 3.16. The above equations are called the **parametric equations for the ellipse**. They are very useful in drawing graphics.

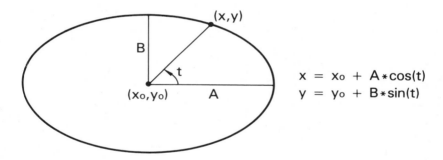

Figure 3.16. An Ellipse in Parametric Form.

For example, here is a program that draws an ellipse with center (320,100) (the center of the screen in high resolution mode) by plotting dots in a "sweep" fashion. (See Figure 3.17.) This graph may be used to simulate the motion of a planet around the sun.

```
5 'planetary orbit
10 SCREEN 2:CLS:KEY OFF
20 FOR T=0 TO 6.28 STEP .05
30      X=320+200*COS(T):Y=100+30*SIN(T)
40      PSET (X,Y)
50      FOR K=1 TO 25:NEXT K
70 NEXT T
```

Note that line 50 provides a delay between plotting of consecutive dots.

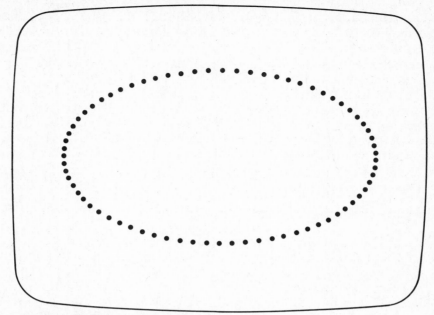

Figure 3.17. Simulating a Planetary Orbit.

Exercises (answers on page 347)

Write BASIC instructions to draw the following:

1. A line connecting (20,50) and (40,100).

2. A line in color 2 connecting the current cursor position and the point (250,150).

3. A line in color 1 connecting (125,50) to a block 100 blocks to the right and 75 units down from it.

4. A rectangle with corners at (10,20), (200,20), (200,150), (10,150).

5. The rectangle of Exercise 4 with its sides and interior in color 3.

6. A circle with radius 20 and center (30,50).

7. A circular arc of the circle of Exercise 6 with a starting angle 1.5 and ending angle of 3.1.

8. Draw the circular arc of Exercise 7 with sides.

9. Write a program that simulates the movement of sweep second hand around the face of a clock.

3.5　Computer Art

The graphics statements of PC BASIC may be used to draw interesting computer art on the screen. As just a taste of what can be done, the program below draws random polygons on the screen. The program is written in high-resolution graphics mode, so that the screen has dimensions 640 x 200. The program first chooses the number N% of sides of the polygon. We allow our polygon to have up to 6 sides. Next, the program picks out N%+1 random points (it takes N%+1 points to draw a polygon of N sides). The points are stored in the arrays X%(J%) and Y%(J%), where J% = 0,1,2,...,N%. In order to generate only closed polygons, we define the point (X%(N%+1),Y%(N%+1)) to be the initial point (X%(0), Y%(0)). The program then draws lines between consecutive points. In Figure 3.18, we show a typical polygon.

The program then erases the polygon and repeats the entire procedure to draw a different polygon. The program draws 50 polygons.

```
10 'Computer art
20 SCREEN 2:CLS:KEY OFF
30 RANDOMIZE VAL(RIGHT$(TIME$,2))
40 FOR M%=1 TO 50
50       C%=3:GOSUB 90       'Draw random polygon
60       C%=0:GOSUB 190      'Erase polygon
70 NEXT M%
80 END
90 'Draw random polygon
100      'Determine number of sides
110      N%=INT(5*RND(1) + 1)    'N=# sides <= 6
120      'Compute coordinates of vertices
130      FOR J%=0 TO N%
140          X%(J%)=INT(640*RND(1))
150          Y%(J%)=INT(200*RND(1))
160      NEXT J%
```

```
170       X%(N%+1)=X%(0):Y%(N%+1)=Y%(0)
180       'Draw sides
190        FOR J%=1 TO N%+1
200             LINE (X%(J%-1),Y%(J%-1))-(X%(J%),Y%(J%)),C%
210        NEXT J%
220 RETURN
```

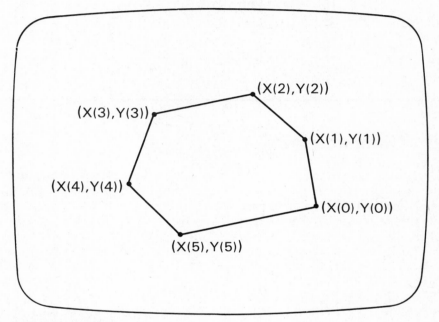

Figure 3.18. A Typical Polygon.

Here is a second program that draws a regular polygon (one with sides of equal length) and then draws inscribed replicas of the original polygon, each of smaller size, until the interior of the original polygon is filled with the inscribed replicas. (See Figure 3.19.)

Here is the mathematics necessary to draw a regular polygon. Suppose that you wish to draw a regular polygon having N sides and inscribed in a circle of radius R and centered at the point X0,Y0. (See Figure 3.20.) The vertices are then the points (X(J),Y(J)) (J=0,1,2,...,N), where

X(J) = X0 + R*COS(2*PI*J/N)

Y(J) = Y0 + R*(5/12)*SIN(2*PI*J/N)

(The factor 5/12 corrects for the aspect ratio so that the circle in which the polygons is inscribed will appear visually as a circle.) For our program, we will let the user choose the value of N (up to 20). The center of the polygon will be the center of the screen (320,100) in high resolution. We use an initial value of 100 for the radius R. Then we draw polygons corresponding to the same value of N, but with successively smaller values of R. Shrinking the

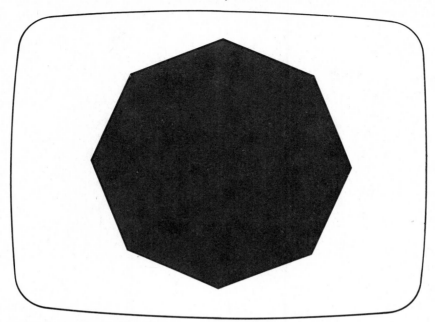

Figure 3.19. Inscribed Polygons.

radius circle in which the polygon is inscribed gives the illusion that the polygon is growing inward.

Here is the program.

```
100 DIM X%(21),Y%(21)
110 INPUT "NUMBER OF SIDES";N%
120 IF N%>20 THEN 110
130 SCREEN 2:CLS:KEY OFF
140 PI=3.14159
150 FOR R%=100 TO 0 STEP -4
160         GOSUB 190
170 NEXT R%
180 END
185 'Calculate vertices
190     FOR J%=0 TO N%
200             X%(J%)=320+R%*COS(2*PI*J%/N%)
210             Y%(J%)=100+R%*(5/12)*SIN(2*PI*J%/N%)
220     NEXT J%
230     X%(N%+1)=X%(0):Y%(N%+1)=Y%(0)
235     'Draw polygon
240     FOR J%=0 TO N%
250             LINE (X%(J%),Y%(J%))-(X%(J%+1),Y%(J%+1))
260     NEXT J%
270 RETURN
```

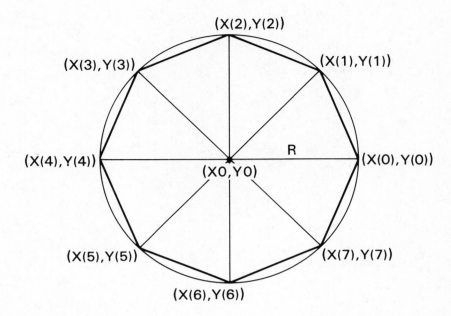

Figure 3.20. An Inscribed Polygon, N = 8

3.6   Drawing Pie Charts

As an application of the CIRCLE command, let's draw the pie chart in Figure 3.21.

To draw this pie chart, let's begin by creating an array to contain the various data and to list the data as shown on the left. We put the category names (Food, Clothing, and so forth) in an array B$( ). The numerical quantities we put in an array A( ). The first part of our program then consists of reading the data from DATA statements and setting up the two arrays. Also, we perform screen intialization by choosing SCREEN 2 (high-resolution graphics mode), and turning the function key display off. Here is the section of the program that accomplishes all these tasks.

```
100 'Program initialization
110 DIM A(7), B$(7),ANGLE(7)
120 DATA food, .20, rent, .18, clothing, .10, taxes, .20
130 DATA entertainment, .10, car, .15, savings, .07
140 FOR J=1 TO 7
150    READ B$(J), A(J)
```

```
160 NEXT J
170 SCREEN 2:              'high resolution
180 KEY OFF:               'turn off function keys
```

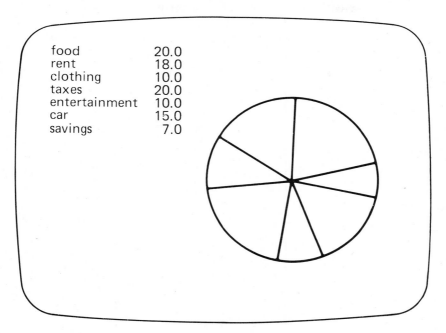

Figure 3.21.

Our next step is to create the left portion of the display. This requires some care and planning. Let's skip the top 4 lines and begin the display in the 5th line. We set up the numbers in our data statements as decimals rather than percentages since the computation of angles that follows is more conveniently carried out in terms of decimals. However, to display percentages, we multiply each number A(J) by 100. To get a formatted display, we use the PRINT USING statement. Let's put the category description in print zone 1 and the percentage in print zone 2. Here are the instructions corresponding to this section of the program. Pay particular attention to the print statements in lines 240 and 250.

```
200 'Display listed data
210 CLS
220 PRINT: PRINT:PRINT:PRINT
230 FOR J=1 TO 7
240     PRINT B$(J),;: 'print and move to 2nd print field
250     PRINT USING "##"; 100*A(J);"%"
260 NEXT J
```

Finally, we come to the section of the program in which we draw the pie. The Jth data item corresponds to the proportion A(J) of the total pie. In angular measure, this corresponds to A(J)*(2*PI) (recall that 2*PI radians corresponds to the entire pie). The first slice of the pie begins at angle ANGLE(0), which we set at 0; it ends at ANGLE(1) = A(1)*(2*PI). The second slice begins where the first slice ends, namely at ANGLE(1). It ends at ANGLE(1) + A(2)*(2*PI). And so forth. Here is the section of the program that draws the various pie slices. Notice that each of the sides of the pie slices is drawn twice, once in each of the slices to which it belongs. This does no harm.

```
300 'Draw Pie
310 ANGLE(0)=0
320 PI=3.14159
330 FOR J=1 TO 7
340    T=A(J)*(2*PI):    'T=angle for current data item
350    ANGLE(J)=ANGLE(J-1)+T
360    CIRCLE (450,100),100,,-ANGLE(J),ANGLE(J-1)
370 NEXT J
```

Note that in line 360, we did not specify a color. Nevertheless, we left space for the color parameter by inserting an extra comma. (The space for the color is an imaginary one between the two commas.) If BASIC calls for a parameter in a certain place, you may usually omit the parameter as long as you leave a place for it. If you don't, BASIC can't understand your statement.

You might wonder how we chose the center of the circle at (450,100) and the radius of 100. Well, it was mostly trial and error. We played around with various circle sizes and placements and chose one that looked good! In graphics work, you should not be afraid to let your eye be your guide.

For convenience, we now assemble then entire program into one piece.

```
100 'Program initialization
110 DIM A(7), B$(7),ANGLE(7)
120 DATA food, .20, rent, .18, clothing, .10, taxes, .20
130 DATA entertainment, .10, car, .15, savings, .07
140 FOR J=1 TO 7
150    READ B$(J), A(J)
160 NEXT J
170 SCREEN 2:              'high resolution
180 KEY OFF:               'turn off function keys
200 'Display listed data
210 CLS
220 PRINT: PRINT:PRINT:PRINT
230 FOR J=1 TO 7
240    PRINT B$(J),;: 'print and move to 2nd print field
250    PRINT USING "##.#"; 100*A(J)
260 NEXT J
300 'Draw Pie
310 ANGLE(0)=0
320 PI=3.14159
```

```
330 FOR J=1 TO 7
340    T=A(J)*(2*PI):    'T=angle for current data item
350    ANGLE(J)=ANGLE(J-1)+T
360    CIRCLE (450,100),100,,-ANGLE(J),ANGLE(J-1)
370 NEXT J
```

This program is subject to a number of enhancements, some of which will be suggested in the exercises.

Exercises

1. Alter the program above so that it accepts the data from the keyboard. Allow it to keep asking for data until it receives a data name "@". Allow for up to 20 data items.

2. Modify the above program so that the pie is drawn in color 2 of palette 1. (This will involve some respacing since you are now in medium resolution, a 40-character width.)

3.7   PAINT and DRAW

In this section, we discuss two of the more advanced graphics statements, PAINT and DRAW. Each of these statements is available only in BASICA.

PAINT

Using the graphics commands of PC BASIC, it is possible to draw a tremendous variety of shapes. For example, Figure 3.22 shows a triangle drawn using several LINE statements. Figure 3.23 shows a circle drawn using the CIRCLE statement. Underneath each shape is a statement to draw the shape. The boundary lines of each shape are specified in the graphics statements used to draw it. The triangle is drawn in color 2. No color is indicated in the case of the circle, so it is drawn in color 3.

The PAINT statement allows you to color the "inside" of a region, just as if the region were in a coloring book and you used a crayon to color it. For example, we may use the PAINT command to paint the interiors of the triangle of Figure 3.21 and the circle of Figure 3.22.

The format of the PAINT command is

```
PAINT (x,y),color,boundary
```

Here **(x,y)** is a point of the region to be painted, **color** is the color paint to use, and **boundary** is the color of the boundary. PAINT starts from the point (x,y) and begins to paint in all directions. Whenever it encounters the boundary color, it stops PAINTING in that direction.

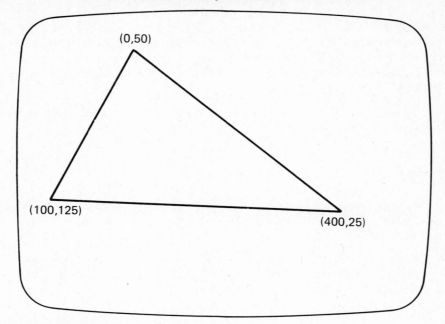

Figure 3.22. A Triangle.

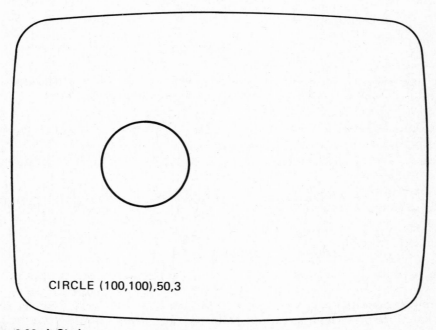

Figure 3.23. A Circle.

For example, consider the triangle in Figure 3.24. The point (75,75) lies inside the triangle. And the triangle itself is drawn in color 2. Suppose that we wished to color the interior of the triangle in color 3. The appropriate PAINT statement would be

```
PAINT (75,75),3,2
```

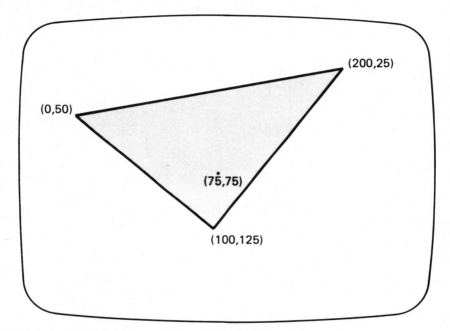

Figure 3.24. PAINTing the Interior of the Triangle.

TEST YOUR UNDERSTANDING 1 (answer on page 58)

Write a statement which will color the interior of the circle of Figure 3.23 in color 1.

PAINT is a very straightforward statement to understand. The main difficulty, however, is in specifying the point within the region. Or, to put it more precisely, if we are given a region, how do we specify a point within it? Well, that's a mathematical question. And I just happen to be a mathematician! So I can't resist explaining a little mathematics at this point.

Let's begin by considering the case of the rectangle $(x1,y1)-(x2,y2)$. The center of the rectangle is at the point $((x1+x2)/2, (y1+y2)/2)$. That is, to obtain the coordinates of the center of the rectangle, we average the values of the coordinates of the opposite corners. See Figure 3.25.

Another way of getting the same answer is to average the values of the coordinates of all 4 corners: $(x1,y1)$, $(x1,y2)$, $(x2,y2)$, $(x2,y1)$. Now there are 4

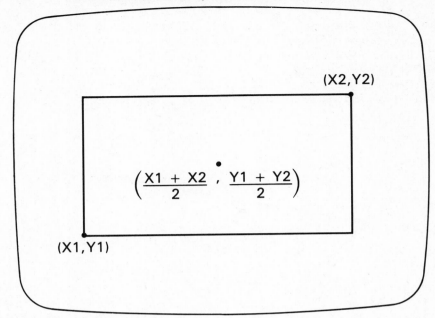

Figure 3.25. The Center of a Rectangle.

x-coordinates to add up, but we must divide by 4: We obtain $(2*x1 + 2*x2)/4$ = $(x1 + x2)/2$, and similarly for the y-coordinate.

Let's now consider a triangle with vertices $(x1,y1)$, $(x2,y2)$, $(x3,y3)$. Suppose that you average the coordinates to obtain

  ($(x1 + x2 + x3)/3$, $(y1 + y2 + y3)/3$).

This point is called the **centroid** of the triangle and is always inside the triangle.

Well, what works for 3- and 4-sided figures works in a more general setting. For many figures bounded by straight lines, you may compute a point within the figure simply by averaging the coordinates of the vertices. For which figures does this apply? The simplest such figures are the so-called **convex bodies**. We say that a figure is **convex** if, whenever you connect two point within the figure by a line, all points of the line are inside the figure. (See Figure 3.26.)

A convex figure bounded by line segments is a type of polygon. Suppose that the vertices of such a polygon are $(x1,y1)$, $(x2,y2)$, ..., (xn,yn). Then the point

  ($(x1 + ... + xn)/n$, $(y1 + ... + yn)/n$)

obtained by averaging the x- and y- coordinates is called the **centroid** of the polygon. And the centroid is always inside the polygon.

So if you wish to PAINT a convex polygon, just compute the centroid. And this will give you the point to use in the PAINT statement!

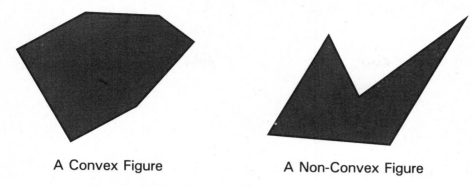

A Convex Figure   A Non-Convex Figure

Figure 3.26. Convex and Non-Convex Figures.

DRAW

Using the various statements of PC BASIC, you may draw some very complex screen images. However, the programs can become rather complex. Many drawings consist only of straight lines, in various positions on the screen. Such drawings may be concisely described and drawn using the DRAW command.

In order to understand the DRAW command, it helps to think of an imaginary pen you may use to draw on the screen. The motion of the pen is controlled by a graphics language used by DRAW. The format of the DRAW command is

```
DRAW <string>
```

Here "string" is a sequence of commands from the graphics language.

In giving commands, you will refer to points on the screen. The action of many of the commands will depend on the **last point referenced**. This is the point most recently referred to in a graphics command associated with DRAW. The CLS and RUN statements both set the last point referenced to the center of the screen (this is (160,100) in medium-resolution graphics and (320,100) in high-resolution graphics).

The graphics commands associated with DRAW are indicated by single letters. The most fundamental is the M command

```
DRAW "M x,y"
```

which draws a straight line from the last point referenced to the point with coordinates (x,y). After the statement is executed, the point (x,y) becomes the last point referenced.

Here are two variations on the M command.

1. If M is preceded by N, then the last point referenced is not changed. For example, here is a DRAW command to draw an angle, as in Figure

3.27. (The vertex of the angle is at (360,100) and the computer is assumed to be in SCREEN 2.)

```
DRAW "M 500,100 NM 200,50"
```

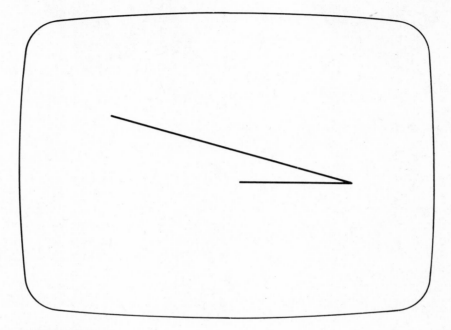

Figure 3.27. An Angle.

2. If M is preceded by B, then the last referenced point is changed, but no drawing takes place. The BM command is used to relocate the pen. For example, here is a command to draw the angle of Figure 3.28, with the vertex located at (300,110):

```
DRAW "BM 300,110 M 500,100 NM 200,50"
```

TEST YOUR UNDERSTANDING 2 (answer on page 58)

Use the DRAW command to draw the triangle of Figure 3.22.

Using Relative Coordinates

In our above discussion, all of our coordinates were **absolute**; that is, we specified the actual coordinates. However, you may also use this form of the M command.

```
M +r,+s
```

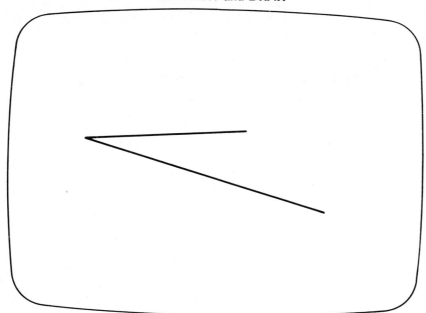

Figure 3.28. Another Angle.

It will draw a line from the last reference point to the point that is r units to the right and s units down. (Down is in the direction of increasing y coordinates!) In a similar fashion, we may use the commands

```
M -r,+s
M -r,-s
M +r,-s
```

Specifying Coordinates Using Variables

The coordinates in an M command may be specified by variables <variable1> and <variable2>, respectively. Here is the form of the command.

```
M =<variable1>;,=<variable2>;
```

Note the semicolons and the comma. You need these. For example, to draw a line from the last referenced point to the point specified by the values of the variables A and B, we could use the command

```
M =A;,=B;
```

By preceding = signs with a + sign, we may use variables to specify a relative coordinate position. For example, to draw the line to the point that is A units to the right and B units down, we could use the command

```
M +=A;,+=B;
```

Note that the signs of A and B give the actual direction of motion. For example, if A is negative, then the motion will be ABS(A) units to the left.

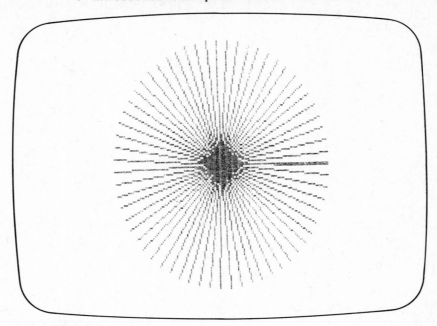

Figure 3.29. A Complex Display.

Figure 3.29 is an example of the sophisticated pictures you can compose using DRAW. Here is a program to create this display.

```
10 SCREEN 1:CLS:KEY OFF
20 FOR R=0 TO 6.3 STEP .1
30 A=160+70*COS(R):B=100+70*SIN(R)
40 DRAW "NM =A;,=B;"
50 NEXT R
```

TEST YOUR UNDERSTANDING 3 (answer on page 58)

Use the random number generator to generate 50 pairs of random points. Use DRAW to draw a line associated with each pair.

More About Relative Motions

In most drawing, coordinates are given in relative rather than absolute form. In order to shorten the lengths of the strings involved in describing such motions, DRAW includes the following commands:

U n —Move n units up

D n —Move n units down

L n —Move n units left

R n —Move n units right

E n —Move n units northeast
   (n units to the right, n units up)

F n —Move n units southeast
   (n units to the right, n units down)

G n —Move n units southwest
   (n units to the left, n units down)

H n —Move n units northwest
   (n units to the left, n units up)

The effect of these commands is illustrated in Figure 3.30.

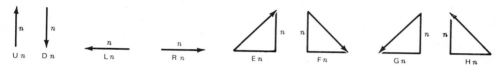

Figure 3.30. The Relative Motion Commands U-G.

You may use the N and B options with the commands U-G. For example, the command

```
DRAW "NU 50"
```

will draw a line from the last referenced point upward for 50 units. However, the last referenced point is not updated. Similarly, the command

```
DRAW "BU 50"
```

will update the last referenced point to the point 50 units up from the current point. However, no line is drawn.

You may also use variables in connection with the commands U-G. For example, consider the command

```
DRAW "U =A;"
```

It will draw a line from the last referenced point A units upward. (If the value of A is negative, then the motion will be downward.)

Color

You may specify color within DRAW by using the command

```
C n
```

Here n is 0, 1, 2 or 3 and refers to a color in the current palette.
Here is a program to draw the sailboat of Figure 3.31.

```
10 SCREEN 1,0: CLS: KEY OFF
20 COLOR 7,0
30 DRAW "C1 L60 E60 D80 C2 L60 F20 R40 E20 L20"
```

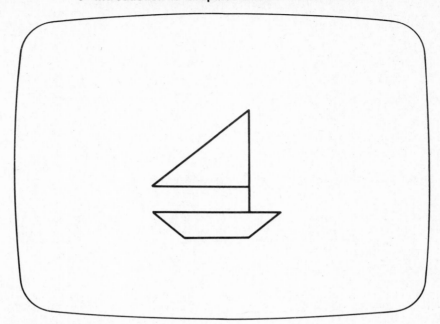

Figure 3.31. A Sailboat.

The background is white, the sail green, and the boat red.

Angle

You may rotate a figure through an angle that is a multiple of 90 degrees. Just precede the DRAW string (describing the figure in unrotated form) with the command

    A n

Here:

n = 0 : no rotation
n = 1 : 90-degree rotation clockwise
n = 2 : 180-degree rotation clockwise
n = 3 : 270-degree rotation clockwise

For example, here is a program that illustrates the sailboat of Figure 3.31 rotated through the various possible angles. (See Figure 3.32.)

```
10 CLS: SCREEN 1: KEY OFF: PSET (160,100)
20 INPUT "ANGLE (0-3)";N
30 DRAW "A=N; BU40 L30 E30 D40 L30 F10 R20 E10 L10"
```

Scale

You may automatically scale figures (make them larger or smaller) using the command

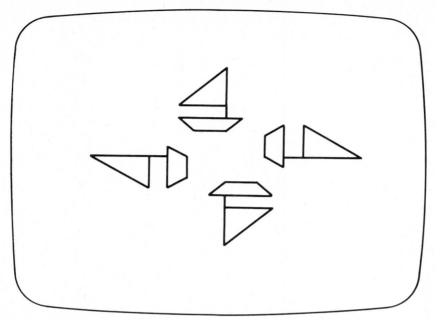

Figure 3.32. Rotated Sailboats.

    S n

All line lengths will be multiplied by n/4. Here n is an integer in the range 1 to 255.

TEST YOUR UNDERSTANDING 4 (answer on page 58)

Write a command to draw the sailboat of Figure 3.31, but at half scale.

Substrings

You may define a string, A$, outside a DRAW statement and then use it in the form

    DRAW A$

Often, you will wish to use one string several times within a single picture. (This is convenient, for example, if you wish to draw the same figure in several parts of the screen.) You may incorporate a string A$ within a larger string by preceding it with the letter X. For example, here is a statement that draws A$, moves up 50 units and draws A$ again:

    DRAW "XA$; BU50; XA$"

Note that X commands are separated from adjacent commands with semicolons.

Exercises

1. Write a program to draw the following figure.

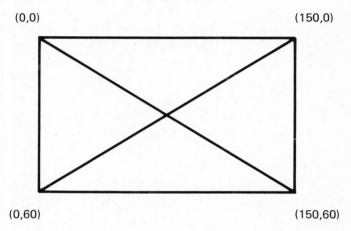

(0,0)   (150,0)

(0,60)   (150,60)

2. Write a program that draws the figure of Exercise 1, but rotates it 270 degrees clockwise.

3. Write a program that draws the figure of Exercise 1, but makes it twice the size.

ANSWERS TO TEST YOUR UNDERSTANDING

1: PAINT (100,100),1,3

2: DRAW "BM 0,50 M 100,125 M 400,25 M 0,50"

3:
```
10 DIM X(50),Y(50)
20 CLS: SCREEN 2: KEY OFF
30 FOR J=1 TO 50
40     X(J)=INT(RND*620)): X*(J)=INT(RND*620))
50     Y(J)=INT(RND*200)): Y*(J)=INT(RND*200))
60        DRAW "BM =X(J); =Y(J); M =X*(J);=Y*(J);"
70 NEXT J
```

4: DRAW "S2 C1 L60 E60 D80 C2 L60 F20 R40 E20 L20"

3.8   Saving and Recalling Graphics Images

Advanced BASIC contains commands that allow you to save and recall the contents of any rectangle on the screen. This is extremely convenient in many graphics applications, particularly animation.

Let's begin our discussion with a description of the image to be saved. The image must consist of a rectangular portion of the screen. The rectangle in question may start and end anywhere, and may contain text characters, portions of text characters, or a graphics image. You specify the rectangle by giving the coordinates of two opposite vertices, either the upper-left and lower-right or the lower-left and upper-right. Thus, a rectangle is specified in the same way as in using the LINE statement to draw a rectangle. Here are some specifications of rectangles.

(0,0)-(100,100)

(3,8)-(30,80)

In specifying rectangles, remember to indicate the coordinates in terms of the current graphics mode (either medium or high resolution). In either graphics mode, text characters occupy 8 by 8 rectangles. For example, the character in the upper left corner of the screen occupies the rectangle (0,0)-(7,7). Lines of text are always 8 pixels high.

TEST YOUR UNDERSTANDING 1 (answer on page 62)

Specify the rectangle consisting of the second text line of the screen. (Assume that you are in the medium-resolution graphics mode.)

The GET statement allows you to store the contents of a rectangle in an array. You may use any array as long as it is big enough. Suppose that the rectangle is x pixels long and y pixels high. Then the size of the array must be at least

$$4 + (2*x+7)*y/32$$

in medium resolution and

$$4 + (x+7)*y/32$$

in high resolution. (Recall that the size of the array is specified in a DIM statement.) For example, suppose that the array is 10 pixels wide and 50 pixels high and is in medium resolution. Then the array required to store the rectangle must contain at least

$$4 + (2*10+7)*50/32 \text{ or } 46$$

elements. We could use an array A( ) defined by the statement

```
DIM A(46)
```

Once a sufficiently large array has been dimensioned, you may store in it the contents of the rectangle using the GET statement, which has the form

```
GET (x1,y1)-(x2,y2), arrayname
```

For example, to store the rectangle (0,0)-(9,49) (this rectangle is 10 by 50) in the array A, we could use the statement

```
GET (0,0)-(9,49), A
```

To summarize: To store the contents of a rectangle in an array, you must:

1. Use a DIM statement to define a rectangle of sufficient size.
2. Execute a GET statement.

You may redisplay the rectangle at any point on the screen by using the PUT statement. For example, to redisplay the rectangle stored in A, you could use the statement

```
PUT (100,125), A
```

This particular statement would redisplay the rectangle in A, with the upper left corner of the rectangle at the point (100,125).

To see GET and PUT in action, let's examine the following program:

```
10 SCREEN 1
20 DIM LETTER(9)
30 LOCATE 1,1
40 PRINT "A"
50 GET (0,0)-(7,7),LETTER
60 CLS
70 PUT (100,100),LETTER
```

Line 10 puts BASIC in medium-resolution graphics mode. We are out to store an 8 by 8 array, so we use the above formulas to calculate the required array size, which works out to 9. In lines 30-40, we print a letter "A", and in line 50, we store the image in the array LETTER. We then clear the screen. Line 70 recovers the image from the array and places it with its upper left corner at the point (100,100).

Don't erase the screen yet. Type

```
PUT (100,100),LETTER
```

and press ENTER. Note that the letter A at (100,100) disappears. If you type the same line again, the A reappears. This feature may be used to create the illusion of motion across the screen. Suppose that you wish to create the illusion that the letter A is moving across the screen. Merely display it and erase it from consecutive screen positions. The screen creates the displays faster than the eye can view them. What you see is a continuous motion of the letter across the screen. Here is a program to create this animation.

```
10 SCREEN 1
20 DIM LETTER(9)
30 LOCATE 1,1
40 PRINT "A"
50 GET (0,0)-(7,7),LETTER
60 CLS
```

```
70 FOR XPOSITION = 0 TO 311
80   PUT (XPOSITION,0),LETTER
90   PUT (XPOSITION,0),LETTER
100 NEXT XPOSITION
```

Note that the XPOSITION runs from 0 to 311. Although the screen is 319 pixels wide, the variable XPOSITION specifies the upper left corner of the rectangle, which is 8 by 8. So 311 is the largest possible value of the variable.

Animation is the backbone of all the arcade games that have become so popular in recent years.

Saving a Screen Image on Diskette

Storing large graphics images (such as the entire screen) takes a great deal of memory. To store the entire screen takes more than 16,000 bytes. Compare this with the fact that BASIC can use a maximum of 65,536 bytes. Because graphics images tend to use such large amounts of memory, it is often necessary to save the screen image on diskette. Here is a program for saving the current screen image on diskette under the filename "SCREEN."

```
10 DEF SEG = &HB800
20 BSAVE "SCREEN",0,&H4000
```

To recall the stored image to the screen, use the program

```
10 DEF SEG = &HB800
20 BLOAD "SCREEN",0
```

We will explain why these programs work in our discussion of BLOAD and BSAVE in Chapter 5.

Exercises (answers on page 348)

1. Specify the rectangle of length 80 and height 40 whose upper left corner is at (10,10).
2. Specify the rectangle that consists of the first two text columns of the screen.
3. Write a dimension statement for the rectangle specified in Exercise 1.
4. Write a dimension statement for the rectangle specified in Exercise 2.
5. Store the current screen contents on diskette.
6. Clear the screen and recall the screen contents stored in Exercise 5.
7. Store a happy face (ASCII character 2) in an array.
8. Display the happy face at the following points:
   a. (0,0)
   b. (50,50)
   c. (0,100)

9. Construct an animation that moves the happy face across the screen in text line 10.

10. Construct an animation that moves the happy face diagonally across the screen from upper left to lower right.

ANSWER TO TEST YOUR UNDERSTANDING

1:   (0,8)-(319,15)

3.9 VIEW and WINDOW

In this section, we will discuss the VIEW and WINDOW statements, two of the very powerful graphics enhancements provided in BASIC 2.00.

The WINDOW statement allows you to define your own coordinate system on the screen. For example, consider the statement

```
WINDOW (-2,0)-(2,100)
```

It causes the screen coordinates to be redefined, as shown in Figure 3.33. Note that the lower left corner becomes the point (-2,0) and the upper right corner becomes the point (2,100). The x coordinates of the screen run from -2 on the left to 2 on the right. The y coordinates run from 0 at the bottom to 100 on the top. The point in the middle of the screen is (0,50).

Figure 3.33. Cartesian Coordinates (-2,0)-(2,100).

After using a WINDOW command, all graphics commands work with the new coordinates. For example, suppose that we execute the above WINDOW statement. The statement

```
PSET (0,50)
```

turns on the pixel at the center of the screen.

TEST YOUR UNDERSTANDING 1 (answer on page 67)

Assume that the screen coordinates are defined by the WINDOW command of Figure 3.33. Describe the location of the points:

(a) (1,75)   (b) (-1,100)   (c) (2,10)

The WINDOW statement does not disturb the contents of the screen. So you may use several different coordinate systems within a single program. Moreover, the placement of text is still governed by the usual text coordinate system (lines 1-25, columns 1-40 or 80), so you can mix text and graphics determined by a WINDOW command.

The WINDOW statement automatically reorders the values of the extreme x- and y-coordinates so that the lesser x-coordinate is on the left, the greater on the right, the lesser y-coordinate is at the bottom, and the greater on the top. Thus, for example, the following WINDOW statements are all equivalent:

```
WINDOW (-1,1)-(1,-1)
WINDOW (1,1)-(-1,-1)
WINDOW (-1,-1)-(1,1)
WINDOW (1,-1)-(-1,1)
```

Note that the above statements turn the screen into a portion of a Cartesian coordinate system, of the same type used in graphing points and equations in algebra. Note also that increasing values of the y-coordinate correspond to moving up the screen. This is the exact opposite of the normal graphics coordinates, in which the pixel rows are numbered from 0 (top of screen) to 199 (bottom of screen). A coordinate system in which increasing values of the y-coordinate correspond to moving **down** the screen are called **screen coordinates**. You may use the WINDOW statement to create a set of screen coordinates using the SCREEN option. For example, the statement

```
WINDOW SCREEN (-2,0)-(2,100)
```

creates a coordinate system as shown in Figure 3.34. Note that y-coordinate 0 is now at the top of the screen.

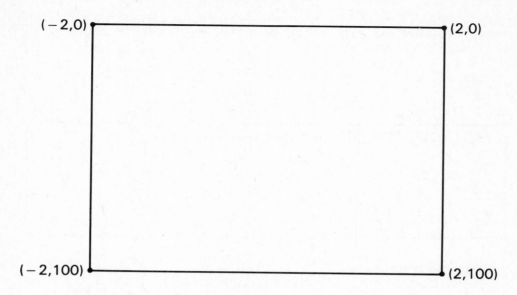

(−2,0)   (2,0)

(−2,100)   (2,100)

Figure 3.34. Screen Coordinates (-2,0)-(2,100).

EXAMPLE 1   Use the WINDOW command to draw an expanding family of rectangles beginning at the center of the screen.

SOLUTION   Let's use a single line statement, namely

```
Line (-.1,-.1)-(.1,.1),,B
```

to draw a rectangle with center (0,0). But let's use a sequence of WINDOW commands to redefine the coordinate system so that the radius .1 corresponds to successively larger distances on the screen. That is, we will let the Jth coordinate system be generated by the statement

```
WINDOW (-1/J,-1/J)-(1/J,1/J)
```

for J = 1, 2, . . . ,10. For the first coordinate system, the screen corresponds to (-1,-1)-(1,1). So the distance .1 seems small. (It corresponds to only .05 of the way across the screen). On the other hand, for J = 10, the coordinate system corresponds to (-.1,-.1)-(.1,.1). So .1 is halfway across the screen. Here is our program.

```
10 SCREEN 2:KEY OFF
20 CLS
30 FOR J=1 TO 10
40      WINDOW (-1/J,-1/J)-(1/J,1/J)
50      LINE (-.1,-.1)-(.1,.1)
60 NEXT J
```

The output of the program is shown in Figure 3.35.

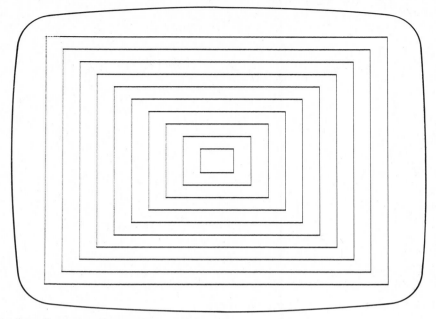

Figure 3.35. Expanding Rectangles.

The WINDOW statement ignores points corresponding to positions off the screen. This procedure is known as **clipping**.

RUN, SCREEN, and WINDOW with no parameters disable any previous WINDOW command.

The VIEW statement allows you to restrict screen activity to a portion of the screen. For example, to restrict all screen activity to the rectangle (20,10)-(100,200), we would use the statement

```
VIEW SCREEN (20,10)-(100,200)
```

This statement turns the rectangle (20,10)-(100,200) in a **viewport**. While a viewport is in effect, you may not plot any points outside the viewport. For example, if a circle statement refers to a circle that lies partially outside a viewport, then only the portion within the viewport will be drawn.

If you execute CLS while a viewport is in effect, you will erase **only** the inside of the viewport.

Note that the viewport applies only to graphics commands. Text commands may apply to any position on the screen, even though a viewport is in effect. Thus, for example, you may use LOCATE and PRINT as if the viewport were not present.

The full form of the VIEW statement is

```
VIEW [SCREEN] (x1,y1)-(x2,y2),[color],[boundary]
```

The color option allows you to fill in the viewport with a particular color (0-3). The boundary option allows you to put a rectangular boundary around the viewport. The value of [background] (0-3) determines the color of the bounding rectangle.

For example, the statement

```
VIEW SCREEN (10,20)-(200,100),3,2
```

defines a viewport colored in color 3 with a boundary in color 2, and the statement

```
VIEW SCREEN (10,20)-(200,100),,2
```

defines a viewport with a boundary in color 2. The interior of the viewport is the background color.

You may omit the SCREEN parameter to obtain plotting relative to the viewport. For example, consider the statement

```
VIEW (10,20)-(200,100)
```

It defines the same viewport as above. However, the point (x,y) in a graphics statement will be interpreted to mean $(x + 10, y + 20)$. In other words, the upper left corner of the viewport is considered as the corner of the screen. The same clipping rules as for VIEW SCREEN apply: If a point (as computed relative to the viewport) lies outside the viewport, then it is not plotted.

You may disable a viewport using the statement

```
VIEW
```

Similarly, using RUN or SCREEN will cancel a viewport.

You may combine VIEW and WINDOW. For example, consider the statements

```
10 VIEW (80,16)-(559,167),,3
20 WINDOW (0,0)-(20,100)
```

They define a viewport in the rectangle (80,16)-(559,167) and then redefine the coordinates **within the viewport** as the Cartesian coordinates (0,0)-(20,100). So (0,0) corresponds to the lower left corner of the viewport and (20,100) to the upper right corner.

On the other hand, consider the statements

```
10 VIEW SCREEN (80,16)-(559,167),,3
20 WINDOW (0,0)-(20,100)
```

Now the WINDOW command refers to the entire screen. (0,0) corresponds to the lower left corner of the screen and (20,100) to the upper right corner of the screen. The viewport serves as a mask to clip off all points that (in the coordinates specified by WINDOW) land outside the viewport.

As we'll see in the next section, viewports are ideal for generating business graphics. We'll use a combination of VIEW and WINDOW to create a custom coordinate system on which to draw a bar graph.

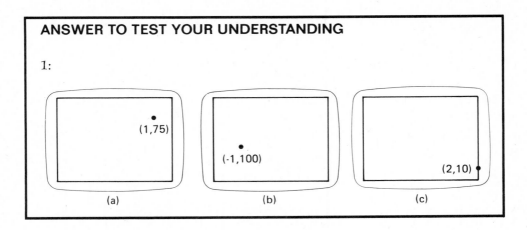

ANSWER TO TEST YOUR UNDERSTANDING

1:

(a) (1,75)

(b) (-1,100)

(c) (2,10)

3.10   Bar Charts — A Case Study, I

In this section, we will launch a major illustration, an actual case study that will show you how a large program is designed and built. Our goal is to build a bar chart program that accepts data from either screen input or a data file and draws the bar chart, along with descriptive titles and labels. At first this might seem like a tall order. But we'll approach this case study step-by-step. And before we know it, we'll have a working program.

Our bar chart program will be built from a number of separate pieces, collected as subroutines and sequenced by a controlling program. In this section, let's concentrate on the design of the portion of the program that actually draws the bar chart from the data. (We'll worry about data input later.)

Let's assign variables to some of the important quantities which our program must reference.

Our requirements, drawn up in Chapter 2, state that the program should allow for display of up to three separate sets of data, as shown in Figure 3.36. The number of different sets (or **series**) of data will be contained in the variable SER%. So SER% will equal either 1, 2, or 3. Each set of data may contain as many as 20 data items. (This will allow up to 3 X 20 or 60 sets of bars. This is the maximum that our screen layout can accomodate.)

The data for the bar chart will be contained in an array DTA$(N%,J%). Here N% is the number of the data set and J% will be the number of the data item within the particular data set. Here is a typical set of data:

	Data Series 1	Data Series 2	Data Series 3
Jan	1580	38.35	48.55
Feb	1312.11	1450.00	12.11

For example, DTA$(2,1)="38.35". The month designations on the left are called **labels** and will be stored as the zero elements in the array. So, for example, DTA$(1,0)="Jan".

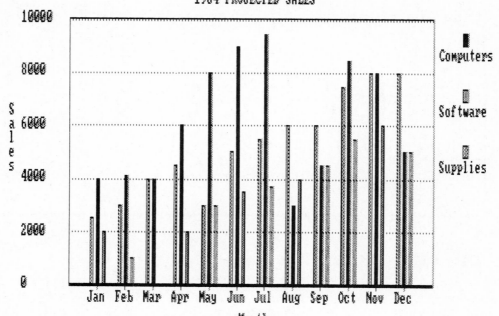

Figure 3.36. A Typical Bar Chart.

You may wonder why we are using a string array to store the data rather than a numerical array. There are two good reasons. First, a string array allows us to store the labels in the same array as the data. Second (and more important), a numerical array allows BASIC to reformat our numbers. For example, 1450.00 will be converted to the number 1450. Of course, we could reformat our numbers on output with PRINT USING, but it is by far easier not to keep track of formats and simply store the data as a string, exactly as it was input. When we use the data for numerical purposes, we will convert it to numerical form using the VAL function.

Let's draw our bar chart in high-resolution graphics (SCREEN 2). We will confine our bar chart to the portion of the screen (16,80)-(169,559). This gives us a 152 x 480 region for our chart. It also leaves the top 2 lines and the bottom 4 lines of the screen for titles. Also, we have room for labels 8 characters wide on either side of the graph.

For the time being, let's set aside the problem of displaying the labels. This involves the problem of precise placement of text in graphics mode, which we will solve in Chapter 6. For now, let's concentrate on drawing the bars.

The coordinate system for the bar chart will be described by the following parameters:

YMIN = the beginning Y-value on the Y-axis
YMAX = the final Y-value on the Y-axis
XMAX = the maximum number of data items in a data series
GRID$ = "Y" if horizontal grid lines are to be displayed
       = "N" otherwise

Our program begins by defining the above screen area as a viewport. Next, we WINDOW to define the coordinate system (0,YMIN)-(XMAX + 1,YMAX) on the viewport. Note that we use XMAX + 1 (rather than XMAX) so that the value XMAX is within the viewport, leaving space for the last bar.

The width of the bars will be (XMAX + 1)/120. This makes each bar 4 pixels wide. (The viewport is 480 pixels wide.) We will store half of this number, or (XMAX + 1)/240, in the variable BW (=bar width). We will draw a bar by locating the center of the lower edge and drawing the sides of the bar at a distance of BW on either side of the center. At each of the integer positions along the X-axis, we will center the bar corresponding to data series 1. We will place the bar for data series 2, 8 pixels to the right and the bar for data series 3, 8 pixels to the left. We store this data in the array ADJ():

ADJ(1) = 0 (center)

ADJ(2) = (XMAX + 1)/60 (8 pixels to the right)

ADJ(3) = -(XMAX + 1)/60 (8 pixels to the left)

Here is the program.

```
1 YMIN=-500:YMAX=500:XMAX=5:YSTEP=100
5 SER%=3
100 'Dimension statements
110 DIM DTA$(4,20)
120 DATA 150,175,300,400,450,-300,-200,500,125,175,
        -200,-100,425,120,-200
200 'Variable initialization
240 FOR J%=1 TO 5
250     FOR N%=1 TO 3
260             READ DTA$(N%,J%)
270     NEXT N%
280 NEXT J%
3000 '**************DRAWBAR ROUTINE**************
3005     CLS
3010     KEY OFF
3015     SCREEN 2:SER%=3
3020     YMIN=VAL(YMIN$)
3025     YMAX=VAL(YMAX$)
3030     YSTEP=VAL(YSTEP$)
3035     IF YMIN>YMAX THEN SWAP YMIN,YMAX
3040     IF YMIN=YMAX THEN 3095
3045     IF YSTEP=0 THEN 3095
```

```
3055     STYLE$(1)=CHR$(&HFF):STYLE$(2)=CHR$(&HAA):
         STYLE$(3)=CHR$(&H99)+CHR$(&H55)
3060     BW=(XMAX+1)/240
3065     ADJ(1)=0:ADJ(2)=(XMAX+1)/60:ADJ(3)=-(XMAX+1)/60
3070     GOSUB 3195:'Write Titles
3075     GOSUB 3305:'Write x-axis labels
3080     GOSUB 3360:'Write y-axis labels
3085     GOSUB 3415:'Draw coordinate system
3090     GOSUB 3435:'Draw bars
3095     E$="":GOTO 920:'Return to control routine
3100 **************SUBROUTINES****************
3195 'Write titles
3200  RETURN
3305 'Write x-axis labels
3355  RETURN
3360 'Write y-axis labels
3410  RETURN
3415 'Draw coordinate system and bars
3420     VIEW (80,16)-(559,167),,3
3425     WINDOW (0,YMIN)-(XMAX+1,YMAX)
3430     LINE (0,0)-(XMAX+1,0):'Draw x-axis
3435     'Draw bars
3440     FOR N%=1 TO SER%
3445         FOR J%=1 TO XMAX(N%)
3450             IF DTA$(N%,J%)="" THEN 3470
3455             HT=VAL(DTA$(N%,J%))
3460             LINE (J%+ADJ(N%)-BW,0)-
                             (J%+ADJ(N%)+BW,HT),,B
3465             PAINT (J%+ADJ(N%),HT/2),STYLE$(N%)
3470         NEXT J%
3475     NEXT N%
3480     'Draw grid lines
3485     FOR J%=0 TO (YMAX-YMIN)/YSTEP
3490        H=YMIN+J%*YSTEP
3495        LINE (0,H)-(XMAX+1,H),,,&H8888
3500     NEXT J%
3505     RETURN
```

Note that the initial lines provide some data you may use to test the program. Note also that we have indicated subroutines to insert titles, but we'll work out those routines in Chapter 6.

One further point. Note the array STYLE$(). It defines the various shading types for the bars. STYLE$() is used in the PAINT statement in line 3465. We'll learn about PAINTing with various styles in Chapter 6. For now, just realize that the STYLE$() setting produces the various shadings in the bars of Figure 3.36.

Exercises

1. Test the above bar chart program by running it with the given test data.
2. Modify the above bar chart program so that the screen image is saved in a diskette file.
3. Recall the image stored in Exercise 2.

3.11   Sound and Music on the PC

The PC has a speaker located in the front left corner of the system unit. You may use this speaker to introduce sound and even music into your programs. There are three sound commands on the PC—BEEP, SOUND, and PLAY. Let's survey the capabilities of these commands.

BEEP

This command is the simplest of the sound commands. It allows you to sound the speaker for 1/4 second. This command gives you no control over the pitch or the duration of the sound. Here is an example of BEEP in a subroutine that responds to a mistake in input.

```
80 PRINT "YOU MADE A MISTAKE, TRY AGAIN!"
90 BEEP
100 RETURN
```

You may also use a **BEEP** statement within other statements, as in

```
10 IF X=100 THEN BEEP
```

Professional programs employ sophisticated input routines that subject user input to a number of tests to determine if the input is acceptable. (Is the length correct? Does the input employ any illegal characters?) Here is a simple subroutine of this type. The main program assigns a value to the variable LENGTH, which gives the maximum length of an input string. The subroutine illuminates a box, beginning at location 1,1 (top left corner of the screen) to indicate the maximum field size for the input. The routine then allows you to input characters and to display them in the appropriate position in the illuminated field. For each character displayed, part of the illumination disappears. Moreover, using the backspace key restores one character space of illumination. If you attempt to input characters beyond the illuminated field, the routine beeps the speaker.

```
5000 'Input routine
5001 'LENGTH is the maximum number of characters in input
     string
5002 'COUNT is the current cursor position in the input field
5010 COUNT=1
5020 CLS
5030 LOCATE 1,1
5040 PRINT ""
5050 LOCATE 1,1
5060 FOR I=1 TO LENGTH
5070      LOCATE 1,I:PRINT CHR$(219);
5080 NEXT I
5090 LOCATE 1,1
5100 A$=INKEY$
5110 IF A$="" THEN 5100
5120 IF A$=CHR$(8) THEN 5200
5130 IF A$= CHR$(13) THEN 5240
5140 IF COUNT= LENGTH+1 THEN 5180
5150 LOCATE 1,COUNT:PRINT A$;
5160 COUNT=COUNT+1
5170 GOTO 5100
5180 BEEP
5190 GOTO 5090
5200 COUNT=COUNT-1
5210 IF COUNT=0 THEN BEEP:COUNT=COUNT+1
5220 LOCATE 1,COUNT:PRINT CHR$(219);
5230 GOTO 5090
5240 RETURN
```

Input routines are so critical to successful programming that we will be returning to this subject in Chapter 4, where we will enhance the design of the above input routine.

Sound

The second speaker command is called **SOUND**. This handy little command enables you to access any frequency between 37 and 32767 Hertz (cycles per second). The duration of your sound is measured in clock ticks, and there are 18.2 clock ticks per second. A numeric expression in the range 0 to 65535 (that's slightly over one hour) is used. To produce a sound at 500 Hz and make it last for 40 ticks of the clock, we would use this statement

```
SOUND 500, 40
```

Here is an elementary graphics program that has been enhanced by the SOUND command. It draws fixed triangles and random circles and blinks them in a manner suitable for illuminating a rock concert. SOUND provides some audio accompaniment.

```
10 KEY OFF
15 'turns the key line off
20 SCREEN 1
25 ' switches from text mode to graphics mode
30 FOR I=1 TO 100
40    CIRCLE (RND*250, RND*200), 30
45     ' draws a circle with random coordinates and a
          diameter of 30
50    SOUND RND*1000+37, 2
55    ' creates a random sound from 37 to 1037 Hz. with a
          duration of 2 clock ticks
60    CLS
70    DRAW "E15; F15; L30"
75    ' draws a triangle
80    SOUND RND*1000 + 37, 2
90    CLS
100 NEXT I
110 END
```

Music on the PC

Next on the level of sound sophistication is the PLAY command. It enables you to turn your PC into a piano and play musical compositions as simple or as complex as you would like. (There is even an arrangement of Beethoven's *Moonlight Sonata* for PC!)

There are a few musical facts that will help you a great deal in your programming:

1. Just like a piano, the PC uses 7 octaves, numbered 0 to 6. Each octave starts with C and goes to B.

2. Octave 3 starts with middle C.

3. The tempo of a song is the speed at which it is played. On the PC, tempo is measured by the number of quarter notes per second. The tempo may range from 32 to 255.

4. The PC allows you to style your notes as normal, legato, or staccato. Normal means that notes are held down for 7/8 of their defined length. Legato means that each note will play for the full time period that you set it to play, while staccato means that each note is held for only 3/4 of the time specified. Legato notes sound "smooth," whereas staccato notes are "crisp."

PLAY

The **PLAY** command allows you to show your creative musical genius, even if you can't play a comb. It uses a language that allows you to write music in the form of strings. Once the music has been transcribed, the PLAY statement allows you to play it on the speaker.

To use the PLAY command:

1. Code the desired musical notes as a string.

2. Use the PLAY command in the form

     PLAY <string>

For example, consider this program. Why not type it in and listen to the results:

```
10 A$="O3L4EDCDEE"
20 PLAY "XA$; E2DDD2EGG2; T255XA$; EEDDEDP2C1"
```

The program probably makes the music look quite mysterious. However, the musical language is quite simple. Here is a summary.

NOTES Indicated by the letters A to G with an optional #, +, or -. The # or + after a letter indicates a sharp, while the - indicates a flat. For example, the note "A sharp" is written A#, whereas "G flat" is written G-.

LENGTH L defines the LENGTH of a note. L1 is a whole note, L2 is a half note, L4 is a quarter note, . . . , L64 a 64th note. The L command defines the length of all subsequent notes, until another L command is given. For example, to play the string of notes CDEFG in quarter notes, we would use this string:
     L4 CDEFG
If you wish to define the length of a single note, omit the L and put the number indicating the length after the note. For example, C4 would indicate C held for a quarter note. Subsequent notes would be held for an amount defined by the most recent L command.

As in musical notation, a dot after a note indicates that the note is to be held for one-and-one-half times its usual length.

REST P1 is a whole note rest, P2 a half note, and so forth.

OCTAVE Initially, all notes are taken from octave 4 (the octave above the one beginning with middle C). The octave is changed by giving the O command. For example, to change to octave 2, the command would be O2. After you give an octave command, all notes are taken from the indicated octave unless you change the octave or temporarily overrule the octave (see below).

TEST YOUR UNDERSTANDING 1 (answer on page 76)

Write a string that plays an ascending C major scale in eighth notes, pauses for a half-note, and then plays the same scale descending.

TEST YOUR UNDERSTANDING 2 (answer on page 76)

Write a string that plays the scale of TEST YOUR UNDERSTANDING 1 in octave 5.

TEMPO Tempo is the speed at which a composition is played. Tempo is measured in terms of quarter beats per second. Unless you specify otherwise, the tempo is set at 120. You may set the tempo using the T command. For example, to set the tempo to 80, use the command T80. The tempo remains unchanged until you give another T command. The tempo may range from 32 to 255.

TEST YOUR UNDERSTANDING 3 (answer on page 76)

Write a string that plays the scale of TEST YOUR UNDERSTANDING 1 at a tempo of 80 and at a tempo of 150.

STYLE You may select the style of notes from among: Normal, Legato, or Staccato. The respective commands are MN, ML, and MS. The style chosen remains in effect until it is canceled by another style selection.

TEST YOUR UNDERSTANDING 4 (answer on page 76)

Write a string that plays the scale of TEST YOUR UNDERSTANDING 1, but with legato style, and with staccato style.

Ordinarily, the PLAY command will cause BASIC to stop while the specified notes are played. However, you may also use the PLAY command in **background mode**. In this mode, while the speaker plays the notes, BASIC continues executing the program, beginning with the statements immediately after the PLAY statement. The background mode may be started with the command MB. You may return to normal mode (also called **foreground mode**) with the command MF.

In coding music, you may wish to use the same string a number of times. This would occur, for example, in the case of a refrain. The X command allows you to repeat a string without retyping it. Just store the desired string in a string variable, say A\$. Whenever the string is required, type

    XA$;

Exercise

1. Choose a piece of piano music and transcribe it for the PC.

ANSWERS TO TEST YOUR UNDERSTANDING

```
1:  A$="CDEFGAB O5 C O4 P2 CBAGFEDC"

2:  A$="O5CDEFGAB O6 C P2 C O5 BAGFEDC"

3:  A$="T80 CDEFGAB O5 C P2 C O4 BAGFEDC"
    A$="T150 CDEFGAB O5 C P2 C O4 BAGFEDC"

4:  A$="ML CDEFGAB O5 C P2 C O4 BAGFEDC"
    A$="MS CDEFGAB C O5 P2 C O4 BAGFEDC"
```

4

Input the Professional Way

4.1 Why You Need an Input Routine

When you saw the title of this chapter, you probably thought: "I know about input. I can use INPUT and LINE INPUT to handle my programs' input needs." Well, I have some bad news. If you want to write professional level programs, the BASIC input statements INPUT and LINE INPUT leave much to be desired.

For example, suppose that your program has just set up a menu with choices to be input by the user. Suppose that INPUT is used to accept the user response. BASIC will respond to a type mismatch (string instead of number or vice versa) with the prompt

Redo from start?

This will usually wreck the carefully planned screen layout you have just created.

INPUT will accept as numerical input any number legal in BASIC, such as 1.7839E-18. For each input to your program, it is your responsibility to check that numbers are of the required type (say, positive or an integer between 1 and 10). But how do you prevent the program user from inputting a number such as 1E40, which is beyond the limits allowed by BASIC? Before you can analyze the input, BASIC declares an overflow error. And you can't RESUME after an overflow!

As for string input, you usually must control the length of input. (Say a name cannot have more than 20 characters.) Or, suppose that a question calls for a Y or N response. Your program should also accept y or n and reject all other letters.

As you can see from the above recitation, input is a complicated business. And, if you wish to write professional level programs, you must be able to control your input so that you force the user to provide input the program can use. That's the purpose of an input routine.

In this chapter, I'll describe an input routine I've developed that avoids all the problems mentioned above. It is a complex routine, but you'll have no trouble understanding it. It was more complicated to build than it is to comprehend. And now that the work's done, you can use it in your own programs.

Our input program is called INPUT and is composed of three main routines, called KEYIN, SCREENIN, and NUMBERCK. KEYIN reads the keyboard, one character at a time. On the basis of user-supplied information, KEYIN accepts certain characters and rejects others. You may request KEYIN to change input to all capital letters.

SCREENIN is a screen entry routine, which displays input characters in a specific field on the screen. SCREENIN allows some character editing and passes on extended ASCII codes for further analysis.

NUMBERCK is a routine that analyzes a string to determine if it is in an acceptable format to be converted into a number. If possible, NUMBERCK performs the conversion and passes the number back to the main program. NUMBERCK also determines whether the converted number is an integer.

Together, these three routines allow you to input data to your program knowing that you are in total control.

We begin this chapter with four preliminary Sections: In Section 2, we discuss the INKEY$ variable, a crucial ingredient in our three input routines. In Section 3, we discuss how you may use the function keys to provide input to a program. In Section 4, we discuss the extended ASCII codes, which are necessary if our input routines are to be able to recognize all possible keyboard input. In Sections 5 and 6, we build our three input routines. Finally, in Section 7, we apply the routines to construct a portion of our case study program, THE BAR CHART GENERATOR.

4.2   The INKEY$ Variable

The Keyboard Buffer

Many programs depend on input from the operator. We have learned to provide such input using the INPUT and LINE INPUT statements. When the program encounters either of these statements, it pauses and waits for input. The program will not proceed unless valid input is provided. The INKEY$ function provides an alternative method of reading the keyboard.

When a key is pressed, BASIC interrupts what it is doing and places the ASCII code corresponding to the key in a reserved section of memory called the **keyboard buffer**. The keyboard buffer has space to record as many as 15 keystrokes. The process of recording information in the keyboard buffer usually proceeds so that you don't even realize that the keyboard buffer is there. For instance, in typing program lines, BASIC is constantly reading the keyboard buffer and displaying the corresponding characters on the screen. In a similar fashion, an INPUT statement reads the keyboard buffer and displays the corresponding characters on the screen. A carriage return (generated by ENTER) tells the INPUT statement to stop reading the buffer.

As characters are read from the buffer, the space they occupy is released. If the buffer is full and you attempt to type a character, you will hear a beep on the speaker. This is to inform you that, until the buffer is read, further typed characters will be lost.

Note that you may type on the keyboard while a program is running. Even though BASIC is busy executing a program, it will pause to place your typed characters in the keyboard buffer, and then return to execution. When the buffer is next read, it will read the characters in the order they were typed. In this way, you may "type ahead" of required program input, at least until the keyboard buffer is full.

Clearing the Buffer

In certain applications, you may wish to prevent the user from typing ahead. One way to do this is to empty the buffer prior to requesting input. You may empty the buffer using the statement line

```
DEF SEG = 0:POKE 1050,PEEK(1052):DEF SEG
```

(We will discuss the DEF SEG, PEEK, and POKE statements in the next chapter. For now just accept this sequence of statements as something that works to clear the keyboard buffer.)

Actually, there are **two** keyboard buffers in BASIC. When accepting program lines or commands in command mode, BASIC stores partial program lines in the **BASIC line buffer**. This buffer stores lines until they are complete (which you indicate by pressing ENTER). The keyboard buffer, on the other hand, accepts keyboard entries only while BASIC is in the execute mode.

The INKEY$ Variable

The INKEY$ function allows you to read one character from the keyboard buffer. When the program reaches INKEY$, it will read the "oldest" character in the keyboard buffer and return it as a string. This procedure counts as reading the character, so that the character is removed from the buffer. If there is no character in the keyboard buffer, INKEY$ will equal the empty string (i.e. INKEY$ = """).

INKEY$ has many uses. For example, suppose that you wish to pause your program until some key is pressed. Here is a statement that accomplishes this task:

```
100 IF INKEY$ = "" THEN 100
```

The program will continually test the keyboard buffer. If there is no character to be read, the test will be repeated, and so on until some key has been pressed.

Caution We have explained the operation of INKEY$ in terms of the keyboard buffer so that you could understand the following trap. If the keyboard buffer is not empty, a reference to INKEY$ will remove a character. If you use INKEY$ a second time, you will be referring to the keyboard buffer anew and the value of the first INKEY$ will be lost. Moral: If you wish to use the value of INKEY$ again, store the value in a string variable. For example, suppose that the keyboard buffer is holding the letters "A" and "B", with "A" the first letter in the buffer. Consider the following an example of a statement NOT to use:

```
10 IF INKEY$ <> "" THEN PRINT INKEY$
```

This statement will print the letter "B". The first reference to INKEY$ will fetch the "A" from the buffer. The second reference fetches the "B". It is much safer to store the value of INKEY$ in a variable, so that it will not be lost in subsequent references to INKEY$, as in the above statement. That is, line 10 above should be replaced by the statement

```
10 C$=INKEY$:IF C$ <> "" THEN PRINT C$
```

Exercises (answers on page 349)

Suppose that the keyboard buffer is originally empty and you type A followed by F followed by c.

1. What is the value of INKEY$?

2. Suppose that the INKEY$ of Exercise 1 has been executed. Suppose that it is followed by the statement:

    ```
    IF INKEY$ = "A" THEN PRINT INKEY$
    ```

    What letter will be displayed on the screen?

3. Write a program that tests the keyboard and displays the keys pressed in a single line, with no spaces between them.

4.3   The Function Keys and Event Trapping

The function keys are the 10 keys labeled F1 through F10 on the left side of the PC keyboard.

The Function Keys as User-Defined Keys

Each function key may be assigned a string constant containing as many as 15 characters. When a function key is pressed, the corresponding string is input to BASIC. In this way, you may reduce typing standard inputs to single keystrokes. This tends to eliminate typing errors. For example, suppose that an input statement asked for a response of HIGH, LOW, or AVERAGE. You could define function keys F1, F2 and F3 to be, respectively, the strings

F1: HIGH <carriage return>

F2: LOW <carriage return>

F3: AVERAGE <carriage return>

Then, pressing F1, for example, would be equivalent to responding to the input statement with the string HIGH followed by ENTER.

Setting Function Keys

You may assign strings to the function keys in either command or execution mode. To assign <string> to the function key n, use the statement

```
KEY n, string
```

Suppose for example that you wish to assign key F1 the string

```
LLIST <carriage return>,
```

This may be done by the statement

```
10 KEY 1, "LLIST"+CHR$(13)
```

Subsequently, whenever you press key F1, the desired string will be input to BASIC. In particular, suppose that the BASIC prompt Ok is displayed, so that you are in the immediate mode. Then pressing F1 will have the same effect as typing LLIST and pressing ENTER. That is, pressing F1 will cause the current program to be listed on the printer. In effect, you have customized the F1 key to a special application. In a similar fashion, you may customize other keys with commands or keystroke sequences that come up often in your work.

If you assign a null string to a function key (via a command of the form KEY n,""), you will disable the function key.

Note that function key strings may contain characters with ASCII codes from 0 to 127.

To display the current function key string assignments, use the command

```
KEY LIST
```

The current string assignments will be displayed on the usual text area of the screen (lines 1-24).

In writing or running a program, it is often convenient to have a reminder of the various key string assignments on the screen at all times. This may be accomplished by giving the command

```
KEY ON
```

The first 6 characters of each function key string will then be displayed in line 25 of the screen. (In case of line width 40, only the first 5 function key strings are displayed.) To turn off the function key display in line 25, use the command

```
KEY OFF
```

TEST YOUR UNDERSTANDING 1 (answer on page 86)

(a)   Write commands to assign the following strings to function keys
      1-3.
      F1—"ADDITION"
      F2—"SUBTRACTION"
      F3—"MULTIPLICATION"
Disable all other function keys.
(b)   Display the function key assignments in line 25.

Event Trapping (BASICA Only)

To use this section, you must use the BASICA version (Advanced BASIC)
of PC BASIC.

We have described how to input data using INPUT, LINE INPUT, and
INKEY$. All of these input methods have the following feature in common:
The program decides when to ask for the input. You may use the function
keys for a very different form of input.

Suppose that you wish the program to monitor function key 1. The instant
F1 is pressed, you wish the program to go to the subroutine in line 1000. This
may be accomplished first by turning on event trapping for key F1 via the
statement

```
10 KEY(1) ON
```

This tells the program to examine F1 after every program statement is executed. Next, we tell the program that whenever F1 is pushed, go to the subroutine starting in line 1000. We tell the program this in the statement

```
20 ON KEY(1) GOSUB 1000
```

The program will inspect the keyboard buffer at the end of each program
statement. When it detects that F1 has been pushed, it will GOSUB 1000.

You may use event trapping to implement a menu, as illustrated in the
following example.

EXAMPLE 1.   Write a program to test addition, subtraction, and multiplication of two-digit numbers. Let the user select the operation via function
keys F1 through F3. Let function key F4 cause the program to end.

SOLUTION.   We create four subroutines, corresponding to addition,
subtraction, multiplication and END. These four subroutines begin in line
1000, 2000, 3000, and 4000, respectively. What is of most interest to us, however, are lines 10-210. We first clear the screen and define the strings associated with function keys F1 to F4 to be, respectively, ADD, SUBTR, MULT,
and EXIT. These definitions are displayed on line 25 of the screen. We then

disable all the rest of the function keys. In lines 140-170, we set up the event trapping lines for function keys F1-F4. And in lines 180-200, we turn the event trapping on.

In line 210, we select the two numbers to use in our arithmetic. And in line 220, we set up an infinite loop that continuously goes from 220 to 210 and back to 220. Note that this infinite loop accesses different random numbers in each repetition. Thus, the problem you get will depend on how long you take to press one of the function keys. So it is really unnecessary to use the randomize command to guarantee non-repeatability. The program keeps executing the loop until one of the function keys F1-F4 is pressed. Then it goes to the appropriate subroutine. Notice that the strings attached to F1-F4 are displayed in line 25 of the screen. This is accomplished in line 130.

```
10   'Initialize function keys
20      CLS
30      KEY 1, "ADD"
40      KEY 2, "SUBTR"
50      KEY 3, "MULT"
60      KEY 4, "EXIT"
70      KEY 5,""
80      KEY 6,""
90      KEY 7,""
100     KEY 8,""
110     KEY 9,""
120     KEY 10,""
130     KEY ON
140     ON KEY(1) GOSUB 1000
150     ON KEY(2) GOSUB 2000
160     ON KEY(3) GOSUB 3000
170     ON KEY(4) GOSUB 4000
180     FOR J=1 TO 4
190         KEY(J) ON
200     NEXT J
210     X=INT(100*RND):Y=INT(100*RND)
220     GOTO 210
1000 'Addition
1010        CLS
1020        PRINT "ADDITION"
1030        PRINT "PROBLEM"
1040        PRINT X;" +";Y;" EQUALS?"
```

```
1050        INPUT ANSWER
1060        IF ANSWER=X+Y THEN 1070 ELSE 1090
1070        PRINT "CORRECT"
1080        GOTO 1100
1090        PRINT "INCORRECT. THE CORRECT ANSWER IS";X+Y
1100 RETURN
2000 'Subtraction
2010        CLS
2020        PRINT "SUBTRACTION"
2030        PRINT "PROBLEM"
2040        PRINT X;" -";Y;" EQUALS?"
2050        INPUT ANSWER
2060        IF ANSWER=X-Y THEN 2070 ELSE 2090
2070        PRINT "CORRECT"
2080        GOTO 2100
2090        PRINT "INCORRECT. THE CORRECT ANSWER IS";X-Y
2100 RETURN
3000 'Multiplication
3010        CLS
3020        PRINT "MULTIPLICATION"
3030        PRINT "PROBLEM"
3040        PRINT X;" *";Y;" EQUALS?"
3050        INPUT ANSWER
3060        IF ANSWER=X*Y THEN 3070 ELSE 3090
3070        PRINT "CORRECT"
3080        GOTO 3100
3090        PRINT "INCORRECT. THE CORRECT ANSWER IS";X*Y
3100 RETURN
4000 'Exit
4010        CLS
4020        KEY OFF
4030 END
```

There may be certain sections in the program in which you wish to disallow trapping of function key n. This may be done using either of the statments

```
KEY(n) STOP
KEY(n) OFF
```

You may resume trapping of function key n using the statement

```
KEY(n) ON
```

If function key n is pressed while a STOP is in effect, the event will be remembered. When trapping is turned on, the program will immediately jump to the appropriate subroutine. If you use a KEY(n) OFF statment, then the event is not remembered when trapping is turned back on.

In addition to the function keys, you may trap the cursor motion keys. (These are the four keys on the numeric keypad with arrows pointing in the four possible directions of cursor motion.) The commands for trapping these keys are

```
ON KEY(n) GOSUB
KEY(n) ON
KEY(n) OFF
KEY(n) STOP
```

where n = 11 corresponds to cursor up, n = 12 to cursor left , n = 13 to cursor right, and n = 14 to cursor down.

Be Wary of the Function Keys

The function keys and their associated BASIC statements are one of the significant features of the PC. However, it is easy to misuse them. I like the function keys so much that I use them to control menu choices in practically all my programs. In such an application, you want the program to respond to a function key by going to a subroutine. At first glance, you might be tempted to implement a scheme such as we did in the above example, using the ON KEY . . . GOSUB statement. However, in building serious programs, this approach has serious defects. For one thing, if you compile your program (as you will almost surely want to do for serious applications programs), any event trapping statements cause extra code to be generated. And the extra code is quite burdensome. The only way the compiler can check for event trapping is to put a check after each statement in the program. This can easily add several thousand bytes to your program. But that's not the whole story. All those tests for event trapping will slow your program considerably. This is not to say that event trapping with the function keys is not a valuable feature. It surely is. However, before you use it, you should ask yourself: Do I really want the program to test for a function key after each instruction? If you are just implementing choices from a menu, the answer should be: No! We'll describe how you should use the function keys to implement menu choices in the next section.

Exercises (answers on page 349)

1. Write a statement that disables function key 5.

2. Write a statement that assigns function key 1 the string 'LIST'<carriage return>.

3. Write a program that causes function key 1 to erase the screen and start a new program.

4. Modify the program of example 1 to disallow function key trapping during the subroutines beginning in lines 1000, 2000, and 3000.

5. Write a statement that traps the cursor up key.

ANSWER TO TEST YOUR UNDERSTANDING

1 (a):

```
10 DATA ADDITION,SUBTRACTION,MULTIPLICATION
20 FOR J=1 TO 3
30     READ A$(J)
40 NEXT J
50 FOR J=1 TO 10
60     KEY J,A$(J)
70 NEXT J
```

(b):   `KEY ON`

4.4   Extended ASCII Codes

Each printable character is assigned a number called its ASCII code. For example, A is assigned the number 65. The ASCII codes are the numbers from 0 to 255 inclusive. Certain of these ASCII codes correspond to control actions rather than to letters. For example, the Escape key has the ASCII code 27. In Table 1, we have included a list of the ASCII codes 0-255 and their interpretations.

The IBM PC keyboard allows for many more key combinations than the standard set of ASCII codes allows. For this reason, the IBM uses **extended ASCII codes** in addition to the standard ones. An extended ASCII code consists of two numbers: a zero followed by one of the numbers 0-255. Here are some examples of extended ASCII codes:

0 15

0 71

0 131

The extended ASCII codes are generated from the keyboard as follows:

ASCII Value	Character	ASCII Value	Character	ASCII Value	Character
000	(null)	041	)	082	R
001	◙	042	*	083	S
002	◙	043	+	084	T
003	♥	044	,	085	U
004	♦	045	—	086	V
005	♣	046	.	087	W
006	♠	047	/	088	X
007	(beep)	048	0	089	Y
008	◙	049	1	090	Z
009	(tab)	050	2	091	[
010	(line feed)	051	3	092	\
011	(home)	052	4	093	]
012	(form feed)	053	5	094	∧
013	(carriage return)	054	6	095	—
014	♫	055	7	096	`
015	☼	056	8	097	a
016	►	057	9	098	b
017	◄	058	:	099	c
018	↕	059	;	100	d
019	‼	060	<	101	e
020	¶	061	=	102	f
021	§	062	>	103	g
022	▬	063	?	104	h
023	↨	064	@	105	i
024	↑	065	A	106	j
025	↓	066	B	107	k
026	→	067	C	108	l
027	←	068	D	109	m
028	(cursor right)	069	E	110	n
029	(cursor left)	070	F	111	o
030	(cursor up)	071	G	112	p
031	(cursor down)	072	H	113	q
032	(space)	073	I	114	r
033	!	074	J	115	s
034	''	075	K	116	t
035	#	076	L	117	u
036	$	077	M	118	v
037	%	078	N	119	w
038	&	079	O	120	x
039	'	080	P	121	y
040	(	081	Q	122	z

Table 1–The ASCII Codes.

Input the Professional Way

ASCII Value	Character	ASCII Value	Character	ASCII Value	Character	ASCII Value	Character
123	{	164	ñ	205	=	246	÷
124	¦	165	Ñ	206	╬	247	≈
125	}	166	ª	207	╧	248	°
126	~	167	º	208	╨	249	•
127	⌂	168	¿	209	╤	250	·
128	Ç	169	⌐	210	╥	251	√
129	ü	170	¬	211	╙	252	ⁿ
130	é	171	½	212	╘	253	²
131	â	172	¼	213	╒	254	■
132	ä	173	¡	214	╓	255	(blank 'FF')
133	à	174	«	215	╫		
134	å	175	»	216	╪		
135	ç	176	░	217	┘		
136	ê	177	▒	218	┌		
137	ë	178	▓	219	█		
138	è	179	│	220	▄		
139	ï	180	┤	221	▌		
140	î	181	╡	222	▐		
141	ì	182	╢	223	▀		
142	Ä	183	╖	224	α		
143	Å	184	╕	225	β		
144	É	185	╣	226	Γ		
145	æ	186	║	227	π		
146	Æ	187	╗	228	Σ		
147	ô	188	╝	229	σ		
148	ö	189	╜	230	μ		
149	ò	190	╛	231	τ		
150	û	191	┐	232	Φ		
151	ù	192	└	233	θ		
152	ÿ	193	┴	234	Ω		
153	Ö	194	┬	235	δ		
154	Ü	195	├	236	∞		
155	¢	196	—	237	$\emptyset$		
156	£	197	+	238	ϵ		
157	¥	198	╞	239	$\cap$		
158	Pt	199	╟	240	≡		
159	ƒ	200	╚	241	±		
160	á	201	╔	242	≥		
161	í	202	╩	243	≤		
162	ó	203	╦	244	⌠		
163	ú	204	╠	245	⌡		

Table 1—The ASCII Codes (Continued).

Second Number of Extended ASCII Code	Key(s) Generating Code
15	Shift tab ( )
16-25	Alt-Q,W,E,R,T,Y,U,I,O,P
30-38	Alt-A,S,D,F,G,H,J,K,L
44-50	Alt-Z,X,C,V,B,N,M
59-68	Function Keys F1-F10 (when disabled as soft keys)
71	Home
72	Cursor Up
73	Pg Up
75	Cursor Left
77	Cursor Right
79	End
80	Cursor Down
81	Pg Down
82	Ins
83	Del
84-93	Shift- F1-F10
94-103	Ctrl- F1-F10
104-113	Alt- F1-F10
114	Ctrl-PrtSc
115	Ctrl-Space
116	Ctrl-Backspace
117	Ctrl-End
118	Ctrl-PgDn
119	Ctrl-Home
120-131	Alt- 1,2,3,4,5,6,7,8,9,0,-,=
132	Ctrl- PgUp

Any ASCII codes that don't appear in the above list may not be generated from the keyboard.

Here is how the extended ASCII codes work. Suppose, for example, that you push the key **Home**. BASIC inserts its extended ASCII code into the keyboard buffer. So the keyboard buffer contains the two numbers 0, 71. As an experiment, run this program.

```
10 C$=INKEY$
20 IF C$="" THEN 20
30 PRINT LEN(C$)
40 PRINT ASC(LEFT$(C$,1))
50 PRINT ASC(RIGHT$(C$,1))
```

In response to the INPUT statement, hit the Home key. The program will print out the three numbers 2, 0 and 71. That is, in response to an extended ASCII code, INKEY$ returns the two character string CHR$(0)+CHR$(71). The first character, CHR$(0), indicates an extended ASCII code. The second character, CHR$(71), indicates the key pushed, according to the above table.

Using the extended ASCII codes, you may keep track of input from all the keyboard keys.

TEST YOUR UNDERSTANDING 1 (Answer on page 91)

Suppose that you press they keys Alt-A followed by End. What will be the contents of the keyboard buffer?

TEST YOUR UNDERSTANDING 2 (Answer on page 91)

Write a program that reads a single key from the keyboard buffer. The program should allow you to read a key with an extended ASCII code.

An important note about the function keys: If a function key is enabled, then pressing it will cause its associated string to be placed in the keyboard buffer. **However, no extended ASCII code will be generated.** On the other hand, if a function key is disabled, then pressing it will generate the corresponding extended ASCII code. For example, if F1 has the associated string "HELP" + CHR$(13), then pressing F1 will put a string of five ASCII codes in the keyboard buffer, namely the ASCII codes corresponding to the four letters "HELP" and ASCII code 13. On the other hand, if F1 is disabled, then pressing F1 will cause the ASCII codes 0 and 59 (the extended code for F1) to be entered into the keyboard buffer.

I prefer to use my function keys by avoiding ON KEY ... GOSUB. To do this, I first disable all the function keys as soft keys. I then use a custom input routine that passes on all keyboard characters to an analysis routine. If the key pressed was a function key, the analysis routine passes the extended ASCII code in the variable E$. By inspecting E$, I can then direct the program to the appropriate subroutine. In this way, all inputs to my program are treated alike. And the savings in memory and run speed are usually considerable.

As an example, consider the following program, which is the command structure we will use in writing our bar chart program in Chapter 7.

```
10 KEY OFF
20 MENU$="1 DEF 2 DATA 3 DRAW 4 SAVE 5 RCLL 6 FILE
        7 EXIT"
30 FOR J%=1 TO 10:KEY J%,"":NEXT J%
100 'Main Menu Choice-Bar Chart Program
110 'E$ is returned by the input routine, =the second
120 'character of extended ASCII code
130 LOCATE 25,1
140 PRINT MENU$;
150 C=ASC(E$)
160 IF C=59 THEN 1000
170 IF C=60 THEN 2000
```

```
180 IF C=61 THEN 3000
190 IF C=62 THEN 4000
200 IF C=63 THEN 5000
210 IF C=64 THEN 6000
220 IF C=65 THEN 7000 ELSE 25000
1000 'Define bar chart parameters
2000 'Input bar chart data
3000 'Draw bar chart
4000 'Save bar chart
5000 'Recall bar chart
6000 'Read data file
7000 'Exit
25000 'Input routine
```

Note the following aspects of this program.

1. Line 30 disables the function keys as soft keys so that pressing the function keys will return an extended ASCII code.

2. Lines 130-140 simulate the usual function key display that was turned off in line 10.

3. Lines 150-210 send the program to the appropriate routine selected by the user. Note that these lines use GOTO rather than GOSUB. Each of the routines will accept its own input from the keyboard buffer by repeatedly calling on the input routine. Whenever a function key is spotted, the routine will send the program back to the above control routine.

4. Line 25000 indicates the beginning of the input routine that we will write in Sections 5 and 6.

ANSWERS TO TEST YOUR UNDERSTANDING

```
1:  CHR$(0)+CHR$(30)+CHR$(0)+CHR$(79)

2:  10 C$=INKEY$
    20 IF C$="" THEN PRINT "NO CHARACTER IN BUFFER"
    30 IF ASC(LEFT$(C$,1))<>0 THEN 100 ELSE
       C$=RIGHT$(C$,1)
    40 PRINT "EXTENDED CODE: 0,";
    100 PRINT ASC(C$)
```

4.5 Inputting Characters

As the first part of our professional input package, let's build the routine KEYIN, which inputs characters from the keyboard. KEYIN continually inspects the keyboard buffer to determine if a key has been pressed. If so, the keyboard buffer is read via INKEY$ and the result is put into the variable

C$. Next, KEYIN determines if the key corresponds to an extended ASCII code. (Is the length of C$ 2?) If so, C$ is replaced by its second byte.

After reading the keyboard buffer, KEYIN goes to one of two analysis sections to determine whether the character is acceptable. There is one analysis section for ordinary ASCII codes and one for extended ASCII codes.

In general, the acceptable characters will vary with the section of the program. For one input you may wish to accept only the characters Y, y, n, or N; for another, you may wish to accept only the digits 1,2,3,4,5; and so forth. So there is a variable CALLER that identifies a set of acceptable characters. For each value of CALLER used, you must define six values:

MINKEY(CALLER), MAXKEY(CALLER), SPECIALKEY$(CALLER)

EXTMINKEY(CALLER), EXTMAXKEY(CALLER), EXTSPECIALKEY$(CALLER)

The first three values correspond to ordinary ASCII codes and the second three to extended ASCII codes. For example, suppose that CALLER = 1 and

```
MINKEY(1)=32, MAXKEY(1)=127,
SPECIALKEY$(1)=CHR$(8)+CHR$(13)+CHR$(27)
```

Then KEYIN will accept any character with an ASCII code from 32 to 127 inclusive (these are the displayable, non-graphics characters), as well as the special characters CHR$(8) (backspace), CHR$(13) (carriage return) and CHR$(27) (Esc). Similarly, suppose that

```
EXTMINKEY(1)=59, EXTMAXKEY(1)=68,
EXTSPECIALKEY$(1)=""
```

Then KEYIN will accept extended ASCII codes 59 through 68 (function keys F1 through F10) and no other extended ASCII codes.

TEST YOUR UNDERSTANDING 1 (Answer on page 96)

What are the values of the six variables if KEYIN is to accept all displayable, non-graphics characters, as well as the four cursor motion keys?

Actually, there is a seventh variable that can depend on the particular CALLER, namely CAPSON(CALLER). If CAPSON = -1 then KEYIN converts letters to capitals; if CAPSON = 0 then KEYIN returns the character as input. If conversion to uppercase is requested, then it is performed in line 26195. We will explain how this line works in the next chapter.

TEST YOUR UNDERSTANDING 2 (Answer on page 96)

What are the values of the seven variables if KEYIN is to accept numerical input and all extended ASCII codes?

TEST YOUR UNDERSTANDING 3 (Answer on page 96)

What are the values of the seven variables if KEYIN is to accept the two responses Yes and No (as indicated by the characters Y and N)?

If you type an unacceptable character, KEYIN will beep the speaker and wait for another character.

We have made certain assumptions in writing KEYIN. First, we assume that the arrays MINKEY(), MAXKEY(), SPECIALKEY$(), EXTMINKEY(), EXTMAXKEY(), and EXTSPECIALKEY$() are dimensioned in the main program. Their size should be dictated by the number of different types of input required by the program.

Second, the variables TRUE = -1 and FALSE = 0 are assumed to be assigned in the main program. Using TRUE and FALSE, we can write statements such as

IF EXTENDED = TRUE THEN . . .

IF MENUEND = FALSE THEN . . .

Using TRUE and FALSE makes programs so much more readable that I include these definitions at the beginning of every program that I write.

Here is the routine KEYIN.

```
26000 '****************KEYIN********************
26005 '
26010 'This routine reads a character from the keyboard
26015 'and accepts or rejects it based on the caller's
          specifications.
26020 'Subroutine variables:
26025 '     CALLER = number of caller
26030 '     MINKEY(CALLER)=minimum ASCII code
                          allowed for CALLER
26035 '     MAXKEY(CALLER)=maximum ASCII code
                          allowed for CALLER
26040 '     CAPSON(CALLER)=Convert to CAPITALS?
26045 '     SPECIALKEYS$(CALLER)=String containing any
                          special acceptable keys
26050 '                          for CALLER
26055 '     EXTMINKEY(CALLER)=minimum extended ASCII code
                          allowed for CALLER
26060 '     EXTMAXKEY(CALLER)=maximum extended ASCII code
```

```
                                  allowed for CALLER
26065 '      EXTSPECIALKEY$(CALLER)=special extended ASCII
                                        codes allowed
26070 '                                 for CALLER
26075 'The above arrays must be dimensioned in the main
          program.
26080 'The array values must also be assigned in the main
          program.
26085 'The values of TRUE and FALSE must also be assigned
26090 'in the main program.
26095 '      C$=the character returned
26100 '      EXTENDED=-1 if C$ is the second byte of an
                             extended ASCII code,
26105 '            = 0 otherwise
26110 'Input character string from INKEY$
26115    C$=INKEY$
26120    IF C$="" THEN 26115: 'Wait for input
26125    C=ASC(C$)
26130    IF LEN(C$)=2 THEN EXTENDED=TRUE ELSE
                            EXTENDED=FALSE
26135    IF EXTENDED=FALSE THEN 26155
26140    C$=RIGHT$(C$,1)
26145    C=ASC(C$)
26150    GOTO 26205
26155 'Ordinary ASCII Codes
26160 '  Test for range
26165        IF C>=MINKEY(CALLER) AND C<=MAXKEY(CALLER)
             THEN 26255
26170 '  Handle special characters
26175        IF SPECIALKEY$(CALLER)=""
             THEN 26240 :'No special characters
26180        IF INSTR(SPECIALKEY$(CALLER),C$)=0
             THEN 26240
26185 '  Convert to capitals if necessary
26190        IF CAPSON(CALLER)=FALSE THEN 26255
26195        IF C>96 AND C<123 THEN C$=CHR$(C AND 223)
26200        GOTO 26255
```

```
26205 ' Extended ASCII codes
26210 '   Test for range
26215          IF C>=EXTMINKEY(CALLER)
               AND C<=EXTMINKEY(CALLER) THEN 26255
26220 '   Handle special characters
26225          IF EXTSPECIALKEY$(CALLER)="" THEN 26240
26230          IF INSTR(EXTSPECIALKEY$(CALLER),C$)=0
               THEN 26240
26235          GOTO 26255
26240 ' Illegal character
26245             BEEP
26250             GOTO 26115: 'Try again
26255 RETURN
```

To try out KEYIN, use a program of this type:

```
1 TRUE=-1:FALSE=0
2 DIM MINKEY(5),MAXKEY(5),EXTMINKEY(5),EXTMAXKEY(5)
3 DIM SPECIALKEY$(5), EXTSPECIALKEY$(5),CAPSON(5)
4 MINKEY(1)=0:MAXKEY(1)=0
5 SPECIALKEY$(1)= "1234567890-+E "
6 EXTMINKEY(1)=0:EXTMAXKEY(1)=0
7 EXTSPECIALKEY$(1)=CHR$(59)+CHR$(60)
8 CAPSON(1)=TRUE:CALLER=1
9 FOR J=1 TO 10:KEY J,"":NEXT J
10 GOSUB 26000
20 IF EXTENDED=TRUE PRINT "EXTENDED ASCII CODE"
21 PRINT ASC(C$),C$
30 GOTO 8
```

This program allows for five different callers (only one is actually used). The acceptable characters for CALLER 1 are the digits 0-9, and the characters +,-,E, space, and the extended ASCII codes 59 and 60 (functions keys F1 and F2). Note that if you type e, it is converted to E since CAPSON(1) = TRUE. The program prints out the ASCII code of the character and the character itself and then awaits another character. You should run this program to convince yourself that KEYIN does, in fact, work.

```
ANSWERS TO TEST YOUR UNDERSTANDING

1:  MINKEY(1)=32:MAXKEY(1)=127:SPECIALKEY$(1)=""
    EXTMINKEY(1)=0:EXTMAXKEY(1)=0:EXTSPECIALKEY$(1)=
    CHR$(72)+CHR$(75)+CHR$(77)+CHR$(80)

2:  MINKEY(1)=0:MAXKEY(1)=0:SPECIALKEY$(1)="1234567890-
    +E."
    EXTMINKEY(1)=0:EXTMAXKEY(1)=127:EXTSPECIALKEY$(1)=""
    CAPSON=-1

3:  MINKEY(1)=0:MAXKEY(1)=0:SPECIALKEY$(1)="YN"
    EXTMINKEY(1)=0:EXTMAXKEY(1)=127:EXTSPECIALKEY$(1)=""
    CAPSON=-1
```

4.6   Inputting Strings and Numbers

Now that we have a character input routine, let's extend our sights and build routines that input strings and numbers.

The routine SCREENIN uses KEYIN to accept input from the keyboard and displays it at a specified position on the screen. When you call SCREENIN, you must specify, in addition to the values needed by KEYIN, the values

XFLD = column position where output is to begin

YFLD = row where output is to be displayed

LNGTH = maximum number of characters allowed

By specifying the allowable characters for KEYIN, you may control the characters that are allowed in your display. You may use the backspace key to erase a character, just as in the BASIC editor. ENTER signifies the end of output, and Esc causes the display field to be erased and the cursor to be positioned at the beginning of the field. (In order for these keys to have the functions indicated, however, you must define the corresponding keys to be acceptable to KEYIN.)

Any extended ASCII code automatically ends input.

The end of input is indicated by setting the variable INPUTEND = TRUE. When input has ended, SCREENIN reads the display field using the SCREEN function. SCREEN(row,column) equals the ASCII code of the character at position (row,column). The resulting string is stored in the variable S$. If input was ended by an extended ASCII code, then EXTENDED is set equal to true and E$ contains the second character of the extended code. Note that S$ does not include any reference to an extended ASCII code.

You will note in several places the statements

```
LOCATE ,,0
LOCATE ,,1
```

The first turns the cursor off and the second turns the cursor on. I have found that watching the cursor motion is very annoying, especially when using SCREEN. So in order to preserve my sanity while using SCREENIN, I turned off the cursor whenever cursor motion proved annoying.

Here is the code for SCREENIN. Note that the code for KEYIN is required to operate SCREENIN. (We numbered KEYIN beginning with 26000 with this in mind.)

```
25000 '***********SCREENIN ROUTINE**************
25005 ' This routine inputs data as a string S$.
25010 ' It allows input to have the following parameters:
25015 ' LNGTH = maximum length of input string
25020 ' XFLD = cursor column for beginning of input field
25025 ' YFLD = cursor row for input field
25030 'CALLER = number of caller
25035 'CAPSON(CALLER) = -1 if letters are to be
                              capitalized for CALLER
25040 '               = 0 otherwise
25045 'FLDBEG = first character position in field
25050 'FLDEND = last character position in field
25055 'S$=Contents of the field from beginning up
         to space before cursor
25060 'T$=contents of the field from the cursor
          to the end of the field
25065 'At end of routine, the contents of the field
        are returned in S$
25070 'LASTPOS=position currently occupied by last
         character
25075 'If a key with an extended ASCII code is pressed,
         it ends processing the current field.
25080 ' The contents of the field are returned in S$ ,
25085 'the second byte of the extended ASCII code in E$.
25090 'CSR = the current column of the cursor
25095 '**************************************************
25100 '
25105 '******MAIN ROUTINE******
25110 '
25115     S$="":E$="":INPUTEND=FALSE:KEYHIT=FALSE
25120     FLDEND=XFLD+LNGTH-1
```

```
25125    CSR=XFLD
25130    GOSUB 25450:'Compute initial LASTPOS
25135    LOCATE YFLD,XFLD
25140    WHILE INPUTEND=FALSE
25145         GOSUB 26000:'Input character
25150         IF EXTENDED=TRUE THEN 25225
              ELSE 25195:'Analyze character
25155    WEND
25160    GOSUB 25365:'Read screen
25165    S$=S$+T$
25170    RETURN
25175 '***********************************************
25180 '
25185 '****** Subroutines ******
25190 '
25195 'Handle ordinary ASCII codes
25200    KEYHIT=TRUE
25205    IF C$=CHR$(8) THEN  25260: 'Backspace
25210    IF C$=CHR$(13) THEN 25295: 'ENTER
25215    IF C$=CHR$(27) THEN 25310: 'Esc
25220    IF C$>=CHR$(32) THEN
         GOTO 25340:'Handle displayable character
25225 'Handle extended ASCII codes
25230    E$=C$
25235    INPUTEND=TRUE
25240    GOTO 25155
25245 'Reject character
25250    BEEP
25255    GOTO 25155
25260 'Handle Backspace
25265    IF LASTPOS<XFLD THEN 25245
25270    GOSUB 25365:'Read field
25275    IF CSR<>XFLD THEN CSR=CSR-1:
25280    LOCATE YFLD,CSR
25285    LASTPOS=LASTPOS-1
25290    GOTO 25155
```

```
25295 'Handle ENTER
25300    INPUTEND=TRUE
25305    GOTO 25155
25310 'Handle ESC (Erase field)
25315    LOCATE YFLD,XFLD
25320    PRINT STRING$(LNGTH,32);
25325    LASTPOS=0:CSR=XFLD
25330    LOCATE YFLD,XFLD
25335    GOTO 25155
25340 'Display character
25345    PRINT C$;
25350    IF LASTPOS<CSR THEN LASTPOS=CSR
25355    IF CSR=FLDEND THEN
         PRINT CHR$(29); ELSE CSR=CSR+1
25360    GOTO 25155
25365 'Read field from screen
25370    LOCATE ,,0
25375    S$="": T$=""
25380    IF LASTPOS=0 THEN 25420
25385    FOR J%=XFLD TO CSR-1
25390             S$=S$+CHR$(SCREEN(YFLD,J%))
25395    NEXT J%
25400    FOR J%=CSR TO LASTPOS
25405             T$=T$+CHR$(SCREEN(YFLD,J%))
25410    NEXT J%
25415    LOCATE ,,1
25420    RETURN
25425 'Erase field
25430    LOCATE YFLD,XFLD:CSR=XFLD:LASTPOS=0
25435    PRINT STRING$(LNGTH,32);
25440    LOCATE YFLD,XFLD
25445    RETURN
25450 'Compute LASTPOS (For inital non-blank field)
25455    LASTPOS=FLDEND:CSR=XFLD
25460    GOSUB 25365:'Read field
25465    WHILE RIGHT$(T$,1)=CHR$(32)
25470             T$=LEFT$(T$,LEN(T$)-1)
```

```
25475                LASTPOS=LASTPOS-1
25480     WEND
25485     RETURN
25490 'Clear keyboard buffer
25495     DEF SEG=0:POKE 1050, PEEK(1052):
          DEF SEG:'Clear keyboard buffer
25500     RETURN
25505 '*************************************************
```

You may test SCREENIN using a program of the following sort.

```
1 TRUE=-1:FALSE=0
2 DIM MINKEY(5),MAXKEY(5),EXTMINKEY(5),EXTMAXKEY(5)
3 DIM SPECIALKEY$(5), EXTSPECIALKEY$(5),CAPSON(5)
4 MINKEY(1)=0:MAXKEY(1)=127
5 SPECIALKEY$(1)= ""
6 EXTMINKEY(1)=0:EXTMAXKEY(1)=0
7 EXTSPECIALKEY$(1)=CHR$(59)+CHR$(60)
8 CAPSON(1)=TRUE:CALLER=1
9 FOR J=1 TO 10:KEY J,"":NEXT J
20 CLS
21 XFLD=5:YFLD=10:LNGTH=20
30 GOSUB 25000
40 GOTO 8
```

This program allows input of any ordinary ASCII codes and F1 and F2.

Note that SCREENIN returns all input in string form. But suppose that your input is a number? You can, of course, convert a string such as "1234" to the number 1234 using the VAL function; i.e. VAL("1234") is equal to 1234. However, some care must be exercised. VAL will accept any string at all. It scans the string to determine the first character that shouldn't be in a number, ignores all characters from there on, and converts the initial string into a number. Thus, for example,

VAL("1NUMBER")=1

VAL("NUMBER")=0 (the null string is converted into 0).

Using KEYIN, we can set up a CALLER that allows our string to contain only the characters

1,2,3,4,5,6,7,8,9,0,+ ,E, and space

This goes a long way toward disallowing incorrect input. However, what about the following strings?

"1.2.3", "1EEE", "1.0E + +", "1.783E.78-"

All contain only characters acceptable to KEYIN with the above CALLER. Clearly, we need a routine that checks whether a string is in proper format to be converted to a number. This is the routine NUMBERCK.

NUMBERCK starts with the string S$, which is an output of SCREENIN, and determines whether S$ may be converted to a number. If so, the variable NUMBERCK is set equal to a negative value. If S$ is not in correct numerical format, NUMBERCK is set equal to 0. If S$ may be converted, then NUMBERCK converts it via the statement

```
S=VAL(S$)
```

So S holds the converted number, which is passed back to the calling program. The routine then sets the value of NUMBERCK as follows:

NUMBERCK = -3 : 'S is an integer (decimal part = 0,
$$-32768 <= S <= 32767$$

NUMBERCK = -2 : 'S has 0 decimal part

NUMBERCK = -1 : 'S has non-zero decimal part

The routine NUMBERCK takes no action if S$ cannot be converted, other than to set the value of NUMBERCK equal to 0. It is up to the calling program to take any action, such as requesting the user to repeat the input.
Here is the code for the routine NUMBERCK.

```
27000 '**********NUMBERCK**********
27005 'This routine checks the format of the string
        S$ to determine if
27010 'it may successfully be converted to a number.
        It returns the result
27015 'of the check in the variable NUMBERCK.
27020 'NUMBERCK = 0: S$ not in numerical format
27025 '          =-1: S$ may be converted into a
                    single-precision real
27030 '          =-2: S$ may be converted with 0
                    fractional part
27035 '          =-3: S$ may be converted to an integer
27040 'If conversion is possible, S contains the converted
27045 'real,S$ the corresponding string.
27050 '************MAIN ROUTINE***************
27055 'Initialize and handle leading sign
```

```
27060          N$="":NUMBERCK=TRUE:DIGIT$="1234567890"
27065          DECPT=FALSE:EXPNT=FALSE:SIGN=FALSE
27070          IF S$="" THEN 27185
27075          T$=LEFT$(S$,1)
27080          IF T$="+" OR T$="-" THEN N$=T$:S$=MID$(S$,2)
27085          IF S$="" THEN NUMBERCK=FALSE:GOTO 27210
27090          IF INSTR(DIGIT$,LEFT$(S$,1))=0 THEN
               NUMBERCK=FALSE:GOTO 27210
27095 WHILE S$ <> ""  :'Loop strips spaces and
                              checks format.Result in N$
27100          T$=LEFT$(S$,1):S$=MID$(S$,2)
27105          IF T$=" " THEN 27135: 'Delete space
27110          IF (T$="+" OR T$="-") AND RIGHT$(N$,1)<>"E"
               THEN NUMBERCK=FALSE:GOTO 27135
27115          IF T$="." THEN IF DECPT=TRUE  OR EXPNT=TRUE
               THEN NUMBERCK=FALSE ELSE N$=N$+T$:DECPT=TRUE
27120          IF T$="+" OR T$="-" THEN
               IF SIGN=TRUE OR EXPNT=FALSE THEN NUMBERCK=FALSE
               ELSE N$=N$+T$:SIGN=TRUE
27125          IF T$="E" THEN IF EXPNT=TRUE THEN NUMBERCK=FALSE
               ELSE N$=N$+T$:EXPNT=TRUE:DECPT=TRUE
27130          IF T$<>"." AND T$<>"+" AND T$<>"-" AND T$<>"E"
               THEN N$=N$+T$
27135 WEND
27140 'Check for overflow(<10^-38 or >10^38)
27145          N%=INSTR(N$,"E")
27150          IF N%=0 THEN 27190
27155          IF N%=1 THEN NUMBERCK=FALSE:GOTO 27210
27160          S$=LEFT$(N$,N%-1):S1$=MID$(N$,N%+1)
27165          S=VAL(S$)
27170          IF S=0 THEN D=0 ELSE D=INT(LOG(ABS(S))/LOG(10))
27175          IF S1$<>"" THEN D=D+VAL(S1$)
27180          IF D<-37 OR D>37 THEN NUMBERCK=FALSE
27185 'Perform the conversion
27190          IF NUMBERCK=TRUE THEN S=VAL(N$)
27195          IF NUMBERCK=TRUE AND S=INT(S) THEN NUMBERCK=-2
27200          IF NUMBERCK=-2 AND S>=-32768! AND S<=32767
               THEN NUMBERCK=-3
```

```
27205      S$=N$
27210 RETURN
```

You may test NUMBERCK using a program such as

```
1 INPUT S$
2 GOSUB 27000
3 PRINT NUMBERCK
4 IF NUMBERCK<0 THEN PRINT "NUMBER ACCEPTED":PRINT S
5 GOTO 1
```

The three routines KEYIN, SCREENIN, and NUMBERCK allow you to put your input on a professional basis. They allow you to control what comes in to your program and to deal with it in a totally controlled manner.

IMPORTANT NOTE   Although the three input routines give you control over your input, they do not totally lift the responsibility from your shoulders. When calling for numerical input, you must still check the returned values to determine that they are in the proper range (positive, less than 10, more than 20, and so forth). The input routines can guarantee that string input is the correct length and contains only predetermined characters. However, You must still check that string input is valid in a particular context. (Did the user type NEP instead of PEN?)

4.7   Bar Charts—A Case Study, II

Our bar chart program has two program modules that require keyboard input—the chart definition module and the data entry module. Let's now build these two modules using the input routines developed in Sections 1-3.

The Bar Chart Definition Module

By pressing a function key, you will be able to start the bar chart definition module. This part of the bar chart program allows you to enter the bar chart parameters into predetermined fields on the screen. When you start the chart definition module, the screen is cleared and the program creates a display like the one in Figure 4.1.

The program is requesting the following pieces of data:

TITLE$	=	chart title (at most 50 characters)
SER1TITLE$	=	data series 1 title (at most 10 characters)
SER2TITLE$	=	data series 2 title (at most 10 characters)
SER3TITLE$	=	data series 3 title (at most 10 characters)
YMIN$	=	minimum displayable Y-value in string form
YMAX$	=	maximum displayable Y-value in string form

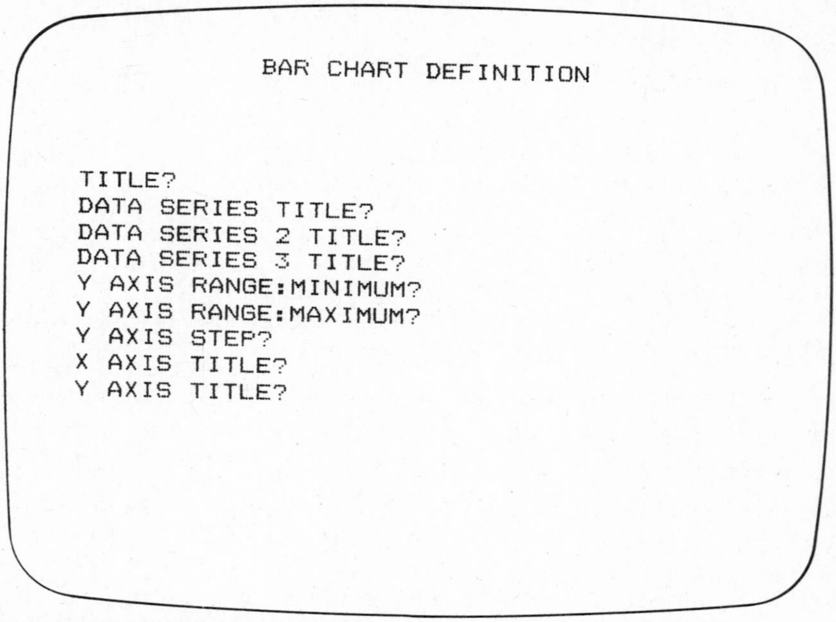

```
                    BAR CHART DEFINITION


        TITLE?
        DATA SERIES TITLE?
        DATA SERIES 2 TITLE?
        DATA SERIES 3 TITLE?
        Y AXIS RANGE:MINIMUM?
        Y AXIS RANGE:MAXIMUM?
        Y AXIS STEP?
        X AXIS TITLE?
        Y AXIS TITLE?
```

Figure 4.1. The Chart Definition Menu.

YSTEP\$ = value of each subdivision along the Y-axis in string form
XTITLE\$ = Title for X-axis (at most 10 characters)
YTITLE\$ = Title for Y-axis (at most 10 characters)

The program allows you to use the cursor up and down keys to move from line to line of the menu. In each line, the cursor is positioned in the first position of the input field. You may type your input into the field, using the backspace and Esc keys for editing. When an extended ASCII code (cursor motion key or function key) is detected, the program reads the field at the current cursor position and assigns the value S\$, returned by the input routine, to the appropriate program variable. In the case of inputs to be converted into numbers, the program calls on NUMBERCK to check for numerical format. If the format test fails, then the value of S\$ is not assigned to the program variable and the field is erased. If a function key is pressed, then it causes the program to read the current field, assign the program variable, if possible, and then to GOTO the main control program, which we assume begins in line 900.

Here is our program.

```
5  '**********INITIALIZATION ROUTINE**********

10 'Dimension Statements

15      DIM MINKEY(5),MAXKEY(5),EXTMINKEY(5),EXTMAXKEY(5)

20      DIM CAPSON(5),SPECIALKEY$(5),EXTSPECIALKEY$(5),
            DTA$(3,20)

25      DIM MENU$(11)

30 'Define parameters for input routine
```

```
35      MOTION$=CHR$(71)+CHR$(72)
40      FUNCTION$=CHR$(59)+CHR$(60)+CHR$(61)+CHR$(62)
                +CHR$(63)+CHR$(64)+CHR$(65)
45 '    **Text input(CALLER=1)**
50      MINKEY(1)=32:MAXKEY(1)=127:
        SPECIALKEY$(1)=CHR$(8)+CHR$(27)
55      CAPSON(1)=0
60      EXTMINKEY(1)=59:EXTMAXKEY(1)=68
65      EXTSPECIALKEY$(1)=MOTION$+FUNCTION$
70 '    **Numerical input (CALLER=2)**
75      MINKEY(2)=0:MAXKEY(2)=0
80      CAPSON(2)=-1:SPECIALKEY$(2)=
85      EXTMINKEY(2)=59:EXTMAXKEY(2)=68
90      EXTSPECIALKEY$(2)=MOTION$+FUNCTION$
95 'Variable initialization
100      TRUE=-1:FALSE=0
105      MENU$(1)="BAR CHART DEFINITION"
110      MENU$(2)="TITLE? "
115      MENU$(3)="DATA SERIES 1 TITLE? "
120      MENU$(4)="DATA SERIES 2 TITLE? "
125      MENU$(5)="DATA SERIES 3 TITLE? "
130      MENU$(6)="Y AXIS RANGE:MINIMUM? "
135      MENU$(7)="Y AXIS RANGE:MAXIMUM? "
140      MENU$(8)="Y AXIS STEP? "
145      MENU$(9)="X AXIS TITLE? "
150      MENU$(10)="Y AXIS TITLE? "
900 '****************CONTROL ROUTINE******************
1000 '**********BAR CHART PARAMETERS INPUT**************
1005 SCREEN 0:CLS:LOCATE 25,1:PRINT FKEY$;
1010 'Display template
1015 LOCATE 1,1:PRINT TAB(27) MENU$(1);
1020 FOR J%=2 TO 10
1025     LOCATE J%+2,1
1030     PRINT MENU$(J%);
1035 NEXT J%
1040 MENUEND=FALSE
1045 GOSUB 1170:'Display current parameter values
```

```
1050 XFLD=25:YFLD=4
1055 WHILE MENUEND=FALSE
1060    LOCATE YFLD,XFLD
1065    IF YFLD=4 THEN CALLER=1:LNGTH=50
1070    IF YFLD>4 AND YFLD<7 THEN CALLER=1:LNGTH=10
1075    IF YFLD>7 AND YFLD<11 THEN CALLER=2:LNGTH=10
1080    IF YFLD>10 THEN CALLER=1:LNGTH=10
1085    GOSUB 25000: 'Call input routine
1090    IF YFLD>7 AND YFLD<11 THEN GOSUB 27000:'Numberck
1095    IF YFLD>7 AND YFLD<11 AND NUMBERCK=FALSE
        THEN GOSUB 25425:GOTO 1085
1100    IF YFLD=4 THEN TITLE$=S$
1105    IF YFLD=5 THEN SER1TITLE$=S$
1110    IF YFLD=6 THEN SER2TITLE$=S$
1115    IF YFLD=7 THEN SER3TITLE$=S$
1120    IF YFLD=8 THEN YMIN$=S$
1125    IF YFLD=9 THEN YMAX$=S$
1130    IF YFLD=10 THEN YSTEP$=S$
1135    IF YFLD=11 THEN XTITLE$=S$
1140    IF YFLD=12 THEN YTITLE$=S$
1145    IF E$=CHR$(80) THEN IF YFLD<12 THEN YFLD=YFLD+1
1150    IF E$=CHR$(72) THEN IF YFLD>4 THEN YFLD=YFLD-1
1155    IF INSTR(FUNCTION$,E$)>0 THEN MENUEND=TRUE
1160 WEND
1165 GOTO 900: 'Return to control routine
1170 'Display current parameter values
1175    LOCATE 4,25:PRINT TITLE$
1180    LOCATE 5,25:PRINT SER1TITLE$
1185    LOCATE 6,25:PRINT SER2TITLE$
1190    LOCATE 7,25:PRINT SER3TITLE$
1195    LOCATE 8,25:PRINT YMIN$
1200    LOCATE 9,25:PRINT YMAX$
1205    LOCATE 10,25:PRINT YSTEP$
1210    LOCATE 11,25:PRINT XTITLE$
1215    LOCATE 12,25:PRINT YTITLE$
1220    RETURN
```

Note that we have defined CALLERs 1 and 2 to correspond to the text input and numerical input, respectively. The only extended ASCII codes allowed are Cursor Up (E$ = CHR$(72)) and Cursor Down (E$ = CHR$(80)) and the function keys F1-F7, which return you to the main control routine in line 900.

The Data Input Module

The data input module is the part of the program in which you enter the numerical values for the various bars and the corresponding identifying labels, which will be displayed below the bars. This module is very similar to the bar chart definition module. When it is called, it clears the screen and creates a display like the one in Figure 4.2.

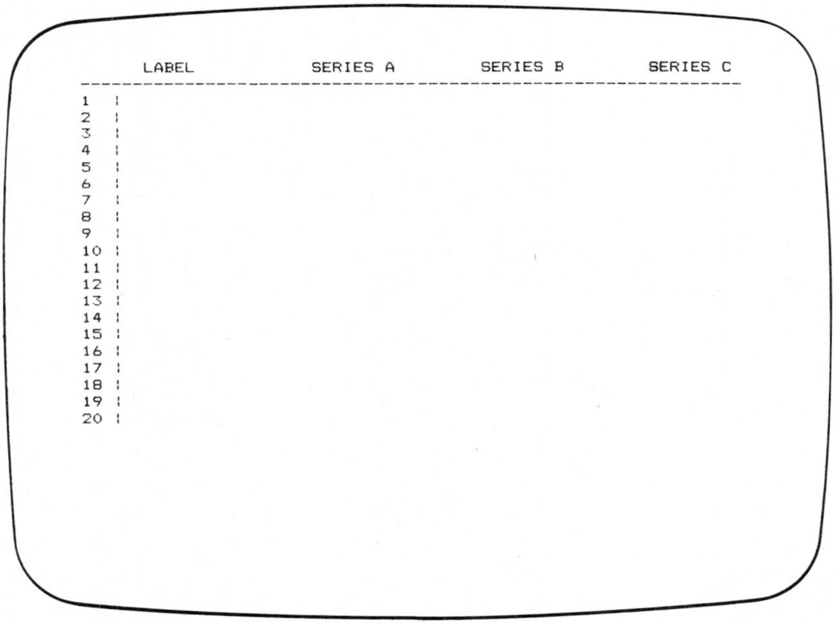

Figure 4.2. The Data Input Matrix.

You type your data into the various positions in the matrix. The cursor motion keys move you around within the matrix. Function keys 1-7 return you to the main control routine in line 900.

Here is the code for the data input module.

```
2000 '**********DATA INPUT ROUTINE**********
2005 SCREEN 0:CLS:LOCATE 25,1:PRINT FKEY$;
2010 LOCATE 1,1:GOSUB 2055:'Display spreadsheet
```

```
2015 ROW%=1:COL%=0
2020 DATAEND=FALSE
2025 WHILE DATAEND=FALSE
2030      GOSUB 2335:'Locate cursor
2035      GOSUB 2150:'Input data
2040 WEND
2045 GOTO 900:'Return to control routine
2050 **************SUBROUTINES*****************
2055 'Display spreadsheet
2060 CLS
2065 LOCATE 1,34
2070 PRINT "DATA VALUES"
2075 PRINT
2080 PRINT TAB(8) "LABEL";TAB(26) "SERIES A";
          TAB(44) "SERIES B";TAB(62) "SERIES C"
2085 PRINT STRING$(80,45);
2090 FOR J%=1 TO 20
2095 LOCATE J%+4,1
2100      PRINT J%; TAB(5) "|";
2105 NEXT J%
2110 FOR ROW%=1 TO 20
2115    FOR COL%=0 TO 3
2120            GOSUB 2335:'Convert to screen coordinates
2125            LOCATE R%,C%
2130            PRINT DTA$(COL%,ROW%);
2135    NEXT COL%
2140 NEXT ROW%
2145 RETURN
2150 'Input data
2155 IF COL%=0 THEN CALLER=3 ELSE CALLER=4
2160 XFLD=C%:YFLD=R%:LNGTH=10
2165 GOSUB 25000
2170 IF S$="" THEN 2195
2175 IF CALLER=3 THEN NUMBERCK=TRUE
2180 IF CALLER=4 THEN GOSUB 27000
2185 IF NUMBERCK<0 THEN DTA$(COL%,ROW%)=S$
2190 IF NUMBERCK=FALSE THEN GOSUB 25425:GOTO 2330
```

```
2195 IF INSTR(FUNCTION$,E$)>0
     THEN DATAEND=TRUE:GOTO 2330
2200 IF E$=CHR$(72) THEN 2230:'Cursor up
2205 IF E$=CHR$(75) THEN 2245:'Cursor left
2210 IF E$=CHR$(77) THEN 2260:'Cursor right
2215 IF E$=CHR$(80) THEN 2275:'Cursor down
2220 IF E$=CHR$(71) THEN 2290:'Home (To position 1,1)
2225 IF E$=CHR$(79) THEN 2310:'End (To position 20,3)
2230 'Cursor up
2235 IF ROW%>1 THEN ROW%=ROW%-1
2240 GOTO 2330
2245 'Cursor left
2250 IF COL%>0 THEN COL%=COL%-1
2255 GOTO 2330
2260 'Cursor right
2265 IF COL%<3 THEN COL%=COL%+1
2270 GOTO 2330
2275 'Cursor down
2280 IF ROW%>0 THEN ROW%=ROW%+1
2285 GOTO 2330
2290 'Home (To position 1,1)
2295 COL%=1
2300 ROW%=1
2305 GOTO 2330
2310 'End (To position 20,3)
2315 COL%=3
2320 ROW%=20
2325 GOTO 2330
2330 RETURN
2335 'Compute screen coordinates
2340 R%=ROW%+4
2345 C%=18*COL%+8
2350 LOCATE R%,C%
2355 RETURN
2360 RETURN
```

Note that it was necessary to define two new CALLERs, CALLER 3 and
CALLER 4, since this module allows you to use all six cursor motion keys,

whereas the bar chart definition module only allows you to use Cursor Up and Cursor Down.

Note how easy it was to force the program user to give correct input. That's the whole point of using an input routine rather than BASIC's prepackaged input statements.

5

Your Computer as a File Cabinet

In this chapter we will discuss techniques for using your computer to store and retrieve information.

5.1   What Are Files?

A **file** is a collection of information stored on a mass storage device (diskette, cassette, or hard disk). There are two common types of files: program files and data files.

Program Files

When a program is stored on diskette, it is stored as a **program file**. You have already created some program files by saving BASIC programs on diskette. In addition to the programs you create, your DOS diskette contains program files that are necessary to run your computer, such as DOS and the BASIC language.

Data Files

Computer programs used in business and industry usually refer to files of information that are kept in mass storage. For example, a personnel department would keep a file of data on each employee: name, age, address, social security number, date employed, position, salary, and so forth. A warehouse would maintain an inventory for each product, with the following information: product name, supplier, current inventory, units sold in the last reporting period, date of the last shipment, size of the last shipment, and units sold in the last 12 months. These files are called *data files*.

In this chapter, we will discuss the procedures for handling files in general and data files in particular.

Consider the following example. Suppose that a teacher stores grades in a data file. For each student in the class, there are four exam grades. A typical entry in the data file would contain the following data items:

111

student name, exam grade #1, exam grade #2, exam grade #3, exam grade #4

In a data file, the data items are organized in sequence. So the beginning of the above data file might look like this:

"John Smith", 98, 87, 93, 76, "Mary Young", 99, 78, 87, 91, "Sally Ronson", 48, 63, 72, 80, . . .

The data file consists of a sequence of string constants (the names) and numeric constants (the grades), with the various data items arranged in a particular pattern (name followed by four grades). This particular arrangement is designed so the file may be read and understood. For instance, if we read the data items above, we know in advance that the data items are in groups of five with the first one a name and the next four the corresponding grades.

In this chapter, we will learn to create data files containing information such as the data in the above example. As we shall see, data may be stored in either of two types of data files—sequential and random access. For each type of file we will learn to perform the following operations.

1.   Create a data file.

2.   Write data items to a file.

3.   Read data items from a file.

4.   Alter data items in a file.

5.   Search a file for particular data items.

5.2   Sequential Files

A **sequential file** is a data file in which the data items are accessed in order. That is, the data items are written in consecutive order into the file. The data items are read in the order in which they were written. You may add data items only to the end of a sequential file. If you wish to add a data item somewhere in the middle of the file, it is necessary to rewrite the entire file. Similarly, if you wish to read a data item at the end of a sequential file, it is necessary to read all the data items in order and to ignore those that you don't want.

OPENing and CLOSEing Sequential Files

Before you perform any operations on a sequential file, you must first open the file. You should think of the file as being contained in a file cabinet drawer (the diskette). In order to read the file, you must first open the file drawer. This is accomplished using the BASIC instruction OPEN. When OPENing a file, you must specify the file and indicate whether you will be reading from the file or writing into the file. For example, to OPEN the file B:PAYROLL for input (for reading the file), we use a statement of the form

```
10 OPEN "B:PAYROLL" FOR INPUT AS #1
```

The #1 is a reference number we assign to the file when opening it. As long as the file remains open, you refer to it by its reference number rather than the more cumbersome file specification B:PAYROLL. The reference number is quite arbitrary. You may assign any positive integer you wish. Just make sure that you don't assign two files that are to be open simultaneously to the same reference number. (If you try this, BASIC will give you an error message.)

Here is an alternate form of the instruction for opening a file for input:

```
10 OPEN "I",#1,"B:PAYROLL"
```

(Here the letter "I" stands for "Input.")

To OPEN the file B:GRADES.AUG for output (that is, to write in the file), we use an instruction of the form

```
20 OPEN "B:GRADES.AUG" FOR OUTPUT AS #2
```

Here is an alternate way to write the same instruction:

```
20 OPEN "O",#2,"B:GRADES.AUG"
```

(The letter "O" stands for "Output.")

BASIC initially allows you to work with three open diskette files at a time. This number may be increased by giving the appropriate command when you start BASIC. For example, to allow use of as many as 5 files at once, start BASIC with the command:

```
BASIC /F:5
```

The "switch" /F:5 is what tells BASIC to set aside memory for simultaneous manipulation of up to 5 files.

In maintaining any filing system, it is necessary to be neat and organized. The same is true of computer files. A sequential file may be opened for input or for output, but not both simultaneously. As long as the file remains open, it will accept instructions (input or output) of the same sort designated when it was opened. To change operations, it is necessary to first close the file. For example, to close the file B:PAYROLL in line 10 above, we use the instruction

```
40 CLOSE #1
```

After giving this instruction, we may reopen the file for output using an instruction similar to that given in line 20 above. It is possible to close several files at a time. For example, the statement

```
50 CLOSE #5,#6
```

closes the files with reference numbers 5 and 6. We may close all currently open files with the instruction

```
50 CLOSE
```

In an OPEN or CLOSE statement, the # is optional. Thus, it is perfectly acceptable to use

```
50 OPEN 1,2
```

```
50 CLOSE 5,6
```

Good programming practice dictates that all files be closed after use. In any case, the BASIC commands NEW, RUN, and SYSTEM automatically close any files that might have been left open by a preceding program.

WRITEing Data Items Into a Sequential File

Suppose that we wish to create a sequential file called INVOICE.001, which contains the following data items:

DJ SALES   50357 4 $358.79   4/5/81

That is, we would like to write into the file the string constant "DJ SALES" followed by the two numeric constants 50357 and 4, followed by the two string constants "$358.79" and "4/5/81". Here is a program that does exactly that:

```
100 OPEN "B:INVOICE.001" FOR OUTPUT AS #1
110 WRITE#1, "DJ SALES", 50357,4,"$358.79", "4/5/81"
120 CLOSE #1
```

The #1 portion of line 110 refers to the identification number given to the file in the OPEN instruction in line 100, namely 1. In a WRITE# statement, a comma must follow the file number.

Note that the WRITE instruction works very much like a PRINT statement, except that the data items are "printed" in the file instead of on the screen.

While a file is open you may execute any number of WRITE instructions to insert data. Moreover, you may WRITE data items that are values of variables, as in the statement

```
200 WRITE #1, A, A$
```

This instruction will write current values of A and A$ into the file.

EXAMPLE 1.   Write a program to create a file whose data items are the numbers 1, 1^2, 2, 2^2, 3, 3^2, . . . , 100, 100^2.

SOLUTION.   Let's call the file "SQUARES" and store it on the diskette in drive A:.

```
10 OPEN "A:SQUARES" FOR OUTPUT AS #1
20 FOR J=1 TO 100
30   WRITE#1, J,J^2
40 NEXT J
50 CLOSE #1
60 END
```

EXAMPLE 2.   Create a data file consisting of names, addresses, and telephone numbers from your personal telephone directory. Assume that you will type the addresses into the computer and will tell the computer when the last address has been typed.

SOLUTION.   We use INPUT statements to enter the various data. Let A\$ denote the name of the current person, B\$ the street address, C\$ the city , D\$ the state, E\$ the zip code, and F\$ the telephone number. For each entry, there is an INPUT statement corresponding to each of these variables. The program then writes the data to the diskette. Here is the program.

```
5 OPEN "TELEPHON" FOR OUTPUT AS #1
10 INPUT "NAME"; NME$
20 INPUT "STREET ADDRESS"; ADDRESS$
30 INPUT "CITY"; CITY$
40 INPUT "STATE"; STATE$
50 INPUT "ZIP CODE"; ZIPCODE$
60 INPUT "TELEPHONE"; TELEPHONE$
70 WRITE#1, NME$, ADDRESS$, CITY$, STATE$, ZIPCODE$,TELEPHONE$
80 INPUT "ANOTHER ENTRY (Y/N)"; G$
90 IF G$="Y" THEN 10
100 CLOSE #1
110 END
```

There are several noteworthy points about the above program. First note the unusual spelling of NAME (NME). We are forced into this queer spelling since NAME is a BASIC reserved word. Second, note that the program uses INPUT rather than the input routine of Chapter 4. We did this to keep the program short. In any serious application program, you should stick to the input routine. You should use the above program to set up a computerized telephone directory of your own. It is very instructive. Moreover, when coupled with the search program given below, it will allow you to look up addresses and phone numbers using your computer.

TEST YOUR UNDERSTANDING 1

Use the above program to enter the following addresses into the file.
John Jones
1 South Main St. Apt. 308
Phila. Pa. 19107
527-1211

Mary Bell
2510 9th St.
Phila. Pa. 19138
937-4896

Reading Data Items

To read items from a data file, it is first necessary to open the file for INPUT (that is, for INPUT from the diskette.) Consider the telephone file in Example 2. We may open it for input, via the instruction

```
300 OPEN "TELEPHON" FOR INPUT AS #2
```

Once the file is open, it may be read via the instruction

```
400 INPUT #2, NME$,ADDRESS$,CITY$,STATE$, ZIPCODE$,TELEPHONE$
```

This instruction will read six data items from the file (corresponding to one telephone-address entry), assign A$ the value of the first data item, B$ the second, and so forth.

In order to read a file, it is necessary to know the precise format of the data in the file. For example, the form of the above INPUT statement was dictated by the fact that each telephone-address entry was entered into the file as six consecutive string constants. The file INPUT statement works like any other INPUT statement: Faced with a list of variables separated by commas, it assigns values to the indicated variables in the order in which the data items are presented. However, if you attempt to assign a string constant to a numeric variable or vice versa, BASIC will report an error.

As long as a file is open for INPUT, you may continue to INPUT from it, using as many INPUT statements as you like. These may, in turn, be inter-mingled with statements that have nothing to do with the file you are read-ing. Each INPUT statement begins reading the file where the preceding INPUT statement left off.

Here's how to determine if you have read all data items in a file. BASIC maintains the functions EOF(1), EOF(2),..., one for each open file. These functions may be used like logical variables. That is, they assume the possi-ble values TRUE or FALSE. You may test for the end of the file using an IF . . . THEN statement. For example, consider the statement

```
100 IF EOF(1) THEN 2000 ELSE 10
```

This statement will cause BASIC to determine if you are currently at the end of file #1. If so the program will go to line 2000. Otherwise, the program will go to line 10. Note that you are not at the end of the file until **after** you read the last data item.

If you attempt to read past the end of a file, BASIC will report an **Input Past End** error. Therefore, before reading a file it is a good idea to determine whether you are currently at the end of the file.

EXAMPLE 3.   A data file, called NUMBERS, consists of numerical entries. Write a program to determine the number of entries in the file.

SOLUTION.   Let us keep a count of the current number we are reading in the variable COUNT. Our procedure will be to read a number, increase the count, then test for the end of the file.

```
10 COUNT=0
20 OPEN "NUMBERS" FOR INPUT AS #1
30 IF EOF(1) THEN 100
40 INPUT #1,A
50 COUNT=COUNT+1
60 GOTO 30
100 PRINT "THE NUMBER OF NUMBERS IN THE FILE IS",COUNT
110 CLOSE
120 END
```

EXAMPLE 4.   Write a program that searches for a particular entry of the telephone directory file created in Example 2.

SOLUTION.   We will INPUT the name corresponding to the desired entry. The program will then read the file entries until a match of names occurs. Here is the program:

```
5 OPEN "TELEPHON" FOR INPUT AS #1
10 INPUT "NAME TO SEARCH FOR"; Z$
20 INPUT #1, NME$,ADDRESS$,CITY$,STATE$,ZIPCODE$,TELEPHONE$
30 IF NME$ = Z$ THEN 100
40 IF EOF(1) THEN 200
50 GOTO 20
100 CLS
110 PRINT NME$
120 PRINT ADDRESS$
130 PRINT CITY$,STATE$,ZIPCODE$
140 PRINT TELEPHONE$
150 GOTO 1000
200 CLS
210 PRINT "THE NAME IS NOT ON FILE"
1000 CLOSE 1
1010 END
```

TEST YOUR UNDERSTANDING 2

Use the above program to locate Mary Bell's number in the telephone file created in TEST YOUR UNDERSTANDING 1.

EXAMPLE 5.   (Mailing List Application) Suppose that you have created your computerized telephone directory, using the program in Example 2. Assume that the completed file is called TELEPHON and is on the diskette in drive A:. Write a program that reads the file and prints out the names and addresses onto mailing labels.

SOLUTION.   Let's assume that your mailing labels are of the "peel-off" variety, which can be printed continuously on your printer. Further, let's assume that the labels are six printer lines high, so that each label has room for five lines of print with one line space between labels. (These are actual dimensions of labels you can buy.) We will print the name on line 1, the address on line 2, the city, state, and zip codes all on line 3, with the city and state separated by a comma.

```
10 OPEN "TELEPHON" FOR INPUT AS #1
20 IF EOF(1) THEN 1000
30 INPUT #1, NME$,ADDRESS$,CITY$,STATE$,ZIPCODE$,TELEPHONE$
40 LPRINT NME$
50 LPRINT ADDRESS$
60 LPRINT CITY$;
70 LPRINT ",";            :'PRINT COMMA
80 LPRINT TAB(10) STATE$;
90 LPRINT TAB(20) ZIPCODE$
100 LPRINT:LPRINT:LPRINT   :'NEXT LABEL
110 GOTO 20
1000 CLOSE 1
1010 END
```

Adding to a Data File

Here is an important fact about writing data files: Writing a file destroys any previous contents of the file. (In contrast, you may read a file any number of times without destroying its contents.) Consider the file "TELEPHON" created in Example 2 above. Suppose we write a program that opens the file for output and writes what we suppose are additional entries in our telephone directory. After this write operation, the file "TELEPHON" will contain *only* the added entries. All of the original entries will have been lost! How, then, may we add items to a file that already exists? Easy. The IBM Personal Computer has a special instruction to do this. Rather than OPEN the file for OUTPUT, we OPEN the file for APPEND, using the instruction

```
500 OPEN "TELEPHON" FOR APPEND AS #1
```

The computer will locate the current end of the file. Any additional entries to the file will be written beginning at that point. However, the previous entries in the file will be unchanged.

EXAMPLE 6.   Write a program that adds entries to the file TELEPHON. The additions should be typed via INPUT statements. The program may assume that the file is on the diskette in drive A:.

SOLUTION.   To add items to the file, we first OPEN the file for APPEND. We then ask for the new entry via an INPUT statement and write the new entry into TELEPHON. Here is the program.

```
10 OPEN "TELEPHON" FOR APPEND AS #1
210 PRINT "TYPE ENTRY:NAME,STREET ADDRESS,CITY, STATE,"
220 PRINT "ZIP CODE, TELEPHONE NO."
230 INPUT #1, NME$,ADDRESS$,CITY$,STATE$,ZIPCODE$,TELEPHONE$
240 WRITE#1, NME$,ADDRESS$,CITY$,STATE$,ZIPCODE$,TELEPHONE$
250 INPUT "ANOTHER ENTRY (Y/N)": Z$
260 IF Z$ <> "Y" THEN 500
300 CLS
310 GOTO 210
500 CLOSE 1
510 END
```

TEST YOUR UNDERSTANDING 3

Use the above program to add you name, address and telephone number to the telephone directory created in TEST YOUR UNDERSTANDING 1.

Exercises (answer on page 349)

1. Write a program creating a diskette data file containing the numbers 5.7, -11.4, 123, 485, and 49.

2. Write a program that reads the data file created in Exercise 1 and displays the data items on the screen.

3. Write a program that adds to the data file of Exercise 1 the data items 5, 78, 4.79, and -1.27.

4. Write a program that reads the expanded file of Exercise 3 and displays all the data items on the screen.

5. Write a program that records the contents of checkbook stubs in a data file. The data items of the file should be as follows:

    check #, date, payee, amount, explanation

    Use this program to create a data file corresponding to your previous month's checks.

6. Write a program that reads the data file of Exercise 5 and totals the amounts of all the checks listed in the file.

7. Write a program that keeps track of inventory in a retail store. The inventory should be described by a data file whose entries contain the following information:

item, current price, units in stock

The program should allow for three different operations: Display the data file entry corresponding to a given item, record receipt of a shipment of a given item, and record the sale of a certain number of units of a given item.

8. Write a program that creates a recipe file to contain your favorite recipes.

9. (For Teachers) Write a program that maintains a student file containing your class roll, attendance, and grades.

10. Write a program maintaining a file of your credit card numbers and the party to notify in case of loss or theft.

5.3   More About Sequential Files

When you WRITE a data item to a sequential file, BASIC automatically includes certain "punctuation" that allows the data to be read:

1. Strings are surrounded by quotation marks.

2. Data items are separated by commas.

3. The last data item in the WRITE# statement is followed by <ENTER>. Here <ENTER> means the ENTER key. To the computer, <ENTER> is a character, just like "A" or ";". It tells the computer to end the current line and move the cursor to the start of the following line. Actually, <ENTER> generates **two** characters: One is a carriage return that returns the cursor to the left side of the line. The other is a line feed that advances the cursor to the next line. In what follows we will continue to use <ENTER> to stand for the combination of these two characters.

4. Positive numbers are inserted in the file without a leading blank.

For example, suppose that A$ = "JOHN",B$ = "SMITH",C = 1234, and D = -14. Consider the following WRITE# statement:

```
10 WRITE#1, A$,B$,C,D
```

Here is how this statement would WRITE the data into file #1:

```
"JOHN","SMITH",1234,-14<ENTER>
```

When the above data is read by an INPUT# statement, the quotation marks, commas, and ENTER enable BASIC to separate the various data items from one another. For this reason, the punctuation marks are called **delimiters**. In using the WRITE# statement, you need not worry about delimiters. However, in other sequential file statements you are not so lucky.

Consider, for instance, the PRINT# statement. This statement may be used to PRINT data to a file exactly as if the data were being printed on the screen. All of the usual features of PRINT, such as TAB, SPC, and semicolons are active. However, the PRINT# statement does not include any delimiters. Consider the above variables A$, B$, C, and D. The statement

```
20 PRINT#1, A$;B$;C;D
```

will write the following image to file #1:

```
JOHNSMITH 1234-14<ENTER>
```

Note that:

1. The space before the positive number 1234 is included in the file,
2. There are no separations between the data items.
3. There are no quotation marks around the strings.

In order to correctly read the individual data items, you must supply delimiters in your PRINT# statement. Here's how. First, put commas as strings in PRINT#:

```
20 PRINT#1, A$;",";B$;",";C;",";D
```

Here's how the image in the file will now look:

```
JOHN,SMITH, 1234,-14<ENTER>
```

The individual data items now may be read.

This is not quite the end of the story, however! Notice that the strings still do not have quotation marks around them. In this example, no harm will be done. To understand why, let's discuss the operation of the INPUT# statement.

INPUT recognizes the following list of delimiters: commas, ENTER, and form feed (we'll learn about this character later). When faced with a stream of data in a file, here is what INPUT# does:

1. INPUT# scans the characters and peels off characters until it finds a delimiter. This indicates the end of the current data item. (The delimiter is not included as part of the data item.)
2. If a numeric data item has been requested, INPUT# checks that the data item is a number (no illegal characters such as A, $, or ;). If illegal characters are detected, a Type Mismatch error occurs.
3. If a string data item has been requested, INPUT# checks to see whether the data item is surrounded by quotation marks. If so, it removes them.

Understanding the above sequence can prevent embarrassing errors. One such error can occur if you wish to include a comma within a data item. For example, suppose that A$="SMITH,JOHN", B$="CARPENTER". The PRINT# statement

```
30 PRINT#1, A$;",";B$
```

will write the following image to the file:

```
SMITH,JOHN,CARPENTER<ENTER>
```

A subsequent INPUT# statement

```
40 INPUT#1, A$,B$
```

will result in A$ = "SMITH" and B$ = "JOHN". To get around this problem, you must explicitly include quotation marks around strings that include a comma. A string that consists of a quotation mark is just CHR$(34). (34 is the ASCII code for a quotation mark.) So to include the quotation marks around the string A$ = "SMITH,JOHN" you may use the statement

```
50 PRINT#1, CHR$(34);A$;CHR$(34);",";B$
```

The file image will now be

```
"SMITH,JOHN",CARPENTER<ENTER>
```

Quotation marks must enclose strings containing commas, semicolons, beginning or ending blanks, or ENTERs.

As you can see, the PRINT# statement is much less convenient than WRITE#. In most cases, it is much simpler to use WRITE#. However, PRINT# has its advantages. With a PRINT#, you may include the USING option to format your data. For example, to write the value of the variable A to the file in the format ##.#, we could use the statement

```
60 PRINT#1, USING "##.#";A
```

The INPUT# statement reads a single data item at a time. However, in some applications you may wish to read an entire line from a file. That is, you wish to read data until you encounter an ENTER. This may be done with the LINE INPUT# statement. For example, suppose that the following data is contained in file #1:

```
SMITH,JOHN,CARPENTER<ENTER>
```

The statement

```
70 LINE INPUT #1, A$
```

will set A$ = "SMITH,JOHN,CARPENTER". Note the following curious twist, however. If you saved your string data with quotation marks around it, those quotation marks would be included as part of the string read by LINE INPUT#. If you plan to read data lines via a LINE INPUT# statement, it is usually wise to save the data using PRINT# so that no extraneous quotation marks are generated.

File Buffers

You may have noticed that the drive light does not always turn on when you are writing a file. For example, try this experiment: OPEN a data file and write a single numerical data item to the file, but don't CLOSE the file. The disk drive does nothing. However, if you run this program a second time, the drive light will go on. This may seem strange. However, it has to do with the way BASIC writes (and reads) diskette files.

Diskette drives are very slow when compared with the speed at which BASIC executes non-diskette operations. In order to speed up diskette operations, BASIC writes to diskette using **file buffers**. A file buffer (or "buffer" for short) is an area of RAM where BASIC temporarily stores data to be written to a file. There is one buffer corresponding to each open file. BASIC reserves the space for a buffer as part of the OPEN operation. When you use any file write operation, BASIC writes the corresponding information into the file's buffer. When the buffer is full, BASIC writes the data to the file.

The CLOSE operation forces all buffers (full or not) to be written to their corresponding files. When you don't close a file (as in our above experiment), the buffer may be sitting with some data that has not yet been written to diskette. In this case, a RUN or END command will also cause the buffers to be written to diskette. Also, as soon as you modify the program in RAM, the buffers will be written to diskette. In our experiment, it was the RUN statement that caused the drive lights to go on, to write the final results of the previous run.

Exercises (answers on page 350)

Suppose that A$ = "MY", B$ = "DOG", C$ = "SAM", D = 1234. What is the format of the data written to file #1 by the following statements?

1. `WRITE#1, A$,B$,C$,D`
2. `PRINT#1, A$,B$,C$,D`
3. `PRINT#1, A$;",";B$;",";C$;",";D`
4. `PRINT#1, CHR$(34);A$;", ";B$;", ";CHR$(34);",";C$;",";D`

Consider the file as written by Exercise 1. What will be displayed by the following statements?

5. `INPUT#1, E$:PRINT E$`
6. `LINE INPUT #1, E$:PRINT E$`

Consider the files as written by Exercises 2-4. What will be displayed by the following statements?

7. `INPUT#1, E$:PRINT E$`

Consider the file as written by Exercise 4. Write a program to display:

MY DOG, SAM

1234

5.4   Random Access Files

The files considered so far in this chapter are all examples of **sequential files**. That is, the files are all written sequentially, from beginning to end. These files are very easy to create, but are cumbersome in many applications, since they must be read sequentially. In order to read a piece of data from the end of the file, it is necessary to read all data items from the beginning of the file. **Random access files** do not suffer from this difficulty. Using a random access file, it is possible to access the precise piece of data you want. Of course, there is a price to be paid for this convenience. (No free lunches!) You must work a little harder to learn how to use random access files.

A random access file is divided into segments of fixed length called **records**. (See Figure 5.1.) The length of a record is measured in terms of **bytes**. For a string constant, each character, including spaces and punctuation marks, counts as a single byte. For example, the record consisting of the string

ACCOUNTING-5

is of length 12.

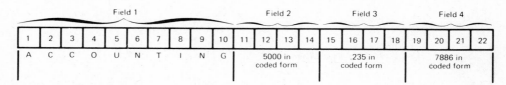

Figure 5.1. A Random Access File.

In order to store a data item in a random access file, all data must be converted into string form. This applies to numeric constants and values of numeric variables. (See below for the special instructions for performing this conversion.) A number (more precisely, a single-precision number) is converted into a string of length 4, no matter how many digits this number has. A record may contain the four data items ACCOUNTING, 5000, .235, and 7886. These pieces of data are stored in order, with no separations between them. The length of this particular record is 22 bytes (10 for ACCOUNTING and four each for the numerical data items). (See Figure 5.2.)

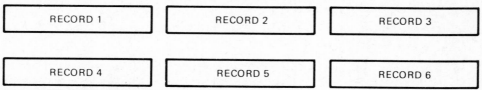

Figure 5.2. A Typical Record.

In order to write data to a random access file, it is necessary to first open it. To open a file named "DEPTS" as a random access file with a record length of 22, we would use the instruction

```
10 OPEN "DEPTS" AS #1 LEN=22
```

Next, we must describe the structure of the records of the file. For example, suppose that each record of file #1 is to start with a 10-character string followed by three numbers (converted to string form). Further, suppose that the string represents a department name, the first number the current department income, the second number the department's efficiency rating, and the third number the current department's overhead. We would indicate this situation with the instruction

```
20 FIELD #1, 10 AS DEPT$, 4 AS INCOME$, 4 AS EFFICIENCY$,
   4 AS OVERHEAD$
```

This instruction identifies the file via the number used when the file was opened. Each section of the record is called a field. Each field is identified by a string variable and the number of bytes reserved for that variable.

To write a record to a random access file, it is first necessary to assemble the data corresponding to the various fields. This is done using the LSET and RSET instructions. For example, to set the DEPT$ field to the string "ACCOUNTING", we use the instruction

```
30 LSET DEPT$="ACCOUNTING"
```

To set the DEPT$ field to the value of the string variable N$, we use

```
40 LSET DEPT$=N$
```

If N$ contains fewer than 10 characters, the rightmost portion of the field is filled out with blanks. This is called **left justification**. If N$ contains more than 10 characters, the field is filled with the leftmost 10 characters.

The instruction RSET works exactly the same as LSET, except that the unused spaces appear on the left side of the field. (The strings are **right justified**.)

To convert numbers to strings for inclusion in random access files, we use the MKS$ (or MKI$ or MKD$) function. For example, to include .753 in the EFFICIENCY$ field, we first replace it by the string MKS$(.753). To include the value of the variable INC in the INCOME$ field, we first replace it by MKS$(INC). After the conversion, we use the LSET (or RSET) commands to insert the string in the field. In the case of the two examples cited, the sequence is carried out by the respective instructions

```
50 LSET EFFICIENCY$=MKS$(.753)
```

```
60 LSET INCOME$=MKS$(INC)
```

Once the fields of a particular record have been set (using LSET or RSET), you may write the record to the file using the PUT instruction. Records are numbered within the file, starting from one. The significant feature of a random access file is that you may record or retrieve information from any particular record. For example, to write the current data into record 38 of file #1, we use the instruction

```
80 PUT #1, 38
```

TEST YOUR UNDERSTANDING 1 (answer on page 131)

Write a program that creates a file containing the following records:

ACCOUNTING	5000	.235	7886
ENGINEERING	3500	.872	2200
MAINTENANCE	4338	.381	5130
ADVERTISING	10832	.95	12500

To read a random access file, you must first open it using an instruction of the form

```
90 OPEN "DEPTS" AS #1 LEN=23
```

Note: This is the same as the instruction for opening a random access file for writing. Random access files differ from sequential files in this respect. By opening a random access file you prepare it for both reading and writing. Before closing the file, you may read some records and write others.

The next step in reading a random access file is to define the record structure using a FIELD statement, such as

```
100 FIELD #1, 10 AS DEPT$, 4 AS INCOME$, 4 AS EFFICIENCY$,
      4 AS OVERHEAD$
```

This is the same instruction we used for writing the file. Until the FIELD instruction is overridden by another, it applies to all reading and writing for file #1.

To perform the actual reading operation, we use the GET statement. For example, to read record #4 of the file, we use the statement

```
110 GET #1, 4
```

The variables DEPT$, INCOME$, EFFICIENCY$, and OVERHEAD$ are now set equal to the appropriate values specified in record #4 of file #1. We could, for example, print the value of DEPT$ using the statement

```
120 PRINT DEPT$
```

If we wish to use the value of EFFICIENCY$ (in a numerical calculation or in a PRINT statement, for instance), it is necessary to first convert it back into numerical form. This is accomplished using the CVS function. The statement

```
130 PRINT CVS(EFFICIENCY$)
```

will print out the current value of EFFICIENCY$; the statement

```
140 LET N=100*CVS(EFFICIENCY$)
```

sets the value of N equal to 100 times the numerical value of EFFICIENCY$.

It is important to note that field variables such as DEPT$ and EFFI-CIENCY$ contain the values assigned in the most recent GET statement. In order to manipulate data from more than one GET statement, it is essential to assign the values from one GET statement to some other variables before issuing the next GET statement.

TEST YOUR UNDERSTANDING 2 (answer on page 131)

Consider the random access file of TEST YOUR UNDERSTANDING 1. Write a program to read record 3 of that file and print the corresponding four pieces of data on the screen.

Random access files use no delimiters to separate data items within the file. Rather, the data items are sandwiched together, using the number of characters specified for each field. In order to peel those data items back apart, you must divide the file into records of the correct length and each record into fields of the proper numbers of bytes.

In our discussion above, we have used the instructions MKS$ and CVS to convert numerical data to string format and back to numerical format. These functions apply to single-precision numbers. In addition to single-precision numbers, there are double-precision numbers (up to 17 digits) and integers (whole numbers between -32768 and +32767). To convert a double-precision number to a string, we use the function MKD$; to convert back to numerical form, CVD. To convert an integer to a string, use the function MKI$; to convert back to numerical form, use CVI.

In either numerical form or string form an integer is represented by 2 bytes, a single-precision number by 4 bytes and a double-precision number by 8 bytes. In particular, this means that MKI$ produces a 2-byte string, MKS$ a 4-byte string, and MKD$ an 8-byte string.

BASIC provides several functions that help you keep track of random access files. In BASIC 1.1, the LOF (Length of File) function gives the number of bytes in the file rounded up to the nearest multiple of 128. In BASIC 2.00, LOF gives the actual number of bytes in the file. For example, suppose that file #2 contains 140 bytes. Then:

LOF(#2) is equal to 256   (BASIC 1.1)

LOF(#2) is equal to 140   (BASIC 2.00)

In BASIC 2.00, the LOF function may be used to determine the number of records currently in the file, according to the formula

<number of records> = LOF(<filenumber>)/<record length>

You may also use this formula in BASIC 1.1, but only if the record length is 128 (the default length).

Note that random access files cannot have any "holes." That is, if you write record 150, BASIC sets aside space for records 1 through 149, even if you write nothing in these records.

The LOC (Location) function gives the number of the last record read or written to the file. For example, if the last record written or read to file #1 was record 58, then LOC(#1) is equal to 58.

Here is an example that illustrates most of the procedures for using random access files.

EXAMPLE 1.   Write a program to create an address/telephone directory using a random access file. The program should allow for updating the directory and for directory search corresponding to a given name.

SOLUTION.   The program first opens the random access file TELEPHON, used to store the various directory entries. Note that the record length is set equal to 128. This allows us to use LOF to calculate the number of records in the file using either BASIC 1.1 or 2.00. The program then displays a menu allowing you to choose among the various options: Add an entry to the directory, Search the directory, Exit from the program. After an option is completed, the program redisplays the menu to allow you to make another choice. The code corresponding to the three options begins at program lines 1000, 2000 and 3000, respectively. Here is the program:

```
1000 'Telephone File
1010 'Open File For Random Access
1020      OPEN "TELEPHON" AS #1 LEN=128
1030      FIELD#1, 20 AS NME$, 20 AS ADDRESS$, 20  AS CITY$,
          20 AS STATE$, 5 AS ZIPCODE$, 20 AS TELEPHONE$,
          23 AS BLANK$
1040      LSET BLANK$=""
1050 'Option Menu
1060      PRINT "OPTIONS"
1070      PRINT "1. MAKE ENTRY IN DIRECTORY"
1080      PRINT "2. SEARCH DIRECTORY"
1090      PRINT "3. EXIT PROGRAM"
1100      INPUT "CHOOSE OPTION (1/2/3)";OPT
1110      ON OPT GOSUB 2000,3010,4010
1120      GOTO 1060
2000 'Add to file
2010      CLS
2020      INPUT "NAME";N$
2030      LSET NME$=N$
2040      INPUT "ADDRESS";N$
```

```
2050      LSET ADDRESS$=N$
2060      INPUT "CITY";N$
2070      LSET CITY$=N$
2080      INPUT "STATE";N$
2090      LSET STATE$=N$
2100      INPUT "ZIPCODE";N$
2110      LSET ZIPCODE$=N$
2120      INPUT "TELEPHONE NUMBER";N$
2130      LSET TELEPHONE$ = N$
2140      PUT #1
3000 RETURN
3010 'Search for a name
3020      NREC=LOF(1)/128
3030      INPUT "NAME TO SEARCH FOR";N$
3040      R=1
3050      GET #1, R
3060      GOSUB 5000: IF M$=N$ THEN 3100
3070      R=R+1
3080      IF R>NREC THEN PRINT "NAME IS NOT ON FILE":
          GOTO 4000
3090      GOTO 3050
3100      PRINT NME$
3110      PRINT ADDRESS$
3120      PRINT CITY$
3130      PRINT STAE$
3140      PRINT ZIPCODE$
3150      PRINT TELEPHONE$
4000 RETURN
4010 'Exit from program
4020      CLOSE
4030 END
5000 'Strip trailing blanks
5010      M$=NME$
5020      IF RIGHT$(M$,1) <> CHR$(32) THEN 5050
5030      M$ = LEFT$(M$,LEN(M$)-1)
5040      GOTO 5020
5050 RETURN
```

Note that line 3020 computes the number of records using the LOF function. In searching the file for a given name N$, the records are read one by one and the first field compared with N$. Note, however, that the first field is always 20 characters long. If the corresponding name has less than 20 characters, the field contains one or more trailing blanks. In comparing the first field with N$, it is necessary to first remove these blanks. This is done in the subroutine beginning in line 5000.

Setting the Random File Buffer Size

When BASIC is started, it sets aside a portion of RAM to aid in reading and writing random access files. This piece of RAM is called a **random file buffer**. Its size places a limit on the record size of your random access files. You may specify any record size you wish (see below). However, if you don't specify the size of the random access buffer, BASIC will allow only 128 bytes.

Suppose, for example, that you wish to use random access files with record lengths as large as 200 bytes. You may arrange for this by starting BASIC as follows:

1.   Obtain the DOS prompt A> .

2.   Type

```
BASIC /S:200
```

and press ENTER.

BASIC will then display the Ok prompt and you may program as usual.

If you attempt to use a FIELD statement requiring more bytes than are contained in the random access buffer, a **Field Overflow** error will result.

Exercises (answer on page 351)

1.   Write a program that writes the file TELEPHON of Section 5.2 (page) as a random access file. Leave 20 characters for the NAME entry, 25 for the address, 10 for the city, 2 for the state, 5 for the ZIP code, and 10 for the telephone number.

2.   Here is a record from a personnel file. (For ease in reading this record, we have replaced all blanks with @.)

```
JONES@@@@@@@JOHN@@@@@@@JFILECLERK4@@@04/15/82HOURLY$5.85
```

Write a field statement that will correctly separate the fields of the record.

3.   Suppose that a file named "SALES" consists of 20 records, each containing four numbers. Write a program that reads the file and prints the numbers in four columns on the screen.

4. Write a program that allows you to specify a name in the file TELEPHON. The program locates the file entry and prints out an address label corresponding to the name.

ANSWERS TO TEST YOUR UNDERSTANDING

```
1:  10 OPEN "DEPTS" AS #1, LEN=23
    20 FIELD #1, 11 AS DEPT$, 4 AS INCOME$, 4 AS
          EFFICIENCY$, 4 AS OVERHEAD$
    30 FOR J=1 TO 4
    40    READ A$,B,C,D
    50    LSET DEPT$=A$
    60    LSET INCOME$=MKS$(B)
    70    LSET EFFICIENCY$=MKS$(C)
    80    LSET OVERHEAD$=MKS$(D)
    90    PUT #1,J
    100 NEXT J
    110 DATA "ACCOUNTING",5000,.235,7886
    120 DATA "ENGINEERING",3500,.872,2200
    130 DATA "MAINTENANCE",4338,.381,5130
    140 DATA "ADVERTISING",10832,.95,12500
    150 CLOSE #1
    160 END

2:  10 OPEN "DEPTS" AS #1, LEN=23
    20 FIELD #1, 10 AS DEPT$, 4 AS INCOME$, 4 AS
       EFFICIENCY$,4 AS OVERHEAD$
    30 GET #1, 3
    40 PRINT "DEPARTMENT","INCOME","EFFICIENCY",
       "OVERHEAD"
    50 PRINT DEPT$,CVS(INCOME$),CVS(EFFICIENCY$),
       CVS(OVERHEAD$)
    60 CLOSE #1
    70 END
```

5.5   An Application of Random Access Files

In this section, we work out a detailed example illustrating the application of random access files. We will design and build a "list manager" program, which allows you to manipulate a list. A program of this sort is sometimes called a **data base management program**.

Our program will manipulate quite general lists. A typical list is structured into a series of entries, with each entry divided into a series of data items. We have allowed each entry of our list to contain as many as five string items and five numerical items. The string items are listed first. A typical list entry has the form

ITEM #1 (STRING)
ITEM #2 (STRING)
ITEM #3 (STRING)
ITEM #4 (STRING)
ITEM #5 (STRING)
ITEM #6 (NUMBER)
ITEM #7 (NUMBER)
ITEM #8 (NUMBER)
ITEM #9 (NUMBER)
ITEM #10 (NUMBER)

It is not necessary to use all 10 items. Then entries of a particular list might consist of three strings followed by two numbers, for example. The program asks for the structure of the list entries (number of strings and number of numbers). The program then assumes that all entries of the list contain the specified numbers of data items of each type.

The list manager allows you to perform the following activities:

1. Give a name to a list and create a corresponding random access file to contain the list.

2. Give titles to the various items ("NAME", "ADDRESS", "SALARY", "TELEPHONE #"). An item title may be up to 12 characters long.

3. Enter list items. The program displays the various item names and allows you to type in the various items for the list entry. You may repeat the entry operation as many times as you wish, thereby compiling lists of any length.

4. Change list entries. You may change a list entry by re-entering its data items.

5. Display list entries. You may display a single list entry or an entire set of consecutive list entries.

6. Search the list. You may search the list for entries in which a particular item (say ZIPCODE) has a particular value (say 20001). The program will inform you of a match and give the entry number. It will then ask you if you wish to see the corresponding list entry. If so, it will display the entry for you. After you are done examining the entry, you hit ENTER and the program will continue to search for further matches.

The following program is highly structured (major tasks correspond to subroutines) and the listing is reasonably self-explanatory. However, you should note the following:

A. The titles of the list are stored in record #1.

B. The actual list entries are stored beginning in record 2. The entry number (list entry 5) is always one less than the corresponding record (record 6).

C.   There are two menus. The main menu allows you to choose among the following activities:

Specify Titles
Specify List Entry
Search and Display
Exit

The second menu is displayed if you choose the Search and Display option on the main menu. The various options in this second menu are:

Display Single List Entry
Display Consecutive List Entries
Search

D.   Entry items are numbered from 1 to 10, with the strings 1 to 5 and the numbers 6 to 10. This numbering holds even if some items are not used. That is, the first numerical item is always denoted 6.

```
10 'List Manager
20 'Main Program
30 GOSUB 4200:              'Obtain file name and open file
40 GOSUB 1010:                'Display Main Menu
50 ON REPLY GOSUB 2000,3000,4100,4140
60 GOTO 40
1000 'Display main menu
1010      CLS
1020      PRINT "THE LIST MANAGER"
1030      PRINT:PRINT
1040      PRINT "PROGRAM ACTIVITIES"
1050      PRINT
1060      PRINT "1. ASSIGN DATA ITEM TITLES"
1070      PRINT "2. SPECIFY LIST ENTRY"
1080      PRINT "3. SEARCH AND DISPLAY LIST"
1090      PRINT "4. EXIT FROM LIST MANAGER"
1100      PRINT
1110      INPUT  "DESIRED ACTIVITY(1-4)";REPLY
1120 RETURN
2000 'Assign Data Item Titles
2010      CLS
2020      IF LOF(1)=1 THEN 2040:      'New File ?
2030      GOSUB 4400:                 'Get old titles
2040      FOR ITEMNUMBER=1 TO 10
```

```
2050          PRINT "DATA ITEM #";ITEMNUMBER;TAB(20) "CURRENT
              DEF'N ";
2060          PRINT A$(ITEMNUMBER)
2070          INPUT "NEW DEF'N: ";TITLE$(ITEMNUMBER)
2080          LSET A$(ITEMNUMBER)=TITLE$(ITEMNUMBER)
2090     NEXT ITEMNUMBER
2100     PUT #1,1:                          'Record new titles.
2110  RETURN
3000 'Specify List entry
3010     CLS
3020     INPUT "LIST ENTRY NUMBER (0=NEW ENTRY)";ENTRYNUMBER
3030     IF ENTRYNUMBER=0 THEN ENTRYNUMBER=LOC(1)+1 ELSE
         ENTRYNUMBER=ENTRYNUMBER+1
3040     GOSUB 4400:                        'Obtain titles
3050     PRINT "LIST ENTRY #";ENTRYNUMBER-1;TAB(20)
         "SPECIFY ENTRY ITEMS"
3060     FOR ITEMNUMBER=1 TO STRINGFIELDS
3070          PRINT "Data Item Title: ";TITLE$(ITEMNUMBER)
3080          INPUT "ENTRY (STRING)";ENTRY$
3090          LSET A$(ITEMNUMBER)=ENTRY$
3100     NEXT ITEMNUMBER
3110     FOR ITEMNUMBER=6 TO 5+NUMERICFIELDS
3120          IF TITLE$(ITEMNUMBER)="" THEN 3160
3130          PRINT "Data Item Title: ";TITLE$(ITEMNUMBER)
3140          INPUT "ENTRY (NUMBER)";ENTRY
3150          LSET A$(ITEMNUMBER)=MKS$(ENTRY)
3160     NEXT ITEMNUMBER
3170     PUT #1,ENTRYNUMBER
3180  RETURN
4000 'Various Subroutines
4100 'Search and Display List
4110     GOSUB 4700:              'Search and Display Menu
4120     ON REPLY GOSUB 4800,4900,5100
4130  RETURN
4140 'Exit
4150  CLS
4160  CLOSE #1
```

```
4170   END
4180  RETURN
4200  'Obtain file name and open file
4210     CLS
4220     CLOSE
4230     PRINT "THE LIST MANAGER"
4240     INPUT "NAME OF FILE";FILENAME$
4250     INPUT "NUMBER OF STRING FIELDS (1-5)";
         STRINGFIELDS
4260     INPUT "NUMBER OF NUMERIC FIELDS (1-5)";
         NUMERICFIELDS

4270     OPEN FILENAME$ AS #1
4280     FIELD #1, 12 AS A$(1), 12 AS A$(2), 12 AS A$(3),
         12 AS A$(4),12 AS A$(5),12 AS A$(6), 12 AS A$(7),
         12 AS A$(8), 12 AS A$(9), 12 AS A$(10)

4290     GOSUB 4400:              'Read Old titles
4300   RETURN
4400  'Read old titles
4410     GET #1,1
4420     FOR J=1 TO 10
4430          TITLE$(J)=A$(J)
4440     NEXT J
4450   RETURN
4500  'Display entry
4510     CLS
4520     PRINT:                  'Advance to 2nd line
4530     GOSUB 4400:             'Read titles
4540     IF DISPLAYENTRY > LOF(1)/128 THEN 4680:
         'Non-existant record
4550     GET #1, DISPLAYENTRY
4560     FOR ITEMNUMBER=1 TO STRINGFIELDS
4570          ENTRY$(ITEMNUMBER)=A$(ITEMNUMBER)
4580          PRINT TITLE$(ITEMNUMBER);
               TAB(21) ENTRY$(ITEMNUMBER)
4590     NEXT ITEMNUMBER
```

```
4600      FOR ITEMNUMBER=6 TO 5+NUMERICFIELDS
4610            IF A$(ITEMNUMBER)="" THEN 4620 ELSE 4640
4620            PRINT TITLE$(ITEMNUMBER)
4630            GOTO 4660
4640            ENTRY(ITEMNUMBER)=CVS(A$(ITEMNUMBER))
4650            PRINT TITLE$(ITEMNUMBER);
                TAB(21) ENTRY(ITEMNUMBER)
4660      NEXT ITEMNUMBER
4670      LOCATE 1,1
4680    RETURN
4700  'Display and Search Menu
4710      CLS
4720      PRINT "DISPLAY AND SEARCH MENU"
4730      PRINT : PRINT
4740      PRINT "1. DISPLAY ENTRY WITH GIVEN NUMBER"
4750      PRINT "2. DISPLAY CONSECUTIVE ENTRIES"
4760      PRINT "3. SEARCH"
4770      PRINT
4780      INPUT "ACTIVITY(1-3)";REPLY
4790    RETURN
4800  'Display entry with given number
4810      CLS
4820      PRINT:                    'Advance to 2nd line
4830      INPUT "Number of entry to display";
          DISPLAYENTRY
4840      DISPLAYENTRY=DISPLAYENTRY+1
4850      IF DISPLAYENTRY > LOF(1)/128 THEN 4890
4860      GOSUB 4500
4870      INPUT "TO CONTINUE, HIT ENTER KEY";REPLY$
4880      IF REPLY$="" THEN 4790 ELSE 4670
4890    RETURN
4900  'Display consecutive entries
4910      CLS
4920      PRINT:                    'Advance to 2nd line
4930      INPUT "NUMBER OF FIRST ENTRY TO DISPLAY";
          DISPLAYENTRY
4940      DISPLAYENTRY=DISPLAYENTRY+1
```

```
4950    IF DISPLAYENTRY > LOF(1)/128 THEN 5020
4960    GOSUB 4500
4970    LOCATE 1,1
4980    INPUT "DISPLAY NEXT ENTRY=0,RETURN TO
        MAIN MENU=1";REPLY
4990    IF REPLY=1 THEN 5020
5000    DISPLAYENTRY=DISPLAYENTRY+1
5010    GOTO 4950
5020  RETURN
5100  'Search
5110    CLS
5120    INPUT "ITEM NUMBER TO SCAN";ITM
5130    PRINT "LOOK FOR ITEM NUMBER";ITM;" EQUAL TO";
5140    IF ITM<6 THEN INPUT MATCHSTRING$
5150    IF ITM>5 THEN INPUT MATCHNUMBER
5160    L=LEN(MATCHSTRING$):
        'L=length of the match string
5170    MATCHSTRING$=MATCHSTRING$+SPACE$(12-L):
        'Add blanks
5180    LNGTH=LOF(1)/128
5190    FOR J=2 TO LNGTH
5200            GET #1, J
5210            IF ITM > 5 THEN A=CVS(A$(ITM))
                ELSE A$=A$(ITM)
5220            IF ITM < 6 AND A$=MATCHSTRING$
                THEN GOSUB 5300
5230            IF ITM > 5 AND A=MATCHNUMBER
                THEN GOSUB 5300
5240    NEXT J
5250  RETURN
5300  'Response to a match
5310    CLS
5320    LOCATE 1,1
5330    PRINT "MATCH IN ENTRY";J-1
5340    INPUT "Do You Wish to Display
        Entry(1=Yes,0=No)";REPLY
5350    IF REPLY=1 THEN 5360 ELSE 5400
5360    DISPLAYENTRY=J
```

```
5370     GOSUB 4500
5380     INPUT "TO CONTINUE, HIT ENTER KEY";REPLY$
5390     IF REPLY$="" THEN 5400 ELSE 5380
5400   RETURN
```

Note that the fields of the file records are all 12 characters wide. This is to accommodate the titles in record 1. Since we do not specify a record length, BASIC assumes that the records are 128 characters long. We are using 120 (12 characters per field x 10 fields) of these characters. If you wish, you may redesign this program to accommodate more data items and longer string items and titles. However, if you use more than 128 characters per record, it will be necessary to initialize BASIC to allow for a sufficiently large random access file buffer.

Exercises

1. Type in the list manager program.

2. Use the list manager program to create a Christmas card list.

3. Practice using the search feature to locate particular data items.

5.6   Sorting Techniques

In the preceding sections, we have discussed the mechanisms to create, read, and write data files. In this section, we discuss the organization of data within such files.

If a data file is to be of much use, we must be able to easily access its data. At first this might seem like a simple requirement. After all, we can always search through a data file, examining records until we find the one we want. Unfortunately, this is just not always possible. Until now, we have been working with rather short data files. However, many applications require dealing with data files containing thousands or even tens of thousands of records. When a data file is large, even the great speed of the computer is insufficient to guarantee a speedy search. Indeed, if we are required to search through an entire file for a piece of data, we might be required to wait for hours! For this reason (as well as others), we usually organize the contents of a file in some way so that access to its data is improved. Here are some examples of common file organizations:

1. A file of data on customers may be arranged in alphabetical order, according to the customer name.

2. A mailing list may be arranged according to ZIPCODE.

3. An inventory list might be arranged according to part number.

4. A credit card company most likely arranges its customer account files according to their credit card number.

In each example, the records in the data file are arranged in a certain order, based on the value of a particular field in the record (name field, ZIPCODE field, part number field, card number field). In maintaining such files, it is essential to be able to arrange the records in the desired order. The process of arranging a set of data items is called **sorting**. Actually, sorting is an extremely important topic to computer programmers and has been the subject of many research papers and books. In this section, we will give an introduction to sorting by describing one of the more elementary sorting techniques—the **bubble sort**.

Let's begin by stating our problem in simple terms. Let's suppose that we wish to arrange the records of a file according to a particular field, say field 1.

PROBLEM: Arrange the records so that the values in field 1 are in ascending order.

For the sake of our initial discussion, let's suppose that the field values are numbers. (Later, we will deal with fields containing strings.)

Let's set up arrays A() and B() as follows: Read the various values of field 1 into the array A().

A(1) = the value of field 1 for record 1,

A(2) = the value of field 1 for record 2,

A(3) = the value of field 1 for record 3,

and so forth. We wish to rearrange the records according to certain rules. Because the actual records may be quite long, we will deal only with the contents of field 1. In order to keep track of the record to which a particular field value belongs, we will use the array B(). That is,

B(1) = the record number for the field value A(1),

B(2) = the record number for the field value A(2),

B(3) = the record number for the field value A(3),

and so forth. Assume that we initially read the values into array A() according to increasing record number. Then we initially have

B(1) = 1, B(2) = 3, B(3) = 3, ...

The Bubble Sort Procedure

The **bubble sort** procedure allows you to arrange a set of numbers in increasing order. It involves repeatedly executing a simple reordering process that involves reordering consecutive items. Each repetition of the process is called a **pass**. Let's illustrate the procedure to arrange the following list of numbers in increasing order:

90, 38, 15, 48 , 80, 1

Pass 1. Start from the right end of the list. Compare the adjacent numbers. If they are out of order, switch them. Otherwise leave them alone. Continue this procedure with each pair of adjacent numbers, proceeding from right to left. Here are the results:

90, 38, 15, 48, 1, 80   (1 < 80 so the pair 80,1 is reversed)

90, 38, 15, 1, 48, 80   (1 < 48 so the pair 48,1 is reversed)

90, 38, 1, 15, 48, 80   (1 < 15 so the pair 15,1 is reversed)

90, 1, 38, 15, 48, 80   (1 < 38 so the pair 38,1 is reversed)

1, 90, 38, 15, 48, 80   (1 < 90 so the pair 90,1 is reversed)

This is the end of Step 1. Note that the number 1 has assumed its correct place in the list.

Pass 2. Apply the procedure of Step 1 to the rightmost five numbers of the current list.

1, 90, 38, 15, 48, 80   (48 < 80 so no exchange)

1, 90, 38, 15, 48, 80

1, 90, 15, 38, 48, 80

1, 15, 90, 38, 48, 80

Note that the number 15 has now been moved to its proper position on the list.

Pass 3. Apply the procedure of Step 1 to the rightmost four numbers of the current list.

1, 15, 90, 38, 48, 80

1, 15, 90, 38, 48, 80

1, 15, 38, 90, 48, 80

Pass 4. Apply the procedure of Step 1 to the rightmost three numbers of the current list.

1, 15, 38, 90, 48, 80

1, 15, 38, 48, 90, 80

Pass 5. Apply the procedure of Step 1 to the rightmost two numbers of the current list.

1, 15, 38, 48, 80, 90

The list is now in order.

Note the following characteristic of the bubble sort procedure. At each step, the smallest remaining number is moved to its proper position in the list. Suppose that we view the original list as written vertically:

the algorithm is terminated. Otherwise, SORTFLAG is set equal to 0, and the algorithm goes on to the next pass. Here is the code for the modified bubble sort routine.

```
200  'Modified Bubble Sort Subroutine
210  SORTFLAG=0
220  FOR I=2 TO N
230       FOR J=N TO I STEP -1
240                IF A(J-1) > A(J) THEN SWAP A(J-1), A(J):
                   SORTFLAG=1
250       NEXT J
260  IF SORTFLAG=0 THEN I=N ELSE SORTFLAG=0
270  NEXT I
280  RETURN
```

Note the logic in line 260. If SORTFLAG is equal to 0, then the loop variable I is set equal to N. In this case, the NEXT I in line 270 causes the I loop to terminate. Otherwise, SORTFLAG is set equal to 0 and the next value of I is considered.

TEST YOUR UNDERSTANDING 1

Compare the times required by both the original and modified bubble sort routines in sorting the following list of numbers into ascending order:

$1,2,3,4,5, \ldots , 95,100,99,98,97,96$

We may use the bubble sort procedure (either the original or the modified version) to arrange a string array A$() in alphabetical order. Just replace A(J) everywhere in the code with A$(J). That is, we compare and interchange the consecutive pairs of strings A$(J-1) and A$(J). In order to understand exactly what this routine does, however, it is necessary to understand the meaning of the string comparison A$ < B$.

Single characters are compared via their respective ASCII codes. For example, the following are valid comparisons:

"A" < "B" ("A" has ASCII code 65, "B" has ASCII code 66)
"a" < "b" ("a" has ASCII code 97, "b" has ASCII code 98)

Note that arranging alphabetic characters in ascending order amounts to arranging them in alphabetic order. However, we have the following additional valid comparisons, which are not usually considered in alphabetic arrangements:

"A" < "a"
"0" < "a" ("0" has ASCII code 48)
"*" > "#" ("*" has ASCII code 42, "#" has ASCII code 35)
"" < "0" ("" has ASCII code 32)

Strings having more than a single letter are compared as follows: First compare first letters. If they are the same, compare second letters. If the first two letters are the same, compare third letters. And so forth. For example, consider the two strings "Smith" and "SMITH". Their first letters are the same, so we compare their second letters "m" and "M", respectively. According to their ASCII codes "M" comes before "m", so that we have:

"SMITH" < "Smith"

If the compared strings consist of only uppercase or only lower case letters, then this comparison procedure will arrange the strings in the usual alphabetic order. However, the procedure may be used to compare any strings. For example, we have:

"**#" < "**0"

Using this comparison procedure, here is the modified bubble sort procedure for a string array A$():

```
200 'Modified Bubble Sort Subroutine for Strings
210 SORTFLAG=0
220 FOR I=2 TO N
230     FOR J=N TO I STEP -1
240                 IF A$(J-1) > A$(J) THEN SWAP
                    A$ (J-1), A$(J): SORTFLAG=1
250     NEXT J
260 IF SORTFLAG=0 THEN I=N ELSE SORTFLAG=0
270 NEXT I
280 RETURN
```

In this section, we have only scratched the surface of the subject of sorting. For an extensive treatment, see *Algorithms + Data Structures = Programs* by Niklaus Wirth, Prentice-Hall,Inc. Englewood Cliffs, New Jersey, 1976.

Exercises

1. Write a program to alphabetize the elements of the array A$() using the bubble sort procedure.

2. Test the program of Exercise 1 using the array A$(1) = "Z", A$(2) = "Y", ... , A$(26) = "A".

3. Write a program that creates an array of N random numbers, where N is given in an INPUT statement. The program should arrange the array in increasing order and should use the clock to time the operation. Make a table of sort times for various values of N. (Be sure to use RANDOMIZE to create non-repetitive arrays.)

4. Write a program that determines the smallest element in field 1 in the various records of the file "TEST". (Assume that the file is 25600 bytes long, the record length is 128 bytes, and field 1 is 4 bytes.

5.7 BASIC File Commands

BASIC on the IBM PC has a number of useful commands which you may use to perform various manipulations on files.

The Directory

You may request, from within BASIC, a directory of the files on a given diskette. This may be done using the FILES command. For example, to list all the files on the current diskette, type

```
FILES
```

and press ENTER. This command is similar to the DOS command DIR, except that this command is used within BASIC.

The FILES command is very versatile. You use it to provide a listing of all files matching a given filespec. For example, to list all files having an extension .BAS on drive B:, use the command

```
FILES "B:*.BAS"
```

Similarly, to list all files on drive B:, use the command

```
FILES "B:*.*"
```

Note that in BASIC 2.00, this last command may be abbreviated to:

```
FILES "B:"
```

TEST YOUR UNDERSTANDING 1 (answer on page 148)

Write a command that lists all files on the current drive with an extension that begins with the letter B.

Erasing Files

You may erase files using the command KILL. The format of this command is

```
KILL <file specification>
```

For example, to erase the file EXAMPLE.TXT, use the command

```
KILL "EXAMPLE.TXT"
```

To erase all files on the diskette in drive B:, use the command

```
KILL "*.*"
```

This last form of the KILL command is very dangerous. You might be erasing some files you don't really want to erase. Use this form of the KILL command with some care.

Note that the KILL command may be used to erase program files as well as data files.

In order to KILL a file, you must include any file name extension. Be careful here. If the file is a BASIC program and if you saved it without specifying an extension, BASIC automatically added the extension BAS. In order to specify the file name for the KILL command, you must include the extension BAS.

TEST YOUR UNDERSTANDING 2 (answer on page 148)

Write BASIC commands to erase the following files:

(a)   The BASIC program named "COLORS"
(b)   The BASIC program "INVOICE.001"

Renaming a File

You may rename a file by using the **NAME** command. To change the name of ROULETTE to GAME, we use the command:

```
NAME "ROULETTE" AS "GAME"
```

Note that the old name always comes **first**, followed by the new name. An error will occur if either (a) ROULETTE doesn't exist or (b) if there is already a file on the diskette with the name GAME.

To rename a program file, you must include any file name extension in the old file name. Be careful here. If the old file is a BASIC program and if you saved it without specifying an extension, BASIC automatically added the extension BAS. To specify the file name for the NAME command, you must include the extension BAS.

Saving Programs

As we learned in Chapter 2, you may save the current program on diskette, using the SAVE command. Let's take this opportunity to point out a few additional features of this command. BASIC allows a program to be saved in any of three alternate formats—compressed format, ASCII format, and protected format.

Compressed Format

This is the format we have used to save programs up till now. In this format, the various words of BASIC (LET, PRINT, IF, THEN, etc.) are reduced to a numerical shorthand, which allows the program to be stored in reduced space. The compressed format is also called **tokenized.**

ASCII Format

In ASCII format, the program is stored letter for letter as you typed it. This requires more diskette space. However, it allows the program to be MERGEd and CHAIN MERGEd. (See below.) Also, a program file must be saved in ASCII format if it is to be used as a source code file for the BASIC compiler. To save a program in ASCII format, use the command

```
SAVE <filespec>, A
```

For example, to save the program TAXES on the diskette in drive B: in ASCII format, we could use the command

```
SAVE "B:TAXES",A
```

Protected Format

Once a program has been saved in protected format, it may not be listed. It provides a mild degree of protection against snoopers. To save TAXES on drive B: in protected format, we could use the command

```
SAVE "B:TAXES",P
```

BASIC provides no way to translate a protected program back into a listable format, so use the protected format with some care.

Merging Programs

BASIC has the ability to merge the program currently in RAM with any other program on a diskette. This is especially useful in inserting standard subroutines into a program and is accomplished via the MERGE command. For example, to merge the current program with the program PAYROLL we use the command

```
MERGE "PAYROLL"
```

Suppose the program currently in RAM contained lines 10, 20, 30, and 100, and PAYROLL contained lines 40, 50, 60, 70, 80, 90, and 100. The merged program would contain the lines 10, 20, 30, 40, 50, 60, 70, 80, 90, 100. The line 100 would be taken from PAYROLL. (The lines of PAYROLL would replace those of the current program in case of duplicate line numbers.) To use the merge feature, the program from diskette must have been SAVEd in ASCII format. In the case of the above example, the command that SAVEd PAYROLL must have been of the form

```
SAVE "PAYROLL", A
```

In case PAYROLL was not SAVEd using such a command, it is first necessary to LOAD "PAYROLL" and resave it using the above command. (Watch out! If you type in a program, say OX as an example, to merge with PAYROLL, remember to save it before giving the MERGE command. If you don't, you will lose OX.)

TEST YOUR UNDERSTANDING 3 (answer on page 148)

(a.) Save the following program in ASCII format under the name GHOST.

```
10 PRINT 5+7
100 END
```

(b.) Type in the program

```
30 PRINT 7+9
40 PRINT 7-9
```

(c.) MERGE the programs of a and b.

Exercises (answers on page 351)

1. a. Write a program that computes $1^2 + 2^2 + \ldots + 50^2$.
    b. SAVE the program under the name SQUARES. Use the SAVE, A command.
2. a. Write a program that computes $1^3 + 2^3 + \ldots + 30^3$. Write this in such a way that the line numbers do not overlap with those of the program in 1a.
    b. MERGE the program of 1a with the program of 2a.
    c. LIST the MERGEd program.
    d. RUN the MERGEd program.
    e. SAVE the MERGEd program under the name COMBINED.
3. Recover the program of 2a without retyping it.
4. Erase the program SQUARES of 1a.

ANSWERS TO TEST YOUR UNDERSTANDING

```
1:  FILES "*.B??"
2:  (a)   KILL "COLORS.BAS"
    (b)   KILL "INVOICE.001"
```

3: (a) Type in the program, then give the command: SAVE "GHOST",A
    (b) Type NEW followed by the given program.
    (c) Type MERGE "GHOST".

6

Memory Management

In this chapter, we will explore the memory of the IBM PC. We will describe the way in which numbers and text are stored and the way the memory is organized. To carry out this program we will need to know something about the binary and hexadecimal number systems. Actually, as we shall see, binary and hexadecimal arithmetic will arise throughout the book. So let's begin with a discussion of these important number systems.

6.1   Binary and Hexadecimal Numbers

Decimal Representation of Numbers

In grade school, we learn to perform arithmetic using the decimal number system. In this system, numbers are written as strings of digits chosen from among the 10 numbers 0, 1, 2, 3, 4, 5, 6, 7, 8, 9. Here are some examples of these familiar numbers:

14312, -928372, 29831029831902938290

Such strings of digits are interpreted according to a system of place value. We proceed from right to left. The digit in the extreme right position represents the number of 1's, the next digit the number of 10's, the next digit the number of 100's, the next digit the number of 1000's, and so forth. For example, the number 1935 stands for:

```
1   1000's    1*1000 =  1000
9   100's     9* 100 =   900
3   10's      3*  10 =    30
5   1's       5*   1 =     5
                        1935
```

The values of the various digit positions, that is, the numbers 1, 10, 100, 1000, . . . are all powers of 10:

$1 = 10^0, 10 = 10^1, 100 = 10^2, 1000 = 10^3$ . . .

So another way of expressing the number 1935 is

1*10^3 + 9*10^2 + 3*10^1 + 5*10^0

149

(Note that we have arranged the digits in their usual order, which corresponds to decreasing powers of 10.)

Binary Representation of Numbers

In the binary number system, numbers are represented by strings formed from the two digits 0 and 1. Here are some examples of binary numbers

10, 01110000111, 100100100100

Just as the decimal number system is based on powers of 10, the binary number system is based on powers of 2, that is on the numbers

$2^0 = 1, 2^1 = 2, 2^2 = 4, 2^3 = 8, 2^4 = 16, \ldots$

We interpret a binary number by examining the digits from right to left. The rightmost digit of a binary number corresponds to the number of 1's, the next digit to the number of 2's, the next digit to the number of 4's, and so forth. So, for example, the binary number 1101 stands for

1	8's	=	8
1	4's	=	4
0	2's	=	0
1	1's (rightmost digit)	=	1
1101		=	13

That is, the binary number 1101 corresponds to the decimal number 13.

TEST YOUR UNDERSTANDING 1 (Answer on page 155)

What decimal number corresponds to the binary number 10101010?

The above calculations for converting a binary number into its decimal equivalent may be tedious. However, we may let the computer do the work for us. Here is a simple program that performs the conversion.

```
100 'Convert binary to decimal
110 INPUT "NUMBER TO CONVERT";N$
120 E=0:      'E=current power of 2
130 D=0:      'D=decimal equivalent
140 L=LEN(N$)
150 IF L=0 THEN 230
160 IF RIGHT$(N$,1) = "1" THEN D=D+2^E:GOTO 200
170 IF RIGHT$(N$,1) <> "0" THEN 250
200 E=E+1
210 N$=LEFT$(N$,L-1)
220 GOTO 140
```

```
230 PRINT "Decimal Equivalent=";D
240 GOTO 260
250 PRINT "Input Not In Proper Format"
260 END
```

Converting From Decimal To Binary

As we have seen, every binary number has a decimal equivalent. The reverse is also true: Every decimal number has a binary equivalent. For example, consider the decimal number 61. Let's divide it by 2 to obtain a quotient 30 and remainder 1. Write these results in the form

$$61 = 30*2 + 1$$

Next, we divide the quotient 30 by 2 to obtain the quotient 15 and remainder 0. Write this result in the form

$$30 = 15*2 + 0$$

If we insert this expression for 30 into the expression for 61, we obtain the result

$$61 = (15*2+0)*2 + 1$$
$$= 15*2^2 + 0*2 + 1$$

Let's now repeat the above procedure using the number 15 instead of 30: First we divide by 2 to obtain a quotient of 7 and a remainder of 1. Next, we write the equation

$$15 = 7*2 + 1.$$

And last, we substitute this equation into our preceding expression for 61

$$61 = (7*2 + 1)*2^2 + 0*2 + 1$$
$$= 7*2^3 + 1*2^2 + 0*2 + 1$$

Repeat the procedure using the number 7.

$$7 = 3*2 + 1$$
$$61 = (3*2+1)*2^3 + 1*2^2 + 0*2 + 1$$
$$= 3*2^4 + 1*2^3 + 1*2^2 + 0*2 + 1$$

Repeat the procedure using the number 3.

$$3 = 1*2 + 1$$
$$61 = (1*2+1)*2^4 + 1*2^3 + 1*2^2 + 0*2 + 1$$
$$= 1*2^5 + 1*2^4 + 1*2^3 + 1*2^2 + 0*2 + 1$$

From this last representation of 61, we may read off the binary representation of 61, namely

$$61 \text{ (decimal)} = 111101 \text{ (binary)}$$

If you don't believe the computation, just proceed in reverse and convert 111101 to its corresponding decimal number. You will obtain 61 as the result.

The above procedure may be programmed for the computer. However, it is necessary to perform division to obtain an integer quotient and remainder. If you use the operation / to perform the division, you will obtain a decimal answer and no remainder. For example, the result of 61/2 is 30.5 (rather than the desired quotient 30 and remainder 1). To obtain the desired information, it is simplest to use the BASIC operations \ and MOD.

The operation \ is called **integer division** and may be used to calulate the quotient of one integer by another. (Recall that an integer is a whole number in the range -32768 to 32767.) Integer division yields only the integer part of the quotient. For example,

$3\backslash2 = 1$

$16\backslash2 = 8$

$72\backslash7 = 10$

The operation MOD allows you to compute the remainder that results from an integer division. For example, 5 MOD 2 yields the remainder of the integer division $5\backslash2$. That is, 5 MOD 2 equals 1.

A word about the order in which operations are performed:

1. Functions are evaluated first.

2. Next comes arithmetic in this order:

    a. ^
    b. sign change —
    c. *, /
    d. \
    e. MOD
    f. +, -

3. Parentheses may be used to override the above order of operations. If parentheses are present, they are evaluated beginning with the inner-most set and proceeding outward.

TEST YOUR UNDERSTANDING 2 (Answer on page 155)

What is the value of $(7\backslash3 + 1)*(18\backslash5 -1)$?

TEST YOUR UNDERSTANDING 3 (Answer on page 155)

What is the value of
   (a)   17 MOD $7\backslash5$ (b) 5^2 MOD $25\backslash2^2$?

Using the operations \ and MOD, we may easily convert a decimal number to its binary equivalent. We repeatedly perform integer division by 2. The remainders of the division provide the digits of the binary number, proceeding from right to left. Here is a program to perform the calculations.

```
100 'Convert from decimal to binary
110 INPUT "NUMBER TO CONVERT";N
120 A$ = ""
130 REMAINDER = N MOD 2
140 A$ = RIGHT$(STR$(REMAINDER),1)+A$
150 N=N\2
160 IF N=0 THEN 170 ELSE 130
170 PRINT "The Binary Equivalent Is "; A$
180 END
```

A binary digit (0 or 1) is called a **bit**. The number 1011 is 4 bits long, whereas the number 10010011 is 8 bits long.

TEST YOUR UNDERSTANDING 4 (Answer on page 155)

(a)   List all possible 2 bit numbers.
(b)   List all possible 3 bit numbers.

In carrying out TEST YOUR UNDERSTANDING 4, you should have found that there are 4 2-bit numbers and 8 3-bit numbers. There are 16 possible 4-bit numbers:

0000, 0001, 0010, 0011, 0100, 0101, 0110, 0111

1000, 1001, 1010, 1011, 1100, 1101, 1110, 1111

It can be proven (in a mathematics text) that the number of possible N-bit numbers is equal to $2^{\wedge}N$. This fact generalizes the particular cases (N = 2,3,4) observed above.

As we shall see, 8-bit and 16-bit binary numbers play a special role in the internal workings of the IBM PC. The number of 8-bit binary numbers is $2^{\wedge}8 = 256$. They represent the numbers 0 through 255. Similarly, the number of 16-bit binary numbers is $2^{\wedge}16 = 65536$. They represent the numbers 0 through 65535.

The IBM PC (and all other digital computers) use the binary number system for their operation. It may appear as if the computer uses decimal numbers. However, all data must be converted into binary form if the computer is to process it. And this applies to text data and program statements as well as numerical data. Each type of information is translated into binary according to its own translation scheme. (More about this later.) Computer operations are performed only on binary numbers. When output is required, the computer translates from binary to either numeric or text format.

154   6—Memory Management

Hexadecimal Representation of Numbers

The hexadecimal number system is closely connected with the binary number system and is much easier to work with in many applications. There are 16 possible hexadecimal digits

0,1,2,3,4,5,6,7,8,9,A,B,C,D,E,F

The digits 0-9 have their usual numerical values, and A,B,C,D,E,F have the respective values

10, 11, 12, 13, 14, 15
 A   B   C   D   E   F

A typical hexadecimal number is string of hexadecimal digits, such as

A1EFF78A

The rightmost digit indicates the number of 1's, the next digit the number of 16's, the next digit the number of 256's ($256 = 16^2$), and so forth. For example, the above hexadecimal number corresponds to

$$10*16^7 + 1*16^6 + 14*16^5 + 15*16^4 + 15*16^3 + 7*16^2 + 8*16 + 10*1$$

The real advantage of hexadecimal is that it offers a shorthand way of writing numbers in binary. The 16 hexadecimal digits correspond to the following 4-digit binary numbers:

Hexadecimal	Binary	Decimal
0	0000	0
1	0001	1
2	0010	2
3	0011	3
4	0100	4
5	0101	5
6	0110	6
7	0111	7
8	1000	8
9	1001	9
A	1010	10
B	1011	11
C	1100	12
D	1101	13
E	1110	14
F	1111	15

A binary number may be blocked off in groups of four digits and translated into hexadecimal according to the above table. For example, consider the 25-digit binary number

1111100111001010111100111

To convert it into hexadecimal, first we block it off into groups of four digits, proceeding from right to left:

1 1111 0011 1001 0101 1110 0111

We complete the leftmost group by adding three zeros on the left:

0001 1111 0011 1001 0101 1110 0111

Finally, we translate each 4-digit group into a hexadecimal digit:

0001 1111 0011 1001 0101 1110 0111
  1   F   3   9   5   E   7

So the hexadecimal equivalent of the binary number is 1F395E7. It is clearly simpler to work with the hexadecimal form rather than the binary form of the number.

Hexadecimal numbers may be used in IBM PC BASIC on a par with decimal numbers. That is, wherever you can use a decimal number, you may use a hexadecimal number and vice versa. In BASIC, a hexadecimal number is indicated with the prefix &H. Thus, for example, the hexadecimal number 1A2F is denoted &H1A2F.

It is possible to write a simple program for converting decimal to hexadecimal. However, BASIC has a built-in function that saves us the bother. This function HEX$ returns a string that is the hexadecimal representation of a given decimal number. For example, we have

HEX$(10) equals "A"

HEX$(30) equals "1E"

Note that HEX$ returns a string, which may not be used in calculations. On the other hand &H1E is a number. As far as BASIC is concerned, &H1E is just another name for 30.

ANSWERS TO TEST YOUR UNDERSTANDING

1:   170
2:   6
3:   (a)   0   (b) 1
4:   (a)   00,01,10,11   (b)   000, 001, 010, 011, 100, 101, 110, 111

6.2   Bits, Bytes, and Memory

Our first application of the binary and hexadecimal number systems will be to describe the addressing scheme used by the PC. At the same time, we describe the various data present in RAM while you are using BASIC.

RAM is broken into a series of 8-bit binary numbers called **bytes**. The size of your RAM is measured in units of 1024 bytes. One 1024 byte unit is called 1K. So a system with 32K of RAM contains 32 x 1024 or 32768 bytes. A system with 64K contains 64 x 1024 or 65536 bytes. Your IBM PC's ram can be expanded to contain as much as 512K.

You should think of RAM as divided into a large number of cubbyholes with each cubbyhole containing a single byte. The cubbyholes of RAM are called **memory locations**. The contents of each memory location may be described by two hexadecimal digits (= 8 bits). So, for example, here are the contents of four memory locations

7E 0F FF 81

The memory locations of a computer are numbered, usually beginning with 0. The number associated with each memory location is called its **address**. For example, in a simple computer system (not the PC) with 4K of RAM, the memory locations have addresses from 0 to 4095 (decimal). At a particular moment, the contents of addresses 3001-3004 might be as follows:

Address	3001	3002	3003	3004
Contents	1A	B0	E8	F1

The computer makes use of addresses in its internal calculations. For this reason, addresses are usually expressed in hexadecimal. Be careful not to confuse an address (a memory location number) with its contents (the data stored in that address).

We observed in the preceding section that 16-bit binary numbers correspond to the decimal numbers 0 through 65535. On the other hand 64K = 65536. Thus, we see that the 16-bit binary numbers provide exactly enough addresses to handle a 64K memory. To address more memory than 64K requires binary numbers longer than 16 bits. Actually, the IBM PC is designed to economically handle 16-bit numbers, so rather than use addresses consisting of, say 24 or 32 bits, it uses pairs of 16-bit numbers. So a typical address on the PC is of the form

(segment, offset)

where **segment** and **offset** are 16-bit numbers having the following meanings.

Bytes are numbered beginning with 0. The byte corresponding to a particular address pair (segment, offset) is byte number

16*segment + offset.

For example, consider the address pair (00FF,1F58). The segment portion, 00FF, equals 255 in decimal. The offset portion, 1F58, equals 8024 in decimal So the particular address pair corresponds to byte number 16*255 + 8024 = 12104.

Suppose that we hold the segment portion of an address pair fixed and allow the offset portion to vary. The corresponding address pair runs over a set of 64K consecutive memory locations. Such a section of memory is called a 64K segment. In programming the 8088 chip (in machine language), such 64K segments play an important role.

The following notation is used to denote an address:

segment:offset

Thus, for example, the address in the above example is

00FF:1F58

TEST YOUR UNDERSTANDING 1 (Answer on page 161)

The maximum address theoretically possible is FFFF:000F. To what byte
number does this correspond?

If your computations are correct, you just found that the PC can address
more than 1 million bytes of RAM. Actually, not all these addresses represent RAM locations. Certain addresses refer to ROMs that contain portions
of BASIC and DOS. Other addresses are reserved for future expansion of
the system's capabilities. Here is a diagram of memory organization when
BASIC is in use. (A diagram of this sort is called a **memory map**.)

Memory Location	Contents
0000:0000	DOS
DS:0000	BASIC
	(approximately 17K)
DS:xxxx	Current Program
DS:yyyy	Variables
	Arrays
	String Space
	BASIC Stack
Top of Memory or DS:FFFF	
	Unused by BASIC
A000:0000	System Use
F400:0000	ROM

The memory map requires a bit of explanation. The memory locations
beginning at 0000:0000 are reserved by DOS. The precise amount of memory required depends on the version of DOS. When BASIC is loaded into
RAM, one of the internal registers of the 8088 processor is loaded with the
segment address corresponding to the beginning of the BASIC interpreter
program. The register containing this information is called the Data Segment
register and its contents are denoted DS on the memory map.

The offsets xxxx and yyyy give the beginning of the current program and
the beginning of the program variables, respectively. Their precise values
depend on the version of BASIC. However, they may be obtained from certain memory locations. (See Section 6.5.) Note that BASIC is allowed only
one 64K segment. A corollary of this fact is that a BASIC program must lie

within that segment, regardless of the amount of memory present in your machine. (This only applies to interpreted BASIC. Compiled programs may be longer than 64K. In fact, they may take advantage of as much memory as you own!)

The BASIC segment of memory ends at either DS:FFFF or at the Top of Memory. If there is less than 64K that may be allocated to BASIC, then the Top of Memory is set equal to the highest location in your RAM.

You may artificially limit the space occupied by BASIC. You may wish to do this to make room for machine language subroutines or communications buffers, for example. To limit the size of BASIC's segment, call up BASIC with a command of the form

```
BASIC /M:numberofbytes
```

Here **numberofbytes** is equal to the desired number of bytes in BASIC's segment. For example, to limit BASIC to 32K, we could use the command

```
BASIC /M:32767
```

If you do not limit the size of BASIC, DOS will automatically reserve all available memory up to a maximum of 64K.

The memory locations beginning A000:0000 are reserved for system functions such as storing the contents of the screen. (Later, we'll show you how to write on the screen by making direct access to the screen memory.)

The locations beginning F000:0000 correspond to ROM. In these locations is stored large portions of both DOS and BASIC. Moreover, these locations contain the master program, called the BIOS, which controls the input and output operations between the various system components. This program is the one responsible for reading and interpreting the keyboard input, displaying characters on the screen, reading and writing on diskette, and so forth.

Snooping Into Memory

It's both fun and instructive to snoop around in your computer's memory. The simplest way to do this is to use the program DEBUG, which is on your DOS diskette. Let's snoop around within the BASIC interpreter. To use DEBUG, obtain the DOS prompt A>, insert your DOS diskette into the current drive and type

```
DEBUG BASIC <ENTER>
```

After a few seconds, you will see the DEBUG prompt

```
-
```

Type D followed by any address. For example, to display the contents of memory beginning at location 0D00:0000, type

```
D 0D00:0000 <ENTER>
```

The DEBUG program will display the contents of 80 consecutive memory locations beginning with 0D00:0000. The display will consist of lines of the form

```
0D00:0000 33 1E 4F 4A A1 09 01 00 00 00 00 00 00 FF FF
```

The address at the beginning of the line corresponds to the first entry following.

DEBUG is quite a powerful program. It allows you to snoop anywhere in memory. For example, we may display the beginning of BASIC by typing

```
DS:0000<ENTER>
```

The DEBUG program will then display 80 consecutive bytes of memory beginning with the address DS:0000. The memory contents are displayed in hexadecimal form. When the desired information has been displayed, DEBUG will redisplay its prompt. To see another section of memory, just give another D command followed by the beginning address. If you omit the address, the program will display the 80 bytes that follow those most recently displayed.

TEST YOUR UNDERSTANDING 2

Use the DEBUG program to display:

(a)   The first 800 bytes of the BASIC interpreter

(b)   The contents of memory location 0000:0076

You say you don't understand what you see? Well, that's because you are looking at a program in machine language. This is the form in which the computer reads and executes programs. We'll have more to say about the meaning of these hexadecimal numbers later.

Addresses Within a BASIC Program

In most BASIC programs you are shielded from dealing directly with specific memory locations. You can name variables, create loops, make decisions, and BASIC automatically keeps track of all the various goings-on in memory. However, in some applications, it is necessary to access a memory location directly. And BASIC has statements that allow you to do this.

At any given moment, there is a current segment number, which is understood as the segment portion of any needed addresses. You specify this segment number by using the DEF SEG statment. The format of this statement is

```
DEF SEG = segment number
```

This statement defines the segment required for the adresses in the PEEK, POKE, CALL, BLOAD, BSAVE, VARPTR, and USR instructions. (All will be discussed subsequently.) Once you specify a segment number via a DEF SEG instruction, the segment number will remain the same until you change it by another DEF SEG instruction.

When BASIC is initialized, the segment number is set equal to the beginning address of the BASIC interpreter. (DS in the above memory map.) Unless you change this segment number via a DEF SEG instruction, all adresses in BASIC are assumed to have the beginning of the BASIC interpreter as their segment number. After giving a DEF SEG instruction, you may return the segment number to its initial setting with the instruction

```
DEF SEG
```

(The segment number is omitted.)

To read the contents of a memory location, you may use the PEEK statement. It has the format

```
x = PEEK(offset)
```

This statement assigns the contents of segment:offset to the numerical variable x. The segment number is the number assigned by the most recent DEF SEG instruction. The contents of a memory location are given as an integer between 0 and 255. For example, the instruction

```
CONTENTS = PEEK(35873)
```

will assign the contents of memory location :35873 to the numerical variable contents, where is the current segment number.

TEST YOUR UNDERSTANDING 3

Use the PEEK instruction to determine the contents of the first 4 memory locations in which the BASIC interpreter is stored. Compare your results with the information determined in TEST YOUR UNDERSTANDING 2(a). (Remember that the results of the preceding TEST YOUR UNDERSTANDING were provided in hexadecimal, whereas PEEK gives its results in decimal.)

You may store a number in a memory location using the POKE instruction, which has the format

```
POKE offset, contents
```

For example, consider the instruction

```
PEEK 5000, 217
```

It stores the number 217 in location :5000. The contents assigned to a memory location must be an integer between 0 and 255.

The PEEK and POKE instructions give you untold power. However, you must use them with care. Be sure not to POKE into a memory location that contains part of the BASIC interpreter, DOS, or any other "non-user" area of memory. You may cause your program to crash!

The various dots of light that comprise the screen display at any given moment are stored, in coded form, in a section of memory. The monochrome display interface uses 4,096 bytes of memory beginning at &HB000, whereas the color/graphics interface uses 16,384 bytes beginning at &HB800:0000. You may write in these memory locations and see what you write. Here is a program that accomplishes this in the case of the color/graphics interface, in medium-resolution graphics mode. The program requests a memory offset. It then stores 255 in the corresponding memory location. Visually, this corresponds to 4 dots in a row. The position of the dots will correspond to the memory offset selected.

```
10 KEY OFF
20 SCREEN 1
30 DEF SEG = &HB800
40 LOCATE 1,1
50 INPUT OFFSET
60 CLS
70 POKE OFFSET,255
80 GOTO 40
```

In many graphics applications, it is most efficient to manipulate displays by writing into or reading directly from the screen memory.

If you consult the memory map provided above, you can see the relative position of your variables, strings and arrays within the memory. You may locate the exact position of any one of these program elements using the VARPTR instruction. For example, suppose that your program uses the variable ALPHA. The instruction

```
X = VARPTR(ALPHA)
```

will set X equal to the offset of the first byte of memory which is used to store ALPHA. The assumed segment is always the beginning of the BASIC interpreter. This assumed segment is not affected by DEF SEG instructions. We will discuss at a later time the precise way in which variables are stored. At that time, we will use the VARPTR instruction to snoop on some variables in action.

ANSWER TO TEST YOUR UNDERSTANDING

1: 1,048,575

6.3   How Data Is Stored in Memory

In the previous section, we discussed the memory of the PC and how the various memory locations are identified by means of addresses. Let's now turn to the actual contents of the memory locations and discuss how BASIC stores various sorts of data in RAM. We should begin by saying that all locations of RAM and ROM contain binary numbers. What we are really after, however, is the way in which various kinds of data (integers, single-precision numbers, double-precision numbers, strings) are represented as binary numbers.

Positive and Negative Integers

An **integer** is a whole number in the range -32768 to 32767. An integer is stored in RAM as a 16-bit binary number. So let's spend a moment discussing the layout of such storage.

The bits of a binary number are numbered as in the diagram below:

bit number	15	14	13	12	11	10	9	8	7	6	5	4	3	2	1	0
bit	1	0	1	0	1	1	0	1	1	0	1	0	0	1	1	1

Bit 0 is called the **least significant** and bit 15 the **most significant**.

A 16-bit binary number is called a **word**. Storage of a word requires two (8-bit) bytes. Now here is the confusing part. The two bytes are stored in consecutive memory locations, with the least significant bits in the first byte and the most significant bits in the second byte. This may seem perfectly natural, but results in the following confusion. Consider the following 16-bit number in hexadecimal form: 1A3F . (Recall that each hexadecimal digit corresponds to 4 bits.) The most significant 8 bits correspond to 1A and the least significant to 3F. Therefore, this 16-bit number is stored in memory as

3F 1A

And, indeed, if you use DEBUG to look at memory, you will see the bytes displayed in this order. Before you interpret a 16-bit number from RAM, remember to reverse the order of the bytes!

TEST YOUR UNDERSTANDING 1 (Answer on page 166)

Here are two consecutive bytes in memory: A3 1F. To what decimal number does this correspond?

In our discussion so far, we have avoided any mention of negative numbers in binary and hexadecimal. Let's fill in that gap. BASIC uses only the 15 least significant bits (bits 0 through 14) to represent a positive number. The most significant bit (bit 15) is always 0 for a positive number. (See Figure 6.1)

This coding method allows representation of 2^{16} = 32,768 binary numbers, corresponding to the decimal numbers 0 through 32,767.

0 b b b b b b b b b b b b b b b

Figure 6.1. A Positive 16-bit Number

The most significant bit (bit 15) is used to indicate the sign of the number. Perhaps the most significant way of indicating the sign would be to have bit 15 = 0 to mean a positive number and bit 15 = 1 to mean a negative number. **However, this is not what is done.** Instead, negative numbers are indicated using the so-called **two's complement**.

To form the **two's complement of a binary number**, proceed as follows:

1. Change every 0 bit to a 1 and vice versa.

2. Add 1 to the resulting number.

For example, to form the two's complement of 0110, we first reverse each bit to obtain

1001

Then, we add 1 to this last number. We could do this by converting to decimal, performing the addition, and then reconverting to binary. However, it is easy to add directly in binary. Just add corresponding places from right to left, just as if you were adding decimal numbers, and follow the rules:

0 + 0 = 0

0 + 1 = 1

1 + 1 = 0 and carry the 1 to the next place

For example, we have

```
   1001
+     1
   1010
```

Thus, the two's complement of 0110 is 1010.

Here is the connection between two's complements and negative numbers: A negative number -n is represented in binary by the two's complement of n, considered as a 16-bit number. Thus, for example, the binary number 0110 equals the positive decimal number 6. The binary representation of -6 is obtained as follows: First consider 0110 as the 16-bit number

0000 0000 0000 0110

Now form the two's complement:

1111 1111 1111 1001

$$+ \underline{\hspace{10em} 1}$$

1111 1111 1111 1010

So -6 is represented by the binary number 1111111111111010.

Here is an easy way to recognize a negative integer directly from its binary representation: A negative always has its high order bit equal to 1. Moreover, you may recover the original number by taking the two's complement a second time. For example, the two's complement of 1111111111111010 is:

0000 0000 0000 0101

$$+ \underline{\hspace{10em} 1}$$

0000 0000 0000 0110

So we retrieve our original number 0110.

TEST YOUR UNDERSTANDING 2 (Answer on page 166)

Determine the number represented by the binary number:
1111 1111 1001 1100

TEST YOUR UNDERSTANDING 3 (Answer on page 166)

Determine the binary representation of

(a)   32767
(b)   -32767

The two's complement of an integer n may be calculated in decimal notation using a very simple procedure:

[two's complement of n] = 65536 - n

For example, the two's complement of 6 is equal to 65530. And it is easy to check that 65530 in binary is equal to

1111111111111010

TEST YOUR UNDERSTANDING 4 (Answer on page 166)

(a)   Store the number -15 in memory location 30000.

(b)   Use a PEEK instruction to display the contents of memory location 30000. What are the contents? Can you explain the results?

The two's complement procedure may seem to be an obscure way of representing negative numbers. However, it is designed to aid in performing arithmetic among binary numbers with the greatest possible speed.

ASCII Characters

The IBM PC has 255 displayable characters. Each of these characters is given an ASCII code, which is an integer between 0 and 255. A character is represented in memory by this ASCII code and therefore occupies exactly one byte. For example, here is how the string "This is a test." is stored in memory.

	T	h	i	s		i	s		a		t	e	s	t	.
ASCII Decimal	84	104	105	115	32	105	115	32	97	32	116	101	115	116	46
ASCII Hexadecimal	54	68	69	73	20	69	73	20	61	20	74	65	73	74	2E

So the given string is stored in memory as the consecutive bytes:

54,68,69,73,20,69,73,20,61,20,74,65,73,74,2E

TEST YOUR UNDERSTANDING 5 (answer on page 166)

How is this display stored in memory?

Line 1
Line 2
Line 3

Single-Precision Numbers and Variables

A single-precision number is stored in a "scientific notation" requiring 4 bytes, regardless of the size of the number. The actual algorithm used for the storage is rather complicated and is designed for efficiency in carrying out computations rather than the convenience of the programmer. One of the four bytes is used to store an exponent which is used as a scaling factor. The other three bytes are used to store a scaled version of the number, called the **mantissa**. We will omit a precise description of the storage algorithm until Appendix B.

Double-Precision Numbers

Double precision numbers are stored using 8 bytes. The first byte is the exponent, exactly as for single-precision numbers. The next 7 bytes are used for the mantissa. The fact that 56 bits are used for the mantissa rather than 24 allows for the greater number of digit precision in double-precision numbers.

ANSWERS TO TEST YOUR UNDERSTANDING

1:   6719

2:   -100

3:   (a)   0111 1111 1111 1111

     (b)   1000 0000 0000 0001

4:   (a)   POKE -15,3000

     (b)   What you see is the decimal equivalent of the two's complement of -15.

5:   In decimal, the list of ASCII codes is:

    76, 105, 110, 101, 32, 49, 13
    76, 105, 110, 101, 32, 50, 13,
    76, 105, 110, 101, 32, 51, 13,

6.4   Operations on Bytes

In many applications (we shall see a few shortly) it is necessary to perform operations directly on the bits of a byte. In this section, we will introduce you to these operations.

Shift and Truncate Operations

It is often required to move all the bits of a byte to the left or to the right. Such operations are called, respectively, a **left shift** and a **right shift**. For example, consider the following byte:

1101 0110

If we apply a left shift, we obtain the byte

1010 1100

Note that the rightmost bit is a 0 and the original leftmost bit has been "pushed off the end." Similarly, a right shift applied to the original byte yields

0110 1011

Note that the leftmost bit is replaced by a zero and the original rightmost bit is "pushed off the end."

How may operations such as those just described be carried out in BASIC? Before we describe a method, let's recall that the binary number system is based on powers of 2. If we multiply a decimal number by 10, we shift all the digits to the left one place. Similarly, in the binary number system, if we multiply a number by 2, we shift the bits to the left one place. Similarly, if we divide a binary number by 2 (integer division), then we shift the digits to the right by one bit.

In the case of multiplcation by 2, there may be a bit shifted into bit position 9. We may rid ourselves of this bit by using MOD 256. (The remainder on division by 256 is exactly the rightmost 8 bits.)

So here is how to perform shifts on the value of the integer variable A%:

Left Shift: 2*A% MOD 256

Right Shift: A%\2

The above use of the MOD operation may be generalized. The remainder on dividing by 2^N is precisely the rightmost N bits. The bits beyond N are replaced by zeros. This process is called **truncation**.

TEST YOUR UNDERSTANDING 1 (Answer on page 170)

Write an instruction that shifts the value of A% to the right 3 bits.

TEST YOUR UNDERSTANDING 2 (Answer on page 170)

Write an instruction that truncates the most significant 3 bits of the value of B%.

Logical Operations on Words

BASIC has a number of built-in operations that you may perform on 16-bit quantities (integers).

NOT

The NOT operation reverses all the bits of a number. For example, consider the number

NOT 0000 1010 1111 0101

We may compute this number by changing every 0 to a 1 and every 1 to a 0.

In BASIC, we may apply the NOT operation to any integer, written in either decimal or hexadecimal form. The NOT operation converts the number to binary form, performs the above computation, and reconverts the number to decimal form.

For example, let's compute NOT 18. We have

18 decimal = 0000 0000 0001 0001 binary

so

NOT 18 = 1111 1111 1110 1110 binary
= -19 decimal

AND

The operation A AND B produces a 16-bit number from the 16-bit numbers A and B. More precisely, if A and B are 16-bit quantities, then

A AND B

is the 16-bit number obtained as follows: Compare A and B bit by bit. For a given bit position, if both A and B have a one, then the corresponding bit of A and B is a one. If either A or B has a zero, the corresponding bit of A AND B is a zero. For example, consider the 16-bit quantities

A = 1101 1011 1000 0000
B = 1001 0001 0011 1111

Then

A AND B = 1001 0001 0000 0000

If A and B are integers given in decimal form, we may also apply the operation AND. The answer will be a decimal number, which is obtained by computing A and B using the respective binary representations of A and B. (In using these binary representations, remember that a negative number is represented in two's complement form.) For instance, suppose that A = 3 and B = 5. Then

A = 0000 0000 0000 0011
B = 0000 0000 0000 0101
A AND B = 0000 0000 0000 0001

That is,

5 AND 3 = 1

OR

The operation A OR B produces a 16-bit number from the two 16-bit numbers A and B. More precisely, if A and B are 16-bit quantities, then

A OR B

is the 16-bit number obtained as follows: Compare A and B bit by bit. For a given bit position, if either A or B have a one, then the corresponding bit of A and B is a one. If both A and B have a zero, the corresponding bit of A OR B is a zero. For example, consider the 16-bit quantities

A = 1101 1011 1000 0000

B = 1001 0001 0011 1111

Then

A OR B = 1101 1011 1011 1111

If A and B are integers given in decimal form, we may also apply the operation OR. The answer will be a decimal number which is obtained by computing A and B using the respective binary representations of A and B. (In using these binary representations, remember that a negative number is represented in two's complement form.) For instance, suppose that A = 3 and B = 5. Then

$$A = 0000\ 0000\ 0000\ 0011$$
$$B = 0000\ 0000\ 0000\ 0101$$
$$A\ AND\ B = 0000\ 0000\ 0000\ 0111$$

That is,

5 OR 3 = 7

XOR

The operation A XOR B is called the **exclusive OR** of A and B and produces a 16-bit result from the two 16-bit numbers A and B. If A and B are 16-bit quantities, then

A XOR B

is the 16-bit number obtained as follows: Compare A and B bit by bit. For a given bit position, if A and B have different bits, then the corresponding bit of A and B is a one. If A and B have the same bits, the corresponding bit of A XOR B is a zero. For example, consider the 16-bit quantities

A = 1101 1011 1000 0000

B = 1001 0001 0011 1111

Then

A XOR B = 0110 1010 1011 1111

If A and B are integers given in decimal form, we may also apply the operation XOR. The procedure is similar to that described in our discussion of AND and OR.

Caution Do not confuse the use of AND, NOT, OR, and XOR within numerical operations and the use of the corresponding words to construct statements in conditional (IF-THEN) instructions. For example, note the use of AND in the expression

A>1 AND B<3

In this case, the AND serves as a logical connector. The statement given is true only if both of the statements A>1 and B<3 are true. In a similar fashion, we may consider statements of the form

NOT (A>1)

(A>1) OR (B<3)

(A>1) XOR (B<3)

The first of these statements is true provided that the statement A>1 is not true. The second of the statements is true if either of the statements A>1 or B<3 is true. The third statement is true provided that the statements A>1 and B<3 are both not true or are both not false.

ANSWERS TO TEST YOUR UNDERSTANDING

1:   A% = A%\8

2:   A% = (A%*8)\8

6.5   Some Applications of Byte Operations

In this section, we will apply some of what we have learned about binary numbers and bytes. We will present three applications:

1.   We will construct a capitalization function.

2.   We will present some advanced graphics tricks using GET and PUT. These tricks will aid in displaying animations.

3.   We will explain the mechanics of designing custom characters for screen display.

A Capitalization Function

You may have noticed that BASIC turns alphabetic characters within a program listing into capital letters. For example, if you type a program statement containing the letter "a", a subsequent listing of the statement will display the letter as "A." Let's write a program to perform such a conversion.

Of course, we may convert lowercase letters into capital letters using a series of IF . . . THEN statements of the form

```
IF A$="a" THEN A$="A"
```

(Here A$ is a string variable containing the letter to be capitalized.) However, such a program would contain many statements, occupy a great deal of memory, and run very slowly. There is a much better way.

To discover the secret relationship between capital and lowercase letters, let's looks at their respective ASCII codes. Here is a portion of the ASCII table.

Letter	ASCII Code	Letter	ASCII Code
A	65	a	97
B	66	b	98
C	67	c	99
.	.	.	.
.	.	.	.
.	.	.	.
Z	90	z	122

What is the relationship between a letter and its corresponding capital? Well, a quick look at the table shows that the ASCII code of a capital letter is 32 less than the ASCII code of the corresponding lowercase letter. And 32 corresponds to one of the bit positions in a byte, namely bit 5. This is no accident, but a result of good planning! Consider the binary equivalents of the ASCII codes for "A" and "a":

65 decimal = 01000001 binary

97 decimal = 01100001 binary

Note that they differ only in the 32's place, namely bit 5. Similarly, consider the ASCII codes for "B" and "b":

66 decimal = 01000010 binary

98 decimal = 01100010 binary

Again the only difference is in bit 5. By subsequent examination of the other letter pairs, we come up with the following rule:

To Convert a Letter From Lower Case To Capital:
Change bit 5 in its ASCII code from 1 to 0.

And the change in bit 5 may be accomplished by ANDing the ASCII code with the number 11011111 = 223 decimal. Here's why. For all bits except bit 5, we are ANDing with a 1. So if the ASCII code has a 1, the ANDing will have a 1; if the ASCII code has a 0, the ANDing will have a 0. In other words, all bits other than bit 5 will remain unchanged. On the other hand, bit 5 is ANDed with a 0 and so will certainly result in a 0. In particular, if bit 5 was a 1 (lower case), it will be converted to a 0 (upper case).

On the basis of our discussion, we may finally construct a function FNA$(X$), which converts the character X$ into a captial letter if it was lower case and otherwise leaves X$ alone:

```
DEF FNA(X$) = CHR$(ASC(X$) AND 223)
```

This function starts with a string X$ (any string will do) and computes the ASCII code of its first character. (This is the ASC(X$) part.) The ASCII code is then ANDed with 223 and the resulting ASCII code is converted back into a character. You should test this function out with some examples of characters X$. Here is a program to carry out the tests.

```
10 DEF FNA$(X$) = CHR$(ASC(X$) AND 223)
20 INPUT "CHARACTER=";X$
30 Z$=FNA$(X$)
40 PRINT "THE CONVERTED CHARACTER IS "; Z$
50 INPUT "TRY ANOTHER CHARACTER (Y/N)";REPLY$
60 IF FNA$(REPLY$)= "Y" THEN 20
70 END
```

This program is interesting in several respects. First, it allows you to try out the capitalization function FNA(X$). Second, it shows you how the function may be used in practice. Observe the instructions in lines 50-70. Line 50 asks if you wish to type another character. It asks for a reply of "Y" or "N". Most people will not even think much about it and respond with "y" or "n". Good program design should allow for such responses. One way of doing this is to ask separately if REPLY$ = "Y" or if REPLY$="y". A much cleaner approach is the one taken in line 60. We replace REPLY$ by FNA$(REPLY$). This converts a reply of "y" into "Y". Then a single question suffices in line 60.

TEST YOUR UNDERSTANDING 1

Modify the above program so that it leaves X$ unchanged if it begins with a non-letter character (A-Z, a-z).

Some Further Tricks With GET and PUT

In the chapter on graphics, we introduced the GET and PUT statements, which can be used for transporting images from place to place on the screen. There are several features of these commands which we have yet to discuss.
Recall that GET has the format

```
GET (x1,y1)-(x2,y2), <array>
```

where (x1,y1) and (x2,y2) are opposite corners of the rectangle to be stored, and <array> is an array that has been dimensioned of a sufficient size to hold the rectangular image. (See our preceding discussion for determining the size of the array.)
Recall that the PUT statement has the form

```
PUT (x,y), <array>
```

This statement puts the image stored in <array> on the screen, with its upper-left corner at the point with coordinates (x,y). Actually, the PUT command offers five modes of displaying the image on the screen. These five modes are indicated by the words

PSET
PRESET
XOR
OR
AND

The last words should be familiar from our discussion of them earlier in the chapter. Their function in connection with the PUT command is similar to their use in the operations we described.

PUT with the PSET option displays the image in exactly the form in which it was stored. This is done independent of the data that was on the screen. This option is invoked with the command

```
PUT (x,y), <array>, PSET
```

PUT with the PRESET option displays the image in the array, but in inverse color. A pixel that was stored in color 3 will be displayed in color 0 (background color); color 2 will be displayed in color 1; color 1 will be displayed in color 2; and color 0 will be displayed in color 3. On a monochrome display, the PRESET option will simply reverse the roles of background and foreground. The PRESET option is invoked with the command

```
PUT (x,y) <array>, PRESET
```

PUT with the AND option displays the recorded image by ANDing it with the image already at the indicated position on the screen. This ANDing takes place pixel by pixel. A pixel is displayed only if the pixel was previously displayed. The AND option is invoked with the command

```
PUT (x,y), <array>, AND
```

PUT with the OR option displays the recorded image by ORing it with the image already at the indicated position on the screen. This ORing takes place pixel by pixel. A pixel is displayed if either the pixel was previously displayed OR the array has the pixel displayed. The OR option is invoked with the command

```
PUT (x,y), <array>, OR
```

PUT with the XOR option displays the recorded image by XORing it with the image already at the indicated position on the screen. This XORing takes place pixel by pixel. In the XOR option, a pixel is displayed provided that it is displayed in **exactly** one of: the original screen image and the display image. In particular, a pixel currently displayed on the screen and displayed in the current image will not be displayed. If you PUT the same image twice using the XOR option, then you will restore the screen to its original state.

This property of the XOR option is especially useful for animations, since you may move an image across the screen and restore the background to its original state. The XOR option is invoked with either of the commands

```
PUT (x,y), <array>, XOR
PUT (x,y), <array>
```

(The XOR option is the default option. That is, if you use PUT without specifying an option, then the XOR option is assumed.)

The precise color assignments used with the AND, OR, and XOR options are rather complicated and are summarized in the following charts:

AND Color Assignment

Current Color	0	1	2	3
PUT Color				
0	0	0	0	0
1	0	0	0	0
2	0	0	2	2
3	0	1	2	3

OR Color Assignment

Current Color	0	1	2	3
PUT Color				
0	0	1	2	3
1	1	1	3	3
2	2	3	2	3
3	3	3	3	3

XOR Color Assignment

Current Color	0	1	2	3
PUT Color				
0	0	1	2	3
1	1	0	3	2
2	2	3	0	1
3	3	2	1	0

Let's illustrate the action of each of the options PSET, PRESET, AND, OR, and XOR using the following example. Suppose that A% is an 8-pixel by 8-pixel array which contains the letter **A**, obtained from a previous GET operation. (See Figure 6.2) Further, suppose that we use a PUT to place this image on a portion of the screen which currently has the image in Figure 6.3. The results of each of the various options is described in Fig. 6.4.

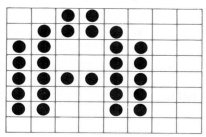

Figure 6.2. The Contents of A%.

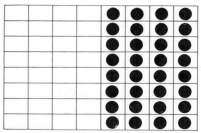

Figure 6.3. The Background.

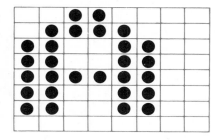

PSET

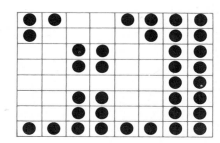

PRESET

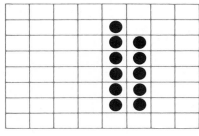

AND

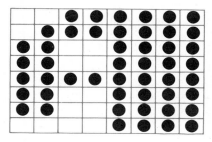

OR

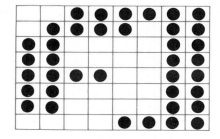

XOR

Figure 6.4. The Results of PUT with Various Options.

Designing Custom Characters

We may combine our recently acquired knowledge of bytes and binary numbers with the PUT command to design custom characters for the screen. Here's how.

A character in graphics mode is displayed in a rectangle 8 pixels wide and 8 pixels high. Note that it does not matter whether the character is displayed in medium-resolution or high-resolution mode. The rectangle is always 8 x 8. For example, Figure 6.5 contains the pixels displayed for the letter A.

Figure 6.5. The letter "A."

Each character may described by a series of bytes, corresponding to the various rows of the rectangle. This description is simplest in high-resolution graphics mode. In this case, each pixel corresponds to a single bit, proceeding from left to right. For example, here are the bits corresponding to the letter A.

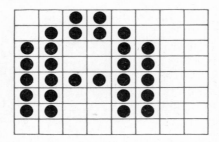

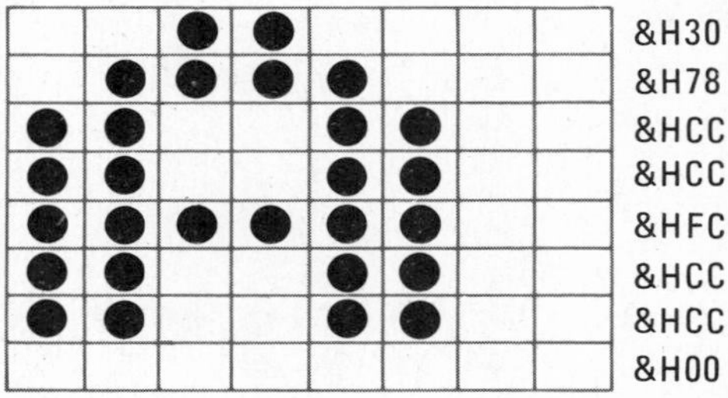

Figure 6.6. The Bits Corresponding to the Letter "A."

Note that each row of the rectangle corresponds to a single byte, or two hexadecimal digits. In hexadecimal, the letter "A" may be represented by the bytes

&H30, &H78, &HCC, &HCC, &HFC, &HCC, &HCC, &H00

When you perform a GET, the bytes are arranged in the array as follows:

A%(0) = the width of the rectangle

A%(1) = the height of the rectangle

A%(2), A%(3), . . . contain the bytes corresponding to the pixels, with two bytes per array element.

For example, the results of GETing the letter "A" to the array A% will yield the following array contents:

A%(0) = 8

A%(1) = 8

A%(2) = &H7803

A%(3) = &HCCCC

A%(4) = &HCCFC

A%(5) = &H00CC

Note the order in which the bytes appear. As usual, the byte to the left (the one containing the higher order bits) is the byte **after** the byte to the right.

The above discussion applies to high-resolution graphics mode, in which each pixel corresponds to one bit. In medium-resolution graphics mode, a pixel may be in any one of four colors, numbered 0, 1, 2, 3. In binary, these choices are coded using two bits:

00 = color 0

01 = color 1

10 = color 2

11 = color 3

Each row of the rectangle now contains two bits per pixel, or 16 bits. That is, each row of the rectangle corresponds to one 16-bit integer. In terms of the array, the first row will now completely fill A%(2), the second A%(3) and so forth.

We have just described how the GET statement fills an array. With this information, we may omit the GET statement entirely. We may fill an array with the data corresponding to a display without first creating the display on the screen. To do this:

1. Use graph paper to draw the pixels of the display.
2. Convert the rows of the display into binary.
3. Convert the binary numbers into hexadecimal.
4. Fill the 0th array element with the display width, the 1st array element with the display height.
5. Fill the array elements beginning with the 2nd with the hexadecimal numbers of step 3. (Be sure to put the later hexadecimal digits on the left of a 16-bit word.)
6. The array is now ready for PUTing.

Let's illustrate this procedure by creating an array that displays the capital Greek letter "phi":

We begin by reducing the letter to pixels, as in Figure 6.7.

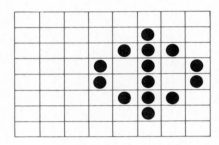

Figure 6.7.

Next, we code the various rows into binary and then hexadecimal form:

row #	binary number	hexadecimal number	array element
1	0000 0000	00	0
2	0010 0000	20	32
3	0111 0000	70	112
4	1010 1000	C8	200
5	1010 1000	C8	200
6	0111 0000	70	112
7	0010 0000	20	32
8	0000 0000	00	0

We may summarize our results in this BASIC program:

```
10 'Create and display the letter "PHI"
20 'at position (100,100).
30 DIM A%(9)
40 A%(0)=8: A%(1)=8: A%(2)=0
50 A%(3)=32: A%(4)=112: A%(5)=200
60 A%(6)=200:A%(7)=112: A%(8)=32: A%(9)=0
70 SCREEN 2:CLS
80 PUT (100,100), A%
```

The ASCII character set (ASCII codes 0-127) is stored in ROM, coded in exactly the fashion we have described above for high-resolution graphics mode. That is, each character is described by a sequence of 8 bytes. This table of bytes begins at memory location F000:FA6E . Here is a program that fills the array A% with the appropriate data from the table for any character you specify.

```
100 'Load character into array
110 DIM A%(10)
120 A%(0)=8
130 A%(1)=8
```

```
140 DEF SEG = &HF000
150 INPUT "CHARACTER TO LOAD";C$
160 OFFSET=8*ASC(C$)+&HFA6E
170 FOR J=0 TO 7
180     B$(J)=HEX$(PEEK(OFFSET+J))
190       IF LEN(B$(J))=1 THEN B$(J)="0"+B$(J)
200 NEXT J
210 FOR J=0 TO 3
220     A%(J+2) = VAL("&H" + B$(2*J+1) + B$(2*J))
230 NEXT J
240 DEF SEG
```

The above program may be used as a subroutine in various character alteration operations. For example, you may create characters that are vertically enlarged by including duplicates of the bytes corresponding to the various display lines. Here is a program that enables you to load an array with a character that is the expansion of a specified character by a given factor.

```
10 'Enlarge a character vertically
100 DIM A%(10),B%(200)
110 INPUT "FACTOR OF ENLARGEMENT";F
120 INPUT "CHARACTER";C$
130 GOSUB 300:
150 B%(0)=8
160 B%(1)=8*F
170 FOR J=0 TO 7
180     FOR K=0 TO F-1
190             B%(F*J+K+2)=A%(J+2)
200     NEXT K
210 NEXT J
220 END
300 'Load character into array
320 A%(0)=8
330 A%(1)=8
340 DEF SEG = &HF000
360 OFFSET=8*ASC(C$)+&HFA6E
370 FOR J=0 TO 7
380     B$(J)=HEX$(PEEK(OFFSET+J))
390       IF LEN(B$(J))=1 THEN B$(J)="0"+B$(J)
400 NEXT J
410 FOR J=0 TO 3
420     A%(J+2) = VAL("&H" + B$(2*J+1) + B$(2*J))
```

```
430 NEXT J
440 DEF SEG
450 RETURN
```

You may print out the character in the array B%() by using a PUT statement.

TEST YOUR UNDERSTANDING 2

Use the above program to display a letter A that is 3 times the usual height.

6.6   Further Graphics Tricks (BASIC 2.0 Only)

In early 1983, IBM introduced its enhanced operating system DOS 2.00. Along with the enhancements to DOS were included various upgrades to BASIC. In particular, the LINE and PAINT statements are enhanced. And since these enhancements use what we have learned about binary and hexadecimal numbers, it seems appropriate to discuss them at this point.

Enhancements to LINE

Recall the format of the LINE statement:

```
LINE (x1,y1)-(x2,y2),color,box
```

Here color is one of the colors 0-3 and box is either the letter B (= open box) or the letter BF (= filled box), and (x1,y1) and (x2,y2) are the coordinates of the endpoints of the line. BASIC 2.00 has added the following enhancement. After the box parameter, you may add the parameter **style**, which determines the line style. Using this option, you may draw an incredible variety of line styles, including dotted and dashed lines. Figure 6.8 shows some of the possibilities.

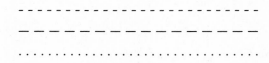

Figure 6.8.

If you make use of the style option, you must code the style as a 16-bit number, input to the program as a hexadecimal number. The LINE command refers to this style designation as it plots the pixels of the line. It starts with the leftmost bit. If it is a one, it plots the pixel. If it is a zero, then it does not plot the pixel. For the next pixel, LINE looks at the second bit of the style designation, and so forth. After 16 pixels, LINE begins over with the leftmost bit. For example, here is a style designator for a dashed line with 8 pixels plotted, followed by 8 pixels not plotted.

11111111 00000000

In hexadecimal, this style designation would be denoted &HFF00. Here is a line that contains a long dash (11 pixels) followed by a one-pixel space, followed by a dot and another space. (See Figure 6.9):

    binary style designation = 11111111 11111010
    hexadecimal style designation = &HFFFA

Figure 6.9. A Line of Style &HFFFA.

To connect the points (50,75) and (100,100) with a line of style &HFFFA, we could use the statement

```
LINE (50,75),,,,&HFFFA
```

Note that you must use the correct number of commas as placeholders for the color and box parameters.

TEST YOUR UNDERSTANDING 1 (answer on page 183)

Describe the line with style designation &HAAAA.

You may use the style designation with the B parameter, in which case, the required rectangle will be drawn with its sides in the requested style. However, you may not use the style designation with the BF parameter. If you do, you will generate a syntax error.

Enhancements to PAINT

As you will recall, the PAINT statement allows you to paint a region of the screen with a particular color. In many graphics applications, you may wish to "crosshatch" the region with a particular pattern rather than a solid color. For example, you may wish to shade a region with horizontal lines, with vertical lines, or with a rectangualr mesh. BASIC 2.00 allows you to accomplish such shading with ease.

Recall that the format for PAINT is

PAINT (x,y), paint, boundary

Here **(x,y)** is a point in the region to be painted, **paint** is the color the region is to be painted, and **boundary** is the color of the boundary of the region.

The BASIC 2.00 enhancement allows the paint parameter to be a string expression describing the figures to be used in shading the region. The string expression may contain as many as 64 bytes. The entire string describes one shading figure. To determine the shading figure, we convert the bytes of the string into binary to obtain an array of the form

```
1 0 0 1 0 1 1 0   byte 1
0 0 1 1 0 0 0 1   byte 2
1 0 0 1 0 1 1 0   byte 3
```

These bytes are translated into pixels in the usual way: In high resolution, the bits are translated into pixels on a one-to-one basis. A one means that the pixel is displayed and a zero means that the pixel is not displayed. In medium resolution, two bits represent one pixel, with the two-bit combination representing one of the four possible colors for the pixel. For example, in high resolution, the above array stands for the shading character

```
■   ■   ■ ■
    ■ ■     ■
■   ■   ■ ■
```

If this shading character is used, then the region to be painted will be filled with shapes of this sort, starting at the point (x,y) and working out to the boundaries.

The above three bytes are specified in hexadecimal as

&H96

&H31

&H96

To construct the corresponding PAINT string, we must convert these bytes into string form using the CHR$ function. That is, the desired PAINT string is

CHR$(&H96) + CHR$(&H31) + CHR$(&H96)

The PAINT string option is extremely powerful. For example, we may shade a region using horizontal lines two pixels apart as follows:

```
1111 1111   byte 1 = &HFF
0000 0000   byte 2 = &H00
0000 0000   byte 3 = &H00
```

paint string = CHR$(&HFF) + CHR$(0) + CHR$(0)

Here is a short program that draws a circle and paints the interior using the last paint string.

```
10 SCREEN 2,0
20 CIRCLE (100,100),75
30 PAINT (100,100),CHR$(&HFF) + CHR$(0) + CHR$(0)
40 GOTO 40
```

TEST YOUR UNDERSTANDING 2 (answer on page 183)

Write a paint string that will allow shading with vertical lines spaced one pixel apart.

ANSWERS TO TEST YOUR UNDERSTANDING

1:    The hexadecimal digit A equals 10, which in binary is 1010. So the given line style consists of dot-space-dot-space-dot-space-dot-space.

2:    CHR$(&HAA)

6.7   Plotting Characters in Graphics Mode

My first business graphics program required me to draw a coordinate system. That was a simple enough task using the LINE statement. I calibrated the axes using tick marks, just as I was accustomed to do in lecturing my calculus students. Still no problem. However, next came the job of labeling the various tick marks. The results were very unsatisfying because I couldn't center the labels on the tick marks. For example, if I wished to label a vertical tick mark as "4.00", I could rarely get the label exactly centered on the tick mark! The reason was that the tick mark was drawn using graphics coordinates and the labels were being plotted with text coordinates. Each character is 8 pixels wide. And BASIC automatically starts characters at positions whose x-coordinate (graphics coordinate) is divisible by 8. If that placement happens to result in a chart that looks good, fine. If not, too bad!

In response to my frustration, I developed the routine PLOTSTRING, which places a string at a particular graphics coordinate. In the following routine, the string is s$. I allow for two types of placement: point and center. In the first type, you specify a set of graphics coordinates (x1,y1). The routine will plot s$, with the upper left corner of the first character of s$ at the point (x1,y1). For center placement, you specify two points, (x1,y1) and (x2,y2). The routine then centers s$ within the rectangle (x1,y1)-(x2,y2).

I had so much fun with this routine that I decided to allow for vertical display of strings. So there are four possible options, specified by the parameter c%:

c% = 1: place at point, horizontal

c% = 2: place at point, vertical

c% = 3: center, horizontal

c% = 4: center, vertical

   PLOTSTRING uses the subroutine of the preceding section to read the
pixels of a character into an array A%, using the table in ROM.
   Here is a listing of the routine PLOTSTRING.

```
1 DIM A%(10),B$(10)
2 MAXWIDTH=639:MAXHEIGHT=199
28000 '**************PLOTSTRING*******************
28005 'This routine allows precise placement of a string
28010 ' in graphics mode.
28015 ' (x1,y1),(x1,y2) are graphics coordinates
28020 ' s$=string to be placed
28025 ' c%=1:place string horizontally, with left corner
28030 '        of 1st character at (x1,y1)
28035 ' c%=2:place string vertically, with left corner
28040 '        of 1st character at (x1,y1)
28045 ' c%=3:center string horizontally in the
28050 '        field (x1,y1)-(x2,y2)
28055 ' c%=4:center string vertically in the
28060 '        field (x1,y1)-(x2,y2)
28065 'Maxwidth=largest allowable x-coordinate
28070 'Maxheight=largest allowable y-coordinate
28075 '******************MAIN ROUTINE*****************
28080    IF C%=1 OR C%=2 THEN X=X1:Y=Y1
28085    ON C% GOSUB 28195,28275,28245,28320
28090    RETURN
28095 ****************SUBROUTINES***************
28100 'Load character into array
28105    A%(0)=8
28110    A%(1)=8
28115    DEF SEG = &HF000
28120    OFFSET=8*ASC(C$)+&HFA6E
28125    FOR J=0 TO 7
28130      B$(J)=HEX$(PEEK(OFFSET+J))
28135      IF LEN(B$(J))=1 THEN B$(J)="0"+B$(J)
28140    NEXT J
28145    FOR J=0 TO 3
28150      A%(J+2) = VAL("&H" + B$(2*J+1) + B$(2*J))
28155    NEXT J
```

```
28160     DEF SEG
28165     RETURN
28170  'Place character at particular coordinates
28175  'Character =c$, coordinates (x,y)
28180     GOSUB 28100
28185     PUT (X,Y), A%
28190     RETURN
28195  'Place string in field beginning at particular
          coordinates.
28200  'Field begins at (x,y), string in S$
28205     WHILE S$ <> ""
28210             IF X>MAXWIDTH THEN 28235
28215             C$=LEFT$(S$,1):S$=MID$(S$,2)
28220             GOSUB 28170: 'place character
28225             IF X<0 THEN 28235
28230             X=X+8
28235     WEND
28240     RETURN
28245  'Center string s$ in field defined by coordinates
          (x1,y1)-(x2,y2)
28250     IF X1>X2 THEN SWAP X1,X2: IF Y1>Y2
          THEN SWAP Y1,Y2
28255     L=LEN(S$): C=INT((X2-X1)/8):
          IF L>C THEN S$=LEFT$(S$,C)
28260     X=X1+(X2-X1+1)/2-8*LEN(S$)/2+4:
          Y=Y1+(Y2-Y1+1)/2-4
28265     GOSUB 28195
28270     RETURN
28275  'Display string s$ vertically beginning at
          coordinate (x,y)
28280     WHILE S$ <> ""
28285             IF Y+7>MAXHEIGHT THEN 28315
28290             C$=LEFT$(S$,1):S$=MID$(S$,2)
28295             IF Y<0 THEN 28305
28300             GOSUB 28170: 'place character
28305             Y=Y+8
28310     WEND
```

```
28315      RETURN
28320    'Center string s$ vertically in field
         (x1,y1)-(x2,y2)
28325      IF X1>X2 THEN SWAP X1,X2:
           IF Y1>Y2 THEN SWAP Y1,Y2
28330      L=LEN(S$): C=INT((Y2-Y1)/8):
           IF L>C THEN S$=LEFT$(S$,C)
28335      Y=Y1+(Y2-Y1+1)/2-8*LEN(S$)/2:
           X=X1+(X2-X1+1)/2-4
28340      IF X<0 THEN X=0 : IF Y<0 THEN Y=0
28345      GOSUB 28275
28350      RETURN
```

PLOTSTRING gives you very precise control of text display in graphics mode. However, you will notice that characters are displayed somewhat more slowly that if you use the PRINT statement. This perceptible difference in speed disappears if PLOTSTRING is used in a compiled program. However, even using the BASIC interpreter, the difference in the appearance of your graphics is worth the slight delay.

You may test PLOTSTRING with a program of the form:

```
100 INPUT "S$";S$
110 INPUT "C%";C%
130 INPUT "x1,y1";x1,y1
140 IF C%=3 OR C%=4 THEN INPUT "x2,y2";x2,y2
150 CLS
160 GOSUB 28000
170 END
```

6.8 Bar Charts—A Case Study, III

When we last left our case study, in Chapter 2, we had constructed a part of the routine that draws bar charts from data collected in other routines. Recall that we used the VIEW and WINDOW statements to set up a coordinate system suitable for drawing the graphs without having to do conversion to the usual screen coordinates. However, recall that we did not display any titles or labels, since the usual text placement in BASIC leads to poor-looking graphics. Now that we have the routine PLOTSTRING, we can finish construction of our bar chart drawing routine.

Before we proceed to labels and titles, however, let's explain a point that we left unexplained earlier. Remember that we PAINTed our bars using a parameter STYLE$(). This is just the stylized painting available in DOS 2.00, which we explained earlier in this chapter. We have selected three bar styles, corresponding to the parameter values:

STYLE$(1) = CHR$(&HFF), STYLE$(2) = CHR$(&HAA),

STYLE$(3) = CHR$(&H99) + CHR$(&H55)

A good bar chart has many titles and labels. In our bar chart definition module, we allowed for the following titles:

CHART TITLE

X AXIS TITLE

Y AXIS TITLE

DATA SERIES 1 TITLE

DATA SERIES 2 TITLE

DATA SERIES 3 TITLE

In addition, we allow each set of bars to have a label, as defined in the data matrix of the data input module.

Figure 6.10 shows a completed bar chart generated by our routine.

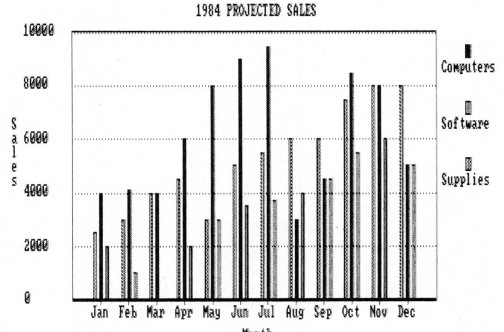

Figure 6.10. A Completed Bar Chart.

Let's place the chart title in text row 1, centered over the graph. The X-axis title will be in text line 24, centered under the graph. The Y-axis title will be arranged vertically, centered on the graph. (A little show-boating there!) The data series titles will be displayed on the right side of the graph, beginning in text column 72, and beginning in text rows 5, 9, and 13. Above each of these titles we include a small square icon, shaded with the same shading as the associated graph.

Finally, we get to the labels along the axis. The X-axis has tick marks at each bar position. Any label specified for the bar position is centered on the tick mark, in text line 23. The Y-axis labels are numerical, beginning with YMIN and proceeding in steps of YSTEP up to YMAX. The Y-axis labels are centered on the horizontal grid lines.

All centering is done using PLOTSTRING.

Here is the code for the routine DRAWBAR, which draws the bar charts from the data supplied. You will note that some of the routine was given previously. The portion of the routine that plots the titles and labels begins in line 3195. Note also, the subroutine that begins in line 3105. This subroutine calculates SER%, the number of data series by looking at the data matrix and determining the number of the last data series that has non-empty data entries. (If data series 3 has data, then it is assumed that there are three valid data series.) Moreover, this routine also determines, for data series N%, the number of the last non-zero numerical data item XMAX(N%). The largest of XMAX(1), XMAX(2), XMAX(3) is taken to be XMAX. (Recall that the number of tick marks is XMAX + 1.)

The subroutine beginning in 3105 saves the user the trouble of inputting a number of parameters that the computer can determine from inspecting the data. And there's no point in making the user do anything that the computer can do, is there?

```
3000  '**************DRAWBAR ROUTINE***************
3005     CLS
3010     KEY OFF
3015     SCREEN 2:SER%=3
3020     YMIN=VAL(YMIN$)
3025     YMAX=VAL(YMAX$)
3030     YSTEP=VAL(YSTEP$)
3035     IF YMIN>YMAX THEN SWAP YMIN,YMAX
3040     IF YMIN=YMAX THEN 3095
3045     IF YSTEP=0 THEN 3095
3050     GOSUB 3105:'Computer SER%
3055     STYLE$(1)=CHR$(&HFF):STYLE$(2)=CHR$(&HAA):
         STYLE$(3)=CHR$(&H99)+CHR$(&H55)
3060     BW=(XMAX+1)/240
```

```
3065    ADJ(1)=0:ADJ(2)=(XMAX+1)/60:ADJ(3)=-(XMAX+1)/60
3070    GOSUB 3195:'Write Titles
3075    GOSUB 3305:'Write x-axis labels
3080    GOSUB 3360:'Write y-axis labels
3085    GOSUB 3415:'Draw coordinate system
3090    GOSUB 3435:'Draw bars
3095    E$="":GOTO 920:'Return to control routine
3100 *************SUBROUTINES****************
3105 'Compute SER%
3110    FOR N%=3 TO 1 STEP -1
3115            XMAX(N%)=20:J%=0
3120            DATAEND=FALSE
3125            WHILE DATAEND=FALSE
3130                    IF DTA$(N%,20-J%)<>"" THEN
                        DATAEND=TRUE:XMAX(N%)=XMAX(N%)+1
3135                    XMAX(N%)=XMAX(N%)-1:J%=J%+1
3140                    IF J%=21 THEN DATAEND=TRUE
3145            WEND
3150    NEXT N%
3155    IF XMAX(3)<=0 THEN SER%=2
3160    IF SER%=2 AND XMAX(2)<=0 THEN SER%=1
3165    IF SER%=1 AND XMAX(1)<=0 THEN SER%=0
3170    XMAX=XMAX(1)
3175    FOR J%=1 TO 3
3180            IF XMAX< XMAX(J%) THEN XMAX=XMAX(J%)
3185    NEXT J%
3190    RETURN
3195 'Write titles
3200    LOCATE 5,72:PRINT SER1TITLE$;
3205 IF SER%=1 THEN 3225
3210    LOCATE 9,72:PRINT SER2TITLE$;
3215 IF SER%=2 THEN 3225
3220    LOCATE 13,72:PRINT SER3TITLE$;
3225    LINE (599,23)-(606,30),,B
3230    PAINT (603,27),STYLE$(1)
3235    IF SER%=1 THEN 3265
3240    LINE (599,55)-(606,62),,B
```

```
3245      PAINT (603,60),STYLE$(2)
3250      IF SER%=2 THEN 3265
3255      LINE (599,87)-(606,94),,B
3260      PAINT (603,93),STYLE$(3)
3265      X1=80:X2=559:Y1=0:Y2=7:C%=3:S$=TITLE$
3270      GOSUB 28000
3275      Y1=191:Y2=184:S$=XTITLE$
3280      GOSUB 28000
3285      X1=0:X2=7:Y1=16:Y2=167:C%=4
3290      S$=YTITLE$
3295      GOSUB 28000
3300      RETURN
3305 'Write x-axis labels
3310      K=480/(XMAX+1)
3315      FOR J%=1 TO XMAX
3320         L=79+K*J%
3325         M%=4*LEN(DTA$(0,J%))
3330         LINE (L,167)-(L,170):'Tick marks
3335         X1=L-M%:X2=L+M%-1:Y1=171:Y2=178:C%=1
3340         S$=DTA$(0,J%)
3345         GOSUB 28000
3350      NEXT J%
3355      RETURN
3360 'Write y-axis labels
3365      IF YSTEP=0 THEN 3410
3370      M=(YMAX-YMIN)/YSTEP
3375      FOR J%=0 TO M
3380         S$=STR$(YMIN+J%*YSTEP)
3385         X1=8:X2=79
3390         Y1=167-J%*152/M-4
3395         Y2=Y1-7:C%=1
3400         GOSUB 28000
3405      NEXT J%
3410      RETURN
3415 'Draw coordinate system
3420      VIEW (80,16)-(559,167),,3
3425      WINDOW (0,YMIN)-(XMAX+1,YMAX)
```

```
3430     LINE (0,0)-(XMAX+1,0):'Draw x-axis
3435 'Draw bars
3440     FOR N%=1 TO SER%
3445         FOR J%=1 TO XMAX(N%)
3450             IF DTA$(N%,J%)="" THEN 3470
3455             HT=VAL (DTA$(N%,J%))
3460             LINE (J%+ADJ(N%)-BW,0)-
                                (J%+ADJ(N%)+BW,HT),,B
3465             PAINT (J%+ADJ(N%),HT/2),STYLE$(N%)
3470         NEXT J%
3475     NEXT N%
3480 'Draw grid lines
3485     FOR J%=0 TO (YMAX-YMIN)/YSTEP
3490         H=YMIN+J%*YSTEP
3495         LINE (0,H)-(XMAX+1,H),,,&H8888
3500     NEXT J%
3505     RETURN
```

We'll return to our case study in the next chapter, when we'll (finally) assemble the pieces into a program.

6.9   Extending the PC's Character Set

In text mode, the PC has 255 characters available. The first 128 ASCII codes 0-127 correspond to the usual displayable characters and control codes. ASCII codes 128 through 255 correspond to the graphics characters. The graphics characters are available only in text mode, however. If you try to print CHR$(175), say, when in SCREEN 1 or SCREEN 2, you will get garbage. However, IBM allows you to define you own character set corresponding to the unused ASCII codes. Here's how.

1. Define the characters in terms of bytes as we have already described. Write them in a list, with eight bytes to a character.

2. Find a section of memory that is unused. (See below for a way to do this.)

3. Use POKE to store the list of bytes in consecutive memory locations.

4. POKE into memory locations 0000:7C through 0000:7F the offset and segment address of the first location you used.

5. The first character in your list now corresponds to ASCII $32 + 128 = 161$, the second to ASCII $33 + 128 = 162$, and so forth.

For example, let's duplicate the ordinary displayable characters in ASCII codes 161-255. The ROM character table begins at F000:FA6E. So we poke 6E into 0000:007C, FA into 0000:007D, 00 into 0000:007E and F0 into 0000:007F. Now ASCII code 161 is a space (= the same as ASCII code 32), ASCII code 193 is an "A", and so forth.

Of course, the real power of the above procedure is that you may design your own character sets. So it doesn't matter whether you wish to display Russian, Hebrew, or a set of scientific symbols. Your IBM allows you to customize your character set to your needs.

APPENDIX A: Some Useful Memory Locations

In a preceding discussion of this chapter, we outlined the layout of memory when BASIC is running. Here are several memory locations useful in working with BASIC.

Location	Contents
0000:007C-000:007F	Address of beginning of graphics character generator
0000:0500-0000:511	Segment address of beginning of BASIC interpreter

In the following addresses, the segment portion is the start of the BASIC interpreter, contained in the addresses given above.

:002E-:002F	Number of line currently being executed
:0347-:0348	Number of line generating last error
:0030-:0031	Offset into current segment of start of program
:0358-:0359	Offset into current segment of start of variables
:006A	Keyboard buffer indicator (non-zero contents means that there are characters waiting to be read).

APPENDIX B: How BASIC Stores Single- and Double-Precision Numbers

We have mentioned that BASIC uses 4 bytes to store a single-precision number and 8 bytes to store a double-precision number. In this section, we will describe the exact method used to code each of these sorts of numbers.

Some Mathematical Preliminaries

We have already learned to convert decimal numbers to binary and binary numbers to decimal, but we discussed this process only in the case of integers. However, it is necessary to deal with numbers with non-zero decimal parts, such as .5, .125, and so forth. Each of these numbers has a representation as a **binary decimal.**

In order to discuss binary decimals, it is necessary to use powers of 2 that are negative as well as positive. So let's review this notion. Recall that

$$2^{\wedge}(-1) = 1/2, 2^{\wedge}(-2) = 1/2^{\wedge}2 = 1/4, 2^{\wedge}(-3) = 1/2^{\wedge}3 = 1/8, \ldots$$

We used the powers $2^{\wedge}0, 2^{\wedge}1, 2^{\wedge}2, \ldots$ to represent the various places in a binary decimal. In a similar fashion, we use the negative powers of 2 to respresent the places to the right of the decimal point in a binary decimal. For example,

$$.5 = 2^{\wedge}(-1) = .1 \text{ binary}$$

$$.125 = 2^{\wedge}(-3) = .001 \text{ binary}$$

TEST YOUR UNDERSTANDING 1 (answer on page 197)

What is the decimal number corresponding to the binary decimal 1.101?

To convert a decimal to a binary decimal, we proceed as follows:

1. Convert the integer portion just as described previously.

2. Subtract the integer portion, so that you are left only with the decimal part of the number.

3. Subtract the negative power of 2, which leaves a positive remainder that is as small as possible. Put a 1 in the corresponding position of the binary decimal.

4. Repeat step 3 as long as there is a non-zero remainder.

For example, consider the decimal 5.23. The integer portion is 5, corresponding to binary 101. So the integer part of the binary decimal is 101. We subtract off the 5 and are left with .23. We try to subtract off negative powers of 2. Clearly $2^{\wedge}-1 = .5$ is too big. So we put a 0 in the first binary decimal place. Now we try $2^{\wedge}(-2) = .25$. Again too big, so we put another 0. Next we try .125. This leaves a positive remainder of .105. So we place a 1 in the binary decimal and repeat the procedure. Our binary decimal so far is

$$5.23 \text{ decimal} = 101.001 \ldots$$

The next negative power of 2 is $2^{\wedge}(-4) = .0625$. This leaves a positive remainder of .0425. So we include another 1 in the binary decimal expansion.

$$5.23 \text{ decimal} = 101.0011 \ldots$$

We continue in this fashion. The binary decimal expansion of 5.23 never terminates. (It's like the decimal expansion of $1/3 = .33333\ldots$). But we may obtain as many binary places in the expansion as we like.

TEST YOUR UNDERSTANDING 2 (answer on page 197)

Convert the decimal number .875 to a binary decimal.

Single Precision Numbers

A single-precision number occupies 32 bits, divided into three parts: exponent, sign, and mantissa (see Figure 6.11). The exponent occupies 8 bits, the sign 1, and the mantissa 23.

Byte 4	Byte 3		Byte 2	Byte 1
31 . . . 24	23	22 . . . 17	16 . . . 9	8 . . . 0
Exponent	Sign	Mantissa	Mantissa	Mantissa

Figure 6.11.

The exponent refers to a power of 2 by which the mantissa is multiplied. To obtain the exponent byte, take the actual exponent and add 128. Thus, for example, if the mantissa is to be multiplied by 2^3, then the exponent byte is $128 + 3 = 131$. This method of coding exponents allows for representation of negative exponents as positive exponent bytes. For example, to multiply the mantissa by $2^{(-8)}$, the exponent byte is $128 + (-8) = 120$. Actual exponents from -128 to +127 (corresponding to exponent bytes of 0 through 255) are allowed.

The sign bit is 0 in case of a positive number and 1 in case of a negative number.

The mantissa portion of a number needs some explaining. Let's take an example. Consider the decimal number 458. In binary, this number equals

1 1100 1010

($458 = 256 + 128 + 64 + 8 + 2 = 2^8 + 2^7 + 2^6 + 2^3 + 2^1$). Note that if we suppress leading zeros, all binary numbers except 0 start out with a 1. So it's not really necessary to include the leading 1. It may be implied. And to make the number 23 bits long, we add the appropriate number of zeros on the right. So we represent the number by the 23-bit mantissa:

110 0101 0000 0000 0000 0000

To determine the exponent, represent the number in the form of a binary decimal:

.111001010

To obtain this form, it was necessary to move the decimal point to the left by 9 places. That is,

458 decimal = .111001010 x 2^9

So the exponent in this case is 9, and the exponent byte is 137 decimal, or 1000 1001 binary. In our example, the sign bit is 0 since 458 is positive. So, finally, we have the result that 458 is represented in memory in the form

1000 1001 0110 0101 0000 0000 0000 0000

TEST YOUR UNDERSTANDING 3 (answer on page 197)

Determine the exponent corresponding to the number 256.

TEST YOUR UNDERSTANDING 4 (answer on page 197)

Determine the representation of the number -832.

Non-integer numbers are handled in a similar fashion. Just make sure to use the binary decimal expansion of the number. For example, the binary decimal

101.1011 0010 0000 1111

would correspond to mantissa

011 0110 0100 0001 1110 0000

and exponent

128 + 3 = 131 = 1000 0011 binary

So the given binary decimal is represented in the form

100 0011 0011 0110 0100 0001 1110 0000

TEST YOUR UNDERSTANDING 5 (answer on page 197)

Determine the way in which the number 5840.75 is stored in memory.

If the binary decimal equivalent of a number goes on for more than 24 bits (including the leading 1, which is assumed), then only the leading 24 bits are used. The remaining bits are just thrown away. This is what is responsible for some of the arithmetic anomalies you may observe in the arithmetic of the PC. Certain fractions that are perfectly natural to use happen to have binary decimal expansions that have bits thrown away. When these numbers are then used in arithmetic, the answers may not be exactly what you expect!

Here is an interesting experiment. Place your PC in BASIC and obtain the BASIC prompt Ok. In immediate mode, type

```
X=5          <ENTER>
```

This action creates a single-precision variable X and sets it equal to the number 5. Let's test what we have just learned by examining what's stored in memory under the variable X. To determine the location of the beginning of the storage area containing X, type

```
PRINT VARPTR(X)        <ENTER>
```

BASIC will respond with a memory location, such as 4161. (Your location may be different, depending on the particular release you are using.) This means that the four bytes corresponding to X are at locations 4161, 4162, 4163, and 4164. Let's retrieve the contents of these memory locations using the PEEK instruction: Here are the results

```
PRINT PEEK(4161)
0
Ok
PRINT PEEK(4162)
0
Ok
PRINT PEEK(4163)
32
Ok
PRINT PEEK(4164)
131
Ok
```

We can see the exponent byte appearing in location 4164. It's 131 corresponding to an exponent of 3. How about the other bytes? In binary, they correspond to

0 010 0000 0000 0000 0000 0000

So the sign bit is zero and the binary decimal corresponding to the mantissa is

.[1]010 0000 0000 0000 0000 0000

To obtain the actual number, we move the decimal point 3 places to the right (recall that 3 is the exponent), to obtain

101.0 0000 0000 0000 0000 0000

That is the number 5. Our description of the internal storage procedure really works.

Double-Precision Numbers

Double-precision numbers work much in the same fashion as single-precision numbers, except that the mantissa is longer, namely 55 bits. The exponent is now in byte 8 and the sign bit is in bit 7 of byte 7.

ANSWERS TO TEST YOUR UNDERSTANDING

1:   1 5/8
2:   .111
3:   136
4:   1000 1010 1101 0000 0000 0000 0000 0000
5:   1000 1100 0011 0110 1000 0111 1000 0000

7

The BAR CHART GENERATOR—A Case Study

We have developed a number of pieces of our BAR CHART GENERATOR. In this chapter, we'll assemble all the pieces into a final program.

7.1 The Initialization and Control Routines

In various sections, we have developed a number of routines that perform particular tasks for the BAR CHART GENERATOR. In order for these routines to work together, we need a control routine that allows us to select among them. When we planned the program, we designated seven main functions for the BAR CHART GENERATOR:

DEFINE BAR CHART PARAMETERS—specify the coordinate system and its various labels and the number of series of data.

DATA INPUT—Input the numerical data corresponding to the various bar heights, and string data naming the various bars.

DRAW BAR CHART—Use the graphics capabilities of the PC to draw the bar chart.

SAVE BAR CHART—Save in a diskette data file the parameters and data corresponding to a particular bar chart.

RECALL BAR CHART—Recall a bar chart that has been saved on diskette.

READ DATA FILE—Read numerical bar chart data that has been saved in a diskette data file produced by another program.

EXIT—Stop executing the program and return to BASIC.

Each of these seven functions corresponds to a routine. The code for the first routine begins in line 1000, for the second in line 2000, and so forth. We call a particular function by pressing a function key: The nth function is called by pressing function key n. So our control routine calls KEYIN, the character input routine, and allows only function keys F1-F7 as input. The control routine responds to an allowable function key by performing the requested function. Note that each of the function routines ends by sending control back to the control routine.

Here is the code for the control routine.

```
900 '**************CONTROL ROUTINE*******************
905 'E$ is returned by the input routine, = the second
910 'character of extended ASCII code
915 KEY OFF:CLS
920 IF E$<>"" THEN 945
925 LOCATE 25,1
930 PRINT FKEY$;
935 CALLER=5:GOSUB 25000
940 GOTO 920
945 C=ASC(E$):EXTENDED=FALSE
950 IF C=59 THEN 1000 :'Bar Chart Definition
955 IF C=60 THEN 2000 :'Data Input
960 IF C=61 THEN 3000 :'Draw Bar Chart
965 IF C=62 THEN 4000 :'Save Bar Chart
970 IF C=63 THEN 5000 :'Recall Bar Chart
975 IF C=64 THEN 6000 :'Read Data File
980 IF C=65 THEN 7000 :'Exit
985 CALLER=5:GOSUB 25000:'Await instructions
```

This routine presupposes that the function keys are disabled as soft keys and that the function key line fkey$ has been specified somewhere. And this brings me to the subject of program organization.

I like to organize my programs (especially the large ones) in a particular order. You may have noticed that the program fragments often had what seemed like "dangling lines" at the beginning, before the documentation. This is because those lines, while necessary to run the particular fragment, really belong in another section of the program, the INITIALIZATION. Here is my INITIALIZATION for the BAR CHART GENERATOR.

```
10 '**********INITIALIZATION ROUTINE**********
100 'Dimension Statements
105     DIM MINKEY(5),MAXKEY(5),EXTMINKEY(5),
        EXTMAXKEY(5)
110     DIM CAPSON(5),SPECIALKEY$(5),EXTSPECIALKEY$(5),
        DTA$(3,20)
115     DIM MENU$(11),A%(10),B$(10),XMAX(3)
```

```
200 'Data Statements
300 'Common Statements
400 'Error Trapping Line
500 'DEF statements
600 'Define parameters for input routine
602      MOTION$=CHR$(71)+CHR$(72)+CHR$(75)+CHR$(77)
                  +CHR$(79)+CHR$(80)
604      MOTION1$=CHR$(72)+CHR$(80)
606      FUNCTION$=CHR$(59)+CHR$(60)+CHR$(61)
                  +CHR$(62)+CHR$(63)+CHR$(64)+CHR$(65)
608 '    **Text input(CALLER=1)**
610      MINKEY(1)=32:MAXKEY(1)=127:
         SPECIALKEY$(1)=CHR$(8)+CHR$(27)
612      CAPSON(1)=0
614      EXTMINKEY(1)=0:EXTMINKEY(1)=0
616      EXTSPECIALKEY$(1)=MOTION1$+FUNCTION$
618 '    **Numerical input (CALLER=2)**
620      MINKEY(2)=0:MAXKEY(2)=0:SPECIALKEY$(2)
         ="1234567890-+ E."+CHR$(8)+CHR$(27)
622      CAPSON(2)=-1
624      EXTMINKEY(2)=0:EXTMAXKEY(2)=0
626      EXTSPECIALKEY$(2)=MOTION1$+FUNCTION$
628 '    **Text input(CALLER=1)**
630      MINKEY(3)=0:MAXKEY(3)=127:SPECIALKEY$(3)=""
632      CAPSON(3)=0
634      EXTMINKEY(3)=0:EXTMINKEY(3)=0
636      EXTSPECIALKEY$(3)=MOTION$+FUNCTION$
638 '    **Numerical input (CALLER=4)**
640      MINKEY(4)=0:MAXKEY(4)=31:
         SPECIALKEY$(4)="1234567890-+ E."
642      CAPSON(4)=-1
644      EXTMINKEY(4)=0:EXTMAXKEY(4)=0
646      EXTSPECIALKEY$(4)=MOTION$+FUNCTION$
648 '    **Control Routine(CALLER=5)**
650      MINKEY(5)=0:MAXKEY(5)=0
652      CAPSON(5)=0
654      EXTMINKEY(5)=0:EXTMAXKEY(5)=0
```

```
656        EXTSPECIALKEY$(5)=FUNCTION$
700   'Initialization of variables
702        TRUE=-1:FALSE=0
704        FOR J%=1 TO 10
706              KEY J%,""
708        NEXT J%
710        FKEY$="1 DEFN  2 DATA  3 DRAW  4 SAVE   5 RCLL
                 6 FILE  7 EXIT"
712        XFLD=1:YFLD=1:LNGTH=0
714        MENU$(1)="BAR CHART DEFINITION"
716        MENU$(2)="TITLE? "
718        MENU$(3)="DATA SERIES 1 TITLE? "
720        MENU$(4)="DATA SERIES 2 TITLE? "
722        MENU$(5)="DATA SERIES 3 TITLE? "
724        MENU$(6)="Y AXIS RANGE:MINIMUM? "
726        MENU$(7)="Y AXIS RANGE:MAXIMUM? "
728        MENU$(8)="Y AXIS STEP? "
730        MENU$(9)="X AXIS TITLE? "
732        MENU$(10)="Y AXIS TITLE? "
734        MAXHEIGHT=199
736        MAXWIDTH=639
```

Note that INITIALIZATION begins with five categories of statements (not all used): DIM, DATA, COMMON, ON ERROR, DEF. These are the "non-executable" statements of the program. When the program encounters these statements, it merely makes a definition or sets aside space or makes a note of a fact to be used later. It is a good idea to put all these statements in one part of the program. For one thing, they are easy to find if, say, you want to increase the size of an array or to insert a new function definition. A second, more compelling reason for grouping these statements together is that the BASIC Compiler requires that all non-executable statements precede all executable statements. So rather than try to rearrange the statements after the program is written, you should develop the discipline to create the INITIAL-IZATION portion of the program as you go along by placing any statements that belong to the INITIALIZATION at the start of a module. After all the modules are constructed, you may assemble the initial statments into the INITIALIZATION.

Note that, in addition to non-executable statements, INITIALIZATION contains variable initializations. You should get in the habit of initializing all variables. I know it's easy to get lazy, especially when dimensioning small arrays. However, if you only need an array with 3 elements, why use 10? Memory is precious. Conserve it. Also, give your variables descriptive names. It is true that they will take up more space in the BASIC interpreter. However, if you plan to compile your program, a descriptive name will lead to no longer a program than a single letter name. (I assume that most large programs will ultimately be compiled.)

We have described the construction of the routines for function keys F1, F2 and F3. Each of the routines was constructed pretty much like the main program. I started with lists of requirements (outputs) and inputs. From these I described the routine in a series of steps. Each step became a subroutine. In each routine, you will note a "main routine," which is really like an outline of the routine.

I construct each subroutine separately and test it with sample data. It's a good idea to debug the small routines first. That way, when a bug arises at the next level, you may usually assume that the trouble is that the output from one subroutine isn't the proper input to another. (That's not always the problem, but in a surprising number of instances, it is!)

After you are sure that the subroutines are working properly, assemble them into a routine and follow the same test procedure again.

When you develop subroutines, don't worry about line numbers. Start all subroutines with line 10 (or 100 or 1000). Add and delete lines at will. After the subroutine is debugged, use the RENUM command to adjust the line numbers so that the subroutine will fit into its intended routine.

When all the main routines are debugged, assemble them into the main program and combine miscellaneous lines to form the INITIALIZATION section. That's all there is to it!

I don't mean to say that the above approach is the only one that can be used to successfully develop large programs. But it's one that works for me. Why not try it? I'm sure that you'll discover convenient variations and improvements. Programming is as much an art as a science. And there is room for artists of all schools.

7.2   Error Trapping

At the moment, our programs have only a single way to respond to an error: The program stops and an error message is displayed. Sometimes the program is stopped with good cause, since a logical error prevents BASIC from making any sense of the program. However, there are other instances in which the error is rather innocent: the printer is not turned on, the wrong data diskette is in the drive, the user provides an incorrect response to a prompt. In each of these situations, it is desirable for the program to report the error to the user and wait for further instructions. Let's learn how to instruct the program to take such action.

Ordinarily, the response to an error is to halt the program. However, an alternative is provided by the

```
ON ERROR GOTO <line number>
```

statement. If your program contains such a statement, BASIC will go to the indicated line number as soon as an error occurs. For example, suppose your program contains the statement

```
ON ERROR GOTO 5000
```

Whenever an error occurs, the program will go to line 5000. Beginning in line 5000, you would program an **error trapping routine**, which would:

1. Analyze the error.
2. Notify the user of the error.
3. Resume the program or wait for further instructions from the user.

The ON ERROR GOTO is called an **error trapping statement** and may occur anywhere in the program. Before a program is run, BASIC scans it for the presence of this line. However, your program will run quicker if you place any error trapping statement at the beginning of the program.

To see how an error trapping routine is constructed, let's consider a particular example. Suppose that your program involves reading a data file, which must be on the diskette in the current drive. The program user may place the wrong diskette in the drive or may not insert any diskette at all. Let's write an error trapping routine to respond to these two types of errors.

Let's place our error trapping routine beginning in line 5000. We begin our program with the error trapping line

```
10 ON ERROR GOTO 5000
```

When an error occurs, BASIC makes a note of the line number in the variable ERL (= error line) and the error number in ERR. It then goes to line 5000. The values of the variables ERL and ERR are at our disposal, just like the values of any other variables.

In our particular example, there are two types of errors to look out for: File Not Found (error number 53) and Disk Not Ready (error number 71) The first error occurs when the file requested by the program is not on the indicated disk. The second error occurs when either the diskette drive door is open or no diskette is in the drive. The error numbers were obtained from either the list of errors on the command card at the end of this book or in Appendix A of IBM's BASIC Reference Manual. In the case of each error, the error trapping routine should notify the user and wait for the situation to be corrected. Here is the routine.

```
5000 'Error trapping routine
5010 IF ERR=53 PRINT "File Not Found"
5020 IF ERR=71 PRINT "Disk Not Ready"
5030 IF ERR<>53 AND ERR<>71 THEN PRINT "Unrecoverable
     Error"
5040 IF ERR<>53 AND ERR<>71 THEN END
5050 PRINT "CORRECT DISKETTE. PRESS ANY KEY WHEN READY."
5060 IF INKEY$="" THEN 5060
5070 RESUME
```

Several comments are in order. Notice that the error trapping routine allows recovery only in case of errors 53 and 71. If the error is any other one, line 5040 will cause the program to END. Line 5050 tells the operator to correct the situation. In line 5060, the program waits until the operator signals that the situation has been corrected. The RESUME in line 5070 clears the error condition and causes the program to resume execution with the line that caused the error.

Note that we analyzed our errors using ERR. We could just as well have used the line number ERL to choose our response to the error.

The RESUME statement has several useful variations:

RESUME NEXT—causes the program to resume with the line immediately after the line that caused the error.

RESUME <line number>—causes the program to resume with the indicated line number.

In designing and testing an error trapping routine, it is helpful to be able to generate errors of a particular type. This may be done using the ERROR statement. For example, to generate an error 50 in line 75, just replace line 75 with

```
75 ERROR 50
```

When the program reaches line 75, it will simulate error 50. The program will then jump to the error trapping routine to be tested.

Exercises (answers on page 352)

1. Write an error trapping routine that allows the program to ignore all errors.

2. Write an error trapping routine that allows detection of a Type Mismatch error in line 500. The response should be to display the error description and go to line 600.

7.3   The BAR CHART GENERATOR

Now that we've constructed all the components, let's unveil the final program. Note that I've included the SAVE and RECALL routines. They make use of what we learned about files in Chapter 5.

Note also that there are two omissions. First of all, I haven't included the DATA FILE routine. I've left this one as an exercise for you. Consider a file containing numerical output from a program. Design a routine that reads the file and includes the information as consecutive data items in a given data series, beginning with a user-specified data item in the series. The routine should then call on the DATA INPUT routine to display the data input from the file (along with any data that was not displaced by file data).

The second omission is an error trapping routine. This is also left as an exercise. Why not go through the program and determine the various errors that can occur (File Not Found, Drive Not Ready, and so forth). From the list of possible errors, you should design an error trapping routine that informs the user of the error and returns the program to the control routine.

```
1 '**********************************************************
2 '**********************************************************
3 '****************BAR CHART GENERATOR********************
4 '**********************************************************
5 '**********************************************************
6 '
7 '
8 '
9 '
10 '**********INITIALIZATION ROUTINE**********
100 'Dimension Statements
105     DIM MINKEY(5),MAXKEY(5),EXTMINKEY(5),
           EXTMAXKEY(5)
110     DIM CAPSON(5),SPECIALKEY$(5),EXTSPECIALKEY$(5),
        DTA$(3,20)
115     DIM MENU$(11),A%(10),B$(10),XMAX(3)
200 'Data Statements
300 'Common Statements
400 'Error Trapping Line
500 'DEF statements
600 'Define parameters for input routine
602     MOTION$=CHR$(71)+CHR$(72)+CHR$(75)+CHR$(77)
               +CHR$(79)+CHR$(80)
604     MOTION1$=CHR$(72)+CHR$(80)
606     FUNCTION$=CHR$(59)+CHR$(60)+CHR$(61)
               +CHR$(62)+CHR$(63)+CHR$(64)+CHR$(65)
608 '   **Text input(CALLER=1)**
610     MINKEY(1)=32:MAXKEY(1)=127:
        SPECIALKEY$(1)=CHR$(8)+CHR$(27)
612     CAPSON(1)=0
614     EXTMINKEY(1)=0:EXTMINKEY(1)=0
616     EXTSPECIALKEY$(1)=MOTION1$+FUNCTION$
618 '   **Numerical input (CALLER=2)**
```

```
620      MINKEY(2)=0:MAXKEY(2)=0:SPECIALKEY$(2)
         ="1234567890-+ E."+CHR$(8)+CHR$(27)
622      CAPSON(2)=-1
624      EXTMINKEY(2)=0:EXTMAXKEY(2)=0
626      EXTSPECIALKEY$(2)=MOTION1$+FUNCTION$
628 '    **Text input(CALLER=1)**
630      MINKEY(3)=0:MAXKEY(3)=127:SPECIALKEY$(3)=""
632      CAPSON(3)=0
634      EXTMINKEY(3)=0:EXTMINKEY(3)=0
636      EXTSPECIALKEY$(3)=MOTION$+FUNCTION$
638 '    **Numerical input (CALLER=4)**
640      MINKEY(4)=0:MAXKEY(4)=31:
         SPECIALKEY$(4)="1234567890-+ E."
642      CAPSON(4)=-1
644      EXTMINKEY(4)=0:EXTMAXKEY(4)=0
646      EXTSPECIALKEY$(4)=MOTION$+FUNCTION$
648 '    **Control Routine(CALLER=5)**
650      MINKEY(5)=0:MAXKEY(5)=0
652      CAPSON(5)=0
654      EXTMINKEY(5)=0:EXTMAXKEY(5)=0
656      EXTSPECIALKEY$(5)=FUNCTION$
700 'Initialization of variables
702      TRUE=-1:FALSE=0
704      FOR J%=1 TO 10
706              KEY J%,""
708      NEXT J%
710      FKEY$="1 DEFN  2 DATA  3 DRAW  4 SAVE  5 RCLL
                6 FILE  7 EXIT"
712      XFLD=1:YFLD=1:LNGTH=0
714      MENU$(1)="BAR CHART DEFINITION"
716      MENU$(2)="TITLE? "
718      MENU$(3)="DATA SERIES 1 TITLE? "
720      MENU$(4)="DATA SERIES 2 TITLE? "
722      MENU$(5)="DATA SERIES 3 TITLE? "
724      MENU$(6)="Y AXIS RANGE:MINIMUM? "
726      MENU$(7)="Y AXIS RANGE:MAXIMUM? "
728      MENU$(8)="Y AXIS STEP? "
```

```
730      MENU$(9)="X AXIS TITLE? "
732      MENU$(10)="Y AXIS TITLE? "
734      MAXHEIGHT=199
736      MAXWIDTH=639
900 '****************CONTROL ROUTINE*******************
905 'E$ is returned by the input routine, = the second
910 'character of extended ASCII code
915 KEY OFF:CLS
920 IF E$<>"" THEN 945
925 LOCATE 25,1
930 PRINT FKEY$;
935 CALLER=5:GOSUB 25000
940 GOTO 920
945 C=ASC(E$):EXTENDED=FALSE
950 IF C=59 THEN 1000 :'Bar Chart Definition
955 IF C=60 THEN 2000 :'Data Input
960 IF C=61 THEN 3000 :'Draw Bar Chart
965 IF C=62 THEN 4000 :'Save Bar Chart
970 IF C=63 THEN 5000 :'Recall Bar Chart
975 IF C=64 THEN 6000 :'Read Data File
980 IF C=65 THEN 7000 :'Exit
985 CALLER=5:GOSUB 25000:'Await instructions
1000 '**********BAR CHART PARAMETERS INPUT**************
1005 SCREEN 0:CLS:LOCATE 25,1:PRINT FKEY$;
1010 'Display template
1015 LOCATE 1,1:PRINT TAB(27) MENU$(1);
1020 FOR J%=2 TO 10
1025     LOCATE J%+2,1
1030     PRINT MENU$(J%);
1035 NEXT J%
1040 MENUEND=FALSE
1045 GOSUB 1170:'Display current parameter values
1050 XFLD=25:YFLD=4
1055 WHILE MENUEND=FALSE
1060     LOCATE YFLD,XFLD
1065     IF YFLD=4 THEN CALLER=1:LNGTH=50
1070     IF YFLD>4 AND YFLD<7 THEN CALLER=1:LNGTH=10
```

```
1075    IF YFLD>7 AND YFLD<11 THEN CALLER=2:LNGTH=10
1080    IF YFLD>10 THEN CALLER=1:LNGTH=10
1085    GOSUB 25000: 'Call input routine
1090    IF YFLD>7 AND YFLD<11 THEN GOSUB 27000:'Numberck
1095    IF YFLD>7 AND YFLD<11 AND NUMBERCK=FALSE
        THEN GOSUB 25425:GOTO 1085
1100    IF YFLD=4 THEN TITLE$=S$
1105    IF YFLD=5 THEN SER1TITLE$=S$
1110    IF YFLD=6 THEN SER2TITLE$=S$
1115    IF YFLD=7 THEN SER3TITLE$=S$
1120    IF YFLD=8 THEN YMIN$=S$
1125    IF YFLD=9 THEN YMAX$=S$
1130    IF YFLD=10 THEN YSTEP$=S$
1135    IF YFLD=11 THEN XTITLE$=S$
1140    IF YFLD=12 THEN YTITLE$=S$
1145    IF E$=CHR$(80) THEN IF YFLD<12 THEN YFLD=YFLD+1
1150    IF E$=CHR$(72) THEN IF YFLD>4 THEN YFLD=YFLD-1
1155    IF INSTR(FUNCTION$,E$)>0 THEN MENUEND=TRUE
1160 WEND
1165 GOTO 900: 'Return to control routine
1170 'Display current parameter values
1175    LOCATE 4,25:PRINT TITLE$
1180    LOCATE 5,25:PRINT SER1TITLE$
1185    LOCATE 6,25:PRINT SER2TITLE$
1190    LOCATE 7,25:PRINT SER3TITLE$
1195    LOCATE 8,25:PRINT YMIN$
1200    LOCATE 9,25:PRINT YMAX$
1205    LOCATE 10,25:PRINT YSTEP$
1210    LOCATE 11,25:PRINT XTITLE$
1215    LOCATE 12,25:PRINT YTITLE$
1220    RETURN
2000 '**********DATA INPUT ROUTINE**********
2005 SCREEN 0:CLS:LOCATE 25,1:PRINT FKEY$;
2010 LOCATE 1,1:GOSUB 2055:'Display spreadsheet
2015 ROW%=1:COL%=0
2020 DATAEND=FALSE
2025 WHILE DATAEND=FALSE
```

```
2030       GOSUB 2335:'Locate cursor
2035       GOSUB 2150:'Input data
2040 WEND
2045 GOTO 900:'Return to control routine
2050 ***************SUBROUTINES******************
2055 'Display spreadsheet
2060 CLS
2065 LOCATE 1,34
2070 PRINT "DATA VALUES"
2075 PRINT
2080 PRINT TAB(8) "LABEL";TAB(26) "SERIES A";
          TAB(44) "SERIES B";TAB(62) "SERIES C"
2085 PRINT STRING$(80,45);
2090 FOR J%=1 TO 20
2095 LOCATE J%+4,1
2100      PRINT J%; TAB(5) "|";
2105 NEXT J%
2110 FOR ROW%=1 TO 20
2115    FOR COL%=0 TO 3
2120            GOSUB 2335:'Convert to screen coordinates
2125            LOCATE R%,C%
2130            PRINT DTA$(COL%,ROW%);
2135    NEXT COL%
2140 NEXT ROW%
2145 RETURN
2150 'Input data
2155 IF COL%=0 THEN CALLER=3 ELSE CALLER=4
2160 XFLD=C%:YFLD=R%:LNGTH=10
2165 GOSUB 25000
2170 IF S$="" THEN 2195
2175 IF CALLER=3 THEN NUMBERCK=TRUE
2180 IF CALLER=4 THEN GOSUB 27000
2185 IF NUMBERCK<0 THEN DTA$(COL%,ROW%)=S$
2190 IF NUMBERCK=FALSE THEN GOSUB 25425:GOTO 2330
2195 IF INSTR(FUNCTION$,E$)>0
     THEN DATAEND=TRUE:GOTO 2330
2200 IF E$=CHR$(72) THEN 2230:'Cursor up
```

```
2205 IF E$=CHR$(75) THEN 2245:'Cursor left
2210 IF E$=CHR$(77) THEN 2260:'Cursor right
2215 IF E$=CHR$(80) THEN 2275:'Cursor down
2220 IF E$=CHR$(71) THEN 2290:'Home (To position 1,1)
2225 IF E$=CHR$(79) THEN 2310:'End (To position 20,3)
2230 'Cursor up
2235 IF ROW%>1 THEN ROW%=ROW%-1
2240 GOTO 2330
2245 'Cursor left
2250 IF COL%>0 THEN COL%=COL%-1
2255 GOTO 2330
2260 'Cursor right
2265 IF COL%<3 THEN COL%=COL%+1
2270 GOTO 2330
2275 'Cursor down
2280 IF ROW%>0 THEN ROW%=ROW%+1
2285 GOTO 2330
2290 'Home (To position 1,1)
2295 COL%=1
2300 ROW%=1
2305 GOTO 2330
2310 'End (To position 20,3)
2315 COL%=3
2320 ROW%=20
2325 GOTO 2330
2330 RETURN
2335 'Compute screen coordinates
2340 R%=ROW%+4
2345 C%=18*COL%+8
2350 LOCATE R%,C%
2355 RETURN
2360 RETURN
3000 '**************DRAWBAR ROUTINE**************
3005    CLS
3010    KEY OFF
3015    SCREEN 2 :SER%=3
3020    YMIN=VAL(YMIN$)
```

```
3025     YMAX=VAL(YMAX$)
3030     YSTEP=VAL(YSTEP$)
3035     IF YMIN>YMAX THEN SWAP YMIN,YMAX
3040     IF YMIN=YMAX THEN 3095
3045     IF YSTEP=0 THEN 3095
3050     GOSUB 3105:'Computer SER%
3055     STYLE$(1)=CHR$(&HFF):STYLE$(2)=CHR$(&HAA):
         STYLE$(3)=CHR$(&H99)+CHR$(&H55)
3060     BW=(XMAX+1)/240
3065     ADJ(1)=0:ADJ(2)=(XMAX+1)/60:ADJ(3)=-(XMAX+1)/60
3070     GOSUB 3195:'Write Titles
3075     GOSUB 3305:'Write x-axis labels
3080     GOSUB 3360:'Write y-axis labels
3085     GOSUB 3415:'Draw coordinate system
3090     GOSUB 3435:'Draw bars
3095     E$="":GOTO 920:'Return to control routine
3100     ***************SUBROUTINES*****************
3105     'Compute SER%
3110     FOR N%=3 TO 1 STEP -1
3115             XMAX(N%)=20:J%=0
3120             DATAEND=FALSE
3125             WHILE DATAEND=FALSE
3130                     IF DTA$(N%,20-J%)<>"" THEN
                         DATAEND=TRUE:XMAX(N%)=XMAX(N%)+1
3135                     XMAX(N%)=XMAX(N%)-1:J%=J%+1
3140                     IF J%=21 THEN DATAEND=TRUE
3145             WEND
3150     NEXT N%
3155     IF XMAX(3)<=0 THEN SER%=2
3160     IF SER%=2 AND XMAX(2)<=0 THEN SER%=1
3165     IF SER%=1 AND XMAX(1)<=0 THEN SER%=0
3170     XMAX=XMAX(1)
3175     FOR J%=1 TO 3
3180             IF XMAX< XMAX(J%) THEN XMAX=XMAX(J%)
3185     NEXT J%
3190     RETURN
3195     'Write titles
```

```
3200      LOCATE 5,72:PRINT SER1TITLE$;
3205 IF SER%=1 THEN 3225
3210      LOCATE 9,72:PRINT SER2TITLE$;
3215 IF SER%=2 THEN 3225
3220      LOCATE 13,72:PRINT SER3TITLE$;
3225      LINE (599,23)-(606,30),,B
3230      PAINT (603,27),STYLE$(1)
3235      IF SER%=1 THEN 3265
3240      LINE (599,55)-(606,62),,B
3245      PAINT (603,60),STYLE$(2)
3250      IF SER%=2 THEN 3265
3255      LINE (599,87)-(606,94),,B
3260      PAINT (603,93),STYLE$(3)
3265      X1=80:X2=559:Y1=0:Y2=7:C%=3:S$=TITLE$
3270      GOSUB 28000
3275      Y1=191:Y2=184:S$=XTITLE$
3280      GOSUB 28000
3285      X1=0:X2=7:Y1=16:Y2=167:C%=4
3290      S$=YTITLE$
3295      GOSUB 28000
3300      RETURN
3305 'Write x-axis labels
3310      K=480/(XMAX+1)
3315      FOR J%=1 TO XMAX
3320          L=79+K*J%
3325          M%=4*LEN(DTA$(0,J%))
3330          LINE (L,167)-(L,170):'Tick marks
3335          X1=L-M%:X2=L+M%-1:Y1=171:Y2=178:C%=1
3340          S$=DTA$(0,J%)
3345          GOSUB 28000
3350      NEXT J%
3355      RETURN
3360 'Write y-axis labels
3365      IF YSTEP=0 THEN 3410
3370      M=(YMAX-YMIN)/YSTEP
3375      FOR J%=0 TO M
3380          S$=STR$(YMIN+J%*YSTEP)
```

```
3385        X1=8:X2=79
3390        Y1=167-J%*152/M-4
3395        Y2=Y1-7:C%=1
3400        GOSUB 28000
3405     NEXT J%
3410     RETURN
3415 'Draw coordinate system
3420     VIEW (80,16)-(559,167),,3
3425     WINDOW (0,YMIN)-(XMAX+1,YMAX)
3430     LINE (0,0)-(XMAX+1,0):'Draw x-axis
3435 'Draw bars
3440     FOR N%=1 TO SER%
3445         FOR J%=1 TO XMAX(N%)
3450             IF DTA$(N%,J%)="" THEN 3470
3455             HT=VAL(DTA$(N%,J%))
3460             LINE (J%+ADJ(N%)-BW,0)-
                            (J%+ADJ(N%)+BW,HT),,B
3465             PAINT (J%+ADJ(N%),HT/2),STYLE$(N%)
3470         NEXT J%
3475     NEXT N%
3480 'Draw grid lines
3485     FOR J%=0 TO (YMAX-YMIN)/YSTEP
3490         H=YMIN+J%*YSTEP
3495         LINE (0,H)-(XMAX+1,H),,,&H8888
3500     NEXT J%
3505     RETURN
4000 '**********SAVE BAR CHART*************
4005 CLS:SCREEN 0
4010 PRINT "SAVE BAR CHART"
4015 INPUT "NAME OF FILE";FILENAME$
4020 OPEN FILENAME$ FOR OUTPUT AS £1
4025 WRITE #1, TITLE$
4030 WRITE #1, SER1TITLE$
4035 WRITE #1, SER2TITLE$
4040 WRITE #1, SER3TITLE$
4045 WRITE #1, YMIN$
4050 WRITE #1, YMAX$
```

```
4055 WRITE #1, YSTEP$
4060 WRITE #1, XTITLE$
4065 WRITE #1, YTITLE$
4070 FOR N%=0 TO 3
4075    FOR J%=1 TO 20
4080            WRITE #1, DTA$(N%,J%)
4085    NEXT J%
4090 NEXT N%
4095 CLOSE #1
4100 LOCATE 25,1:PRINT FKEY$;
4105 E$=""
4110 GOTO 900
5000 '**********RECALL BAR CHART************
5005 CLS
5010 PRINT "RECALL BAR CHAR"
5015 INPUT "NAME OF FILE";FILENAME$
5020 OPEN FILENAME$ FOR INPUT AS £1
5025 INPUT #1, TITLE$
5030 INPUT #1, SER1TITLE$
5035 INPUT #1, SER2TITLE$
5040 INPUT #1, SER3TITLE$
5045 INPUT #1, YMIN$
5050 INPUT #1, YMAX$
5055 INPUT #1, YSTEP$
5060 INPUT #1, XTITLE$
5065 INPUT #1, YTITLE$
5070 FOR N%=0 TO 3
5075    FOR J%=1 TO 20
5080            INPUT £1, DTA$(N%,J%)
5085    NEXT J%
5090 NEXT N%
5095 CLOSE #1
5100 GOTO 3000: 'Display bar chart
6000 '**********READ DATA FILE**********
6005 '(Exercise for the reader)
6010 E$="":GOTO 900
7000 '*************EXIT*****************
```

```
7005 SYSTEM
25000 '************KEYBOARD INPUT ROUTINE**************
25005 ' This routine inputs data as a string S$.
25010 ' It allows input to have the following parameters:
25015 ' LNGTH = maximum length of input string
25020 ' XFLD = cursor column for beginning of input field
25025 ' YFLD = cursor row for input field
25030 'CALLER = number of caller
25035 'CAPSON(CALLER) = -1 if letters are to be
                           capitalized for CALLER
25040 '              =  0 otherwise
25045 'FLDBEG = first character position in field
25050 'FLDEND = last character position in field
25055 'S$=Contents of the field from beginning up
         to space before cursor
25060 'T$=contents of the field from the cursor
          to the end of the field
25065 'At end of routine, the contents of the field
        are returned in S$
25070 'LASTPOS=position currently occupied by last
         character
25075 'If a key with an extended ASCII code is pressed,
        it ends processing the current field.
25080 ' The contents of the field are returned in S$ ,
25085 'the second byte of the extended ASCII code in E$.
25090 'CSR = the current column of the cursor
25095 '*********************************************
25100 '
25105 '******MAIN ROUTINE******
25110 '
25115     S$="":E$="":INPUTEND=FALSE:KEYHIT=FALSE
25120     FLDEND=XFLD+LNGTH-1
25125     CSR=XFLD
25130     GOSUB 25450:'Compute initial LASTPOS
25135     LOCATE YFLD,XFLD
25140     WHILE INPUTEND=FALSE
25145          GOSUB 26000:'Input character
```

```
25150            IF EXTENDED=TRUE THEN 25225
                 ELSE 25195:'Analyze character
25155   WEND
25160   GOSUB 25365:'Read screen
25165   S$=S$+T$
25170   RETURN
25175 '*********************************************
25180 '
25185 '****** Subroutines ******
25190 '
25195 'Handle ordinary ASCII codes
25200    KEYHIT=TRUE
25205    IF C$=CHR$(8) THEN  25260: 'Backspace
25210    IF C$=CHR$(13) THEN 25295: 'ENTER
25215    IF C$=CHR$(27) THEN 25310: 'Esc
25220    IF C$>=CHR$(32) THEN
         GOTO 25340:'Handle displayable character
25225 'Handle extended ASCII codes
25230    E$=C$
25235    INPUTEND=TRUE
25240    GOTO 25155
25245 'Reject character
25250    BEEP
25255    GOTO 25155
25260 'Handle Backspace
25265    IF LASTPOS<XFLD THEN 25245
25270    GOSUB 25365:'Read field
25275    IF CSR<>XFLD THEN CSR=CSR-1:
         PRINT CHR$(29)+T$+CHR$(32); ELSE PRINT T$;
25280    LOCATE YFLD,CSR
25285    LASTPOS=LASTPOS-1
25290    GOTO 25155
25295 'Handle ENTER
25300    INPUTEND=TRUE
25305    GOTO 25155
25310 'Handle ESC (Erase field)
25315    LOCATE YFLD,XFLD
```

```
25320      PRINT STRING$(LNGTH,32);
25325      LASTPOS=0:CSR=XFLD
25330      LOCATE YFLD,XFLD
25335      GOTO 25155
25340 'Display character
25345      PRINT C$;
25350      IF LASTPOS<CSR THEN LASTPOS=CSR
25355      IF CSR=FLDEND THEN
           PRINT CHR$(29); ELSE CSR=CSR+1
25360      GOTO 25155
25365 'Read field from screen
25370      LOCATE ,,0
25375      S$="": T$=""
25380      IF LASTPOS=0 THEN 25420
25385      FOR J%=XFLD TO CSR-1
25390              S$=S$+CHR$(SCREEN(YFLD,J%))
25395      NEXT J%
25400      FOR J%=CSR TO LASTPOS
25405              T$=T$+CHR$(SCREEN(YFLD,J%))
25410      NEXT J%
25415      LOCATE ,,1
25420      RETURN
25425 'Erase field
25430      LOCATE YFLD,XFLD:CSR=XFLD:LASTPOS=0
25435      PRINT STRING$(LNGTH,32);
25440      LOCATE YFLD,XFLD
25445      RETURN
25450 'Compute LASTPOS (For inital non-blank field)
25455      LASTPOS=FLDEND:CSR=XFLD
25460      GOSUB 25365:'Read field
25465      WHILE RIGHT$(T$,1)=CHR$(32)
25470              T$=LEFT$(T$,LEN(T$)-1)
25475              LASTPOS=LASTPOS-1
25480      WEND
25485      RETURN
25490 'Clear keyboard buffer
25495      DEF SEG=0:POKE 1050, PEEK(1052):
```

```
        DEF SEG:'Clear keyboard buffer
25500   RETURN
25505 '*******************************************
26000 '****************KEYIN********************
26005 '
26010 'This routine reads a character from the keyboard
26015 'and accepts of rejects it based on the caller's
        specifications.
26020 'Subroutine variables:
26025 '    CALLER = number of caller
26030 '    MINKEY(CALLER)=minimum ASCII code
                        allowed for CALLER
26035 '    MAXKEY(CALLER)=maximum ASCII code
                        allowed for CALLER
26040 '    CAPSON(CALLER)=Convert to CAPITALS?
26045 '    SPECIALKEYS$(CALLER)=String containing any
                            special acceptable keys
26050 '                        for CALLER
26055 '    EXTMINKEY(CALLER)=minimum extended ASCII code
                        allowed for CALLER
26060 '    EXTMAXKEY(CALLER)=maximum extended ASCII code
                        allowed for CALLER
26065 '    EXTSPECIALKEY$(CALLER)=special extended ASCII
                            codes allowed
26070 '                        for CALLER
26075 'The above arrays must be dimensioned in the main
        program.
26080 'The array values must also be assigned in the main
        program.
26085 'The values of TRUE and FALSE must also be assigned
26090 'in the main program.
26095 '    C$=the character returned
26100 '    EXTENDED=-1 if C$ is the second byte of an
                        extended ASCII code,
26105 '            = 0 otherwise
26110 'Input character string from INKEY$
26115   C$=INKEY$
```

```
26120      IF C$="" THEN 26115: 'Wait for input
26125      C=ASC(C$)
26130      IF LEN(C$)=2 THEN EXTENDED=TRUE ELSE
                              EXTENDED=FALSE
26135      IF EXTENDED=FALSE THEN 26155
26140      C$=RIGHT$(C$,1)
26145      C=ASC(C$)
26150      GOTO 26205
26155 'Ordinary ASCII Codes
26160 '  Test for range
26165          IF C>=MINKEY(CALLER) AND C<=MAXKEY(CALLER)
               THEN 26255
26170 '  Handle special characters
26175          IF SPECIALKEY$(CALLER)=""
               THEN 26240 :'No special characters
26180          IF INSTR(SPECIALKEY$(CALLER),C$)=0
               THEN 26240
26185 '  Convert to capitals if necessary
26190          IF CAPSON(CALLER)=FALSE THEN 26255
26195          IF C>96 AND C<123 THEN C$=CHR$(C AND 223)
26200          GOTO 26255
26205 ' Extended ASCII codes
26210 '  Test for range
26215          IF C>=EXTMINKEY(CALLER)
               AND C<=EXTMINKEY(CALLER) THEN 26255
26220 '  Handle special characters
26225          IF EXTSPECIALKEY$(CALLER)="" THEN 26240
26230          IF INSTR(EXTSPECIALKEY$(CALLER),C$)=0
               THEN 26240
26235          GOTO 26255
26240 ' Illegal character
26245          BEEP
26250          GOTO 26115: 'Try again
26255 RETURN
27000 '*********NUMBERCK**********
27005 'This routine checks the format of the string
      S$ to determine if
27010 'it may successfully be converted to a number.
```

```
             It returns the result
27015 'of the check in the variable NUMBERCK.
27020 'NUMBERCK = 0: S$ not in numerical format
27025 '          =-1: S$ may be converted into a
                       single-precision real
27030 '          =-2: S$ may be converted with 0
                       fractional part
27035 '          =-3: S$ may be converted to an integer
27040 'If conversion is possible, S contains the converted
27045 'real,S$ the corresponding string.
27050 '************MAIN ROUTINE***************
27055 'Initialize and handle leading sign
27060     N$="":NUMBERCK=TRUE:DIGIT$="1234567890"
27065     DECPT=FALSE:EXPNT=FALSE:SIGN=FALSE
27070     IF S$="" THEN 27185
27075     T$=LEFT$(S$,1)
27080     IF T$="+" OR T$="-" THEN N$=T$:S$=MID$(S$,2)
27085     IF S$="" THEN NUMBERCK=FALSE:GOTO 27210
27090     IF INSTR(DIGIT$,LEFT$(S$,1))=0 THEN
          NUMBERCK=FALSE:GOTO 27210
27095 WHILE S$ <> "" :'Loop strips spaces and
                       checks format.Result in N$
27100     T$=LEFT$(S$,1):S$=MID$(S$,2)
27105     IF T$=" " THEN 27135: 'Delete space
27110     IF (T$="+" OR T$="-") AND RIGHT$(N$,1)<>"E"
          THEN NUMBERCK=FALSE:GOTO 27135
27115     IF T$="." THEN IF DECPT=TRUE  OR EXPNT=TRUE
          THEN NUMBERCK=FALSE ELSE N$=N$+T$:DECPT=TRUE
27120     IF T$="+" OR T$="-" THEN
          IF SIGN=TRUE OR EXPNT=FALSE THEN NUMBERCK=FALSE
          ELSE N$=N$+T$:SIGN=TRUE
27125     IF T$="E" THEN IF EXPNT=TRUE THEN NUMBERCK=FALSE
          ELSE N$=N$+T$:EXPNT=TRUE:DECPT=TRUE
27130     IF T$<>"." AND T$<>"+" AND T$<>"-" AND T$<>"E"
          THEN N$=N$+T$
27135 WEND
27140 'Check for overflow(<10^-38 or >10^38)
27145     N%=INSTR(N$,"E")
```

```
27150      IF N%=0 THEN 27190
27155      IF N%=1 THEN NUMBERCK=FALSE:GOTO 27210
27160      S$=LEFT$(N$,N%-1):S1$=MID$(N$,N%+1)
27165      S=VAL(S$)
27170      IF S=0 THEN D=0 ELSE D=INT(LOG(ABS(S))/LOG(10))
27175      IF S1$<>"" THEN D=D+VAL(S1$)
27180      IF D<-37 OR D>37 THEN NUMBERCK=FALSE
27185 'Perform the conversion
27190      IF NUMBERCK=TRUE THEN S=VAL(N$)
27195      IF NUMBERCK=TRUE AND S=INT(S) THEN NUMBERCK=-2
27200      IF NUMBERCK=-2 AND S>=-32768! AND S<=32767
           THEN NUMBERCK=-3
27205      S$=N$
27210 RETURN
28000 '**************PLOTSTRING********************
28005 'This routine allows precise placement of a string
28010 ' in graphics mode.
28015 ' (x1,y1),(x1,y2) are graphics coordinates
28020 ' s$=string to be placed
28025 ' c%=1:place string horizontally, with left corner
28030 '        of 1st character at (x1,y1)
28035 ' c%=2:place string vertically, with left corner
28040 '        of 1st character at (x1,y1)
28045 ' c%=3:center string horizontally in the
28050 '        field (x1,y1)-(x2,y2)
28055 ' c%=4:center string vertically in the
28060 '        field (x1,y1)-(x2,y2)
28065 'Maxwidth=largest allowable x-coordinate
28070 'Maxheight=largest allowable y-coordinate
28075 '*****************MAIN ROUTINE*****************
28080      IF C%=1 OR C%=2 THEN X=X1:Y=Y1
28085      ON C% GOSUB 28195,28275,28245,28320
28090      RETURN
28095 *****************SUBROUTINES****************
28100 'Load character into array
28105      A%(0)=8
28110      A%(1)=8
28115      DEF SEG = &HF000
```

```
28120     OFFSET=8*ASC(C$)+&HFA6E
28125     FOR J=0 TO 7
28130       B$(J)=HEX$(PEEK(OFFSET+J))
28135       IF LEN(B$(J))=1 THEN B$(J)="0"+B$(J)
28140     NEXT J
28145     FOR J=0 TO 3
28150       A%(J+2) = VAL("&H" + B$(2*J+1) + B$(2*J))
28155     NEXT J
28160     DEF SEG
28165     RETURN
28170 'Place character at particular coordinates
28175 'Character =c$, coordinates (x,y)
28180     GOSUB 28100
28185     PUT (X,Y), A%
28190     RETURN
28195 'Place string in field beginning at particular
        coordinates.
28200 'Field begins at (x,y), string in S$
28205     WHILE S$ <> ""
28210             IF X>MAXWIDTH THEN 28235
28215             C$=LEFT$(S$,1):S$=MID$(S$,2)
28220             GOSUB 28170: 'place character
28225             IF X<0 THEN 28235
28230             X=X+8
28235     WEND
28240     RETURN
28245 'Center string s$ in field defined by coordinates
        (x1,y1)-(x2,y2)
28250     IF X1>X2 THEN SWAP X1,X2: IF Y1>Y2
          THEN SWAP Y1,Y2
28255     L=LEN(S$): C=INT((X2-X1)/8):
          IF L>C THEN S$=LEFT$(S$,C)
28260     X=X1+(X2-X1+1)/2-8*LEN(S$)/2+4:
          Y=Y1+(Y2-Y1+1)/2-4
28265     GOSUB 28195
28270     RETURN
28275 'Display string s$ vertically beginning at
        coordinate (x,y)
```

```
28280     WHILE S$ <> ""
28285          IF Y+7>MAXHEIGHT THEN 28315
28290          C$=LEFT$(S$,1):S$=MID$(S$,2)
28295          IF Y<0 THEN 28305
28300          GOSUB 28170: 'place character
28305          Y=Y+8
28310     WEND
28315     RETURN
28320 'Center string s$ vertically in field
      (x1,y1)-(x2,y2)
28325     IF X1>X2 THEN SWAP X1,X2:
          IF Y1>Y2 THEN SWAP Y1,Y2
28330     L=LEN(S$): C=INT((Y2-Y1)/8):
          IF L>C THEN S$=LEFT$(S$,C)
28335     Y=Y1+(Y2-Y1+1)/2-8*LEN(S$)/2:
          X=X1+(X2-X1+1)/2-4
28340     IF X<0 THEN X=0 : IF Y<0 THEN Y=0
28345     GOSUB 28275
28350     RETURN
```

7.4   Further Tips For Planning Large Programs

We have just constructed a rather long program. It took a great deal of work, but each of the steps was rather straightforward. One problem we never considered, however: Will the program fit into memory? This is a question that you may never have even thought of. But it is a real consideration in building a large program. THE BAR CHART GENERATOR will comfortably run in a PC equipped with at least 64K of RAM. However, if we decided to expand the program (say, by adding line graph capability), we would soon find that 64K is just not sufficient. And adding more memory is not necessarily the answer to this dilemma, since BASIC is designed to make use of only one 64K segment of RAM, no matter how much memory the computer has. In this section, we will discuss some techniques, using the CHAIN and COMMON statements, for getting around this limitation.

The CHAIN instruction allows you to call a BASIC program from within a running program. For example, the statement

```
2000 CHAIN "B:SQUARES"
```

will cause the program to load and execute the program "B:SQUARES." The current program will be lost, as will the values of all its variables. BASIC will begin execution of "SQUARES" with its first line. The unadorned CHAIN statement has the same effect as the RUN command. It causes all buffers to be cleared, all files to be closed and all current variables and arrays to be deleted.

You may begin execution of "SQUARES" at line 300 by using the statement

```
2000 CHAIN "SQUARES",300
```

You may carry ALL of the variables of the current program over into "SQUARES" and begin with the first statement of "SQUARES" by using the statement

```
2000 CHAIN "SQUARES",,ALL
```

To carry forward all of the variables of the current program and to begin "SQUARES" at line 300, use the statement

```
2000 CHAIN "SQUARES",300,ALL
```

A CHAIN statement is useful if a particular program is too large for memory. You may break the program into sub-programs and use CHAIN statements to link them together into a single program. In the interest of saving memory, you may wish to carry over only some of the variables of the current program. You may do this with the COMMON statement. For example, to pass the variables A, B and C$ to "SQUARES", we would include the following statement in the chaining program

```
10 COMMON A,B,C$
```

If, in addition, you wish to pass the values of the array SALARY(), the COMMON statement should be of the form

```
10 COMMON A,B,C$,SALARY()
```

You may include as many COMMON statements as you wish. However, a variable may appear in only one of them. COMMON statements may appear anywhere in a program, but it is a good idea to place them in the beginning.

Be careful in using the CHAIN statement. It has the following significant effects.

1. There is no way to pass user-defined functions to the chained program.

2. Any variable types that have been defined by the statements DEFINT, DEFSNG or DEFDBL will not be preserved. If you plan to use CHAINing with variable types, it is better to use declaration tags %, !, and # rather than DEFINT, DEFSNG, or DEFDBL.

3. The error trapping line number (if previously defined) will be deleted.

4. All files are closed.

The CHAIN statement completely eliminates the current program. You may keep a portion (or all) of the current program by using the CHAIN MERGE statement. For example, the statement

```
CHAIN MERGE "SQUARES",300
```

will merge the program "SQUARES" with the current program and resume execution at line 300. The lines of "SQUARES" will be interleaved with the lines of the current program. If a line number in "SQUARES" duplicates a line number in the current program, then the line in the current program will be deleted in favor of the corresponding line in "SQUARES".

The program to be MERGEd must have been stored in ASCII format (SAVE,A). Otherwise, BASIC will report a **Bad File Mode Error**.

In some applications, you may wish to delete a section of the current program before MERGEing. For example, the statement

```
CHAIN MERGE "SQUARES",300,DELETE 300-1000
```

will first delete lines 300-1000 of the current program, merge "SQUARES" with the current program, and resume execution at line 300 of the resulting program.

CHAIN MERGE leaves files currently open and preserves variables, variable types, and user-defined functions.

Exercises (answers on page 352)

1. Write a statement to merge the program "L" into the current program and begin at the first line of the resulting program.

2. Write a program to run the programs "A","B", and "C" one after the other.

8

The IBM/EPSON Printer

Until now, we have used the printer in a rather simple fashion, for listing programs and for printing output. In this chapter, we discuss some of the fine points of printer usage, including an introduction to printer graphics. In Section 3, we will develop a graphics screen dump that will print the contents of the screen in either of the two graphics modes. Each printer is different. Printer capabilities and the techniques for accessing them vary widely among manufacturers and even among models by a single manufacturer. The discussion of this chapter applies only to the following printers:

IBM 80 character per second Matrix Printer

IBM 80 character per second Graphics Printer

EPSON MX/80 or MX/100 with either GRAFTRAX-80 or GRAFTRAX-PLUS

EPSON FX/80

8.1 Printing Fundamentals

The IBM/EPSON printers accomplish printing by means of a print head with 9 wires arranged vertically. A character is sent to the printer as an ASCII code, which is an integer from 0 to 255. Some ASCII codes represent printable characters and some represent commands. In response to a printable ASCII character, the electronics of the printer cause the wires of the print head to "fire" in particular combinations that have been pre-programmed. For a given character, the print wires fire 12 times. After each firing, the print head is advanced by 1/12 of a character (1/120 inch). The result is a set of dot patterns arranged within a rectangular grid 9 dots high and 12 dots wide. For example, in Figure 8.1, we show the dot pattern corresponding to the letter "A."

The above sequence of print head firings happens extraordinarily fast, too fast, in fact, for the eye to observe. Because the print head prints a set of dots within a rectangular matrix, this type of printer is called a **dot matrix printer**. One advantage of a dot matrix printer is its great speed. The IBM Dot Matrix Printer, the IBM Graphics Printer, and the EPSON MX/80 and MX/100 are

Figure 8.1. The Letter "A".

all capable of printing 80 characters per second. (The EPSON FX/80 is capable of 160 characters per second.)

However, speed is not the only virtue of these printers. They are capable of some incredibly sophisticated printing assignments. Before we begin to tell you about the various possibilities, let's discuss the way in which the printer receives and interprets information.

Printer Communications

The IBM PC communicates with the printer through a parallel port, which is cabled to a connector at the rear of the system unit. If you have a monochrome display interface, then the parallel port is mounted on the monochrome display interface card. If you are using the color/graphics interface, then you must get your parallel port on some other card. The parallel port of the PC is connected to the rear of the printer via a rather heavy cable, which you may purchase from you local computer dealer. (The same cable works for all the printers we are discussing.)

When you send data to the printer (say via an LPRINT statement), here is what happens:

1. The data, in the form of a sequence of one-byte ASCII codes, is deposited in a section of the PC's memory called the **printer buffer**. This is a holding area for data awaiting transmission to the printer.

2. At intervals, the printer requests data. (Don't worry about how it does this.)

3. In response, the computer sends a number of bytes from the printer buffer, taking care to note which bytes were sent.

4. When the printer receives the bytes, it deposits them in its own buffer to await printing.

5. Whenever the print mechanism needs a character to print, the printer looks to the buffer for a byte.

6. If the buffer is not empty, the printer takes the next byte in line.

7. The byte is decoded. It may correspond to a command or to a printable character.

8. The printer takes action on the byte. Either the command is executed or the character is printed.

9. Steps 5-8 are repeated until the printer's buffer becomes low.

10. The printer then tells the computer to transmit more data and the process begins again with Step 3.

The above procedure happens so quickly that you are unlikely to be aware of it. However, it is helpful to understand what is happening 'under the hood' if you are to understand the operation (or non-operation) of the printer commands.

Some Elementary Printer Commands

The most rudimentary printer command is the carriage return-line feed sequence. A carriage return is a command to return the print head to the left-most end of the print line. A line feed advances the paper by one line. The carriage return-line feed sequence is used at the ends of most lines to reposition the print head for the beginning of the next line. In fact, the statements LPRINT and LPRINT USING will automatically insert the carriage return-line feed sequence, unless you suppress it by using a semicolon at the end of the statement, as in

```
LPRINT A$;
LPRINT USING "##.##";A,B,C;
```

A carriage return is indicated by ASCII code 13 or ASCII code 141. A line feed is indicate by ASCII code 10. In theory then, a carriage return-line feed sequence should be generated by the string

```
CHR$(13)+CHR$(10)
```

However, there is a slight catch. IBM PC BASIC automatically adds the CHR$(10) whenever it sees CHR$(13). So the carriage return-line feed sequence may be generated with the command

```
LPRINT CHR$(13);
```

If you wish to send a carriage return without a line feed, you must use ASCII code 141.

You may use the carriage return without the line feed to produce some interesting print effects. For example, you may backspace and then overprint some characters. Here is a program that prints the string "BASIC," then back-spaces to the beginning of the string and overprints each letter with a "/" .

```
10 LPRINT "BASIC";
20 LPRINT CHR$(141); :'Carriage return, no line feed
30 LPRINT "/////"    :'Overprint and carriage return-line
                        feed
```

In the above example, we used the carriage return to go back to the beginning of the line. However, in some overprint operations, you may wish to go back only a single space. This may be accomplished with the backspace command. You may backspace the print head one character with ASCII code 8

```
LPRINT CHR$(8);
```

Here is a program that prints the string "BASIC" and overprints the "C" with a "/", then prints "PASCAL" in character position 30 on the same line.

```
10 LPRINT "BASIC";
20 LPRINT CHR$(8);
30 LPRINT "/";
40 LPRINT TAB(30) "PASCAL"
```

A word of caution: Try this program

```
10 LPRINT "BASIC";
```

When you try to run it, nothing seems to happen. Actually, the string "BASIC" is sent to the printer's buffer. However, it is held there until the buffer fills up. (Printing partial buffers is inefficient.) You may force release of the printer buffer by giving a carriage return-line feed sequence. Thus, for example, the program

```
10 LPRINT "BASIC"
```

will result in immediately printing the string "BASIC," since the automatic carriage return-line feed sequence has not been suppressed.

Just as the line feed command allows you to advance the paper by one line, the form feed command allows you to advance the paper to the beginning of the next page. Form feed is indicated by ASCII code 12.

Printing Mailing Labels

You may use your printer to print mailing address labels. Here's how. You can buy peel-off labels on continuous form backing. These labels are available in several layouts, including one and three labels across. Let's assume that we are dealing with labels 3 inches wide and 15/16 inches high, with a 1/16-inch vertical space between labels. So at 6 lines to the inch vertical spacing, each label has room for 5 lines. The 6th line spaces to the beginning of the next label. The layout of two consecutive labels is shown in Figure 8.2. (Of course, one or more of the lines could be blank.)

I usually use labels 3 inches wide. Since the print on the printer is 10 characters to the inch, this allows up to 30 characters per line. When I use labels that are two across, the first label begins in print column 1, and the second begins in print column 50. (These numbers depend on the particular label.)

Below are three programs that do various label printing tasks. The first program allows printing multiple copies of a single label, using forms containing only one label across. The second program performs the same task for forms containing two labels across. I use these programs for generating address labels for people I communicate with often. I also use such labels

```
Line 1
Line 2
Line 3
Line 4
Line 5


Line 1
Line 2
Line 3
Line 4
Line 5
```

Figure 8.2. Two Consecutive Labels.

when I travel. I address the labels to my home address and regularly mail papers home, rather than carry them with me for the duration of the trip.

The third program takes addresses from a mailing list and prints a set of corresponding labels on forms containing one label across. It is assumed that the file containing the addresses is a random access file in which each record contains 5 fields (one per label line) each containing 20 characters.

Here are the three programs.

Copies of a single label, one across

```
10 INPUT "NUMBER OF COPIES";NUMBER
20 FOR J=1 TO 5
30    PRINT "LINE ";J;
40    INPUT L$(J)
50 NEXT J
60 FOR J=1 TO NUMBER
70    FOR K=1 TO 6
80          LPRINT L$(J)
90    NEXT K
100 NEXT J
```

Copies of a single label, two across

```
10 INPUT "NUMBER OF COPIES";NUMBER
20 FOR J=1 TO 5
30    PRINT "LINE ";J;
40    INPUT L$(J)
50 NEXT J
60 FOR J=1 TO NUMBER
70    FOR K=1 TO 6
80          LPRINT L$(J);TAB(50) L$(J)
90    NEXT K
100 NEXT J
```

Print Labels From a Mailing List

```
10 INPUT "FILE NAME OF MAILING LIST";FILENAME$
20 OPEN FILENAME$ AS #1
30 FIELD #1, 20 AS L$(1), 20 AS L$(2), 20 AS L$(3), 20 AS
   L$(4), 20 AS L$(5)
40 IF EOF(#1) THEN 100
50 GET #1
60 FOR K=1 TO 6
70      LPRINT L$(J)
80 NEXT K
90 GOTO 40
100 CLOSE 1
```

Exercises

1. Modify label program 2 so that it prints copies of a label three across. (Assume that the labels begin in print columns 1, 31, and 61.

2. Modify label program 1 so that it allows addition of serial numbers in the lower right corner of the label, on line 5. Write the program so that it generates 100 labels with the serial number 100, . . .,199.

3. Modify label program 3 so that it generates labels from the mailing list using forms containing two labels across.

8.2   Printer Command Sequences

Your printer is capable of a great many options with regard to type style, print spacing, page length, and so forth. This section presents an organized look at the various command sequences available to you.

Certain printer commands are given by means of a single ASCII code. For example, a carriage return is given with ASCII code 13. However, certain printer commands are given as a sequence of ASCII codes. For such commands, the sequence of codes begins with ASCII code 27 (= ESCAPE). This ASCII code tells the printer that the following ASCII codes are to be interpreted as part of a command rather than as printable characters. For example, consider the sequence of ASCII codes

27, 78, 3

It instructs the printer to skip three lines at the end of the page. This allows you to skip over the perforation between consecutive sheets of paper. You may communicate this sequence of ASCII codes to the printer as you would any other ASCII codes, using the LPRINT statement

```
LPRINT CHR$(27);CHR$(78);CHR$(3);
```

Line Spacing

The following commands are available for adjusting the vertical line spacing:

Action	Command Sequence
Set line spacing to 1/6″	27, 50
Set line spacing to 1/8″	27, 48
Set line spacing to 7/72″	27, 49
Set line spacing to n/72″	27, 65, n, 27, 50* 27, 65, n**
*Set line spacing to n/216″	27, 51, n
*Set line spacing to n/216″ for current line only.	27, 74, n

Default setting: line spacing = 1/6″
Here are some samples of various vertical line spacings.

```
LINE SPACING 8 /72 INCHES
LINE SPACING 1o /72 INCHES
LINE SPACING 12 /72 INCHES
LINE SPACING 14 /72 INCHES
LINE SPACING 16 /72 INCHES
LINE SPACING 18 /72 INCHES
LINE SPACING 20 /72 INCHES
LINE SPACING 22 /72 INCHES
LINE SPACING 24 /72 INCHES
```

Figure 8.3. Examples of Vertical Line Spacing.

Page Length and Layout

This group of commands allows you to set the length of the page and the amount of space to skip in order to avoid the perforations in continuous forms.

Action	Command Sequence
Set page length to n lines	27, 67, n
*Set page length to n inches	27, 67, n, 0
*Leave n lines blank at bottom of page (=Skip perforation)	27, 78, n
*Cancel skip perforation	27, 79

Default setting: Page length = 66 lines = 11 inches

---

*IBM Printers only.
**Non-IBM Printers only.

Notes:

1. You must set the page length before giving the Skip Perforation command.

2. The Skip Perforation command causes the number of printed lines to be decreased by the specified skip. For example, a skip of 10 lines and standard page length will cause pages to consist of 56 lines followed by 10 blank lines.

3. You may wish to adjust the paper so that any skip is evenly distributed between bottom of a page and the top of the following one.

4. The beginning of the page is set when the printer is turned on. Any form feed commands make reference to the latest vertical line spacing and the latest page length information in spacing to the top of the next page.

Print Style

The IBM/EPSON printer is capable of a number of print styles, including emphasized, double strike, double width, compressed, underlined, and sub-script/superscript**. We may group these attributes as follows:

Group A: Normal
          Compressed
          Emphasized

Group B: Double Strike
          Subscript
          Superscript

Group C: Double Width

Group D: Underline

You may combine attributes by selecting at most one attribute from each group. For example, you may select print that is simultaneously compressed, subscript, and double width. However, you may not select print simultaneously compressed and emphasized.

Here are some samples of the various print styles possible with your printer.

```
This is the standard type font.
This line is emphasized.
This line is double-struck.
This   line   is   double   width.
This line is condensed.
This line is italics.
```
Figure 8.4. Various Print Styles.

Here are the print commands that govern the various print styles:

Emphasized print ON   27, 69

** IBM printers or EPSON with GRAFTRAX PLUS.

Emphasized print OFF	27, 70
Double strike ON	27, 71
Double strike OFF	27, 72
* Subscript ON	27, 83, 1
*Superscript ON	27, 83, 0
*Subscript/Superscript OFF	27, 84
Compressed ON	15
Compressed OFF	18
Double width ON (current line only)	14
Double width OFF	20
*Underline ON	27, 45, 1
*Underline OFF	27, 45, 0

Notes:

1. The double width style prints 5 characters to the inch, but is the same height as standard print.

2. The compressed print style prints 132 characters per 8 inch line.

Tabs

Set horizontal tabs at columns n1,n2, . . .,nk	27, 68, n1, n2, . . ., nk, 0
Horizontal tab	9
Cancel horizontal tabs	27, 68, 0
Set vertical tabs at columns n1, n2, . . ., nk	27, 66, n1,n2, . . .,nk
Vertical tab	11
Cancel vertical tabs	27, 66, 0

Exercises

Write a command that sets the following parameter of the printer:

1. Vertical line spacing to 9/72″.
2. Vertical line spacing to 8 lines per inch.
3. Vertical line spacing to 12 lines per inch.
4. Vertical line spacing to 6 lines per inch, double spaced.

*IBM Graphics Printer or EPSON with GRAFTRAX PLUS.

5.   Set horizontal tabs at columns 5, 10, 15, and 30.

6.   Set the page length to 33 lines per page.

7.   Suppose that you wish to print 6 lines per inch, triple spaced. Write commands to set the appropriate page length and vertical line spacing.

Print the sentence "THIS IS A TEST." in the following type styles:

8.   Emphasized

9.   Compressed

10.   Double width

11.   Double strike

Print the following equations:

12. X^2

13. H_2O

14. $e^x = 51.3$

8.3   Printer Graphics

In this section, we will discuss the graphics capabilities of the IBM/EPSON printers. Our discussion will not apply to the IBM Matrix Printer, unless you have equipped it with GRAFTRAX 80 or GRAFTRAX PLUS.

As we have mentioned, the print head has 9 wires arranged vertically. In the graphics mode, only the top 8 of these wires are used. Figure 8.5 shows the 8 wires used in the graphics modes and numbers them, from bottom to top with the numbers 0 through 7.

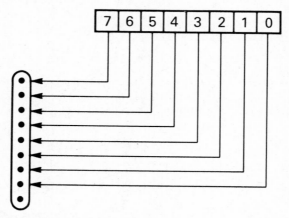

Figure 8.5. The Print Head Wires.

Each print wire corresponds to a single printed dot. You may request the print head to print any combination of dots, corresponding to the 8 wires used in graphics mode. Figure 8.6 shows a number of typical dot patterns.

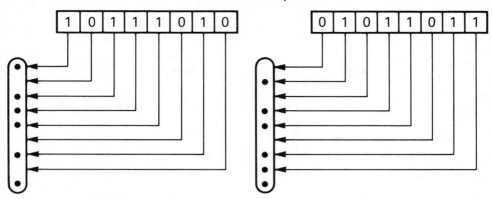

Figure 8.6. Some Typical Dot Patterns.

A dot pattern is specified as a single byte, with wire 0 corresponding to bit 0, wire 1 corresponding to bit 1, and so forth. The most significant bit corresponds to the top print wire. Figure 8.6 indicates the bytes corresponding to each of the given bit patterns.

TEST YOUR UNDERSTANDING 1 (answer on page 243)

Determine the bytes corresponding to the following dot patterns:

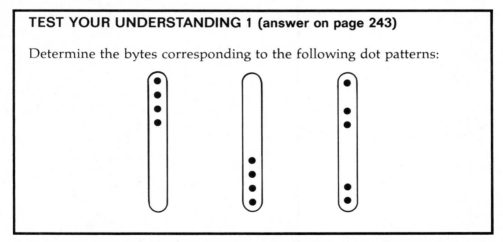

TEST YOUR UNDERSTANDING 2 (answer on page 243)

Determine the dot patterns corresponding to the following bytes:

   (a)   &HFF   (b)   &H0F   (c)   &H1A

You may specify more complex dot patterns by representing them in terms of a number of 8-dot vertical patterns like those above. For example, consider the following dot pattern which forms a letter A. (See Fig. 8.7.) It is formed of a grid 11 × 8 and so may be represented as 11 vertical 8-bit dot patterns. Here are the dot patterns with their corresponding byte representations. (See Fig. 8.8.)

Figure 8.7.

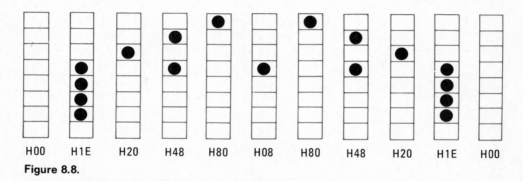

H00   H1E   H20   H48   H80   H08   H80   H48   H20   H1E   H00

Figure 8.8.

TEST YOUR UNDERSTANDING 3 (answer on page 243)

Determine the dot configuration determined by the bytes:

&HFE, &H01, &H00, &H01, &H00, &H01, &H00, &HFE

TEST YOUR UNDERSTANDING 4 (answer on page 243)

Determine the bytes corresponding to the following dot configuration (a mathematical symbol meaning "sum"):

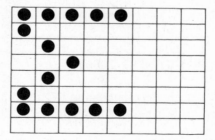

Horizontal Dot Placement

There are three graphics modes, with the following horizontal dot densities:

Medium Resolution   — 480 dots per 8-inch line

High Resolution   — 960 dots per 8-inch line

Ultra-High Resolution*—1920 dots per 8-inch line

In medium resolution, adjacent dots have a noticable horizontal space between them. In high resolution, this space is eliminated. And in ultra-high resolution, adjacent dots actually overlap. For each density you may, in principle, print any 8-dot vertical pattern in each of the horizontal dot positions on a line. (But see below for an exception.) For example, in medium-resolution mode, you may print 480 vertical 8-bit patterns per 8-inch line. Actually, it is possible to mix graphics patterns with text. For example, you might print a line consisting of 50 standard printed characters (at 10 characters to the inch = 5 inches), followed by 120 graphics patterns (at 60 per inch = 2 inches), followed by 10 standard printed characters.

As with most things in life, increasing the resolution comes only at a price. If you wish to use high resolution without any restrictions in dot placement, you can print at only half the speed of medium resolution. A similar statement goes for ultra-high resolution. If you wish to retain the speed, you must live with some restrictions in dot placement. In order for high resolution to run at full printer speed, you cannot print two dots that are horizontally adjacent to one another. In ultra-high resolution, you can print dots only in every third horizontal dot position.

In order to initiate a printer graphics mode, it is necessary to give an escape sequence that tells the computer:

1. The graphics mode

2. The speed

3. The number of vertical 8-bit graphics patterns forthcoming

These three data items are expressed by a four-byte code:

27 m n1 n2

where m is a byte denoting the graphics mode/speed and n1 and n2 are bytes that, together, indicate the number of vertical 8-bit graphics patterns to come.

Here are the meanings of m, n1, and n2:

m = 75 : 480 dots per 8-inch line

m = 76 : 960 dots per 8-inch line, half speed

m = 89 : 960 dots per 8-inch line, full speed, no adjacent dots

m = 90 : 1920 dots per 8-inch line, full speed, can print only every third dot (not available with GRAFTRAX-80)

n1   = the remainder obtained when the number of graphics patterns is divided by 256

n2   = the number of graphics patterns divided by 256 (integer part)

That is,

<number of graphics patterns> = 256*n2 + n1

---

*IBM Graphics Printer or EPSON with GRATRAX PLUS.

For example, suppose that you wish to print 400 graphics patterns in medium-resolution mode. Divide 400 by 256. The quotient is 1 and the remainder is 144. That is,

$$400 = 256*1 + 144$$

Therefore, $n2 = 1$ and $n1 = 144$. The command that specifies 400 graphics patterns in medium-resolution mode is then given by the sequence of bytes

27, 75, 144, 1

As a second example, suppose that we wish to print the letter A, given as the sequence of 9 graphics patterns, as specified in the hexadecimal bytes

&H1E &H20 &H48 &H80 &H08 &H80 &H48 &H20 &H1E

Further, suppose that we wish to use low-speed, high-resolution mode. Since

$$9 = 0*256 + 9$$

we have $n1 = 9$ and $n2 = 0$. So we initiate the desired printing pattern with the sequence of bytes

27, 76, 9, 0

We follow these bytes with the bytes representing the 9 graphics patterns. Here is a program that prints the desired 9 graphics patterns.

```
10 LPRINT CHR$(27);CHR$(76);CHR$(9);CHR$(0);
20 LPRINT CHR$(&H1E);CHR$(&H20);CHR$(&H48);CHR$(&H80);
30 LPRINT CHR$(&H08);CHR$(&H80);CHR$(&H48);CHR$(&H20);
40 LPRINT CHR$(&H1E);
```

Note that we did not allow any carriage returns in any of the LPRINT statements. Furthermore, note that we specified the graphics patterns in hexadecimal rather than decimal. This is because it is easier to go from the actual dot pattern to hexadecimal. Translating the hexadecimal into decimal would provide room for errors. Finally, note that we sent each hexadecimal byte to the printer via a CHR$ statment. You might wonder why we don't just LPRINT the hexadecimal bytes directly, as in, say

```
LPRINT &H1E
```

This approach will not work, however, for it sends the printer the number &H1E. BASIC automatically translates this number into its decimal equivalent 31. BASIC then sends the printer the decimal digits "3" and "1", coded as ASCII codes. So what gets sent are the two bytes: &H33, &H31. And this is not the same thing as sending the hexadecimal byte &H1E.

The above program is extremely hard to read. A better approach is as follows:

```
10 INIT$= CHR$(27)+CHR$(76)+CHR$(9)+CHR$(0)
20 A$ = CHR$(&H1E)+CHR$(&H20)+CHR$(&H48)+CHR$(&H80)+CHR$
        (&H08)+CHR$(&H80)+CHR$(&H48)+CHR$(&H20)+CHR$(&H1E)
30 LPRINT INIT$;
50 LPRINT A$;
```

As a further example, let's draw a box, as in Figure 8.9.

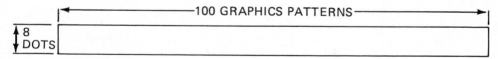

Figure 8.9.

The box is 100 graphics patterns wide in high resolution. The bottom of the box is drawn by print wire 0 and the top by print wire 7. We may draw this box out of two graphics patterns, one consisting of all 8 dots (for both ends) and a second consisting of only the top and bottom dot. The hexadecimal equivalents for these dots are, respectively, &HFF and &H81. (Check this!) So here is a program which draws the box.

```
10 INIT$=CHR$(27)+CHR$(76)+CHR$(100)+CHR$(0)
20 SIDE$=CHR$(&HFF)
30 MIDDLE$=CHR$(&H81)
40 LPRINT INIT$;
50 LPRINT SIDE$;
60 FOR J=1 TO 98
70    LPRINT MIDDLE$;
80 NEXT J
90 LPRINT SIDE$;
```

Note that you may mix ordinary text and graphics. For example, let's print the phrase "WRITE YOUR ANSWER IN THE BOX." immediately to the left of the box, and the phrase "STOP" immediately to the right. Here is what our printed line should look like (Figure 8.10).

WRITE YOUR ANSWER IN THE BOX ⌷━━━━━━━━━━━━━━━━━━━━━━━━⌷ STOP

Figure 8.10.

Here is the program to print this line.

```
10 LPRINT "WRITE YOUR ANSWER IN THE BOX.";
20 INIT$=CHR$(27)+CHR$(76)+CHR$(100)+CHR$(0)
30 SIDE$=CHR$(&HFF)
40 MIDDLE$=CHR$(&H81)
50 LPRINT INIT$;
60 LPRINT SIDE$;
70 FOR J=1 TO 98
```

```
80    LPRINT MIDDLE$;
90 NEXT J
100 LPRINT SIDE$;
110 LPRINT "STOP"
```

This program prints the desired line and does a carriage return to the next line. (There is no semicolon on line 110.)

Note that line 10 prints in ordinary text, lines 40-100 in high-resolution graphics mode. Line 110 returns to ordinary text. It is not necessary to give any special command to return to text mode. After the specified number of graphics patterns, the printer automatically reverts to ordinary text. Any special print modes (emphasized, subscript, compressed, etc.) in effect before entry into graphics mode remain in effect on return to text mode.

If you print two consecutive lines of graphics with default line spacing (1/8 inch), you will notice that there is a small blank area between them. You may eliminate this space, thereby making a continuous graphics pattern. The secret is to use 8/72 inch spacing. (This corresponds to 9 lines to the inch as opposed to the default 8 lines per inch.) You may set this spacing using the command

```
LPRINT CHR$(27);CHR$(65);CHR$(8);CHR$(27);CHR$(50);
```
                          (IBM Graphics Printer)
```
LPRINT CHR$(27);CHR$(65);CHR$(8);
```
                          (Others)

You may print as many consecutive graphics lines as you wish. However, if you then wish to return to printing text, remember to reset the vertical line spacing.

Exercises

1.   Write a program to print the following symbol.

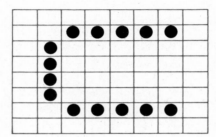

2.   Write a program to print the following line.

                THIS IS A TEST   ⬜ ⬜ ⬜

3. Write a program to draw a box 500 dots long and 80 dots high in high-resolution graphics mode.

ANSWERS TO TEST YOUR UNDERSTANDING

1: (a)   &H11 (b) &H0F (c) &HFA

2:

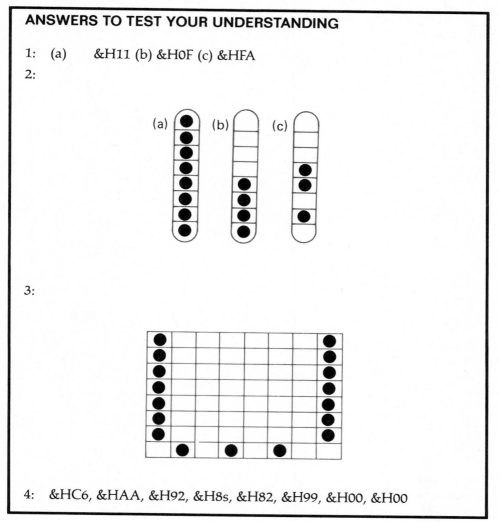

3:

4: &HC6, &HAA, &H92, &H8s, &H82, &H99, &H00, &H00

8.4   A Graphics Screen Dump

Let's use what we have learned in order to write a program that prints the contents of the screen in either medium- or high-resolution graphics mode. Our program is designed as a subroutine to be called within another program. Once you have the desired image on the screen, just call this subroutine and it will print the contents of the screen, pixel by pixel.

To start, let's assume that we are dealing with an image in high-resolution graphics mode. The image is then 640 pixels wide and 200 pixels high. We don't wish to impose any restrictions on printing of adjacent dots, so we are stuck with printing in medium-resolution graphics mode. Of course, this allows us only 480 dots across a line, not enough to print a line of the screen. The solution to this dilemma is to print the screen sideways. The lower left corner of the screen will be printed at the upper left side of the paper. The upper left corner of the screen will correspond to the upper right corner of the paper. (See Figure 8.11.)

Figure 8.11.

Our basic idea is to use the GET statement to read pixels of the screen, from bottom to top, in columns 8 pixels wide. (See Figure 8.12.)

Each GET statement will yield a single byte, one bit for each of the 8 pixels. This byte will be sent to the printer and printed as a graphics pattern. Each row of graphics patterns on the printer will correspond to a single column of 8 pixels. Since the screen is 640 pixels wide, we will need to break the screen into 80 columns.

At 1/9 inch per column, the screen will print as 80/9 = 8.9 inches down the page. On the other hand, the width of the printed image is 200 dots, or 200/60 = 3.3 inches. As you can see, the perspective is quite distorted. The image is almost three times as long as it is high. To make up for this deficiency, let's print each graphics pattern twice. This will expand the printed

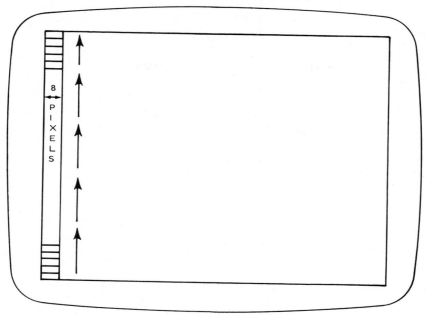

Figure 8.12.

image across the page to 400 dot = 400/60 = 6.7 inches. This is close to the usual 4-to-3 ratio between the horizontal and vertical measurements of the screen.

To center the image vertically on the page, we begin with one inch of space at the top of the page. Since the image will be approximately 8.9 inches down the page, this leaves about a one-inch space at the bottom, which centers the image. Across each printed line, we are using 6.67 inches. To center the image, we must have a space of approximately .9 inches on each side of a line. Since there are 10 characters to the inch, we leave a 9-character space at the beginning of the line.

One last problem before we write our program. BASIC automatically inserts carriage returns at the end of every line. In fact, unless you tell it otherwise, it will assume that a line has ended after 80 characters and will then send a carriage return-line feed sequence. In our graphics screen dump, we will be sending several hundred "characters" per line. (As far as BASIC is concerned, each byte sent is a "character.") We must somehow disable this automatic feature. This may be done using the WIDTH instruction. The statement

```
WIDTH "LPT1:",255
```

tells BASIC to assume an infinite line width for the printer. This statement disables the automatic carriage return-line feed.

After all these considerable preliminaries, here is our screen dump program.

```
1000 'GRAPHICS FILE PRINT SUBROUTINE:IBM GRAPHICS PRINTER
1010 'Initialization
1020 DIM Z%(2)
1030 WIDTH "LPT1:",255
1040 'Print Screen
1050 LINESPACE9$=CHR$(27)+CHR$(65)+CHR$(8)+CHR$(27)+CHR$(50)
1060 LINESPACE6$=CHR$(27)+CHR$(65)+CHR$(12)+CHR$(27)+CHR$(50)
1070 GRAPH400$=CHR$(27)+CHR$(75)+CHR$(144)+CHR$(1)
1080 LPRINT LINESPACE9$;
1090 FOR J%=1 TO 9
1100      LPRINT
1110 NEXT J%
1120 FOR COL%=0 TO 79
1130      LPRINT SPACE$(9);
1140      LPRINT GRAPH400$;
1150      FOR ROW%=199 TO 0 STEP -1
1160           GET (8*COL%+7,ROW%)-(8*COL%,ROW%),Z%
1170           LPRINT CHR$(Z%(2))+CHR$(Z%(2));
1180      NEXT ROW%
1190      LPRINT
1200 NEXT COL%
1210 FOR J%=1 TO 10
1220      LPRINT
1230 NEXT J%
1240 LPRINT LINESPACE6$;
1250 RETURN
```

We have explained the reason behind most of the program already. However, lines 1130 and 1140 deserve some comment. The pixels corresponding to (COL%+7,ROW%)-(COL%,ROW%) go across the column COL% at row ROW%, proceeding from right to left. These pixels are stored in the array Z%. Recall the manner in which GET stores this information. Z%(0) contains the width of the rectangle being stored, in this case 8; Z%(1) contains the height of the rectangle being stored, namely 1; Z%(2) contains the first 8 pixels of the first row of the rectangle. In this case, the entire rectangle has only 8 pixels. So Z%(2) contains precisely the information we want. And the information is stored with the most significant bit corresponding to the rightmost pixel. (The order of storage is guaranteed by the order in which we have stated the endpoints of the rectangle in line 1130.)

A few further comments.

1. The above program is written for the IBM Graphics printer. To use the program on the EPSON printers, replace lines 1050-1060 with

    ```
    1050 LINESPACE9$=CHR$(27)+CHR$(65)+CHR$(8)
    1060 LINESPACE6$=CHR$(27)+CHR$(65)+CHR$(12)
    ```

2. The above program is written to be used in high-resolution graphics mode (SCREEN 2). We leave the modifications necessary to print the screen in medium-resolution graphics mode for the exercises.

Exercises

1. Type in the screen print program and use it to print a graphics image in high-resolution graphics mode.
2. Modify the screen print program for use with medium-resolution graphics mode. (Recall that in this mode GET returns 2 bits for each pixel instead of one.)

8.5 Back to Our Case Study

Our screen dump routine is a useful addition to the BAR CHART GENERATOR. Using the screen dump, we can print out copies of our bar charts on the IBM/EPSON printer.

We leave it to you to carry out the modifications of the BAR CHART GENERATOR. Why not integrate the screen dump using, say, lines 8000 on. Let the user activate the screen dump using function key F8. It will be necessary to modify your error trapping routine to allow for errors caused by printer use (Printer Not Ready, Device Timeout, etc.).

Debugging an addition to an existing program should train you in the possible hazards of adding code to a working program. Try it. I promise it will be an educational experience!

9

Computer Communications

9.1 Fundamentals of Computer Communications

At some point you will almost certainly want to make use of computer communications. Here are some typical applications that use communications.

1. Connecting two IBM PCs to one another, either via a direct cable or through a modem.

2. Connecting an IBM PC to another computer (microcomputer or mainframe), either via a direct cable or through a modem. In this case, you may wish the PC to temporarily serve as a terminal to the other computer, or you may wish to send or receive files.

3. Connecting a PC to another device such as a plotter.

4. Connecting a PC to a printer with a serial interface.

5. Using an external data base, such as The Source or The Dow Jones News Service.

To carry out communications of the above sort, your PC must be equipped with an **asynchronous communications adapter**, also known as an **RS-232C interface**. The asynchronous communications adapter is a board that fits into one of the expansion slots in the system unit of your PC. It is equipped with a 25-pin connector visible on the rear panel of your system unit. You may have one or two asynchronous communications adapters, allowing you to simultaneously connect your PC to several devices. The communications adapters have device names "COM1:" and "COM2:".

In order to communicate with a device, you must first cable the device to the 25-pin connector of your communications interface. (See Figure 9.1.)

WARNING Your cable must be specifically wired to connect the PC to your particular device. Just because a cable has the correct connectors at each end, don't assume that you can use it to establish communications to a particular device. If you have any questions about the suitability of a particular cable, consult your local computer dealer.

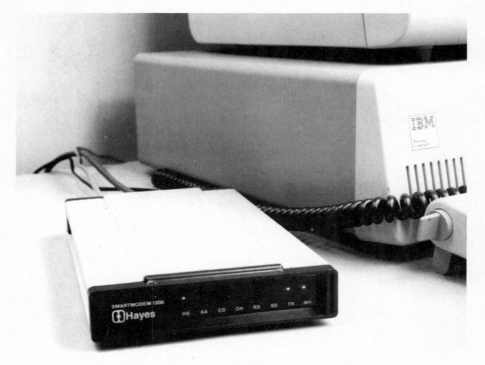

Figure 9.1. A Modem Connected to the PC.

An Elementary Example

As a first illustration of communications, let's suppose that you wish to connect two PCs so that they can exchange files. Each PC must be equipped with a communications interface. The cable connecting them assumes a simple form: It must connect each pin on one connector with the corresponding pin on the other, with the following exception. Pin 2 on connector A must connect to pin 3 on connector B and pin 3 on connector A must be connected to pin 2 on connector B (See Figure 9.2). The reason for this interchange is quite simple. The RS232-C wires 2 and 3 are send and receive, respectively. However, one computer's send wire must be connected to the other computer's receive wire.

Suppose that we wish to transmit a file TEST from computer S (= Send) to computer R (= Receive). Suppose that TEST is contained on the diskette in drive B: and you wish the received copy to go to the diskette in drive A:. This may be accomplished simply using the COPY command. Here's how.

1. Turn on computer R (the receiving computer) and obtain the DOS prompt.

2. Type

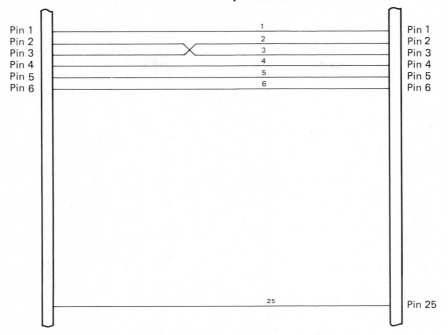

Figure 9.2. Cable for PC-PC Communications.

```
COPY COM1: A:TEST <ENTER>
```

This tells the PC to copy data from the communications adapter COM1: and put the data into the file TEST: (If you get an error message when you type the command, push CTRL-Break and retype.)

3. Turn on computer S (the transmitting computer) and obtain the DOS prompt.

4. Type

```
COPY B:TEST COM1: <ENTER>
```

Notice the light on drive B: of computer S. It lights for a few seconds as the file is copied and sent through the communications interface COM1:. On the receiving end, you will notice nothing for a few seconds. Then the drive light on A: will light. This indicates that a portion of the file is being written on A:. If the file is long, it may be transferred in several parts. In this case, the drive light on A: will go on and off several times. Eventually the following message will appear on the screen:

1 File(s) copied.

The file TEST is now on the diskette in drive A:. Check that it is by asking for the directory of drive A:. Check that TEST is in the directory and that it has the same number of bytes as the file sent.

This elementary example shows, on the one hand, how simple communications can be. On the other, it conceals a good deal of what is going on, since DOS automatically takes care of most of the details. Here are some of these details.

Baud Rate

In order for two devices to communicate with one another, they must "talk" at the same speed. The speed of communications is measured in units called **baud**. This is a term left over from the days of teletype communications. The communications speed is called the **baud rate**. Here are the possible baud rates:

75

110

150

300

600

1200

1800

2400

4800

9600

To translate these rates into more familiar terms, just divide by 10. This will give the approximate speed of transmission in characters per second. For example, 110 baud, which corresponds to a teletype, equals a transmission speed of approximately 11 characters per second. The default baud rate of DOS is 2400, or approximately 240 characters per second. In most communications, transmitting a single character (represented by either 7 or 8 bits) requires addition of several additional bits (parity and stop bits—see below) to bring the total number of bits to 10. So each character requires that 10 bits be transmitted.

Parity

As a means of ensuring that data is transmitted accurately, you may specify a **parity bit** to be attached to each word of data. There are a number of different parity conventions (See below). However, the sender and receiver must agree beforehand on the particular one used. The parity bit is transmitted in a standard position relative to a word and is checked by the receiver. If the parity bit is not what is expected, then a **parity error** is generated at the receiver. Here are the various types of parity:

S = Space   : The parity bit is 0.

O = Odd   : The parity bit is set so that the sum of it and all the bits in the data word add up to an odd number. For example, if the data word is 1011011 and the parity is odd, then the parity bit is set to 0. (There are five 1's in the data word.)

M = Mark   : The parity bit is 1.

E = Even   : The parity bit is set so that the sum of it and all the bits in the data word add up to an even number. For example, if the data word is 1011011 and the parity is even, then the parity bit is set to 1. (There are 5 1's in the data word.)

N = None   : No parity bit is transmitted.

The default parity setting is E = Even.

Data

The data bits may be transmitted in groups (or **words**) of 4, 5, 6, 7 or 8 bits. In most cases, you will be using 7- or 8-bit bytes. The seven-bit option allows you to transmit ASCII codes 0-127, since the seven bits transmitted are the seven least significant bits. This allows you to transmit all of the standard printable characters, both upper and lower case. However, it will not allow you to transmit the contents of the high-order bit, which is used by many word processors to distinguish soft spaces from hard spaces and soft hyphens from hard hyphens. If you wish to preserve the information in the high-order bit, you must transmit all 8 bits.

If you specify a seven-bit code, then the high-order bit is used for the parity bit, if requested. However, if you specify an eight-bit code, then no parity bit is allowed.

Stop Bits

The stop bits are transmitted both before and after the data (and parity, if any). There may be 1 or 2 stop bits. A seven- or eight-bit code usually uses 1 stop bit.

Assembling all of the above information, we have assembled in Figures 9.3 and 9.4 the typical bit transmission for 7- and 8-bit data.

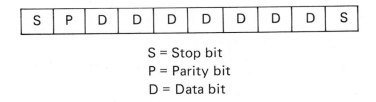

S = Stop bit
P = Parity bit
D = Data bit

Figure 9.3. Typical Bit Transmission for 7-bit Data.

9.2 Communications Files

In this section, we will describe the BASIC instructions you may use to effect communications.

S	D	D	D	D	D	D	D	D	S

S = Stop bit
D = Data bit

Figure 9.4. Typical Bit Transmission for 8-bit Data.

BASIC carries out communications using so-called **communications files**. These files function very much like the diskette data files we have already learned to use. Even the names of the statements and functions used with communications files are the same as those used with diskette files: OPEN, CLOSE, INPUT #, WRITE #, LOF, LOC, EOF, and so forth. Of course, the meanings of these statements in the case of communications files are somewhat different than for diskette files. However, in so far as possible, the operation of communications files is designed to suggest the close analogy with diskette files.

Here, then, is how to conduct communications in BASIC:

1. OPEN the communications adapter (COM1: or COM2:) as a communications file. The OPEN statement for a communications file accomplishes three things:

    a. It assigns a reference number to the file, just as with a diskette file. Subsequent commands may refer to the communications file by its reference number.

    b. OPEN assigns all the relevant communications parameters (baud rate, parity, number of stop bits, number of data bits).

    c. OPEN sets up an area of memory that acts as temporary storage for the communications file. This temporary storage is called a **buffer**.

2A. To send data to the communications interface, you write to the communications file. This is done using any of the usual file write instructions:

```
WRITE #
PRINT #
PUT #
```

These instructions move data to the buffer.

2B. To receive data from the communications interface, you read from the communications file. This is done using any of the usual file read instructions:

```
INPUT #
INPUT $
LINE INPUT #
GET #
```

These instructions move data from the buffer.

3. BASIC automatically monitors the status of the communiciations inter-
    face. When it is time to send a character, BASIC reads the buffer,
    determines the next character to be sent (if any), and passes it to the
    communications interface. Similarly, when the communications inter-
    face receives a character, BASIC automatically accepts the character
    and places it in the buffer.

4. BASIC contains commands to determine the status of the buffer:

    Is the buffer empty?
    How many characters are waiting in the buffer?
    How many bytes of the buffer are currently unused?

By determining the answers to these questions, the program may determine
when to perform the next read or write operation.

Let's now get down to details.

Communication File Buffers

The default communications receive file buffer size is 256 bytes. You may
change this number using the /C: option when you start BASIC (or BASICA).
For example, to make all communications receive file buffers 1024 bytes, you
would start BASIC from DOS with the command

```
BASIC /C:1024
```

BASIC automatically sets aside a file buffer for each communications adapter
in your system. If a program does not use any communications files, you
may increase the amount of available memory by starting BASIC with the
command

```
BASIC /C:0
```

This adds 256 bytes of working memory for each communications adapter
present.

OPENing a Communications File

The OPEN instruction opens a communications file associated with a particular communications adapter COM1: or COM2:. There are a large
number of options that allow you to match your communications to a wide
spectrum of devices. The format of this command is

```
OPEN "COMn:<parameters>" AS <filenumber> [LEN=<length>]
```

Here is the meaning of the various notation:

1. n is the number of the communications adapter (=1 or 2).

2. <filenumber> is the reference number by which you may refer to
    the file in subsequent write and read operations.

3. <length> is the maximum number of bytes that may be written to or read from the file by a single GET or PUT statement. LEN is optional. If it is omitted, then the default is 128 bytes.

4. The various communications <parameters> are described below, but if you wish to use default values for these parameters, then they need not be specified at all.

The format of <parameters> is as follows:

<baud rate,parity,data length,stop bits>

You may omit any of these options. However, it is necessary to insert commas as place holders for omitted parameters. If you omit an option, the default value is substituted. (See below.)

Here are the communications parameters you may specify:

a. baud rate—The acceptable baud rates are 75, 110, 150, 300, 600, 1200, 1800, 2400, 4800, and 9600. The default value is 300. (Be careful. The default in DOS is 2400. However, BASIC's default value is 300.)

b. parity—The valid values for the parity are:
    S = space
    O = odd
    M = mark
    E = even
    N = none
    The default value is E for even parity.

c. data length—The number of bits in each data group can be 4, 5, 6, 7, or 8. The default value is 7.

d. stop bits—The number of bits before and after each data group. Possible values are 1 or 2. The default value is 2 for 75 and 110 baud, 1 for all other baud rates. (A 4 or 5 for data length is an old-fashioned code. It automatically is given three stop bits between groups of data bits.)

For example, consider the statement

```
OPEN "COM1:" AS #1
```

It causes BASIC to set up a communications file corresponding to the communications adapter COM1:. The reference number is #1 and all other parameters assume their default values: baud rate = 300, parity = E, data length = 7, stop bits = 2, GET and PUT size = 128 bytes. The seven bit data length allows us to send ASCII codes 0 through 127. The most significant bit becomes the parity bit. The actual number of bits transmitted with each 7 bits of data is

1 stop bit + 7 data bits + 1 parity bit + 1 stop bit = 10 bits

As a second example, consider the statement

```
OPEN "COM1:2400,N,8,1" AS #1 LEN=256
```

In this case, we OPEN a communications file for COM1: with speed = 2400 baud, no parity, 8-bit data length, 1 stop bit, and buffer size 256 bytes. (Note: If you chose a data length of 8 bits, you must set the parity to N, no parity.) The actual number of bits transmitted with each 7 bits of data is

1 stop bit + 8 data bits + 1 stop bit = 10 bits

TEST YOUR UNDERSTANDING 1

Write a statement that opens communication file #1 at 9600 baud, with the rest of the communications parameters at their default settings.

Writing to a Communications File

You write to a communications file using the same statements as you use to write to a diskette file, namely:

```
WRITE #
PRINT #
PRINT # USING
PUT #
```

When used in connection with a communications file, each of these statements transfers data to the file buffer. The first three statements work exactly as they do in connection with diskette files. In particular, all delimiters are sent to the buffer, exactly as if the statments were being used to write a sequential diskette file. For example, here is a statement that sends the string A$ to the communications file buffer.

```
PRINT #1, A$;
```

The semicolon suppresses the carriage return that PRINT usually sends. Here is a statement that sends A$ and B$, delimited by quotation marks, with a comma between the two strings. After B$, BASIC supplies a carriage return-line feed.

```
WRITE #1 A$,B$
```

Use of PUT to Write to a Communications File

In communications, PUT is used similarly to the way it is used with diskette files:

First use a FIELD statement to define buffer variables and associated lengths. Use LSET and RSET to place data in the file buffer. Next, use a PUT statement of the form

```
PUT #<file number>, <number of characters>
```

to transmit data from the file buffer to the communications file. Here <number of characters> is the total number of characters to be transmitted (usually equal to the number of characters defined by the FIELD statement.) Characters are transmitted from the beginning of the first field statement, in the order specified, until the required number of characters is sent.

The PUT statement may be used to send data in blocks each consisting of a certain number of characters arranged in a certain format (in fields).

Reading From a Communications File

You may read from a communications file using the statements

```
INPUT #
LINE INPUT #
INPUT$
```

The first two of these statements work exactly like their counterparts for diskette files: The INPUT # statement reads the next characters from the buffer up to the first comma or carriage return. The comma or carriage return is ignored. The LINE INPUT # statement reads the next characters from the buffer up to the first carriage return. The carriage return is ignored.

In communications files, it is usually necessary to read all incoming characters, including commas and carriage returns. To accomplish this, we use the INPUT$ function, which has the form

```
INPUT$(<number of characters>,<file number>)
```

For example, the statement

```
A$=INPUT$(10,1)
```

reads 10 characters from file number 1 and assigns A$ the corresponding string. The INPUT$ statement reads all characters, including control characters. For example, suppose that the communications file buffer contains the following 34 characters (including the carriage return):

John, come home. ALL IS FORGIVEN!<carriage return>

Here is a program that reads the file buffer with file number 1, and displays the data on the screen.

```
10 A$=INPUT(34,1)
20 PRINT A$;
```

Note that we used a semicolon to suppress the automatic carriage return in the PRINT statement in line 20. Actually, the data will be displayed on the screen and will be followed by a carriage return. However, the carriage return comes from the last character of the data. Without the semicolon, the PRINT statement would add a second carriage return.

Monitoring The Status of the Buffer

In the program above, we used INPUT$ to read 34 characters of the communications file buffer. This program assumes that, somehow, we know that the buffer contains 34 characters. This information and more can be determined using the three buffer status functions LOC, LOF, and EOF.

The function LOC returns the number of unread characters in the buffer. The format of this function is

LOC(file number)

So, for example, here is a program that reads all characters in the file buffer. If there are no characters currently in the buffer, the program waits for characters to arrive. As characters are read, they are displayed on the screen.

```
10 IF LOC(1) = 0 THEN 10
20 A$=INPUT$(1,1)
30 PRINT A$;
40 GOTO 10
```

The function LOF returns the number of free bytes remaining in the buffer. For example, here is a program that copies a diskette file named "TEST" to a communications file. We open "TEST" as a random access file with record length 128. We use the LOF function to determine if the buffer contains at least 128 bytes of space. If so, we write the next record to the communications file using the PUT command.

```
10 OPEN "TEST" AS #1 LEN=128
20 OPEN "COM1:" AS #2 LEN=128
30 FIELD #1, 128 AS A$
40 FIELD #2, 128 AS B$
50 WHILE NOT EOF(1)
60    IF LOF(2) < 128 THEN 90
70    GET #1
80    LSET B$=A$
90    PUT #2
100 WEND
```

The function EOF returns a true (actually, value = −1) if the communications file buffer is empty and a false (value = 0) otherwise. Here is a program that monitors the status of the communications file buffer. As soon as there are characters to read the program jumps to a subroutine beginning at line 1000. This subroutine reads the character and displays it on the screen.

```
10    IF NOT EOF(1) THEN GOSUB 1000
20    GOTO 10
1000 'Read and display character
1010 A$=INPUT$(1,1)
1020 PRINT A$;
1030 RETURN
```

The statement **CLOSE** may be used to close a communications file. After CLOSE, the corresponding file number is no longer active and any input or output statements to the file number will generate a **Bad File Number** error. Subsequent to a close, the communications file may be reopened, possibly using different parameters and possibly with a different file number.

Communications Protocols

As data is received by the asynchronous communications adapter, it is deposited in the corresponding file buffer. However, the buffer has only a certain limited capacity. If the capacity of the buffer is exceeded, then some of the data will be lost. At baud rates 1200 and above, the characters may arrive more rapidly than the computer can process them. To prevent buffer overflow and consequent loss of data, you must use a **communications protocol**. Simply put, a communications protocol is a set of signals the receiver sends in order to tell the sender when to pause and when to resume transmissions.

There are many common communications protocols. In fact, it is not hard to make up your own. The important feature of a protocol is that it be recognized by both the sender and the receiver. Therefore, if you are communicating with a friend via modem, then the two of you must agree on the pause and resume signals. In many applications, however, you will be exchanging data with a source over which you have no control (say a mainframe computer). In this case, it will be necessary for you to match the protocol dictated by the source.

In this brief introduction, we cannot describe the various common protocols. However, to show you how a protocol works, let's describe just one, the so-called **XON-XOFF** protocol.

XON is a name for the control character with ASCII code 17 and XOFF is a name for the control character with ASCII code 19. When the receiver wishes a pause in transmission, he sends XOFF. When he wishes transmission to resume, he sends XON. A typical place for a pause is when the file buffer is half full. (Assuming the default buffer size, this occurs when the buffer has more than 128 characters waiting to be read.) The following instructions implement this scheme

```
10 IF EOF(1) THEN 10:'Wait for input
20 IF LOC(1) > 128 THEN GOSUB 100: 'Send XOFF
30 WHILE LOC(1) > 0
40    A$ = INPUT$(1,1):'Input character
50    PRINT A$;:'Display character
60    IF LOC(1) < 128 AND PAUSE=1 THEN GOSUB 200
70 WEND
100 'Send XOFF
110 PAUSE=1
120 PRINT #1, CHR$(19);
130 RETURN
```

```
200 'Send XON
210 PAUSE=0
220 PRINT #1, CHR$(17);
230 RETURN
```

Many communications schemes allow for two-way communications. The simplest model for such a scheme is for two computer operators to communicate with one another via messages typed on the PC keyboard and transmitted via the communications adapter. Let's allow only one party to speak at a time. Correspondingly, we define the variable TRANSMIT:

TRANSMIT = 1 if receiving data
= 0 if transmitting data

The sender indicates the end of his message and his switch to receiving status by sending the control code ESC (= ASC 27). The sender may end the conversation by sending EOT (=End of Transmission = ASCII 4). ASCII code 3 may be generated from the keyboard with the key combination CTRL-C; ASCII code 4 by the key combination CTRL-D.

The transmitter must constantly listen for XOFF to pause transmission. Once transmission is paused, the transmitter must listen for XON before resuming transmission.

The conversation scheme just described is similar to that employed in CB radio. Only one party speaks at a time. When a party is done speaking, he says "OVER." To sign off, he says "TEN-FOUR." ESC is our analogue of OVER and EOT our analogue of TEN-FOUR. This form of conversation is called **half-duplex**.

Here is a program for half-duplex conversation.

```
10 ON ERROR GOTO 600
20 CLOSE
30 OPEN "com1:2400,n,8" AS £1
40 CLS:KEY OFF:WIDTH 80
50 PRINT "OPTIONS"
60 PRINT
70 PRINT "1.RECEIVE"
80 PRINT "2.SEND"
90 PRINT
100 INPUT "CHOOSE OPTION (1/2)"; STATUS
110 ON STATUS GOSUB 200, 400
120 GOTO 110
200 'receive
210 PRINT "RECEIVING"
220 IF EOF(1) THEN 220
```

```
230 IF PAUSE=0 THEN 260
240 IF PAUSE=1 THEN 250 ELSE 260
250 IF LOC(1)<=128 AND PAUSE=1 THEN PAUSE=0:
                    PRINT #1, CHR$(17);:GOTO 280
260 IF LOC(1)>128 AND PAUSE = 1 THEN 280
270 IF LOC(1)>128 AND PAUSE=0 THEN
                    PRINT #1, CHR$(19);:PAUSE=1
280 A$=INPUT$(1,1)
290 IF A$=CHR$(4) THEN
                    STATUS=3-STATUS:GOTO 330
300 IF A$=CHR$(3) THEN END
310 PRINT A$;
320 GOTO 220
330 RETURN
400 'send
410 PRINT "SENDING"
420 A$=INKEY$
430 IF A$="" THEN 420
440 IF PAUSE=1 THEN
                    BEEP:GOTO 420
450 PRINT #1,A$;
460 PRINT A$;
470 IF A$=CHR$(4) THEN
                    STATUS=3-STATUS:GOTO 500
480 IF A$=CHR$(3) THEN
                    PRINT #1,A$:END
490 GOTO 420
500 RETURN
600 'Error trapping
610 X=ERL
620 RESUME X
```

Note the error trapping in lines 600-620. If one of the two conversing computers is not yet ready (for instance it might not be turned on yet), the other computer will generate a Device Timeout error when it attempts to establish communications. The purpose of the error trapping lines is to force the computer to keep trying to set up communications.

Note also that the above program incorporates a communications protocol. It is unlikely that this will be needed since it is unlikely that keyboard input could ever be fast enough to overflow the buffer. However, the protocol will definitely be necessary for the variation of the program suggested in Exercise 1 below.

Exercise

1. Modify the above half-duplex communications program so that it allows transfer of a diskette file from one computer to the other. Your program should begin with a transfer of the filename between the two computers. ASCII code 4 (EOT) should cause the receiver to close the file and ask whether another file is to be transmitted.

9.3   Trapping Communications

Communications may be only a portion of your program. Suppose that you don't wish to wait around for data to arrive in you communications file buffer. Rather, during the waiting period, you wish to perform some other task. This situation is ready made for communications trapping, as provided by the ON COM statement.

The ON COM statement is similar to the other event trapping statements in PC BASIC, namely ON KEY, ON PEN, and ON STRIG. (See the next chapter for ON PEN and ON STRIG.) Its format is:

```
ON COM(n) GOSUB line
```

When data begins to enter the communications buffer for communications adapter n, the program executes a GOSUB to the indicated line. Presumably, the subroutine contains instructions to read the buffer and, possibly, to process the input.

The ON COM instruction may be inserted anywhere in the program prior to the desired beginning of communications trapping. The ON COM instruction does not, by itself, turn on the actual trapping. This is done by the COM(n) ON statement. So, for example, here is a program that watches for input to communications adapter 1. After line 20 is executed, any communications input to adapter 1 will cause a jump to line 1000.

```
10 ON COM(1) GOSUB 1000
20 COM(1) ON
  .
  .
  .
1000 'Communications input processing routine
  .
  .
  .
1300 RETURN
```

You may turn off communications trapping for part of your program. There are two instructions for this purpose:

COM(n) OFF

This instruction turns off communications trapping for adapter n in an absolute fashion. While COM(n) OFF is in effect, no communications trapping takes place. You may reinstate communications trapping at any point in the program by using the COM(n) ON statement. The computer will not remember any communications activity that occurred while COM(n) OFF was in effect. However, the communications buffer will contain any information that arrived during that time period (assuming that buffer overflow did not occur).

Even if communications trapping is turned off, you may still read the communications buffer as if trapping were not present in the program.

COM(n) STOP

This instruction turns off communications trapping for adapter n, but remembers if any communications take place. When a subsequent COM(n) ON instruction is given, the program will immediately execute a trap to the communications trapping subroutine if any communication took place while trapping was stopped.

When your program traps to a communications subroutine, BASIC executes a COM(n) STOP routine. That is, the communications subroutine cannot be interrupted by a trap to itself. (You can see where this would lead to problems in program organization!) The same is true for any other kind of trapping (KEY, PEN, and STRIG, as well as ERROR). After trapping to a communications subroutine, BASIC automatically turns trapping back on before returning to the main program. You may turn off this automatic trap enabling if you execute a COM(n) OFF within the trapping routine.

Exercises

Explain the action of the following instructions.

1. COM(2) ON
2. COM(1) OFF
3. ON COM(2) GOSUB 100
4. COM(1) STOP

Consider the following program:

```
10 ON COM(1) GOSUB 1000
20 COM(1) ON
30 FOR J=1 TO 10
40 PRINT J
```

```
 50 NEXT J
 60 COM(1) OFF
 70 FOR J=1 TO 10
 80 PRINT J^2
 90 NEXT J
100 COM(1) ON
110 GOTO 30
1000 'Communications subroutine
   .
   .
   .
1200 RETURN
```

5. Explain what would happen if communications activity occurred in adapter 1 while line 30 was being executed. Line 80. Line 1030.

10

Using Your PC with Other Devices

In this chapter, we will discuss the use of certain optional devices on your PC, namely:

light pens

joy sticks

plotters

This list certainly is not comprehensive. The PC has heated creative juices to the boiling point and has sparked an incredible number of add-on devices from many independent (non-IBM) manufacturers. And more such devices are being introduced all the time. This chapter is designed to give you a brief look at how a few of these devices may be used.

10.1   Using a Light Pen

A light pen is a marvelous device that allows you to input information to the computer without using the keyboard. A light pen is a rod-shaped device connected to the PC via a cable attached to a connector mounted on the rear of your system unit and, in turn connected to the color/graphics adapter. (In particular, you cannot use a light pen if you do not have the color/graphics adapter.)

You use the light pen to point to a screen position, either in text or graphics mode. To identify a particular point P, point the light pen at P, just above the surface of the screen. Most light pens have an adjustment that controls how close you must hold the light pen in order to get a reading. (See Fig. 1)

A program may read the coordinates of the point P at any given moment. In addition, you may "mark" a point for later reading by the light pen. This is done by pushing the button on the light pen and is called **activating the light pen**. If BASIC is in a graphics mode, then the light pen coordinates may be given either as graphics coordinates (x,y) or as a character position (row,column). In text mode, light pen coordinates may be given only as a character position.

Of course, at certain moments, you may not be able to read the position of the light pen: it may be too far from the surface of the screen or it may be

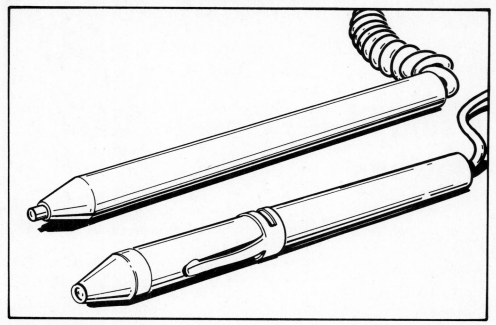

Figure 10.1. Light Pens.

pointed at a position off the screen. In such cases, the light pen remembers the coordinates of the last legal position it pointed to.

BASIC reads the light pen coordinates using the function PEN(n), where n is an integer in the range 0 through 9. The format of this function is

```
<numeric variable> = PEN(n)
```

Here <numeric variable> is set equal to the value of PEN(n). A reading of light pen coordinates via PEN(n) is called a **poll** of the light pen.

Here are the values of PEN(n) corresponding to the various values of n:

Flags

n=0: Returns TRUE (-1) if the pen was activated since the last poll, 0 otherwise.

n=3: Returns TRUE (-1) if the pen is currently activated, 0 otherwise.

Graphics Coordinates

(Valid only in medium- or high-resolution graphics modes.)

n=1,2: Return the x and y coordinates, respectively, where the pen was last activated.

n=4,5: Return the x and y coordinates, respectively, of the last valid point pointed to by the light pen.

Character Position

(Valid in either graphics mode or text mode.)

n = 6,7: Return the row and column, respectively, where the pen was last activated.

n = 8,9: Return the row and column, respectively, of the last valid character position pointed to by the light pen.

You may also use PEN(n) as a variable in statements such as

```
100 IF PEN(6) < 100 THEN GOSUB 800
200 WHILE PEN(8) > 50 AND PEN(8) < 100
```

Controlling the Light Pen

In order to use the light pen, you must first execute the statement

```
PEN ON
```

This enables BASIC to use PEN(n). To turn off the light pen, use the statement

```
PEN OFF
```

An Application

In the following program, we use the light pen to choose the background and foreground colors for text mode. The program begins by displaying small blocks (CHR$(219)) in all the possible background colors. The program then waits for the light pen to be activated. It reads the character position of the pen and interprets the position to determine the background color selected. If the position is not the location of one of the color samples, then the light pen reading is rejected and the program requests the background color again. The program then repeats the process for the foreground (text) color.

```
100 DIM A$(16)
110 CLS:KEY OFF: SCREEN 0,1:WIDTH 40
120 DATA black,blue,green,cyan,red,magenta,brown,white
130 DATA gray, light blue, light green, light cyan, light
         red, light magenta
140 DATA yellow, high int. white
150 FOR J=0 TO 15
160      READ A$(J)
170 NEXT J
```

```
180 PRINT TAB(10) "COLOR SELECTION GUIDE"
190 FOR J=0 TO 7
200     LOCATE 2*J+3,1
210     COLOR J
220     PRINT CHR$(219);
230     COLOR 7
240     PRINT TAB(5) A$(J);
250     NEXT J
260 FOR J=8 TO 15
270     LOCATE 2*(J-8)+3,20
280     COLOR J
290     PRINT CHR$(219);
300     COLOR 7
310     PRINT TAB(25) A$(J);
320 NEXT J
330 COLOR 7
340 LOCATE 20,1
350 PRINT "CHOOSE FOREGROUND COLOR"
360 GOSUB 1000
370 PRINT "FOREGROUND COLOR IS ";A$(C)
380 FORE=C
390 PRINT "CHOOSE BACKGROUND COLOR"
400 GOSUB 1000
410 PRINT "BACKGROUND COLOR IS ";A$(C)
420 BACK=C
430 COLOR FORE,BACK
440 END
1000 'select color
1010 PEN ON
1020 X = PEN(0)
1030 IF X=0 THEN 1020
1040 ROW = PEN(6)
1050 COLUMN = PEN(7)
1060 IF COLUMN <> 1 AND COLUMN <> 20 THEN 1020
1070 IF COLUMN=1 THEN C= ROW-3
1080 IF COLUMN=20 THEN C= ROW+5
1090 RETURN
```

Trapping Light Pen Activity

You may trap light pen activity in the same way that you trap function key activity. That is, when you request light pen trapping, BASIC checks after every statement to determine if the light pen was activated. If so, BASIC jumps to an indicated subroutine. Light pen trapping is defined by the statement

```
ON PEN GOSUB <line>
```

This statement merely defines the line number to jump to in case of light pen activity. However, in order for the jump to take place, you must execute a statement

```
 PEN ON
```

As with function key trapping, there are two ways to stop trapping. The statement

```
 PEN STOP
```

causes BASIC to cease trapping light pen activity. This statement remains in effect until canceled by a PEN ON statement. However, BASIC will remember any light pen activity while the PEN STOP is in effect. As soon as trapping is turned back on, BASIC will jump to the indicated line number before executing any other statements if pen activity occurred while trapping was STOPped.

The second method of stopping light pen trapping is to use the statement

```
 PEN OFF
```

This statement works similarly to the PEN STOP statement. However, BASIC does not remember any light pen activity while the pen is turned off (unless PEN OFF was executed within the trap routine).

BASIC executes a PEN STOP when it jumps to a light pen trapping routine. This is to prevent light pen activity from interrupting the trapping subroutine. When BASIC executes the RETURN from the trapping subroutine, it executes a PEN ON so that light pen trapping is again enabled. Of course, if light pen activity occurrs during execution of the trapping routine, then an immediate jump back to the trapping routine will occur.

In our application above, we monitored the light pen by continually polling it. We could modify the program to take advantage of light pen trapping.

10.2   Using a Joystick

Anatomy of a Joystick

A joystick is a small box connected to the PC by a cable. (See Figure 10.2) Sticking out of the top of the box is a lever you can push in any direction. The position of the lever is expressed in terms of a pair of coordinates (x,y).

The precise correspondence between lever position and the coordinates (x,y) depends on the model of joystick. Generally, pushing the lever away from you will result in a positive y-coordinate, whereas pulling the lever towards you results in a negative y-coordinate. Similarly, pushing the lever to the left results in a negative x-coordinate, whereas pushing the lever to the right results in a positive x-coordinate.

In addition to the lever, the joystick has from one to four buttons. (The exact number depends on the particular model of joystick.)

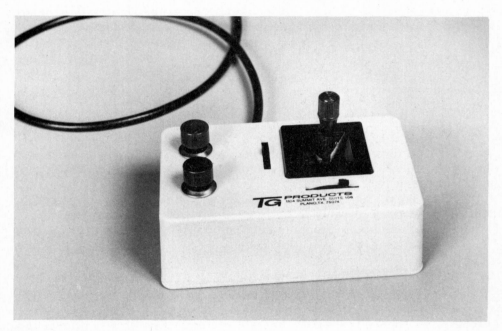

Figure 10.2. A Joystick.

Joysticks, used in many arcade-type video games, are familiar objects in millions of homes. You may use joysticks on the IBM PC, either in connection with arcade games you purchase or with games or programs of your own design.

Joysticks must be plugged into the appropriate socket on the game adapter card. The game adapter allows you to simultaneously connect two joysticks to the IBM, one joystick for each player in a two-person game.

Using a Joystick in BASIC

Some of the BASIC statements involving joysticks are available only in advanced BASIC. To make the exposition as simple as possible, we will assume throughout that advanced BASIC is in effect.

Reading the Joystick Lever

You may read the joystick lever using the STICK function. The format of this function is

```
<numeric variable> = STICK(n)
```

Here n is one of the integers 0,1,2,3. You may also use STICK(n) as a variable as in the statements

```
100 IF STICK(1) = 1 THEN 500
```

```
200 WHILE STICK(2) < 5
```

Corresponding to the various choices of n, STICK(n) has the following meaning:

STICK(0) = the value of the x-coordinate of joystick A

STICK(1) = the value of the y-coordinate of joystick A

STICK(2) = the value of the x-coordinate of joystick B

STICK(3) = the value of the y-coordinate of joystick B

The precise ranges of the x- and y-coordinates will depend on the particular model of joystick you are using.

The function STICK(0) has a special purpose. Whenever you refer to it, STICK(0) updates all of the coordinates STICK(0), STICK(1), STICK(2), and STICK(3) with the current readings from the two joysticks. If you use the values of STICK(1), STICK(2) or STICK(3) without first using STICK(0), you will be using the values obtained from the most recent reference to STICK(0).

TEST YOUR UNDERSTANDING 1 (answer on page 277)

Write a program that sets X1 equal to the current x-coordinate and Y1 equal to the current y-coordinate of joystick B.

In the next example, we illustrate how you may translate the joystick motions into motions on the screen. This type of translation process is used in many arcade games.

EXAMPLE 1.   Write a program that displays a happy face at high-resolution graphics coordinates (320,100). The program should read joystick A. If the x-coordinate is positive, the happy face should be moved one dot to the right; if the x-coordinate is negative, the happy face should be moved one dot to the left. If the y-coordinate is positive, the happy face should be moved one dot up; if the y-coordinate is negative, the happy face should be moved one dot down.

SOLUTION.   We use the GET statement to store the happy face in an array. We also record the initial position of the happy face as (xpos, ypos) = (320,100). We test the joystick. Based on our readings, we erase the happy face at its current position, compute the new coordinates, then display the happy face at its new location.

```
100 'Store happy face in array A%
110 DIM A%(50)
120 KEY OFF:CLS:SCREEN 2
130 PRINT CHR$(1);
140 GET (0,0)-(7,7),A%
150 CLS
160 'Place happy face in initial position
170 'xpos and ypos give the current coordinates of the
    happy face
180 XPOS=320:YPOS=100
190 GOSUB 300
200 'Poll joystick lever
210 X=STICK(0)
220 Y=STICK(1)
230 GOSUB 300 : 'Erase happy face
240 IF X > 0 THEN XPOS=XPOS+1
250 IF X < 0 THEN XPOS=XPOS-1
260 IF Y > 0 THEN YPOS=YPOS+1
270 IF Y < 0 THEN YPOS=YPOS-1
280 GOSUB 300: 'Redisplay happy face at new position
290 GOTO 200
300 'Display happy face at (xpos,ypos)
310 PUT (XPOS,YPOS),A%
320 RETURN
```

Reading the Joystick Buttons

You may read the joystick buttons using the STRIG function. You may determine, for each joystick:

- if a particular button was pressed since you last interrogated the joystick buttons,

- if a particular button is currently pressed.

The format of the STRIG function is

```
<numeric variable> = STRIG(n)
```

Or, alternatively, you may use STRIG(n) as a variable within a statement.
Here are the meanings of STRIG(n) corresponding to the various values of n.

STRIG(0) = -1 if button 1 of joystick A was pressed since the last STRIG(n), =0 otherwise.

STRIG(1) = -1 if button 1 of joystick A is currently pressed, =0 otherwise.

STRIG(2) = -1 if button 1 of joystick B was pressed since the last STRIG(n), =0 otherwise.

STRIG(3) = -1 if button 1 of joystick B is currently pressed, =0 otherwise.

STRIG(4) = -1 if button 2 of joystick A was pressed since the last STRIG(n), =0 otherwise.

STRIG(5) = -1 if button 2 of joystick A is currently pressed, =0 otherwise.

STRIG(6) = -1 if button 2 of joystick B was pressed since the last STRIG(n), =0 otherwise.

STRIG(7) = -1 if button 2 of joystick B is currently pressed, = 0 otherwise.

Note that the values STRIG(4)-STRIG(7) are available only in BASIC versions 2.00 and later.

To be able to use the STRIG function, you must turn it on with the statement

```
STRIG ON
```

The statement

```
STRIG OFF
```

disables testing of STRIG.

Trapping Joystick Button Activity

You may trap pressing a joystick button. This trapping works exactly like all the other event trapping we have discussed. To enable trapping for the function STRIG(n), you must execute the statement

```
STRIG(n) ON
```

Moreover, you must specify a trapping subroutine via the statement

```
ON STRIG(n) GOSUB <line>
```

You may turn off joystick button trapping with the statement

```
STRIG(n) OFF
```

To temporarily ignore joystick button trapping, we use the statement

```
STRIG(n) STOP
```

In this case, if the appropriate button is pushed while trapping is stopped, the trap will occur as soon as trapping is turned back on.

TEST YOUR UNDERSTANDING 2 (answer on page 277)

Write a program which allows you to respond to joystick button 1 by clearing the screen and to joystick button 2 by printing "Joysticks are fun!".

EXAMPLE 2. Enhance the program of Example 1 so that the joystick lever causes no motion until button 1 is pressed. Motion is then allowed for 10 seconds.

SOLUTION. We enable trapping for button 1 of joystick A. The trap routine resets the clock to 0. Then when we are finished with each move of the happy face, we test the current value of the clock. If more than 10 seconds have elapsed, we end the program.

```
100 'Enable button trapping
110 ON STRIG(1) GOSUB 370
120 STRIG(1) ON
130 'Store happy face in array A%
140 DIM A%(50)
150 KEY OFF:CLS:SCREEN 2
160 PRINT CHR$(1);
170 GET (0,0)-(7,7),A%
180 CLS
190 'Place happy face in intial position
200 ' xpos and y pos give the current
      coordinates of the happy face
210 XPOS=320:YPOS=100
220 GOSUB 340
230 'Poll joystick lever
240 X=STICK(0)
250 Y=STICK(1)
260 GOSUB 340 : 'Erase happy face
270 IF X > 0 THEN XPOS=XPOS+1
280 IF X < 0 THEN XPOS=XPOS-1
290 IF Y > 0 THEN YPOS=YPOS+1
300 IF Y < 0 THEN YPOS=YPOS-1
310 GOSUB 340: 'Redisplay happy face at new position
320 TIME=VAL(RIGHT$(TIME$,2))
```

```
330 IF TIME >= 10 THEN END ELSE 230
340 'Display happy face at (xpos,ypos)
350 PUT (XPOS,YPOS),A%
360 RETURN
370 'Button trapping routine
380 STRIG(1) OFF
390 TIME$="00:00:00":'reset clock
```

ANSWERS TO TEST YOUR UNDERSTANDING

```
1:  10 STICK(0)
    20 X1=STICK(3)
    30 Y1=STICK(4)

2:  10 STRIG(1) ON
    20 ON STRIG(1) GOSUB 1000
    30 STRIG(4) ON
    40 ON STRIG(4) GOSUB 1100
    50 GOTO 50
    1000 CLS
    1010 RETURN
    1100 PRINT "Joysticks are fun!"
    1110 RETURN
```

10.3 Using a Plotter

A digital plotter is a device capable of very high quality graphics output. Using a plotter, you can prepare charts, graphs, blueprints, pictures—anything you can draw. And the quality of the picture is much greater than can be drawn on most printers. Many plotters have multiple pens and allow output in several colors. In Figures 10.3 and 10.4 we show two typical plotter graphs.

There are a number of different plotters you may hook up to your PC, and using them may depend on the particular machine you are using. However, as an illustration, let's pick the Hewlett-Packard 7470A Plotter. This device is a two-pen plotter, well within the price range of a personal computer user.

The plotter comes with an RS232-C interface and you connect the RS232C plug on the plotter to the RS232C plug on your asynchronous communications adapter. Since your are using asynchronous communications, it is necessary to set up the various communications parameters so that the computer and the plotter can exchange signals. The first step is to hook up the two devices via a proper cable. Here your local computer store can help. Second, you must set the switches on the plotter for the correct communications. Here, again, your computer store can help.

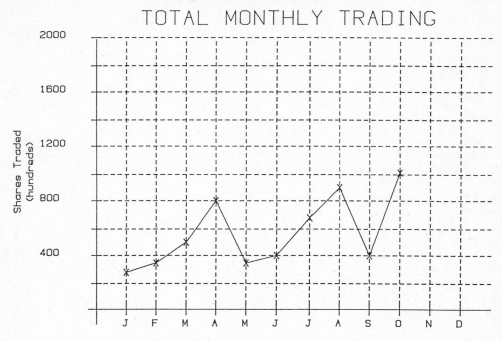

Figure 10.3.

Once the plotter and the computer have been connected, you may send signals to the plotter via a communications file. With the Hewlett-Packard 7470A, you may use a baud rate of 2400. That is, open the communications file with the statement

```
10 OPEN "COM1:2400,S" AS #1
```

The ",S" means that we are using SPACE parity.

At 2400 baud, you will need a communications protocol to prevent buffer overflow. At the end of a data transmission to the plotter, send CHR$(5) and await a response from the plotter before resuming transmission. Suppose, for example, that you are sending a string STRING$ to the plotter. The protocol would work as in this subroutine:

```
1000 PRINT #1, STRNG$;
1010 PRINT #1, CHR$(5);
1020 INPUT #1, D$
1030 RETURN
```

You instruct the plotter via a graphics language. For example, to lower the pen to the paper, the command is PD (Pen Down); to raise the pen from the paper, the command is PU (Pen Up). The Hewlett-Packard graphic com-

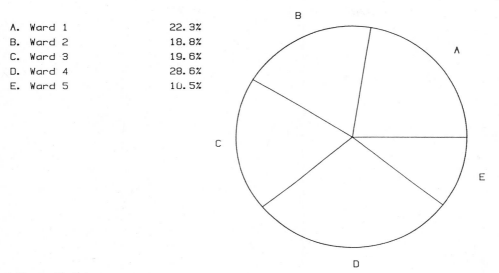

Enrollments

A.	Ward 1	22.3%
B.	Ward 2	18.8%
C.	Ward 3	19.6%
D.	Ward 4	28.6%
E.	Ward 5	10.5%

Figure 10.4.

mands allow you to locate the pen anywhere on the page, with the motion occurring either with the pen up or down. You may draw lines of various styles, write strings in letters of various sizes, or draw customized letters. The character CHR$(3) is used as punctuation between commands. For example, to write a string beginning at plotter coordinate (x1%, y1%), you would send the string

```
100 'Write string
110 STRNG$="PU;PA"+STR$(x1%)+","+STR$(y1%)+";LB"+
    CHR$(3)+";"
120 GOSUB 1000
```

Note that the numbers x1% and y1% must be converted into strings, along with appropriate command letters and separators (;) and CHR$(3). After the string has been assembled, it is sent to the communciations file. Here is a command that sets the size of a character.

```
200 'Size
210 STRNG$="SI .40,.60;"
220 GOSUB 1000
```

For the full range of commands, consult your plotter manual. The only point we wish to make here is that communications with a plotter is just a special case of communications. And all the same principles that we learned in the communications chapter apply to communicating with your plotter (or any other device).

11

The BASIC Compiler

11.1 Why Compile Programs?

We have learned a great deal about writing, debugging and using programs written in both Disk BASIC and Advanced BASIC. The advantages of these two versions of BASIC are many. Programs are both easy to write and easy to debug. Moreover, you have access to many hardware features of the PC that are unavailable if you use other languages. However, there is (at least) one big disadvantage: The programs run SLOWLY. This might come as a surprise to you. After all, we have been touting the great speed and efficiency of computers in general and the PC in particular. Why do we now begin to complain about speed?

Well, the answer is that now we have progressed to the point where the programs are more demanding of the computer. And some programs run at an annoying crawl. For example, consider the sorting program of Chapter 2. We observed that, as the number of items to be sorted increases, the execution speed increases disproportionately. As a second example, consider the graphics screen dump of Chapter 8. It works, but it takes more than 9 minutes to print one graphics image. As a third example, consider the animation displayed in Chapter 3. You might have noticed how slowly the image moved across the screen. Examples like these lead us to ask: Is there some way to improve execution speed? There is. And that's where the BASIC compiler comes in.

Both Disk BASIC and Advanced BASIC are **interpreters**. That is, they interpret each program line as the program is running. The interpretation process is very time-consuming. Here's why. In running a program, BASIC scans program lines as they are encountered. BASIC interprets the meaning of the various commands that it finds, determines the locations of any variables involved, and only then executes the instructions of the line. The process of program interpretation is full of inefficiencies. Suppose, for example, that your program includes GOTO statements that cause a particular line to be executed many times. Each time a line is encountered, it is reinterpreted.

The **BASIC Compiler** is a program that performs the interpretation of a program without actually running the program. The compiler translates a BASIC program into **machine language**, which consists of low-level instructions that can be executed directly by the computer without interpretation. A compiled program does not require the time-consuming interpretation of ordinary BASIC and will generally run much faster. For example, a compiled version of the graphics screen dump program will allow you to print the screen in less than 3 minutes (compared with more than 9 for the interpreted version).

In the next few sections, we will discuss operation of the BASIC Compiler. We will cover all you need to know to start compiling your favorite programs.

11.2   Compiling a Program

Source Code, Object Code, Compiled Program

Let's suppose that you wish to write a program GRAPH, which will ultimately be compiled. Your first job is to write the program in BASIC. Proceed as you would in developing any program. Test the operation of your program by running it in BASIC or BASICA. When you are satisfied that the program works, save it in ASCII format. That is, save the program on diskette using the command

```
SAVE "GRAPH",A
```

This will create an ASCII text file, called GRAPH.BAS, which contains the text of your program stored character by character the way it appears on the screen. (Even the numbers are stored digit by digit.) The file GRAPH.BAS is called the **source code** of your program. It is the source code on which the compiler operates.

In order to translate the source code into a machine language program, you must proceed in two steps:

I.   Allow the compiler to translate the source code into an intermediate form called **object code**. This object code is stored in a diskette file, which the compiler will name GRAPH.OBJ . (You may choose a different name if you wish.) In addition, you may ask the compiler to create an optional listing file that contains a listing of the program in both source and object code.

II. Allow the Linker program to translate the object code into a program. The Linker performs the following tasks:

   1.   The object code contains references to various subroutines it will need from BASIC. The Linker looks up the required routines in one of several libraries of subroutines. The code for the required subroutines is then included with the object code to form the final program.

   2.   The Linker determines the placement of the program in memory.

The Linker program produces a diskette file it names GRAPH.EXE. (You may choose a different name.)

The diskette file GRAPH.EXE contains the machine language version of the program GRAPH.BAS. To run GRAPH.EXE, you start from the DOS prompt A> and type

```
GRAPH
```

DOS will then load and run GRAPH.EXE. Note that after compiling, you no longer need BASIC to run the program. It runs directly from DOS.

Now that we have an overall picture of the compilation process, let's describe some of the operational details.

Generating the Source Code

It is best to follow the discussion with an example. So here is a version of the graphics screen dump. This program assumes that the screen image has been saved in a diskette file. It requests the name of the file, displays the image, and then prints it on the IBM graphics printer.

```
100 'GRAPHICS FILE PRINT ROUTINE
110 DIM Z%(2)
120 'Display screen image file
130 SCREEN 2:KEY OFF
140 PRINT "GRAPHICS SCREEN PRINT"
150 INPUT "NAME OF FILE TO PRINT";FILENAME$
160 ON ERROR GOTO 420
170 DEF SEG= &HB800
180 BLOAD FILENAME$,0
190 DEF SEG
200 'Print Screen
210 LINESPACE9$=CHR$(27)+CHR$(65)+CHR$(8)+CHR$(27)+CHR$(50)
220 LINESPACE6$=CHR$(27)+CHR$(65)+CHR$(12)+CHR$(27)+CHR$(50)
230 GRAPH400$=CHR$(27)+CHR$(75)+CHR$(144)+CHR$(1)
240 LPRINT LINESPACE9$;
250 FOR J%=1 TO 9
260       LPRINT
270 NEXT J%
280 FOR COL%=0 TO 79
290       LPRINT SPACE$(9);
300       LPRINT GRAPH400$;
310       FOR ROW%=199 TO 0 STEP -1
320             GET (COL%+7,ROW%)-(COL%,ROW%),Z%
```

```
330              LPRINT CHR$(Z%(2))+CHR$(Z%(2));
340        NEXT ROW%
350        LPRINT
360 NEXT COL%
370 FOR J%=1 TO 10
380        LPRINT
390 NEXT J%
400 LPRINT LINESPACE6$;
410 END
420 'Error trapping routine
430 IF ERR=53 THEN PRINT "FILE NOT FOUND"
440 IF ERR <> 53 THEN PRINT "PRINTER ERROR"
450 RESUME 140
```

To follow the discussion, type in this program and save it with the command

```
SAVE "GRAPH",A
```

Generating the Object Code

To generate the object code, you will need your source code file GRAPH.BAS and the BASIC Compiler file BASCOM.COM. For simplicity, you may store both files on the same diskette. Obtain the DOS prompt, place this diskette in the current drive, and type

```
BASCOM GRAPH,,/o/e/a
```

Here GRAPH is the name of the source code file. The extension .BAS is understood. The letters /o/e/a are parameters. We will describe the meaning of these particular parameters in the next section.

The diskette drive will light and the compiler will go to work. After it finishes (assuming that no errors were encountered in the source code!), the compiler will display a message of the form

```
xxxxx Bytes Available
xxxxx Bytes Free
    0 Warning Error(s)
    0 Severe Error(s)
```

Type DIR to obtain a directory of the diskette. You will notice that the compiler created a new file, named GRAPH.OBJ. This completes step I.

TEST YOUR UNDERSTANDING 1 (answer on page 293)

Follow the above procedure to create the file GRAPH.OBJ.

Using the Linker

The Linker program is contained in the file LINK.EXE. This program is contained on the DOS diskette and on one of the diskettes supplied with the BASIC compiler. For simplicity, you should copy LINK.EXE onto a fresh diskette containing GRAPH.OBJ and the library file BASCOM.LIB, contained on one of the BASIC compiler diskettes. Obtain the DOS prompt and insert the diskette into the current drive. Type

```
LINK
```

The Linker program will be loaded and will respond with the prompt

```
Object Modules [.OBJ] :
```

Type the name of the object code file, namely GRAPH, and press ENTER. Note that the extension .OBJ may be omitted. The next Linker prompt is

```
Run File [GRAPH.EXE] :
```

Press ENTER to indicate that you wish the final program to be titled GRAPH.EXE. (You could, of course, type in a new program name. The compiler will ignore any extension you specify and automatically assign the extension .EXE .) The Linker now prompts

```
List File [NUL.MAP] :
```

Again press ENTER to indicate that we do not wish a memory map of the final program. Finally, the Linker prompts

```
Libraries [.LIB]
```

We will be using the library BASCOM.LIB, so respond by typing BASCOM and press ENTER. Note that we again omitted the extension.

The Linker will now go to work and create the file GRAPH.EXE.

TEST YOUR UNDERSTANDING 2 (answer on page 293)

Follow the above procedure to create the file GRAPH.EXE .

TEST YOUR UNDERSTANDING 3 (answer on page 294)

(a)   Create a screen image file using the following program. (You will be storing a pretty graphics design.)

```
10 SCREEN 1:CLS:KEY OFF
20 FOR R=0 TO 6.3 STEP .1
30 A=160+70*COS(R):B=100+70*SIN(R)
40 DRAW "NM =A;, =B;"
```

```
50 NEXT R
60 DEF SEG &HB800
70 BSAVE "DESIGN",0,&H4000
80 DEF SEG
```

(b) Use the program GRAPH.EXE to prepare a hard copy of the graphics design stored in (a).

The BASCOM Command

In our example above, we used the BASCOM command in the form

```
BASCOM GRAPH,, /o/e/a
```

The most general form of the BASCOM command is

```
BASCOM <source file>,<object file>,<list file>
       <parameters>
```

<source file> is the name of the source file. The extension .BAS is always assumed, although there is no harm if you include this extension when specifying the source file name. Note that there is no comma between <list file> and <parameters>.

<object file> is the name of the object file to be created by the compiler. The extension .OBJ is assumed, although there is no harm if you include this extension when specifying the object file name. You may omit the object file name completely, in which case the object file name (without extension) is the same as the source file name (without extension, GRAPH in the above example).

<list file> is the name of the file to contain the compiler listing (See below). In the default situation, the listing file has the name NUL.LST, indicating that the listing file is not created. If you specify any other file name, then the list file is created, with the name you specify. The list file is always given the extension .LST.

<parameters> are switches you may set to choose among the various options in compilation. (See the next section for a description of the parameters.)

If you choose not to list all the above components as part of a BASCOM command, you should end the command with a semicolon.

TEST YOUR UNDERSTANDING 4 (answer on page 294)

Write a command to compile the source code file LAMBDA.BAS, with object code file named BETA.OBJ.

The Compiler Listing

You may have the compiler generate a listing that shows each program line and the corresponding code generated, in a symbolic form. For example, to create a listing file with the name GRAPH.LST, we could use the command

```
BASCOM GRAPH,,GRAPH /o/e
```

Note that the extra comma holds the place for the object file that is taken to be the default choice GRAPH.OBJ. Here is the contents of the listing file generated.

```
Offset  Data    Source Line         IBM Personal Computer BASIC Compiler V1.00

 001A   0002    100 'GRAPHICS FILE PRINT ROUTINE
 001A   0002    110 DIM Z%(2)
 001A   0002    120 'Display screen image file
 001A   0002    130 SCREEN 2:KEY OFF
 0026    **            I00001: CALL  $531
 002B    **            L00100:
 002B    **            L00110:
 002B    **            L00120:
 002B    **            L00130: MOV   BX,0002H
 002E    **                    CALL  $SC2
 0033    **                    XOR   BX,BX
 0035    **                    CALL  $KYO
 003A   0008    140 PRINT "GRAPHICS SCREEN PRINT"
 003A    **            L00140: CALL  $PROA
 003F    **                    MOV   BX,OFFSET <const>
 0042    **                    CALL  $PV2D
 0047   0008    150 INPUT "NAME OF FILE TO PRINT";FILENAME$
 0047    **            L00150: MOV   BX,OFFSET <const>
 004A    **                    CALL  $INOA
 004F    **                    DB    00H
 0050    **                    CALL  $IPUA
 0055    **                    DB    01H
 0056    **                    DB    07H
 0057    **                    MOV   BX,OFFSET FILENAME$
 005A    **                    CALL  $IPUB
 005F   000C    160 ON ERROR GOTO 420
 005F    **            L00160: MOV   BX,OFFSET L00420
 0062    **                    CALL  $OEGA
 0067   000C    170 DEF SEG= &HB800
 0067    **            L00170: MOV   BX,0B800H
 006A    **                    CALL  $DS1
 006F   000C    180 BLOAD FILENAME$,0
 006F    **            L00190: MOV   BX,OFFSET FILENAME$
 0072    **                    XOR   DX,DX
 0074    **                    CALL  $BL1
```

```
0079   000C   190 DEF SEG
0079   **         L00190: CALL   $DSO
007E   000C   200 'Print Screen
007E   000C   210 LINESPACE9$=CHR$(27)+CHR$(65)+CHR$(8)+CHR$(27)+CHR$(50)
007E   **         L00200:
007E   **         L00210: MOV    BX,001BH
0081   **                 MOV    DX,BX
0083   **                 CALL   $CHR
0088   **                 MOV    CX,BX
008A   **                 MOV    BX,0041H
008D   **                 CALL   $CHR
0092   **                 XCHG   AX,CX
0093   **                 CALL   $AD$A
0098   **                 MOV    CX,BX
009A   **                 MOV    BX,0008H
009D   **                 CALL   $CHR
00A2   **                 XCHG   AX,CX
00A3   **                 CALL   $AD$A
00A8   **                 MOV    CX,BX
00AA   **                 MOV    BX,DX
00AC   **                 CALL   $CHR
00B1   **                 XCHG   AX,CX
00B2   **                 CALL   $AD$A
00B7   **                 MOV    DX,BX
00B9   **                 MOV    BX,0032H
00BC   **                 CALL   $CHR
00C1   **                 XCHG   AX,DX
00C2   **                 CALL   $AD$A
00C7   **                 MOV    DX,OFFSET LINESPACE9$
00CA   **                 CALL   $SASA
00CF   0010   220 LINESPACE6$=CHR$(27)+CHR$(65)+CHR$(12)+CHR$(27)+CHR$(50)
00CF   **         L00220: MOV    BX,001BH
00D2   **                 MOV    DX,BX
00D4   **                 CALL   $CHR
00D9   **                 MOV    CX,BX
00DB   **                 MOV    BX,0041H
00DE   **                 CALL   $CHR
00E3   **                 XCHG   AX,CX
00E4   **                 CALL   $AD$A
00E9   **                 MOV    CX,BX
00EB   **                 MOV    BX,000CH
00EE   **                 CALL   $CHR
00F3   **                 XCHG   AX,CX
00F4   **                 CALL   $AD$A
00F9   **                 MOV    CX,BX
00FB   **                 MOV    BX,DX
00FD   **                 CALL   $CHR
0102   **                 XCHG   AX,CX
```

```
0103    **              CALL    $AD$A
0108    **              MOV     DX,BX
010A    **              MOV     BX,0032H
010D    **              CALL    $CHR
0112    **              XCHG    AX,DX
0113    **              CALL    $AD$A
0118    **              MOV     DX,OFFSET LINESPACE6$
011B    **              CALL    $SASA
0120    0014    230 GRAPH400$=CHR$(27)+CHR$(75)+CHR$(144)+CHR$(1)
0120    **              L00230: MOV    BX,001BH
0123    **              CALL    $CHR
0128    **              MOV     DX,BX
012A    **              MOV     BX,004BH
012D    **              CALL    $CHR
0132    **              XCHG    AX,DX
0133    **              CALL    $AD$A
0138    **              MOV     DX,BX
013A    **              MOV     BX,0090H
013D    **              CALL    $CHR
0142    **              XCHG    AX,DX
0143    **              CALL    $AD$A
0148    **              MOV     DX,BX
014A    **              MOV     BX,0001H
014D    **              CALL    $CHR
0152    **              XCHG    AX,DX
0153    **              CALL    $AD$A
0158    **              MOV     DX,OFFSET GRAPH400$
015B    **              CALL    $SASA
0160    0018    240 LPRINT LINESPACE9$;
0160    **              L00240: CALL   $PROE
0165    **                      MOV    BX,OFFSET LINESPACE9$
0168    **                      CALL   $PV1D
016D    0018    250 FOR J%=1 TO 9
016D    **              L00250: MOV    AX,0001H
0170    **                      JMP    I00002
0173    0018    260     LPRINT
0173    **              I00003:
0173    **              L00260: CALL   $PROE
0178    **                      MOV    BX,OFFSET <const>
017B    **                      CALL   $PV2D
0180    0018    270 NEXT J%
0180    **              L00270: MOV    AX,J%
0183    **                      INC    AX
0184    **              I00002: MOV    J%,AX
0187    **                      CMP    WORD PTR J%,09H
018C    **                      JNG    $-1BH
018E    001A    280 FOR COL%=0 TO 79
019E    **              L00280: XOR    AX,AX
```

```
0190   **                        JMP    I00004
0193   001A    290    LPRINT SPACE$(9);
0193   **                 I00005:
0193   **                 L00290: CALL  $PROE
0198   **                        MOV   BX,0009H
019B   **                        CALL  $SP$
01A0   **                        CALL  $PV1D
01A5   001A    300    LPRINT GRAPH400$;
01A5   **                 L00300: CALL  $PROE
01AA   **                        MOV   BX,OFFSET GRAPH400$
01AD   **                        CALL  $PV1D
01B2   001A    310    FOR ROW%=199 TO 0 STEP -1
01B2   **                 L00310: MOV   AX,00C7H
01B5   **                        JMP   I00006
01BB   001A    320        GET (COL%+7,ROW%)-(COL%,ROW%),Z%
01BB   **                 I00007:
01BB   **                 L00320: MOV   BX,COL%
01BC   **                        MOV   DX,BX
01BE   **                        ADD   BX,07H
01C1   **                        MOV   CX,DX
01C3   **                        MOV   DX,ROW%
01C7   **                        CALL  $GE0
01CC   **                        MOV   BX,CX
01CE   **                        CALL  $GE1
01D3   **                        MOV   BX,OFFSET Z%
01D6   **                        MOV   DX,0006H
01D9   **                        CALL  $GE2
01DE   001E    330        LPRINT CHR$(Z%(2))+CHR$(Z%(2));
01DE   **                 L00330: CALL  $PROE
01E3   **                        MOV   BX,Z%+0004H
01E7   **                        MOV   DX,BX
01E9   **                        CALL  $CHR
01EE   **                        MOV   CX,BX
01F0   **                        MOV   BX,DX
01F2   **                        CALL  $CHR
01F7   **                        XCHG  AX,CX
01F8   **                        CALL  $AD$A
01FD   **                        CALL  $PV1D
0202   001E    340    NEXT ROW%
0202   **                 L00340: MOV   AX,ROW%
0205   **                        DEC   AX
0206   **                 I00006: MOV   ROW%,AX
0209   **                        CMP   WORD PTR ROW%,00H
020E   **                        JNL   $-58H
0210   001E    350    LPRINT
0210   **                 L00350: CALL  $PROE
0215   **                        MOV   BX,OFFSET <const>
0218   **                        CALL  $PV2D
```

```
021D    001E    360 NEXT COL%
021D    **              L00360: MOV    AX,COL%
0220    **                      INC    AX
0221    **              I00004: MOV    COL%,AX
0224    **                      CMP    WORD PTR COL%,4FH
0229    **                      JG     $+03H
022B    **                      JMP    I00005
022E    001E    370 FOR J%=1 TO 10
022E    **              L00370: MOV    AX,0001H
0231    **                      JMP    I00008
0234    001E    380     LPRINT
0234    **              I00009:
0234    **              L00380: CALL   $PR0E
0239    **                      MOV    BX,OFFSET <const>
023C    **                      CALL   $PV2D
0241    001E    390 NEXT J%
0241    **              L00390: MOV    AX,J%
0244    **                      INC    AX
0245    **              I00008: MOV    J%,AX
0248    **                      CMP    WORD PTR J%,0AH
024D    **                      JNG    $-1BH
024F    001E    400 LPRINT LINESPACE6$;
024F    **              L00400: CALL   $PR0E
0254    **                      MOV    BX,OFFSET LINESPACE6$
0257    **                      CALL   $PV1D
025C    001E    410 END
025C    **              L00410: CALL   $END
0261    001E    420 'Error trapping routine
0261    001E    430 IF ERR=53 THEN PRINT "FILE NOT FOUND"
0261    **              L00420:
0261    **              L00430: CALL   $ERN
0266    **                      CMP    BX,35H
0269    **                      JE     $+03H
026B    **                      JMP    I00010
026E    **                      CALL   $PR0A
0273    **                      MOV    BX,OFFSET <const>
0276    **                      CALL   $PV2D
027B    001E    440 IF ERR <> 53 THEN PRINT "PRINTER ERROR"
027B    **              I00010:
027B    **              L00440: CALL   $ERN
0280    **                      CMP    BX,35H
0283    **                      JNE    $+03H
0285    **                      JMP    I00011
0288    **                      CALL   $PR0A
028D    **                      MOV    BX,OFFSET <const>
0290    **                      CALL   $PV2D
0295    001E    450 RESUME 140
```

```
0295    **              I00011:
0295    **              L00450: MOV   BX,OFFSET L00140
0298    **                      CALL  $RESA
029D    001E
029D    **                      CALL  $ENP
0334    001E
```

    22151 Bytes Available
    21254 Bytes Free

        0 Warning Error(s)
        0 Severe Error(s)

Note that for each BASIC statement, there is included a list of the corresponding assembly language instructions. We'll discuss these instructions
further in Chapter 12.

You may display the listing file on the screen using the DOS command

`TYPE GRAPH.LST`

To generate a copy of the listing on the printer, press Ctrl-PrtSc prior to
giving the TYPE command.

The BASIC Compiler Libraries

The BASIC Compiler comes with two sets of library routines, contained,
respectively, in the files BASCOM.LIB and BASRUN.LIB. If you use the
library BASCOM.LIB, then your program will be stand-alone, that is, it will
run without reference to any data external to itself. If you compile your program with the library BASRUN.LIB, then your program may be run only if
the runtime library file BASRUN.EXE is present on the same diskette as your
program. When you load your program, the library BASRUN.EXE will be
loaded into memory so that the program can make use of its routines. The
advantages of compiling with the BASRUN.LIB library are two:

1. Using BASRUN.LIB results in shorter object code and final program.
2. BASRUN.LIB allows you to use certain commands (see Section 4) not
    available in the library BASCOM.LIB.

Note, however, that BASRUN.EXE is copyrighted by IBM. If you are generating programs for resale, you may not include a copy of BASRUN.EXE
unless you pay a royalty fee to IBM.

Some Comments On the File GRAPH.EXE

In compiling, you start from a source code program and generate a
number of new files. It is useful to get a feel for the sizes of the various files
involved. In the example above, here are the file sizes:

File	Bytes
GRAPH.BAS (source code)	1009
GRAPH.OBJ (object code)	2709
GRAPH.EXE (executable program)	19200

You might be shocked at the above table. After all, here is a program that is only 1009 bytes in source code (it would be less if we had not used ASCII format!). But when compiled the program grows to 19200 bytes. Part of the growth is only illusory, however. Remember that, in order for the source code to run, the BASIC interpreter must be present in memory. And this takes up about 16K. On the other hand, GRAPH.EXE is a stand-alone program. This puts the size comparison in a more favorable light, although the source code version takes up slightly less memory.

What if we had used the library BASRUN.LIB for compilation? In this case, the sizes of the object code and executable program are, respectively, 1975 bytes and 1920 bytes. Quite a difference! But there's a catch. The library run time file BASRUN.EXE must also reside in memory. And BAS-RUN.EXE takes up 31744 bytes. So using the run time library takes considerably more memory. However, if you wish to include several compiled programs on a single diskette, then the run time library file need be present only once. And this results in a considerable savings of diskette space. So there is a definite trade-off in using the run time library file.

Can it be that the compiler is that memory inefficient? To a certain extent, the answer is YES. However, bear in mind the following point. The file BASIC.COM does not contain all of the BASIC interpreter. Actually, most of the interpreter is stored in ROM and you are not even aware of it most of the time. When you include the amount of ROM taken up by BASIC, then the memory comparisons are much more favorable toward the compiled programs.

ANSWERS TO TEST YOUR UNDERSTANDING

1:   Use the command

```
BASCOM GRAPH ,, /a/o/e
```

2:   Use the command

```
LINK
```

Answer the four prompts with

```
GRAPH
ENTER
ENTER
```

BASCOM

3: (a)   Make sure that the diskette in the current drive has at least
          16K bytes of empty space. Obtain the BASIC prompt Ok,
          type in the program and type RUN<ENTER>.

    (b)   Obtain the DOS prompt. Type GRAPH<ENTER>.
          Answer the prompt with DESIGN.

4: BASCOM LAMBDA,BETA;

11.3   Compiler Parameters

You may control the compilation process using compiler parameters.
These parameters are included at the end of the BASCOM command line. A
parameter consists of a letter preceded by a slash /. You may list parameters
one after the other with no punctuation between them, as in

BASCOM ADDER ,,/V/O/E/D/C:1024

Compiler parameters may be given in uppercase, lowercase, or a combination of the two. We won't cover all of the possible compiler parameters, only
the most important.

/O   Compile the program so that the code may be linked using the
     library BASCOM.LIB.

/E   Generate error trapping code. Use this parameter if you use an ON
     ERROR GOTO and a RESUME <line> in your program.

/X   Generate error trapping code. Use this parameter if you use an ON
     ERROR GOTO and some of the statements RESUME <line>,
     RESUME, RESUME NEXT, RESUME 0. Use only one of the parame-
     ters /X and /E.

/V   Generate event trapping code. Use if your program contains event
     trapping for the function keys, light pen, joysticks, or
     communications.

/C   Set size of communications buffer, as in C:1024. Without this param-
     eter, the size of the buffer is 256 bytes.

/N   Allow compilation of source code without line numbers. This param-
     eter allows you to compile programs prepared with an editor. Pro-
     grams without line numbers are easier to read and maintain.
     However, you may not debug them using the BASIC interpreter.
     Also, note that any lines referred to in GOTO or GOSUB statements
     must be numbered.

/D   Allow use of TRON and TROFF in the source code. Useful in debug-
     ging BASIC programs prepared with an editor.

/A   Generate object code in the listing file.

11.4   Differences Between the Compiler and the Interpreter

The BASIC Compiler allows you to compile programs written with the BASIC interpreter. However, there are certain important differences in the BASIC languages used by the two programs. In this section, we summarize the most important of these differences.

Order of Statements

The BASIC interpreter is rather insensitive to the order in which you define your program elements (arrays, functions, etc.) This is because the interpreter can define program elements "on the fly." However, the compiler must pre-plan all its definitions and allocate memory space accordingly. So it is very important to include all your definitions **at the beginning of the program**. More specifically, you must collect all of the following "non-executable statements" at the start of your program.

```
COMMON
DEF FN
DEFINT
DEFSNG
DEFDBL
DIM
```

For similar reasons, you may not delete arrays while a program is running, so the ERASE statement may not be used.

You must be sure that FOR...NEXT loops are properly nested. The compiler will not allow GOTO statements that send you to the inside of a loop. (This is very bad programming practice in any case.) A similar comment applies to WHILE...WEND loops.

Remarks

The REM statement is ignored by the compiler. So remarks in programs do not contribute to final program length.

CHAIN and COMMON

CHAIN and COMMON may not be used with the library BASCOM.LIB. They may be used only in restricted form with the library BASRUN.LIB. Namely, the CHAIN options ALL, MERGE, and DELETE may not be used. You may use the CHAIN statement only to CHAIN an entire program with variables passed via COMMON statements.

The CHAINed program and the CHAINing program must **both** contain COMMON statements listing the variables they have in common. These variables must be listed in the same order. (Any extra variables listed in the CHAINed program COMMON statement are ignored.)

The CHAINed program must be an .EXE file created with the BASIC Compiler. That is, it is not possible for a compiled program to chain to an ordinary (uncompiled) BASIC program.

Function Keys

The function keys are initially disabled by the compiler. However, you may enable them and use them exactly as with the interpreter.

Communications

To use the communications statements OPEN "COM:..." and ON COM(n), you must link the file IBMCOM.OBJ with your object code. For example, if your object file is named TERM.OBJ, then you would respond to the Linker request for the object code file with

```
TERM,IBMCOM
```

11.5   Compilation Errors

The compiler has an extensive set of error messages that tell you of problems with your program. For example, if your source code file is not in ASCII format, the compiler will respond with the message

```
Binary Source File
```

The compiler will then quit and return to DOS.

If at all possible, the compiler will scan your entire program and report errors. It is very explicit. For each error found, the compiler will display the line, a pointer to a position on the line, usually near the cause of the error, and a coded error message.

You can find a list of the meanings of the error codes in the BASIC Compiler Manual. The compiler error codes are similar to the error messages provided by BASIC. For example, DD means that there is a Duplicate Definition of an array.

Compiler error messages are divided into two types: Warning Errors and Severe Errors. A warning error is exactly what it claims to be. It is a warning to you. For example, if you don't dimension an array, the compiler will warn you that it is assuming the default dimension 10. However, warning errors don't interfere with the compilation process.

A Severe Error is an error, like a syntax error, that causes a program not to run. If the compiler encounters severe errors, it will report them to you, but will not generate an object code file. If severe errors are reported, you must correct the source code file (usually using the BASIC interpreter) and then try to compile the program again.

If you use the /D option, the compiler will execute a series of debugging tests on your program. It will check things like: Does every FOR have an associated NEXT? Does every GOSUB have an associated RETURN? And so forth. In addition, the /D option allows you to include TRON and TROFF instructions within your program to trace program activity. It is a good idea to initially run your program through the compiler using the /D option. The compiler may pick up errors that have not shown themselves in the interpreter. If the program passes the debugging test, recompile without the /D option in order to eliminate the debugging code.

11.6   Back to the Case Study Once Again

If you've tried to work with the BAR CHART GENERATOR, you will surely have noticed that portions of it move quite slowly. For one thing, the cursor motions, the data input, and bar chart definition modules are rather slow. And the plotting of titles is quite slow indeed.

The BAR CHART GENERATOR would definitely benefit from compilation. However, as of this writing, this is not possible unless the actual bar chart drawing module is reworked. The problem is that the BASIC Compiler (Version 1.00) does not support the style extensions to LINE and PAINT, nor does it support the statements VIEW and WINDOW. I considered it worthwhile to show how these statements could be used to advantage in the BAR CHART GENERATOR, knowing full well that the program could not be compiled at the moment. I hope that by the time you read this, IBM will have updated the compiler to a version that supports these valuable statements. However, be warned that if you expect to compile a program, make sure to use only statements that the compiler accepts.

Actually, it is not all that hard to modify the BAR CHART GENERATOR so that it may be compiled. You just need to work harder. You can't depend on VIEW and WINDOW to calculate your screen coordinates for you. Instead, you must write a routine that does the necessary coordinate conversion. In addition, you must generate the required styles of shading on your own. (The B and BF options to LINE provide two shades. You'll have to be ingenious to invent the third shade.) Why not try the modifications? You'll learn a lot and you'll end up with a valuable compiled program to boot.

12

Assembly Language Subroutines in BASIC

In this chapter, we discuss the use of assembly language subroutines in BASIC. We will not be discussing assembly language per se. Rather, we will provide a few self-contained examples to illustrate the procedure whereby machine language subroutines are used within a BASIC program. The discussion of this chapter will lay the groundwork for a more detailed study of assembly language programming on the PC, such as contained in *IBM PC and XT Assembly Language: A Guide for Programmers,* by Leo J. Scanlon, Robert J. Brady Co., 1983.

12.1   The 8088 Microprocessor

The IBM PC is controlled by an 8088 microcprocessor, a "chip" manufactured by Intel Corporation. The 8088 has a number of locations in which it may temporarily hold data. These storage places are called **registers**, and function much like memory locations. In addition, the 8088 is able to perform a number of operations, such as:

- Move data between RAM and its registers
- Modify the data in its registers
- React to signals from other devices, such as the keyboard and the printer adapter

The 8088 Registers

The 8088 has 14 registers, each capable of holding 16 bits. It is easiest to understand the structure of the 8088 if we group these registers into five groups.

A.   Data Registers—There are four general-purpose registers, labeled AX, BX, CX, DX.

B.   Pointer and Index Registers—There are four registers in this category:

SP—Stack pointer   SI—Source index
BP—Base pointer   DI—Destination index

C. Segment Registers—There are four registers for holding segment addresses:

> CS—Code segment   SS—Stack segment
> DS—Data segment   ES—Extra segment

D. Instruction Pointer—This register, designated IP, holds the offset address of the instruction currently being executed.

E. Status Flags—The bits of this register report various aspects of the outcome of the preceding operation.

Addressing in the 8088

As we have already discussed, it takes two 16-bit pieces of data to specify an address in memory, namely the segment and the offset. The 8088 is able to store four segment addresses at a time and it does this in the four segment registers CS, DS, SS, and ES. The four segment addresses allow you to address four 64K areas in memory at a time. Each of the 64K areas is called a segment. **Here are the names associated with the four segment registers:**

> CS—Code Segment   SS—Stack Segment
> DS—Data Segment   ES—Extra Segment

These segments may overlap or even coincide. (See Figure 12.1.)

As program execution proceeds, you may change the contents of the four segment registers, in effect, altering the portion of memory under consideration.

Program Execution

A program in machine language consists of a sequence of bytes. For program execution, these bytes are stored in consecutive locations in RAM. To execute a program, the 8088 interprets the bytes as instructions and data. The segment register CS always specifies the segment address for the instructions currently being executed. The instruction pointer (IP) register gives the offset corresponding to the current instruction.

For example, suppose that a program is stored beginning at address &H0100:0000. Then the contents of CS would be &H0100 and IP would be 0. Program execution would begin with the byte at &H0100:0000. Instructions may require more than one byte. (The 8088 knows from the form of the first byte exactly how many bytes are required.) Suppose, for example, that the first instruction is a three-byte instruction. Then the required three bytes would be at offsets 0000, 0001, and 0002. After the instruction is executed, IP is adjusted to read 0003.

The Data Registers

Each of the four data registers may be used as either a 16-bit register or two 8-bit registers. For example, you may consider the AX register as two 8-bit registers, called AH and AL, where AH consists of the most significant 8

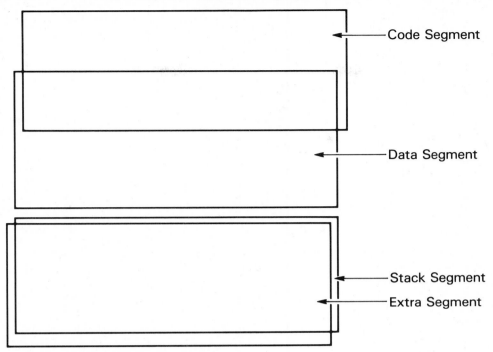

Figure 12.1. The Four Segments of Memory.

bits of AX (bits 8-15) and AL consists of the least significant 8 bits (bits 0-7). Similarly, we may consider the BX register to consist of the two 8-bit registers BH and BL. Similarly for CX and DX.

The 8088 has a very extensive instruction set that allows manipulation of both 8-bit and 16-bit quantities. We will survey the instructions in the next few sections. However, as a roadmap through the instruction set, here are some general guidelines on the functions of the various data registers.

AX is the **accumulator**. This is the main register used to hold data while performing operations on it. Some operations assume that the accumulator contains one of their required data inputs. Some operations store their end results in the accumulator.

BX is the **base register**. It is often used in instructions that address memory. In these instructions, a common use of BX is to hold an offset address.

CX is the **count register**. In loops, CX is often used as a counter.

DX is the **data register** and may be used to hold a second data item in some instructions requiring more than one data input.

12.2   Why Use Assembly Language Subroutines?

The IBM PC works at incredible speed. However, this is not to say that it is fast enough for all practical applications. Indeed, there are many simple applications that require the PC to perform so many statements that the resulting slow execution speed becomes a problem. This is especially true when executing loops nested several levels deep. For example, consider this sequence of nested loops:

```
10 FOR I=1 TO 10
20    FOR J=1 TO 50
30       FOR K=1 TO 50
40          ....
50          ....
60          ....
70       NEXT K
80    NEXT J
90 NEXT I
```

The set of instructions 40-50-60 will be executed 10x50x50 = 25,000 times! Even a small improvement in the execution time of lines 40-60 will have a significant effect on the overall running time of the program. And often, such an improvement may be obtained by replacing lines 40-60 with a machine language subroutine.

A second reason for using a machine language subroutine is that certain calculations are clumsy to perform in BASIC and may be most easily expressed in machine language. For example, any operations that have to do with bytes (as opposed to 16-bit integers) are usually awkward in BASIC, whereas they may be very simply performed in machine language. For example, consider the following problem: The variable A% contains an integer. Suppose that you wish to rotate the rightmost 8 bits of an integer 1 bit to the left, with bit 0 becoming bit 1, bit 1 becoming bit 2 ,..., bit 8 becoming bit 0. The leftmost 8 bits of A% remain unchanged. So, for instance, we wish to change

A% = 1001 0010 1011 1000

to

1001 0010 0111 0001

Try to write a BASIC program that performs this operation. For one thing, it's rather tricky. For another, the program requires several steps. In machine language, it's a snap! Just move the the lower 8 bits of A% to the AL register and perform the machine language instruction ROL (= rotate left). Then we store the resulting 8 bits in the lower 8 bits of A%. In machine language mnemonics, the desired operation may be written

```
MOV SI,<address of A%>
MOV AL,[SI]
ROL AL, 1
MOV [SI],AL
```

The "1" in the third instruction indicates that all AL bits are to be rotated by 1 place. The last line moves the contents of AL, namely the desired result, to the offset address contained in SI, namely the address of A%.

We have just written an assembly language program. We still have a number of things to do before our program may be used as a subroutine by the main program. However, looking ahead to the finished subroutine, here are the steps in using a machine language subroutine in BASIC.

Step 1: Write the assembly language subroutine. Translate it into machine language.

Step 2: Store a copy of the machine language program in a form accessible to your program. (We'll see how to do this later.)

Step 3: Include in the BASIC program instructions to call up the subroutine, where necessary. As part of the calling procedure, BASIC must pass any required data to the subroutine.

Step 4: Execute the subroutine.

Step 5: Return control to the BASIC program that called the subroutine.

12.3   Calling a Machine Language Subroutine

In this section, we will describe Step 3 of the above process, since it is the least technical.

PC BASIC provides two instructions for calling machine language subroutines, CALL and USR, each with its own advantages.

The CALL Statement

The format of this statement is

```
CALL <offset> (variable,variable,variable, . . .)
```

Here, <offset> is the offset address of the first byte of the subroutine. This address is given as the value of a variable, whose name serves as the subroutine name. For example, the offset might be given as the value of the variable SUBROUTINE. The variables listed within the parentheses are variables needed by the subroutine. (We say that the variables are **passed to the subroutine.**)

The CALL statement has the offset address of the subroutine "built-in." The segment address is always given by the most recent DEF SEG instruction. If no DEF SEG instruction has been used prior to executing CALL, then the segment address is taken to be the beginning of BASIC's workspace (= the default value of DEF SEG).

As an example, consider the subroutine for rotation of the lower 8 bits of A% we introduced in Section 1. Suppose that we call this subroutine by the name SUBROUTINE (a numeric variable). Then a CALL instruction that invokes this subroutine would have the form

```
CALL SUBROUTINE (A%)
```

Here SUBROUTINE is a variable whose value is the offset address at which the subroutine has been loaded into memory. Suppose, for example, that the subroutine begins at offset location 65000 of BASIC's current workspace. Then the machine language subroutine call could be carried out by the instructions

```
10 SUBROUTINE=65000
20 CALL SUBROUTINE (A%)
```

For debugging purposes, it is often simplest to have the offset addresses begin with 0 corresponding to the first byte of the subroutine. This may be accomplished using a DEF SEG instruction. For example, suppose that the subroutine begins at location &HF000. Then the segment can be described as beginning at &HF00 and we could use the sequence of instructions

```
10 DEF SEG = &HF00
20 SUBROUTINE = 0
30 CALL SUBROUTINE (A%)
```

TEST YOUR UNDERSTANDING 1

Write a sequence of instructions that calls a subroutine named SCR, beginning at location 00FF:7325 and requires the variables A, B, C$.

Arrays may be passed to machine language subroutines. For example to pass the array D%() to the subroutine SBR, we could use the instruction

```
10 CALL SBR (D%())
```

The USR Statement

USR is the second statment which may be used to call a machine language subroutine from a BASIC program. It is not quite as versatile a statement as CALL, however, since it allows you to pass only a single data item to the subroutine. The format of the USR statement is

```
USR[number](data)
```

Here [number] is one of the integers 0 through 9, and data is either a numeric expression or a string variable, which is to be passed to the machine language subroutine. For example, if user-defined subroutine 5 is to make use of B$, then USR5 may be invoked using the statement

```
USR5(B$)
```

You should think of USR as a user-defined function specified by a machine language subroutine. Just as with any user-defined function, you must define USR using a DEF statement. This must be done before you may invoke the function. In the case of a USR function, the appropriate DEF statement is of the form

```
DEF USR[number] = <offset>
```

As with the CALL statement, <offset> is the offset address of the first byte of the machine language subroutine. The segment address is defined by the most recent DEF SEG statement. If there has not been a DEF SEG statement, then the segment address is assumed to be the beginning of BASIC's workspace. For example, if USR5 begins at offset 65000 into BASIC's workspace, then the appropriate definition statement would read

```
DEF USR5 = 65000
```

Note the following facts about USR:

1. A machine language subroutine called by USR may have only one piece of data passed to it.
2. You may not pass arrays with USR.
3. In a USR call, you may omit the [number]. In this case, USR0 is assumed.

Because of the limitations of the USR statement, in what follows, we will concentrate exclusively on machine language subroutines that make use of the CALL statement.

12.4   Writing a Machine Language Subroutine

In Section 1, we wrote a simple, 4-instruction, machine language subroutine for rotating the lower 8 bits of a 16-bit number. To make use of this subroutine within a BASIC program, we must add instructions that allow us to access the data passed to us by BASIC (the value of A%), and that allow us to return safely to BASIC once the subroutine is completed.

The Stack

BASIC interacts with machine language programs via the stack. The stack is a series of consecutive memory locations in which the 8088-processor stores intermediate information. The stack operates like a stack of dishes. We may place information, one byte at a time, onto the stack. And we may remove bytes from the stack, starting with the byte most recently added. (This is the byte on the "top" of the stack.) However, the only way to remove a byte from the middle of the stack is to remove all the bytes on top of it.

We may place the contents of a register onto the stack using the PUSH instruction. For example, the instruction

```
PUSH AX
```

places the contents of the AX register (2 bytes) onto the top of the stack. The instruction

```
PUSH DL
```

places the contents of the DL register (1 byte) onto the stack.

The current location of the top of the stack is contained in the SP (= stack pointer) register. A PUSH instruction causes the contents of the SP register to be adjusted. For example, in the case of the instruction PUSH AX, the SP register is increased by 2 (2 bytes are PUSHed onto the stack); in the case of the instruction PUSH DL, the SP register is increased by 1 (1 byte is PUSHed onto the stack).

We may recover bytes from the stack using the POP instruction. POP reads a byte from the top of the stack, adjusts the SP register (thereby removing the byte or bytes from the stack), and reads the bytes into a register. For example, the instruction

```
POP AX
```

takes the top 2 bytes from the stack and reads them into the AX register. The instruction

```
POP DL
```

takes the top byte from the stack and reads it into the DL register.

When you execute either a CALL or USR instruction, certain information is placed on the stack. While in the machine language subroutine, you may make use of this information. However, at the end of the subroutine, it is important to return the stack pointer to its position prior to the subroutine call.

Writing a Subroutine for CALL

Execution of the CALL instruction causes the following to happen:

- Six bytes of data needed to return to BASIC are pushed onto the stack. (BASIC takes care of this for you.)
- For each variable passed to the subroutine, a 2-byte address is pushed onto the stack. In the case of our example, this address is the offset address of the variable A%. (The segment address is the beginning of BASIC's workspace.)
- Program execution begins with the first byte of the subroutine.
- The subroutine ends with code that returns execution to the BASIC program.

When the machine language routine gets control, here are the contents of the various registers:

DE, ES, and SS are all equal to the segment address of BASIC's workspace.

CS contains the value specified by the latest DEF SEG instruction. If there was no DEF SEG instruction, CS contains the segment address corresponding to the beginning of BASIC's workspace.

IP contains the offset into the current segment (as specified by CS) at which the subroutine begins.

SP contains the offset into the current segment of the top of the stack.

BP contains information that will be needed on return to BASIC.

If you pass data to your assembly language subroutine, it must begin with the instructions

```
PUSH BP
MOV BP,SP
```

The first of these puts the contents of BP onto the stack for later retrieval. The second instruction moves the contents of the SP (= stack pointer) register into the register BP. This register is used for pointing to the addresses of variables that have been pushed onto the stack by CALL.

If you pass data to your assembly language subroutine, it must end with the instructions

```
POP BP
RET <number>
```

The first restores the contents of BP to what they were at the start of the subroutine. The second instruction peels off all the addresses stored on the stack and does a return from the subroutine. Here <number> is twice the number of variables passed to the subroutine. This is exactly the number of bytes pushed onto the stack by the variable addresses. The RET <number> instruction adjusts the stack pointer so that the stack contains only the 4-byte CS-address stored by CALL. This address is then used to return control to the BASIC program.

If you don't pass data to you machine language program, you need no introductory instructions and your program should end with the instruction

```
RET
```

In our example, we are passing data to the subroutine, so we use the pair of introductory instructions and the pair of ending instructions. These instructions are required. However, they don't do the job of the subroutine itself. Sandwiched in between the two pairs of instructions, you place your subroutine. In our case, the subroutine is almost written. We have gotten this far:

```
MOV SI, <address of A%>
MOV AL, [SI]
ROL AL, 1
MOV [SI],AL
```

In order to complete the program, we must determine the address of A%. But this address has been placed on the stack for us. It is contained in the location [BP]+6. (Remember that [BP] contains the address of the stack just before CALL.) So we write our program

```
MOV SI, [BP]+6
MOV AL, [SI]
ROL AL,1
MOV [SI],AL
```

With the beginning and ending instructions, here is our complete subroutine

```
PUSH BP
MOV BP,SP
MOV SI, [BP]+6
MOV AL, [SI]
ROL AL,1
MOV [SI],AL
POP BP
RET 2
```

In the above subroutine, we passed a single numerical parameter. This was accomplished by PUSHing onto the stack the offset address of the first byte of the parameter. If you wish to pass a string parameter, then the procedure is slightly different. In the latter case, the stack contains the offset address, not of the string itself, but of a three-byte quantity called the **string descriptor**. The first byte contains the length of the string, whereas the second and third bytes contain the offset address of the first byte of the string. Your subroutine must be careful not to change the string descriptor or the length of the corresponding string. You may, however, change the content of the string.

12.5   Using the Assembler

In the preceding section, we arrived at the following machine language program

```
PUSH BP
MOV BP,SP
MOV SI, [BP]+6
MOV AL, [SI]
ROL AL,1
MOV [SI],AL
POP BP
RET 2
```

The program above is in **mnemonic form**. In order for the computer to execute it, we must translate it into the equivalent binary (or hexadecimal) program.

It is possible to code the instructions manually using a table of the 8088 mnemonics and their hexadecimal equivalents. However, this is a time-consuming, tedious chore. It is better to let the computer do the coding by using either of the assemblers available with the IBM Macro Assembler package, namely the Small Assembler, or the Macro Assembler.

To use either of the assemblers, it is necessary to add a certain number of instructions for use of the assembler. Fortunately, at our level, it is not necessary to understand these instructions. They are always the same. At the beginning of the program add

```
CSEG      SEGMENT
          ASSUME CS:CSEG
SUBRT     PROC        FAR
```

At the end of the program add

```
SUBRT     ENDP
CSEG      ENDS
          END
```

Here then is our complete program

```
CSEG      SEGMENT
          ASSUME CS:CSEG
SUBRT     PROC        FAR
          PUSH BP
          MOV BP,SP
          MOV SI, [BP]+6
          MOV AL, [SI]
          ROL AL,1
          MOV [SI],AL
          POP BP
          RET 2
SUBRT     ENDP
CSEG      ENDS
          END
```

Creating the Program Source File

The above assembly language program is called a source program. In order for an assembler to be able to translate a source program into hexadecimal code, you must create a diskette file that contains the above program. There are many ways to create such a file.

- Use a word processing program.
- Use the line editor EDLIN contained on the DOS diskette.
- Use the DOS COPY command. (Copy the file from the keyboard [= CON:] to diskette as described in the chapter on files.)

We will assume that you have used one of these methods (or one of your own devising) to create the file containing the above program. We will assume that the name of the file is MLSUB.ASM. (The extension ASM is required by the assemblers.)

Using The Assembler

To operate the IBM (Small) Assembler, begin with the DOS prompt A> and type

```
ASM <ENTER>
```

Here are the four assembler prompts and the required responses (underlined).

```
Source filename [.ASM]: MLSUB
Object filename [MLSUB.OBJ]: MLSUB.OBJ
Source listing [NUL.LST]: MLSUB.LST
Cross reference [NUL.CRF]: <carriage return>
```

The assembler will translate the source program into an object program located in the file MLSUB.OBJ with a listing in the file MLSUB.LST. For subroutines to be called from BASIC, we will not need the OBJ file at all. Look at the listing file by typing

```
TYPE MLSUB.LST
```

The screen will now display the listing as shown here.(You may obtain a copy of the listing on your printer by pressing CTRL-PrtSc before giving the TYPE command. This will cause the listing to appear on both the screen and the printer.)

The IBM Personal Computer Assembler 04-26-83   PAGE 1-1

```
0000                   CSEG      SEGMENT
                                 ASSUME CS:CSEG
0000                   SUBRT     PROC        FAR
0000   55                        PUSH BP
0001   8B EC                     MOV BP,SP
0003   8B 76 06                  MOV SI, [BP]+6
0006   8A 04                     MOV AL, [SI]
0008   D0 C0                     ROL AL,1
000A   88 04                     MOV [SI], AL
000C   5D                        POP BP
000D   CA 0002                   RET 2
0010                   SUBRT     ENDP
0010                   CSEG      ENDS
                                 END
```

Figure 12.2. Listing of the Subroutine.

From the second column of the listing, we may read off the subroutine in hexadecimal form, namely

55, 8B, EC, 8B, 76, 06, 8A, 04, D0, C0, 88, 04, 5D, CA, 02, 00

WARNING   Note that the last two bytes of the program are 02 and 00, respectively. These come from the last entry of the listing, namely 0002. This is a 16-bit number consisting of 4 hexadecimal digits. Don't forget that 16-bit numbers are stored with their lower 8 bits **first**, followed by the upper 8 bits. Therefore, in our list of bytes, the 02 comes before the 00.

For reference, note that the program contains 16 bytes.

12.6   Placing Your Subroutine Into Memory

Now that we have our machine language subroutine in hexadecimal form, we must put it into memory in a form that the main program can use. Before we can do that, however, we must locate a free section of memory. After all, it won't do for our subroutine to overwrite a section of our main program, DOS, or the BASIC interpreter. Nor can we allow the subroutine to overwrite any of the variables that the main program is using. Since BASIC takes care of its own memory allocation and the process proceeds quite invisibly, finding a portion of memory that is safe is often a tricky business. Here are two reliable methods.

1.   **Stay Outside BASIC's workspace.**
     In BASIC 1.1, the combination of DOS and BASIC requires approximately the first 22K of memory. BASIC utilizes the next 64K as its workspace. Any memory locations above this area may be used for machine language subroutines.

TEST YOUR UNDERSTANDING 1 (answer on page 315)

A system has 128K. Approximately how much memory can be allocated to machine language subroutines?

TEST YOUR UNDERSTANDING 2 (answer on page 315)

Suppose that it is desired to place a machine language subroutine beginning at byte 96K. What is the address (in hexadecimal) of the first location of the subroutine.

---

2.   **Restrict BASIC's Workspace.**
     You may restrict the size of BASIC's workspace to less than 64K, thereby reserving the remainder for machine language subroutines. To do this, use the following statement at the beginning of your program

```
CLEAR , <size of BASIC workspace>
```

For example, to restrict the size of BASIC's workspace to 45000 bytes, you would use the statement:

```
CLEAR , 45000
```

You should not use this statement in the middle of a program since it will cause many side effects, such as erasing variables, undefining user functions, and so forth.

You may determine the segment address of the beginning of BASIC's workspace by PEEKing the memory locations 0000:0510 and 0000:0511. In DOS 1.1, the contents of these addresses are, respectively, 85 and 0B. That is, the BASIC interpreter begins at 0B85:0000.

TEST YOUR UNDERSTANDING 3 (answer on page 315)

Assuming that the BASIC interpreter begins at the above address, and assuming that the system has 64K of RAM, write an instruction that reserves 4K for machine language subroutines.

Let's assume that we have reserved memory space beginning at location 32768 relative to the start of BASIC's workspace. Let's enter our machine language program into the first 16 bytes of this reserved space. One method of doing this is to include the bytes of the program in data statements and put them into the desired memory locations using the POKE statement. This technique is illustrated in the following program:

```
10   CLEAR ,32768!
20   FOR J=1 TO 16
30     READ B%
40     POKE 32767+J, B%
50   NEXT J
110  INPUT "INPUT AN INTEGER";A%
120  ROTATE = 32768!
130  CALL ROTATE (A%): ' Call the subroutine
140  PRINT "THE RESULT IS ";A%
150  END
200  DATA &H55, &H8B, &HEC, &H8B
210  DATA &H76, &H06, &H8B, &H04
220  DATA &HD0, &HC0, &H89, &H04
230  DATA &H5D, &HCA, &H02, &H00
```

Note that line 10 reserves memory beginning at location 32768 relative to the beginning of BASIC's workspace. The loop in lines 20-50 POKEs the machine language program into the desired location in memory. The machine language program is contained in the data statements of lines 200-

230. Note that each byte is preceded by &H. This is to let BASIC know that these numbers are in hexadecimal.

To check out our program, let's run it. It requests

`INPUT AN INTEGER?`

Type 1 followed by ENTER. The computer responds

`THE RESULT IS    2`

Indeed, we have set

A% = 1 decimal = 0000 0000 0000 0001 binary

When we rotate the low 8 bits of A%, we obtain

0000 0000 0000 0010 binary = 2 decimal

Similarly, A%=7 yields a result of 14. This is correct since

7 decimal = 0000 0000 0000 0111 binary

14 decimal = 0000 0000 0000 1110 binary

To check that the upper 8 bits remain unchanged, set A%=256. The result is 256. Indeed,

256 decimal = 0000 0001 0000 0000 binary

Therefore, 256 has no non-zero bits among bits 0-7. So it remains unchanged upon rotation.

TEST YOUR UNDERSTANDING 4 (answer on page 315)

What is the result if the input is 758? Can you confirm this manually?

A Second Method of Entering the Subroutine

Here is another method of entering the subroutine into memory. First, let's create a diskette file, called ROTATE, which contains a binary image of the file. This file will be read into memory by the BASIC program prior to the subroutine call.

To create a binary image of the file, let's first write the file into memory at its proper position. This may be accomplished using the following simple BASIC program.

```
100 'Create a memory image file
110 INPUT "NAME OF DISKETTE FILE";FILENAME$
120 BYTECOUNT=0
130 INPUT "STARTING LOCATION (OFFSET)";START
140 PRINT "ENTER BYTE IN RESPONSE TO PROMPT."
150 PRINT "TYPE ONLY HEXADECIMAL DIGITS OF BYTE."
```

```
160 PRINT "TO INDICATE THE END OF THE PROGRAM, TYPE > ."
170 'Input bytes
180 INPUT "BYTE=";A$
190 IF A$=">" THEN 250
200 BYTECOUNT=BYTECOUNT+1
210 A$="&H"+A$
220 BYTE=VAL(A$)
230 POKE START+BYTECOUNT,BYTE
240 GOTO 180
250 'Write binary file to diskette
260 BSAVE FILENAME$,START,BYTECOUNT
270 END
```

Note that to use this program, you enter the bytes without the prefix &H. Just enter the hexadecimal digits. That is, instead of &HB8, you would enter B8. This approach leads to less typing. Note that the routine POKEs the input bytes into consecutive memory locations beginning with the given starting location, as specified in the variable START. The number of bytes POKEd is recorded in the variable BYTECOUNT.

After the last byte has been specified, the program saves a binary image of the bytes input, using the BSAVE command. The format of this command is

```
BSAVE <filename>, <starting location>, <number of bytes>
```

In our program, the filename is given by FILENAME$, the starting location is given by the variable START, and the number of bytes is recorded in BYTECOUNT. The starting location is an offset address with corresponding segment address equal to that given in the most recent DEF SEG instruction. If no DEF SEG instruction is used, then the segment address is equal to the beginning of BASIC's workspace.

TEST YOUR UNDERSTANDING 5 (answer on page 315)

Write instructions for saving as a binary image the region of memory beginning with location 00FF:FA73 and continuing for 1000 bytes.

TEST YOUR UNDERSTANDING 6 (answer on page 315)

Use the above program to create a binary file called ROTATE that contains the machine language program we have been considering in this chapter.

Once the file ROTATE is saved on diskette, you may call it back using the BLOAD instruction. This instruction has the format

```
BLOAD <file name>, <starting location>
```

Its effect is to load the bytes specified in the file into memory, beginning at the specified location. As usual, the starting location is an offset address, with the segment address determined specified in the usual way. In our case, the proper BLOAD instruction is

```
BLOAD "ROTATE", 32768
```

Here is how this instruction may be incorporated into a program together with the CALL to the subroutine.

```
10 CLEAR ,32768!
20 BLOAD "ROTATE",32768
110 INPUT "INPUT AN INTEGER";A%
120 ROTATE = 32768!
130 CALL ROTATE (A%)
140 PRINT "THE RESULT IS ";A%
150 END
```

Note that the use of the BLOAD instruction simplifies the calling program a great deal.

Exercise

1. The DOS Manual advises that you may print a graphics screen on the IBM Graphics Printer from within a program using the machine language program:

    ```
    PUSH BP
    INT 5
    POP BP
    ```

    (a) Write a machine language subroutine for printing a graphics screen from a BASIC program.

    (b) Compile the program to determine the hexadecimal equivalent of the program.

    (c) Test your subroutine by printing out a graphics image.

ANSWERS TO TEST YOUR UNDERSTANDING

1: 32K

2: 1800:0000

3: CLEAR , 58491

4: 10 11101101

5: ```
    10 DEF SEG = &HOOFF
    20 BSAVE FILENAME, &HFA73, 1000
    30 DEF SEG
    ```

6:  Use the program of TYU 5, with FILENAME replaced by ROTATE.

---
    ```

12.7   Some Final Observations

As we have seen in this chapter, it is reasonably difficult to use machine language subroutines from within a BASIC program. At this point you may be wondering, Why bother? Well, we stated the main reasons at the beginning of the chapter: Increased speed of execution and the ability to perform certain operations that may be clumsy in BASIC. Of course, the suitability of machine language subroutines must be decided on a case-by-case basis. You must decide whether it will be worth the savings in execution time and/or program length to develop an appropriate machine language subroutine. In general, you would not develop such a subroutine for a program that will be used only a few times. Similarly, you would not develop such a subroutine for a program that already runs reasonably quickly. However, if speed and/or program size are critical issues, then perhaps machine language programs are the answer.

13

Some Features of DOS 2.00

In early 1983, IBM released version 2.00 of DOS. This version is a significant enhancement of the previous release 1.00, 1.05 and 1.10. In this chapter, we summarize some of the most significant new features of DOS 2.00.

13.1   Paths, Directories, and Subdirectories

Directories and Subdirectories

DOS 2.00 allows you to manipulate files contained on a hard disk drive, such as the one contained in the system unit of the PC/XT. As far as the user is concerned, a hard disk functions much like a floppy disk, except for its greater storage capacity and its higher speed. However, a hard disk may contain thousands of files at one time. A single directory would be unwieldy. It would be difficult for you to look at and it would be slow for the computer to search for a particular file. To combat this problem, DOS 2.00 allows you to organize your directory in a "tree structure."

To explain what we mean, consider the typical DOS 2.00 directory shown in Figure 13.1.

```
Volume in drive C is DOS
Directory of C:\MIDWEST

.               <DIR>       4-17-83     7:49p
..              <DIR>       4-17-83     7:49p
PAYROLL    83   <DIR>       4-30-83    10:09a
PERSON     83   <DIR>       5-12-83    11:00a
INVENTRY   83   <DIR>       5-12-83     3:45p
MEMO      518   5847        5-18-83     1:12p
MEMO      520   4850        5-20-83     3:24p
```

Figure 13.1. A DOS 2.00 Directory.

The first line of the directory gives the volume title. DOS 2.00 allows you to assign a title to a disk. In this case, the contents of the hard disk are named "DOS" (Drive C: is the hard disk). A typical DOS 2.00 directory has two sorts of entries, files and directories. A file entry is exactly the same sort of entry as used in DOS 1.1 . For example, the directory of Figure 13.1 lists the files MEMO.518 and MEMO.520. The notations <DIR> indicate that all of the other entries are directories: PAYROLL.83, PERSON.83, INVENTRY.83. Each of these directories are **subdirectories** of the directory shown. They may each contain files and directories of their own. (Don't worry about the directories "." and ".." for now. They serve a purely technical role.)

In DOS 2.00, each directory has a name, which may consist of a main part and an extension. The rules for directory names are the same as for file names. (The main name may contain up to 8 characters; the extension up to three; and so forth.) For example, the directory shown in Figure 13.1 has the name MIDWEST. The organization of files into directories may be described as a **tree**. For example, Figure 13.2 shows the relationship of the directory of Figure 13.1 with other directories on the same disk. The main directory RECORDS has three subdirectories: MIDWEST, SOUTH, and NORTH-EAST. Each of these subdirectories has several subdirectories as well as several files.

Note that a file or directory name may be repeated in various parts of a tree. For example, each of the directories MIDWEST, SOUTH, and NORTHEAST has a subdirectory named PERSON. However, each directory named PERSON is independent; their respective contents need have nothing to do with one other.

The Root Directory

When a diskette is formatted, DOS creates a master directory called the **root directory**, designated by the symbol \. (This symbol is called a **backslash**. You may type it from the keyboard using the key just to the right of the left Shift key.) All directories are subdirectories of the root directory. Note the root directory at the bottom of the tree in Figure 13.2.

The Current Directory

At any given moment, each disk drive has a directory designated the **current directory**. If you give a DOS command without specifying a directory, then the current directory is assumed. When DOS is started, the current directory is the root directory for each drive.

Here are some examples of DOS commands that refer to the current directory.

```
C:
DIR A:
```

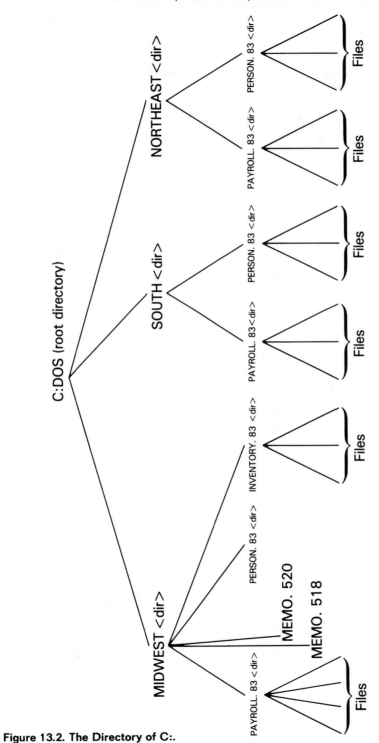

Figure 13.2. The Directory of C:.

The first command changes the current drive to C: and the directory to the current directory of C:. The second command lists the contents of the current directory of the diskette in drive A:.

Paths

To completely specify a file for use in a DOS command, you must give the drive, the file name and the path to the file starting from the current directory. For example, suppose that the current directory is MIDWEST and you wish to refer to FILE.1. You would specify the file with the path

```
INVENTRY\FILE.1
```

This sequence of names is called a **path**. It tells DOS that to find the file, start from the current directory, go to the subdirectory INVENTRY, and then to FILE.1. As a second example, suppose that the current directory is the root directory. Then the path to FILE.1 is

```
MIDWEST\INVENTRY\FILE.1
```

As a third example, suppose that the current drive is A:. The path to FILE.1 is now

```
C:\MIDWEST\INVENTRY\FILE.1
```

(The path begins with \ to indicate that the search should begin with the root directory.)

Most DOS commands may use paths instead of file names. For example, suppose that the current directory is MIDWEST. Then the command

```
DIR INVENTRY
```

will list the contents of the subdirectory INVENTRY. Similarly, suppose that the current drive is A:. Then the command

```
COPY C:\MIDWEST\INVENTRY\*.* A:
```

will copy all files in the subdirectory C:\MIDWEST\INVENTRY to the current directory of the diskette in drive A:.

Any missing parameters in a path mean that the current value of the parameter is to be assumed. For example, if the drive designation is omitted, then the current drive is assumed. If the path is omitted, then the current directory is assumed.

TEST YOUR UNDERSTANDING 1 (answer on page 324)

(a) Write a command to list the directory of NORTH\PERSON.

(b) Write a command to copy all files in NORTH\PERSON to SOUTH\INVENT.

TEST YOUR UNDERSTANDING 2 (answer on page 324)

What does this command do?

    COPY A:*.* C:

TEST YOUR UNDERSTANDING 3 (answer on page 324)

What does this command do?

    COPY *.* A:

The symbol .. may be used in a path to indicate a move one level down the tree, from a subdirectory to its "parent directory." For example, suppose that the current directory is MIDWEST. Then the path

    ..

refers to the root directory. Similarly, if the current directory is the subdirectory INVENTRY of MIDWEST, then the path

    ..\..

describes a move two steps down the tree, to the root directory. As yet another example, suppose that we wish to get to the subdirectory PERSON of SOUTH from the subdirectory INVENTRY of MIDWEST. We must go down to the root directory and back up to PERSON. Here is a path that describes these moves.

    ..\..\SOUTH\PERSON

DOS 2.00 limits the length of paths to 63 characters.

Changing the Current Directory

You may change the current directory by using the DOS command CHDIR. For example, suppose that the current directory is MIDWEST and we wish to change to the subdirectory PERSON. The proper command is

    CHDIR PERSON

The general format of the CHDIR command is

    CHDIR <path>

Here <path> is a path from the current directory to the desired current directory.

If a drive designation is included in the path, then CHDIR will change the current directory on the indicated drive. However, the current drive is not changed. For example, suppose that you wish to perform the directory change ".." for drive A: and the current drive is C:. The command

```
CHDIR A:..
```

will change the current directory on A: but will leave the current drive as C:.

Directory changes occur so often that DOS 2.00 allows you to use the shorthand CD instead of CHDIR.

TEST YOUR UNDERSTANDING 4 (answer on page 324)

(a) Suppose that the current directory is MIDWEST. Write a command that changes the current directory to the root directory.

(b) Suppose that the current directory is MIDWEST. Write a command that changes the current directory to the subdirectory PERSON of SOUTH.

(c) Suppose that the current directory is MIDWEST and the current drive is C:. Change the current drive to A: and perform the directory change .. on C: .

Creating and Deleting Directories

You may create directories using the MKDIR command. For example, suppose that the current directory is the root directory. To create the subdirectory MIDWEST, we would use the command

```
MKDIR \MIDWEST
```

Still assuming that the current directory is the root directory, we may create the subdirectory INVENTRY of MIDWEST using the command

```
MKDIR \MIDWEST\INVENTRY
```

The general form of the MKDIR command is

```
MKDIR [drive:]path
```

If the drive is omitted, then the current drive is assumed. DOS allows you to use the shorthand MD as a substitute for MKDIR.

TEST YOUR UNDERSTANDING 5 (answer on page 324)

Suppose that the current directory is MIDWEST. Write a command to create the directory SOUTH in the root directory.

Note that you cannot copy files into a directory until the directory is created by the MKDIR command. BASIC and DOS will respond to any attempt to reference a non-existent directory with an **Invalid Directory or Filename** error.

The MKDIR command creates the specified directory and enters in it two files, named . and .. . The first of these contains the names of all files and subdirectories contained within the particular directory. Initially, the file . contains no entries. The file .. specifies the directory to which this subdirectory belongs. That is, the file .. contains the information necessary to descend one level in the tree.

The root directory may contain as many as 64 entries in case of a single-sided diskette or 112 entries in case of a double-sided diskette or a hard disk. However, there are no limitations on the number of entries in a subdirectory.

You may delete a directory using the RMDIR command. To remove a directory, it must contain only the files . and .. . (This is a safety feature so that you will not accidentally delete files by mistake.) The RMDIR command works similarly to the command MKDIR. It has the format

```
RMDIR [drive:] path
```

For example, if the current directory is the root directory, then you may remove the subdirectory PERSON of MIDWEST using the command

```
RMDIR /MIDWEST/PERSON
```

If you attempt to remove a directory containing files other than . and .. , then DOS will report an error.

DOS allows the shorthand RM as a substitute for RMDIR.

COPY and ERASE in DOS 2.00

You may add files to a directory in the usual ways, using the COPY command, for instance. Similarly, you may erase files using the ERASE command. The new feature in DOS 2.00 is that both COPY and ERASE may use paths to describe the files involved. Of course, you may omit the paths if you wish to refer to files in the current directory.

For example, to COPY FILE1 to the current directory of drive C:, we use the command

```
COPY FILE1 C:
```

Suppose that the current directory is the root directory and we wish to copy FILE1 into the subdirectory MIDWEST\PERSON. We use the command

```
COPY FILE1 MIDWEST\PERSON
```

After performing this command, we could then erase FILE1 using the command

```
ERASE FILE1
```

NOTE The COPY and ERASE commands refer only to files and not to directories. To copy the contents of a directory, you must first use MKDIR to create a directory with the proper name. Then use the COPY command to copy the desired files into the new directory.

TEST YOUR UNDERSTANDING 6 (answer on page 324)

(a)   Write a command to copy all files in the current directory on A: to the directory MIDWEST\INVENTRY .

(b)   Write a command to erase all files in the root directory of drive A:.

The concept of a tree-structured directory is most useful for systems equipped with a hard disk, since it is a hard disk that most needs a tree-structured directory's organization. But what if you don't have a hard disk? In this case, you have two choices. You may use the tree-structured directories of DOS 2.00 as if your diskette were a hard disk. Or you may ignore them completely and continue to use a single directory a la DOS 1.1.

ANSWERS TO TEST YOUR UNDERSTANDING

1:   (a)   `DIR NORTH/PERSON`
     (b)   `COPY NORTH\PERSON\*.* SOUTH\INVENT`

2:   It copies all files on the diskette in drive A: onto the current directory.

3:   It copies all files in the current directory onto the diskette in drive A:.

4:   (a)   `CD .. <ENTER>`
     (b)   `CD ..\SOUTH\PERSON <ENTER>`
     (c)   `A:<ENTER>`

   `CD C:.. <ENTER>`

5:   `MD ..\SOUTH`

6:   (a)   `COPY A:*.* C:MIDWEST\INVENTRY`
     (b)   `ERASE A:*.*`

13.2   A Survey of Changes in DOS 2.00

In the last section, we discussed the enhanced directory structure of DOS 2.00, and the commands COPY, ERASE, DIR, CHDIR, MKDIR, and RMDIR. Let's now survey the changes in other DOS 1.1 commands.

In describing the format of the various commands, we will enclose in brackets [ ] input data that is optional.

Commands Unchanged in DOS 2.00

Several of the commands in DOS 2.00 work exactly like their counterparts in DOS 1.1 . In this category are the commands DATE, SYS, and TIME.

DATE—Used to set the date or to display the current date. It has the format

```
DATE [mm-dd-yy]
```

Here mm-dd-yy is the date in the form month (1-12), day (1-31), and year (80-99). If the date is included, DATE sets the date. Otherwise, the date is displayed.

TIME—Used to set or display the time. It has the format

```
TIME [hh-mm-ss]
```

Here hh-mm-ss is the time in hours (0-23), minutes (0-59), and seconds (0-59). If the time is included, then TIME sets the time. Otherwise, the time is displayed.

SYS—Allows you to write DOS onto a diskette. Space must have been reserved on the diskette, since DOS must reside only in certain sectors. To record DOS on the diskette in drive d:, use the command

```
SYS [d:]
```

If the [d:] is omitted, then DOS will be written onto the diskette in the default drive.

Commands With Minor Changes in DOS 2.00

The commands COMP, DIR, DISCOMP, DISKCOPY, RENAME, and TYPE are subject to minor changes in DOS 2.00, mainly to allow the use of paths instead of file names.

COMP—Allows you to compare two files to determine whether they are the same. Here is the format of the COMP command.

```
COMP [d:][path][filename] [d:][path][filename]
```

If you omit either of the two sets of file data, DOS will prompt you to supply them. In DOS 2.00, you may use wild card characters * and ? in the file data to compare several files in one operation.

DIR—Allows you to list the directory corresponding to a given set of file data. Here is the format of the DIR command

```
DIR [d:][path][filename] [/P] [/W]
```

You may use this command to display the directory information about a single file or about a collection of files described by a path. The /P option tells DOS to pause after each screenful of data. You may continue with the listing of file data by pressing any key. The /W option displays the files by name only and in a wide format, allowing you to view the contents of especially large directories.

   DISKCOMP—Allows you to compare the contents of two diskettes. Here is the format of the DISKCOMP command.

```
DISKCOMP [d:] [d:] [/1] [/8]
```

If you omit a drive designation, then the default drive is assumed. The /1 option allows you to compare only the first sides of two-sided diskettes. The /8 option allows you to compare only 8 sectors per track (sectors 1-8) even if the diskettes have been formatted with 9 sectors per track.

   DISKCOPY—Allows you to copy the contents of one diskette onto another. Here is the format of the DISKCOPY command

```
DISKCOPY [d:] [d:] [/1]
```

If you omit a drive designation, then the default drive is assumed. The /1 option allows you to copy only one side of a two-sided diskette. If the target diskette is not formatted, then the DISKCOPY command will also format. It will format the target diskette in exactly the same format as the source diskette.

   RENAME—Allows you to rename a file. Here is the format of the RENAME command

```
RENAME [d:][path][filename] [filename]
```

You may use wild card characters * and ? in the filenames. Any portions of a file name that are unambiguous are carried over from the statement of the command. The ambiguous characters are determined from the name of the source file.

   TYPE—Allows you to display the contents of a file. Here is the format of the TYPE command

```
TYPE [d:][path][filename]
```

Commands With Substantive Changes in DOS 2.00

   Let us now discuss the DOS 1.1 commands that underwent more substantial revision in DOS 2.00.

   CHKDSK—Allows you to check the directories and file allocation table for inconsistencies and to display a report on unused disk and memory space. Here is the format of the CHKDSK command:

```
CHKDSK [d:][filename][/F][/V]
```

If you specify a filename, CHKDSK will analyze the memory allocated for the designated file. CHKDSK will look only at the current directory, so no path is allowed. The /F option tells CHKDSK to fix any errors that it finds. The /V option tells CHKDSK to report on its progress with the errors it finds and their locations.

FORMAT—Allows you to format a diskette. Here is the format of the FORMAT command.

```
FORMAT [d:][/S][/1][/8][/V][/B]
```

The /S option allows you to copy the system files onto the diskette. The /1 option allows you to format the diskette as single-sided. The /8 option allows you to format the diskette with 8 sectors per track. The /V option will prompt you for a volume name. The /B option reserves space for any version of DOS. With this option, you may later write DOS 1.00, 1.05, 1.10 or 2.00 onto the diskette with the SYS command. Without the /B option you may place only DOS 2.00 onto the diskette.

The default FORMAT in DOS 2.00 makes the diskette double-sided with 9 sectors per track.

As part of the FORMAT operation, the sectors are verified and any defective sectors are marked so that they will not be included in a file. FORMAT reports on the total number of bytes on the diskette, the number of defective bytes, the number of bytes allocated to system files, and the number of free bytes available.

MODE—Allows you to set parameters for the screen, printer, or asynchronous communications adapter.

Option 1-Printer—Allows you to set parameters for the printer. The format of the MODE command for Option 1 is

```
MODE LPT#:[n][,[m]][,[P]]
```

where # is the number of the printer (1-3), n is the number of characters per line (80 or 132), m is the number of lines per inch vertically (6 or 8), and P specifies a continuous retry in case of time-out errors.

Option 2-Screen—Allows you to set parameters for the screen. The format of the MODE command for Option 2 is

```
MODE [n],m[,T]
```

Here n controls the adapter, color, and line width. The possibilities for n are

```
  40 — color/graphics adapter, 40 characters per line
  80 — color/graphics adapter, 80 characters per line
BW40 — color/graphics adapter, no color, 40 characters per line
BW80 — color/graphics adapter, no color, 80 characters per line
CO40 — color/graphics adapter, color, 40 characters per line
CO80 — color/graphics adapter, color, 80 characters per line
MONO — monochrome display adapter
```

The parameter m allows you to shift the display one character right or left; m is either R (right shift) or L (left shift).

The parameter T tells DOS to display a test pattern to align the display.

Option 3-Asynchronous Communications Adapter—Allows you to define the parameters for the communications adapter. The format of the MODE command for Option 3 is

```
MOD COMn:baud[,parity[,databits[,stopbits[,P]]]]
```

Here:

n is the number of the communications adapter (1-3)

baud is the desired baud rate

parity = N (no parity), O (odd parity), E (even)

databits—7 or 8

stopbits—1 or 2

P—indicates connection to a serial printer. Device time-outs are continuously retried.

The default settings are even parity, 7 databits, and 2 stopbit if baud = 110, and 1 stopbit otherwise. Note that the baud must always be specified.

Option 4-Redirection of Parallel Printer To Asynchronous Communications Adapter—For this option, the MODE command has the format

```
MODE LPT#:=COMn
```

Here # is the number of the printer and n is the number of the asynchronous communications adapter. To use this option, you must first initialize the asynchronous communications adapter by using the MODE command in Option 3.

13.3   New Commands in DOS 2.00

Let's now discuss the commands which are new in DOS 2.00.

ASSIGN

This command allows you to redirect all instructions involving one drive to another drive. For example, the command

```
ASSIGN A=B C=D
```

reroutes all requests involving drive A to B and drive C to drive D. The command

```
ASSIGN
```

returns the drive routing to its default setting: A to A, B to B, and so forth.

An ASSIGN command remains in effect until another ASSIGN command is given or DOS is restarted. Drive reassignments are ignored by DISK-COPY and DISKCOMP.

TEST YOUR UNDERSTANDING 1 (answer on page 334)

Write a command that assigns all diskette commands for drive C: to drive A:.

BACKUP

A hard disk may contain literally thousands of files. To guard against possible data loss, it is advisable to keep backup copies of all hard disk data on diskette. The BACKUP command allows you to make such copies with a minimum of operator input. To use the BACKUP command, you must have formatted diskettes ready with sufficient capacity to contain the files to be backed up. The format of the BACKUP command is

```
BACKUP [d:][path][filename] d:[/S][/M][/A][D:mm-dd-yy]
```

This command instructs DOS to back up the files specified by [d:][path][filename] onto the diskettes to be inserted in drive d: . DOS will instruct you to insert the diskettes, as needed.

The BACKUP process may be quite time consuming. For this reason, there are several options that allow you to be selective in the files you back up.

The /S option tells DOS to back up all files in the subdirectories of the indicated path. For example, suppose that the path was

```
C:MIDWEST
```

where MIDWEST is a subdirectory of the root directory of C:. The /S option tells DOS to back up all files in MIDWEST, all files in any subdirectories of MIDWEST, all subdirectories of those subdirectories, and so forth.

The /M option tells DOS to back up only those files that have been modified since the most recent backup operation. This option is especially useful if you have modified only a few files of a directory since the last backup. Using the /M option may save a lot of time.

The /D:mm-dd-yy operation allows you to backup only those files that have been either created or modified since the given date mm-dd-yy.

The /A option tells DOS to add the backup files to the diskette already in the specified drive.

TEST YOUR UNDERSTANDING 2 (answers on page 334)

Write commands to do the following backup operations.

(a)   Backup all files in the current directory of C: .

(b)   Backup all files in the directory C:MIDWEST that have been modified since the last backup.

(c)   Backup the file specified by MIDWEST\INVENT\STATUS.051 .

(d)   Backup the files in the direcory MIDWEST that have been modified since Dec. 4, 1983.

BREAK

Under default conditions, DOS checks for the Ctrl-Break combination only during screen, keyboard, printer, or communications adapter operations. However, you may instruct DOS to check for Ctrl-Break during any program-requested DOS operations. This would enable you to interrupt a diskette read or write operation, for example. To enable checking for Ctrl-Break, use the command

`BREAK ON`

To disable checking, use the command

`BREAK OFF`

CLS

The CLS command enables you to clear the screen from DOS.

GRAPHICS

The GRAPHICS command allows you to print the screen on the IBM Graphics Printer. This command is invoked by pressing Ctrl-PrtSc. If the computer is in one of the graphics modes, printing may take up to three minutes. In high-resolution graphics mode, the image is printed sideways on the paper.

PATH

Under default conditions, you may run only programs that are in the current directory, and those programs may make reference only to files in the current directory. However, the PATH command allows you to alter these conditions by specifying alternate paths to search for programs of data files. The format of the path command is

```
PATH [d:]path;[[d:]path;...]
```

When you issue a command or make reference to a file, DOS will first look in the current directory. If the program or file is not found, DOS will then look in each of the paths specified by PATH, in the order in which the paths are listed.

TEST YOUR UNDERSTANDING 3 (answer on page 334)

Write a command that tells DOS to refer to the directories MIDWEST, NORTH, and A:CURRENT.

PRINT

The PRINT command is a sophisticated file transfer utility that allows you to transfer a copy of a file to any of the devices LPT1:, LPT2:, LPT3:, COM1:, COM2:, AUX:, or PRN: . Moreover, it allows you to specify up to 10 files to be transferred. The transfer may take place while the computer is being used for other tasks. The format of the PRINT command is

```
PRINT [[d:][filename][/T][/C][/P]...]
```

For example, to PRINT the files FILE1 and FILE2, you would use the command

```
PRINT FILE1 FILE2
```

The files to be printed must be contained in the current directory. However, after the PRINT command has been given, you may change the current directory without affecting the PRINT operation.

The first time you execute a PRINT command after system startup, DOS gives you an opportunity to identify the receiving device. DOS supplies the prompt

```
Name of list device [PRN]:
```

You may type any of the device names given above. If you press ENTER, then you are choosing the default device PRN: .

The /T option terminates printing of the current file and cancels all files waiting to be printed.

The /C option selectively cancels printing of the files listed. Cancellation begins with the file name preceding the /C and continues until a /P is encountered. If no /P is encountered, then cancellation applies to all files listed.

The /P option allows you to add files to the print list. A file name followed by /P is added to the list, as are all subsequent files. Adding files continues until a file name is followed by /C.

TEST YOUR UNDERSTANDING 4 (answer on page 334)

Write DOS commands to perform the following operations:
(a) Print the files FILE1 and FILE2
(b) Add the files FILE3 and FILE4 to the print list.
(c) Cancel printing of FILE4.
(d) Terminate all printing.
(e) Print the files to the communications adapter COM1: .

RECOVER

After you write a file on a diskette, the diskette, for one of many reasons, may develop a bad sector that destroys some of the data of the file. The RECOVER command allows you to recover the undamaged data from such a file. The format of the the RECOVER command is

```
RECOVER [d:][path][filename]
```

or

```
RECOVER d:
```

In the first format, the RECOVER command reconstructs the data file, inserting blanks for the damaged data. The second format is used to RECOVER all files on a diskette in case the directory is damaged.

RESTORE

The RESTORE command is the reverse of BACKUP and allows you to write from a backup diskette to a hard disk. The format of the RESTORE command is

```
RESTORE d: [d:][path][filename][/S][/P]
```

For example, to restore the contents of the backup diskette in drive A: to the current directory of the hard disk, we could use the command

```
RESTORE A: C:
```

To restore all files on drive A: with names MEMO.* to the directory MID-WEST, we could use the command

```
RESTORE A: MIDWEST\MEMO.*
```

The /S option is similar to the /S option of the BACKUP command. It allows you to restore all files in all subdirectories of the indicated directory, as well as all files in sub-sub directories, and so forth.

The /P option tells DOS to prompt you with the names of files that have changed since they were last backed up or that are read-only. You may then decide whether to restore the file.

Note that a BACKUP copy of a file should not be used by a program. The DOS BACKUP command uses all the space on a diskette. If there is not enough space for an entire file, then DOS splits the file between two diskettes. Your program has no way of telling whether or not you have the entire file on the current diskette. So before using a BACKUP copy of a file, do a RESTORE first.

TREE

The TREE command allows you to display the directory of a disk in tree form. The command

```
TREE d:
```

displays all directories on drive d:. Along with each directory, DOS lists all subdirectories; and with each subdirectory, its subdirectories, and so forth.

The option /F allows you to include all files in the tree listing. For example, to list all directories and files on the disk C:, use the command

```
TREE C: /F
```

In most cases, the output of TREE will take up more than a single screen. To inspect the output, you may press Ctrl-Prtsc prior to giving the TREE command. The output will then be sent to both the screen and printer.

VER

This command causes DOS to display the version number in the form

```
IBM Personal Computer DOS Version 2.00
```

VERIFY

Under default conditions, DOS does not verify the accuracy of disk write and read operations. You may enable or disable disk operation verification using the VERIFY command. To enable verification, use the command

```
VERIFY ON
```

To disable verification, use the command

```
VERIFY OFF
```

If verification is enabled, then diskette read and write operations will be slowed considerably.

VOL

The VOL command displays the volume name of a specified diskette. For example, to display the volume name of disk C:, use the command

```
VOL C:
```

The name is displayed in the form

```
Volume in drive C: is RECORDS
```

The volume name is the one given when the disk was formatted.

```
VOL [d:]
```

ANSWERS TO TEST YOUR UNDERSTANDING

```
1:   ASSIGN C=A
2:   (a)    BACKUP C: A:
     (b)    BACKUP C:MIDWEST\*.* A: /M
     (c)    BACKUP C:MIDWEST\INVENT\STATUS.051 A:
     (d)    BACKUP C:MIDWEST A: /D12-04-83
3:   PATH MIDEST;NORTH;A:CURRENT
4:   (a)    PRINT FILE1 FILE2
     (b)    PRINT FILE3/A FILE4
     (c)    PRINT FILE4/C
     (d)    PRINT /T
     (e)    Answer the initial prompt with COM1: and press ENTER.
```

13.4 Enhanced Batch File Capability

DOS 2.00 has a greatly expanded batch file capability from DOS 1.1. In this section, we will survey this capability. Our discussion assumes that you are familiar with batch files in DOS 1.1. More precisely, we assume as background the material in Section 3.8 of [GG].

DOS 2.00 batch files control the execution of sequences of DOS commands and/or user programs. The batch files of DOS 2.00 are actually programs in their own right. In DOS 2.00, you may have a batch file execute a command or not, depending on the truth or falsity of a particular condition. You may also specify looping of commands.

The enhanced features of DOS 2.00 batch commands are controlled by the subcommands

```
ECHO
FOR
GOTO
IF [NOT]
SHIFT
PAUSE
REM
```

You use these commands within a batch file exactly as if they were DOS commands.

ECHO

The ECHO subcommand controls certain aspects of screen display during execution of a batch file. Under default conditions (as well as DOS 1.1), DOS displays each DOS command as it is being performed. For example, suppose that a batch file is executing the command

```
COPY *.* C:
```

Then DOS will display the command while it is being executed.

The subcommand

```
ECHO OFF
```

disables the command display. Note, however, that ECHO OFF does not affect displays other than the display of the current command.

The subcommand

```
ECHO ON
```

cancels the ECHO OFF subcommand. This returns the command display to the default condition.

For example, here is a batch file employing ECHO.

```
ECHO OFF
COPY FILE1 C:
COPY FILE2 C:
COPY FILE3 C:
ECHO ON
```

The ECHO OFF turns off the display of subsequent commands. The ECHO ON returns DOS to the default condition in which commands are displayed. Note, however, that the command ECHO OFF is displayed and will remain displayed while the other commands of the batch file are executed. You may remove the display of the command ECHO OFF by following that command with the DOS command CLS. This clears the screen, erasing ECHO OFF.

You may display a message from a batch file using the subcommand

```
ECHO <message>
```

For example, to display the message "Copying Files . . . Wait", you could use the command

```
ECHO Copying Files...Wait
```

PAUSE

The PAUSE subcommand allows you to pause execution of a batch file to allow you to take some action (such as to change diskettes). The PAUSE subcommand displays the prompt

```
Strike a key when ready
```

Execution of the batch file is suspended until a key is pressed. You may include an optional remark with the PAUSE subcommand. For example, to display "Insert Data Diskette 2" and pause, we would use the command

```
PAUSE Insert Data Diskette 2
```

The display will read

```
Insert Data Diskette 2
Strike a key when ready
```

TEST YOUR UNDERSTANDING 1 (answer on page 341)

Write a batch file that copies FILE1 onto FILE2. The batch file should pause and display the instruction "Insert diskette containing FILE1".

REM

This subcommand allows you to annotate a batch file with remarks. Note, however, that if ECHO is ON, then the remarks will be displayed as the batch file encounters the REM subcommands.

Labels and GOTO

You may insert labels to identify various points in a batch file. A label is a string of up to 8 characters. (You may actually use more than 8 characters, but only the first 8 are significant.) For example, here is a batch file in which we have included the label LABEL1.

```
LABEL1:
COPY FILE1 FILE2
```

Note that the label has a colon following it. Labels are not displayed as commands.

The GOTO subcommand allows you to control the flow of execution of a batch file by causing a jump to a label. For example, to jump to LABEL1, we would use the command

```
GOTO LABEL1
```

When this command is encountered in a batch file, DOS checks the file for the location of LABEL1. If LABEL1 is found, then execution resumes with the command immediately after LABEL1. If the label is not found, then DOS prints the message

```
Label not found
```

and goes to the next command in the batch file.

TEST YOUR UNDERSTANDING 2 (answer on page 341)

Write a batch file to repeatedly display the volume label of the diskette in drive A:. (The only way to stop such a batch file is to use Ctrl-Break.)

FOR

The FOR subcommand allows you to execute loops within a batch file. The format of this subcommand is

```
FOR %%variable IN <set> DO <command>
```

Here %%variable is a dummy parameter that may be used within <command>. This dummy parameter must be preceded by %%. An example is %%FILE.

The dummy parameter %%variable is set equal to the values in <set>. For instance, to let %%FILE assume the values FILE1, FILE2 and FILE3, <set> would assume the form

```
(FILE1 FILE2 FILE3)
```

Note that the items of <set> are enclosed within parentheses and individual items are separated by spaces.

The <command> may be any DOS command or a program that runs under DOS. The FOR subcommand allows %%variable to assume each value in <set>. It then performs <command>. For example, to copy FILE1, FILE2, and FILE3 onto the diskette in drive B:, we could use the command

```
FOR %%FILE IN (FILE1 FILE2 FILE3) DO COPY %%FILE B:
```

At first %%FILE is equal to FILE1 and DOS performs the command

```
COPY FILE1 B:
```

Next %%FILE is equal to FILE2 and DOS performs the command

```
COPY FILE2 B:
```

Finally, %%FILE is equal to FILE3 and DOS performs the command

```
COPY FILE3 B:
```

TEST YOUR UNDERSTANDING 3 (answer on page 341)

Use the FOR command to run the BASIC programs PROG1.BAS, PROG2.BAS, and PROG3.BAS one after another.

IF

The IF subcommand allows you to execute commands conditionally. The possible forms of the IF subcommand are

```
IF <condition> <command>
IF NOT <condition> <command>
```

For the first form, if <condition> is true, then <command> is executed; if <condition> is false, the control skips to the next command in the batch file. For the second form, if <condition> is false, then <command> is executed; if <condition> is true, then control skips to the next command in the batch file.

<command> may be any DOS command or a program name.

There are three possible forms for <condition>:

EXIST filespec—This form allows you to test if the given file specification (filespec) actually corresponds to a file in the current directory. (Paths may not be included.)

string1 = string2—This form allows you to compare two strings, one or both of which may be given by dummy parameters specified when the batch file was invoked.

ERRORLEVEL number—This form allows you to test if the preceding DOS command ended with an ERRORLEVEL at least equal to <number>.

Let's give a few examples of IF commands using each type of condition. Here is a batch file to copy the FILE1 onto A:FILE2.

```
IF EXIST FILE1 COPY FILE1 A:FILE2
IF NOT EXIST FILE1 ECHO File Not Found
```

Note that the second IF statement prints an error message if FILE1 is not found.

In the above batch file, FILE1 and FILE2 were fixed. However, we may specify them as dummy parameters %FILE1 and %FILE2. In this case, the batch file would be

```
IF EXIST FILE1 COPY %FILE1 A:%FILE2
IF NOT EXIST %FILE1 ECHO File Not Found
```

Suppose that the batch file is called COPYA. Then the batch file would be invoked by giving the command

```
COPYA FILE1 FILE2
```

Here FILE1 is the file to be substituted for %FILE1 and FILE2 the file to be substituted for %FILE2.

Here is a command that checks whether two dummy parameters %1 and %2 are equal. If so, it prints out the error message "Incorrect input".

```
IF %1=%2 ECHO Incorrect input
```

DOS commands set a variable called ERRORLEVEL that indicates the level of completion achieved in executing the command. A value of ERRORLEVEL = 0 means that successful execution was achieved. The various values for ERRORLEVEL are found in the DOS manual. For example, here is the listing of values for the command RESTORE:

0—Normal completion

1—No files found to restore

3—Terminated by user

4—Terminated due to error

You may, for example, use the IF command to determine if ERRORLEVEL is at least 1 (non-normal completion), in which case, you could repeat the command.

SHIFT

This command allows you to use more than 10 dummy parameters. SHIFT causes dummy parameter 1 to become dummy parameter 0, parameter 2 to become dummy parameter 1, and so forth. To use more than 10 dummy parameters, you just type the desired parameter values on the command line and use SHIFT to get at the values past the tenth.

A Tip For Hard Disk Users

The PC/XT comes standard with a 10-megabyte hard disk. This disk is capable of containing thousands of files at one time. The tree-structured directory enables you to organize your files so that you may find you way around the disk.

I have organized my disk so that the only entries in the root directory are subdirectories and COMMAND.COM. For example, I have one directory for BASIC, one for DOS and all its commands, one for the BASIC compiler, one for PASCAL, one for each of the books I am working on, one for my word processor, and so forth. Very often, it is necessary to cross over subdirectory lines to perform a task. For example, to edit a file using the word processor, the file and the word processor must be in the same subdirectory. It is possible to solve this problem by keeping multiple copies of the word processor, one copy in each subdirectory possibly requiring editing. However, this is a clumsy solution that wastes disk space.

A better solution is to use an appropriate batch file to copy the word processor into the appropriate subdirectory at the time of editing. For instance, I use WordStar to write my books. I keep WordStar in a subdirectory of the the root directory called Wordstar. This subdirectory contains the three files: WS.COM, WSMSGS.OVR, and WSOVLY1.OVR . WordStar is started from DOS with the command WS. I have decided to retain this command name and to include a parameter to specify the subdirectory containing the files to be edited. I do this by creating a batch file called WS.BAT. To edit a file in the subdirectory IBM.2E, for example, I use the command

```
WS IBM.2E
```

Here is the contents of the file WS.BAT.

```
ECHO OFF
COPY C:WORDSTAR\WS.COM C:%
COPY C:WORDSTAR\WSMSGS.OVR C:%
COPY C:WORDSTAR\WSOVLY1.OVR C:%
CD %
WS
ERASE WS.COM
ERASE WSMSGS.OVR
ERASE WSMSGS.OVR
CD ..
```

The first command turns the echo off. The next three commands copy the three WordStar files to the directory specified by the parameter %. The next commands change the current directory and start WordStar (the copy that was just copied into the directory!). After you leave WordStar, the next three commands erase the WordStar files in the current directory and change the current directory back to the root directory.

Note that the above batch file works only for editing files in a directory that is one level down from the root directory. However, you may easily modify the batch file to allow directories that are two or more levels down the tree.

```
ANSWERS TO TEST YOUR UNDERSTANDING

1:  PAUSE Insert diskette containing FILE1
       COPY FILE1 FILE2
2:  LABEL1:
    ECHO OFF
    VOL
    GOTO LABEL1
3:  FOR PROG% IN (PROG1.BAS PROG2.BAS PROG3.BAS) DO BASIC
    PROG%
```

13.5   Redirecting Input and Output

In its default state, DOS receives its input from the keyboard and its output is sent to the display. However, you may tell DOS to redirect the input or output, replacing the standard devices with either a file or another device.

Redirecting Output

To a File To send output to a file, you may use a DOS command that begins with either > or >>. For example, to send output to the file MIDWEST\INVENT\MEMO.528, use either of the commands

```
>MIDWEST\INVENT\MEMO.528
>>MIDWEST\INVENT\MEMO.528
```

The two commands differ only in case the indicated file currently exists. The first command replaces the existing file, while the second adds to it.

The above commands may be used in conjunction with DOS commands or user programs. For example, here is a command that runs the user program PROG1 and writes the output to the file A:OUTPUT

```
PROG1 >A:OUTPUT
```

(If A:OUTPUT exists, it will be replaced with the output of PROG1.) Here is a command that writes the tree structure onto the file A:TREE .

```
TREE >A:TREE
```

Here is a batch file that runs PROG1 and PROG2 and accumulates the output from the two programs PROG1 and PROG2 in the file A:COMBINED

```
PROG1 >A:COMBINED
PROG2 >>A:COMBINED
```

Note that the second command appends to the file A:COMBINED which is started by the first command.

Redirection of output lasts only for the duration of the command or program. At the completion of the command or program, output is redirected back to the screen.

TEST YOUR UNDERSTANDING 1 (answer on page 342)

Write a command that:

- runs PROG1 and writes its output in the file TEST1
- runs PROG2 and writes its output on the display

Just as you may redirect output to a file, you may redirect output to a device. Just use a device name instead of a file name. For example, to redirect the output of PROG1 to the printer, you may use the command

```
PROG1 >PRN:
```

TEST YOUR UNDERSTANDING 2 (answer on page 342)

Write a command to write the contents of the current directory to the file DRECTRY.CUR .

Redirecting Input

You may redirect a program or DOS command to receive its input from a file. For example, to run the program PROG1 with input from the file A:DIRECT, we would use the command

```
PROG1 <A:DIRECT
```

Redirecting input is trickier than redirecting output. The file used for input must contain all the necessary program input. If you reach the end of the input file before all input needs are met, your program will wait indefinitely for the added input. If this happens, it will be necessary for you to return to DOS by pressing Ctrl-Break.

ANSWERS TO TEST YOUR UNDERSTANDING

```
1:   PROG1 >TEST1
     PROG2
2:   DIR >DRECTRY.CUR
```

13.6   BASIC 2.00

In a number of places in this book, we have introduced various features of BASIC 2.00 and BASICA 2.00. For example, we discussed the BASICA 2.00 enhancements to LINE and PAINT. In this section, let's discuss the changes in BASIC (and BASICA) that support the enhanced directory structure of DOS 2.00.

You may start BASIC 2.00 (or BASICA 2.00) the same way as BASIC 1.1. However, the file BASIC.COM must be either in the current directory or in a directory specified by the PATH command. Otherwise, you will get an error

```
Bad command or file name
```

Redirecting Input and Output

You may redirect input and output just as described in Section 5. You do this by invoking BASIC (or BASICA) with a command of the form:

```
BASIC [filespec] [<input] [>output]
```

Here **filespec** is the program you wish to run, **input** is the file from which to take input and **output** is the file to receive output. You may include any of the other options on the command line (such as /M, /F, and /C), but they must come after any redirection of input.

When you redirect input and/or output, error messages still are displayed on the screen (as well as going to the output file). In case trapping activity is specified, then that input will come from the required device (function keys, light pen, joy stick, communications adapter). Even if input is redirected, you may still stop a program using Ctrl-Break.

INPUT$ and input from the device KYBD: still are read from the keyboard. Output to the device SCRN: still goes to the screen.

Using Paths

In BASIC 2.00, you may use a path plus a filename anyplace BASIC 1.10 would allow a file specification. For example, LOAD, SAVE, and OPEN all may be used with paths.

Using Directories

BASIC 2.00 includes three commands for directory manipulation: CHDIR, MKDIR, RMDIR. These commands have identical functions to their DOS counterparts. However, in BASIC, the paths used with these commands must be inserted in quotation marks. For example, to change the current directory to the one specified by the path ..\NORTH\INVENT, you would use the BASIC statement

```
CHDIR "..\NORTH\INVENT"
```

If a file specification is given without a path, then BASIC assumes that the file belongs to the current directory.

Answers to Selected Exercises

Chapter 3

Section 3.1 (page 15)

1.
```
10 FOR J=1 TO 80
20     LOCATE 18,J: PRINT CHR$(196);
30 NEXT J
40 END
```

2.
```
10 FOR J=1 TO 25
20     LOCATE J,17: PRINT CHR$(179);
30 NEXT J
40 END
```

3.
```
10 FOR J=1 TO 80
20     LOCATE 13,J: PRINT CHR$(196);
30 NEXT J
40 FOR J = 1 TO 25
50     LOCATE J,40: PRINT CHR$(179);
60 NEXT J
65 LOCATE 13,40: PRINT CHR$(197)
70 END
```

4.
```
10 CLS
20 FOR J=1 TO 2
30     FOR K=1 TO 80
40         LOCATE 8*J,K: PRINT CHR$(196);
50     NEXT K
60 NEXT J
70 FOR J=1 TO 2
80     FOR K=1 TO 25
90         LOCATE K,26*J: PRINT CHR$(179)
100    NEXT K
110 NEXT J
112 LOCATE 8,26: PRINT CHR$(197);
113 LOCATE 8,52: PRINT CHR$(197);
114 LOCATE 16,26: PRINT CHR$(197);
115 LOCATE 16,52: PRINT CHR$(197);
120 END
```

5.  ```
    10  FOR J=1 TO 24
    20      LOCATE J,30: PRINT CHR$(219);
    30      LOCATE J,31: PRINT CHR$(219);
    40  NEXT J
    50  END
    ```

6.  ```
    10  FOR J=1 TO 24
    20      LOCATE J,J: PRINT CHR$(219);
    30  NEXT J
    40  END
    ```

7.  ```
    10  FOR J=1 TO 80
    20      LOCATE 12,J: PRINT CHR$(219);
    30  NEXT J
    40  FOR K=1 TO 3
    50      LOCATE 11,20+K*20: PRINT CHR$(219);
    60      LOCATE 13,20+K*20: PRINT CHR$(219);
    70  NEXT K
    80  END
    ```

8.  ```
    10  FOR J=1 TO 25
    20      LOCATE J,40: PRINT CHR$(219);
    30  NEXT J
    40  FOR J=0 TO 4
    50      LOCATE 5+5*J,39: PRINT CHR$(219);
    60  NEXT J
    70  END
    ```

9. Suppose that the name to be displayed is "JOHN JONES".
    ```
    10  LOCATE 2,2
    20  PRINT "JOHN JONES"
    30  LOCATE 1,1
    40  FOR J=1 TO 12
    50      LOCATE 1,J: PRINT CHR$(42);
    60      LOCATE 2,J: PRINT CHR$(42);
    70  NEXT J
    80  LOCATE 2,1: PRINT CHR$(42);
    90  LOCATE 2,12: PRINT CHR$(42);
    100 END
    ```

10. ```
    10  FOR J=1 TO 80
    20  LOCATE 16,J: PRINT CHR$(219);
    30  FOR J=0 TO 10
    40  LOCATE 15,8*J:PRINT CHR$(219);
    50  LOCATE 17,8*J:PRINT CHR$(219);
    60  LOCATE 8*J,18
    70  PRINT 8*J
    80  NEXT J
    90  END
    ```

11. ```
    10  INPUT "ASCII GRAPHICS CODE",A
    20  PRINT CHR$(A)
    30  END
    ```

12.
```
10 CLS
20 LOCATE 1,1
30 PRINT "COST"
40 LOCATE 1,2
50 PRINT "PRICE"
60 LOCATE 1,3
70 PRINT "INDEX"
80 FOR J=1 TO 25
90 LOCATE J,6: PRINT CHR$(219)
100 NEXT J
110 FOR J=1 TO 80
120 LOCATE 22,J: PRINT CHR$(219)
130 NEXT J
140 DATA J,F,M,A,M,J,J,A,S,O,N,D
150 FOR J=1 TO 12
160 READ A$
170 LOCATE 21,6*J: PRINT CHR$(219)
180 LOCATE 23,6*J: PRINT CHR$(219)
190 LOCATE 6*J,24
200 PRINT A$
210 NEXT J
220 LOCATE 72,25
230 PRINT "MONTH"
240 END
```

Section 3.2 (page 23)

2. Delete lines 20-30. Change line 50 to read: INPUT A(M)

3. Type in numbers A(M) as prompted. (Remember: No commas or dollar signs.)

4. Mil. $ should be printed at position 1,2. There is no room for vertical label 1.0. Print .9, .8, .7, ..., .1, respectively, in rows 4, 6, 8, 10, 12, 14, 16, 18, and 20 .

Section 3.3 (page 29)

1. `10 COLOR 5,1`   2. `10 COLOR 12,0`

3. `10 PSET (200,80), 1`   4. `10 COLOR 3,0`
                                `20 PSET (100,100), 2`

5. `10 PSET STEP (-200,-100)` 6. `10 PSET STEP (100,0)`

Section 3.4 (page 40)

1. `10 LINE (20,50)-(40,100)`   2. `10 LINE -(250,150),2`

3. `10 LINE (125,50)-STEP(100,75),1`

4. `10 LINE (10,20)-(200,150),,B`

5. `10 LINE (10,20)-(200,150),3,BF`

6. `10 CIRCLE (30,50),20`

7. `10 CIRCLE (30,50),20,,1.5,3.1`

8.  ```
    10 CIRCLE (30,50),20,,-1.5,3.1
    ```

9.  ```
    10 CLS:KEY OFF: SCREEN 2
    20 CIRCLE (320,100),100
    30 FOR J=0 TO 6.28 STEP .1
    40 X=320+100*COS(J)
    50 Y=100+100*SIN(J)
    60 LINE (320,100)-(X,Y)
    70 LINE (320,100)-(X,Y),0
    80 NEXT J
    ```

Section 3.8 (page 61)

1. (10,10)-(89,49)

2. (0,0)-(639,15) (in high resolution mode)

3.  ```
    DIM Z%(212)
    ```

4.  ```
    DIM Z%(327)
    ```

5. Use the program given in the text.

6. Use the program given in the text.

7.  ```
    10 SCREEN 0
    20 CLS
    30 PRINT CHR$(2);
    40 DIM Z%(9)
    50 GET (0,0)-(7,7),Z%
    ```

8.  ```
    60 SCREEN 1
    70 PUT (0,0), Z%
    80 PUT (50,50), Z%
    90 PUT (0,100), Z%
    ```

9.  ```
    10 SCREEN 0
    20 CLS
    30 PRINT CHR$(2);
    40 DIM Z%(9)
    50 GET (0,0)-(7,7),Z%
    60 SCREEN 1
    70 FOR J=0 TO 312
    80     PUT (J,72), Z%
    90     PUT (J,72), Z%
    100 NEXT J
    ```

10. ```
    10 SCREEN 0
    20 CLS
    30 PRINT CHR$(2);
    40 DIM Z%(9)
    50 GET (0,0)-(7,7),Z%
    60 SCREEN 1
    70 FOR J=0 TO 312
    80     PUT (J,200*J/320), Z%
    90     PUT (J,200*J/320), Z%
    100 NEXT J
    ```

Chapter 4

Section 4.2 (page 80)

1. "A"
2. "c"
3.
```
10 A$=INKEY$
20 IF A$<>"" THEN PRINT A$;
30 GOTO 10
```

Section 4.3 (page 85)

1. `KEY 5, ""`
2. `KEY 1, "LIST"+CHR$(13)`
3. `10 KEY 1, "CLS"+CHR$(13)+"NEW"+CHR$(13)`
4. Let the first line of each subroutine be:

   `FOR J=1 TO 4:KEY(J) STOP :NEXT J`

   Let the last line of each subroutine be:

   `FOR J=1 TO 4:KEY(J) ON :NEXT J`
5. `KEY(11) ON`

Chapter 5

Section 5.2 (page 119)

1.
```
10 DATA 5.7,-11.4,123,485,49
20 OPEN "NUMBERS" FOR OUTPUT AS #1
30 FOR J=1 TO 5
40     READ A
50     WRITE #1, A
60 NEXT J
70 CLOSE 1
80 END
```

2.
```
10 OPEN "NUMBERS" FOR INPUT AS #1
20 FOR J=1 TO 5
30     INPUT #1,A
40     PRINT A
50 NEXT J
60 CLOSE 1
70 END
```

3.
```
10 OPEN "NUMBERS" FOR APPEND AS #1
20 DATA 5, 78, 4.79, -1.27
30 FOR J=1 TO 4
40     READ A
50     WRITE#1,A
60 NEXT J
```

```
70 CLOSE 1
80 END
```

4.
```
10 OPEN "NUMBERS" FOR INPUT AS #1
20 FOR J = 1 TO 9
30     INPUT #1, A
40     PRINT A
50 NEXT J
60 CLOSE 1
70 END
```

5.
```
10 OPEN "CHECKS" FOR OUTPUT AS #1
20 PRINT "TYPE CHECK DATA ITEMS REQUESTED."
30 PRINT "FOLLOW EACH ITEM BY A CARRIAGE RETURN."
40 OPEN "CHECKS" FOR OUTPUT AS #1
50 INPUT "CHECK #";A
60 INPUT "DATE";B$
70 INPUT "PAYEE";C$
80 INPUT "AMOUNT(NO $)";D
90 INPUT "EXPLANATION";E$
100 WRITE #1,A,B$,C$,D,E$
110 INPUT "ANOTHER CHECK(Y/N)";F$
120 CLS
130 IF F$ = "Y" THEN 20
140 CLOSE
150 GOTO 1000
1000 END
```

6.
```
10 OPEN "CHECKS" FOR INPUT AS #1
20 IF EOF(1) THEN GOTO 500
30 INPUT #1, A,B$,C$,D,E$
40 S=S+D
50 GOTO 30
100 CLOSE
110 PRINT "TOTAL OF CHECKS IS",S
120 GOTO 1000
1000 END
```

Section 5.3 (page 123)

1. "MY","DOG","SAM", 1234<ENTER>
2. MYDOGSAM1234<ENTER>
3. MY,DOG,SAM,1234<ENTER>
4. "MY DOG, ",SAM,1234<ENTER>
5. MY
6. "MY","DOG","SAM", 1234
7. MYDOGSAM1234
   MY
   MY DOG,
8.
```
10 INPUT#1,E$
20 PRINT E$;
```

```
30 INPUT#1,E$
40 PRINT " ";E$
50 INPUT#1,E$
60 PRINT E$
```

Section 5.4 (page 130)

1.
```
10 OPEN "TELEPHON" AS #1 LEN=72
20 FIELD #1, 20 AS NAME$, 25 AS ADDRESS$, 10 AS CITY$,
   2 AS STATE$, 5 AS ZIP$, 10 AS TELEPHONE$
30 CLS
40 INPUT "NAME";A$
50 INPUT "STREET ADDRESS";B$
60 INPUT "CITY";C$
70 INPUT "STATE";D$
80 INPUT "ZIP CODE";E$
90 INPUT "TELEPHONE NUMBER";F$
100 LSET NAME$=A$
110 LSET ADDRESS$=B$
120 LSET CITY$=C$
130 LSET STATE$=D$
140 LSET ZIP$=E$
150 LSET TELEPHONE$=F$
160 PUT #1, LOF(#1)+1
170 INPUT "ANOTHER ENTRY (Y/N)";G$
180 IF G$="Y" THEN 20 ELSE 200
190 CLOSE #1
200 END
```

2.
```
10 OPEN "SALES" AS #1 LEN=16
20 FIELD #1, 4 AS NUM1$, 4 AS NUM2$, 4 AS NUM3$, 4 AS
   NUM4$
30 FOR J=1 TO 20
40    GET #1, J
50    PRINT CVS(NUM1$), CVS(NUM2$), CVS(NUM3$),
         CVS(NUM4$)
60 NEXT J
70 CLOSE #1
80 END
```

Section 5.7 (page 148)

1. (a)
```
10 S=0
20 FOR J=1 TO 50
30       S=S+J^2
40 NEXT J
50 PRINT S
60 END
```
(b) Type SAVE "SQUARES",A

2. (a)
```
100  S = 0
110  FOR J=1 TO 30
120       S=S + S+J^3
130  NEXT J
140  PRINT S
150  END
```
    (b)   Type MERGE "SQUARES"

    (c)   Type LIST

    (d)   DELETE 60 (This is the END of SQUARES.) Type RUN.

    (e)   Type SAVE "COMBINED",A (The A is optional.)

3. Type LOAD "COMBINED"

4. Type ERASE "SQUARES"

Chapter 7

Section 7.2 (page 205)

1.
```
10 ON ERROR GOTO 1000
1000 RESUME
```

2.
```
10 ON ERROR GOTO 1000
1000 IF ERR=13 THEN 30 ELSE END
1010 IF ERL=500 THEN 40 ELSE END
1020 PRINT "Type Mismatch Error in Line 500"
1030 RESUME 600
```

Section 7.4 (page 226)

1. CHAIN MERGE "L"

2. End program "A" with the statement: CHAIN "B" . End program "B" with the statement CHAIN "C" .

Index

Accumulator, base register, 301
Adding data to a sequential file, 118
Addresses with a BASIC program, 159
Advanced Basic, 1, 34
Alternate character set, 2
AND, 168, 171, 173
Angle, 35, 52, 56
APPEND, 118
Arc, 34
Array, 157
ASCII character, 165
ASCII code, 86, 87, 100, 165, 171, 260
ASCII format, 147
Aspect ratio, 36, 38
Assembler, 308
Assembly language, 299
Assembly language subroutine, 301
ASSIGN, 328
Asynchronous communications adapter,
   249

Background color, 27
Background mode (music), 76
BACKUP, 329
Bad File Mode error, 226
Bad File Number error, 260
Bar chart, 18
Bar Chart Definition Module, 103, 104
BAR CHART GENERATOR, 1, 5, 67, 103,
   186, 199, 205
BAR CHART GENERATOR, listing of, 206
Bar chart in text mode, 18
BASCOM, 286
BASCOM.LIB, 287, 292
Base pointer, 300
BASIC 2.00, 343
BASIC compiler, 2, 142, 281
BASIC file commands, 144
BASIC interpreter, 157, 281, 312
BASIC line buffer, 79
BASIC stack, 157
BASIC workspace, 311
BASIC's segment, 158
BASICA, 34
BASRUN.LIB, 287, 292
Batch file, 334

Baud rate, 252
BEEP, 71
Beethoven, 73
Binary number, 149, 153
Binary representation of numbers, 150
Binary Source File error, 296
BIOS, 158
Bit, 153
BLOAD, 61, 314
Boundary for PAINT, 47
BREAK, 330
BSAVE, 61, 314
Bubble sort, 139, 141
Bubble sort for file records, 142
Bubble sort for string data, 143
Bubble sort, efficiency of, 142
Buffer, 123
Byte, 124, 154
Byte operations, 170
   applications of, 170
Byte, operations on, 166

Cable between two PC's, 250
CALL, 303, 304, 306, 306, 307
Capitalization function, 170
Carriage return (on printer), 229
Cartesian coordinates, 62
Center, 35
Centroid, 50, 51
CHAIN, 224, 225, 295
CHAIN MERGE, 226
CHAIN MERGE . . DELETE, 226
Changing the current directory, 321
CHDIR, 321
Checking the date integrity of a diskette or
   disk, 326
CHKDSK, 326
Circle, 30, 34, 36
Circular arc, 34
CLEAR, 312
CLOSE, 123
CLOSE (file), 113
CLOSEing a sequential file, 112
CLS, 330
Code segment, 300
Color, 27, 27

Color/graphics adapter, 24
Color/graphics interface, 24, 28
COM(n) OFF, 264
COM(n) ON, 263
COM(n) STOP, 264
COM1:, 249
COM2:, 249
COMMON, 224, 225, 295
Communications, 2, 296
Communications adapter, 249
Communications buffer, 158, 254, 255
   monitoring status, 258
Communications file, 253, 254
   OPENing, 255
   reading, 257
   WRITEing, 256
Communications protocol, 260
COMP, 325
Compare two diskettes, 326
Comparing file contents, 325
Compiled program, 282
Compiler, 281
   differences between interpreter and, 294
   error messages, 296
   libraries, 285, 287
   listing, 287
   parameters, 294
Compressed format, 146
Computer art, 41
Computer communications, 249
Contents of a memory location, 155
Control routine, 8, 199, 206
Converting binary to decimal, 150
Converting decimal to binary, 153
Convex figure, 50, 51
Coordinate system, 5
COPY, 250, 309, 323
Count register, 301
Creating a directory, 322
Ctrl-break, 15
Current directory, 318
Cursor, turning on and off, 96
Custom character sets (screen), 176, 191
CVD, 127
CVI, 127
CVS, 126, 127

Data bit, 253
Data file, 111
Data Input Module, 107
Data register, 300, 301, 301
Data segment, 300
DATE, 325
DEBUG, 158
Decimal number, 165

Decimal numbers, 153
Decimal representation of numbers,
   149
DEF SEG, 79, 159, 160, 304
DEF USR, 305
DEFDBl, 225
DEFINT, 225
DEFSNG, 225
Degree, 34
Deleting a directory, 323
Delimiter, 120
Destination index register, 300
Device Timeout, 247
Device Timeout error, 262
DIR, 325
Directories in BASIC 2.00, 343
Directory, 145, 317
   displaying contents of, 325
DISKCOMP, 326
DOS, 157
DOS 2.00, 2, 317
Dot matrix printer, 228
Double-precision number, 165, 192, 197
DRAW, 47, 51
DRAWBAR routine, 69, 188

ECHO, 335, 336
EDLIN, 309
Ellipse, 37, 38
End of File (EOF), 117, 118
EOF (communications), 258
EPSON printer, 2, 227
ERASE, 323
Erasing files, 145
ERL, 204
ERR, 204
ERROR, 205
Error Trapping, 203
   line, 225
   routine, 204
   statement, 204
ERRORLEVEL, 338
ESC, 232
Escape sequences, 232
Event trapping, 80, 82
Exclusive or, 169
EXIST, 338
Extended ASCII code, 86, 88, 90
Extra segment, 300

FIELD, 125, 126
Field Overflow, 130
File, 2, 111
File buffer, 123
File commands, 145

FILES, 145
Files, number allowed to be open
    simultaneously, 113
FOR in a batch file, 337
FOR . . . NEXT, 295
Foreground color, 27
Forground mode (music), 76
FORMAT, 327
Function key, 80, 83, 85, 90, 296
Function, user-defined, 225

GET (graphics), 59, 172, 244
GET (random access files), 126
GOTO in a batch file, 336
GRAFTRAX-80, 227
GRAFTRAX-PLUS, 227
GRAPHICS, 330
Graphics characters, 9, 12
Graphics coordinates, 25
Graphics screen dump, 243

Half-duplex, 261
Hard disk, 339
Hertz, 73
Hexadecimal digits, 153
Hexadecimal number, 149, 153, 165
High-resolution graphics mode, 24
Home, 88

IBM monochrome display, 28
IBM printer, 2, 227
IF in a batch file, 338
Infinite loop, 15
Initialization, 8
Initialization Routine, 199, 200, 202
INKEY$, 78, 80, 89
INPUT #, 116, 121, 122
Input Past End error, 117
Input routine, 2, 72, 77
Inputting characters, 91
Inputting numbers, 96
Inputting strings, 96
Inscribed polygon, 44
Integer, 162
Integer division, 152

Joystick, 271
    trapping activity of, 277

KEY LIST, 81
KEY OFF, 81
KEY ON, 81
KEY(n) OFF, 84, 85
KEY(n) ON, 82, 85
KEY(n) STOP, 84, 85

Keyboard buffer, 78
    clearing, 79
KEYIN routine, 91, 93
KILL, 145

Labels in batch files, 336
LAINT, 2
Last point referenced, 25, 51
Least significant bit, 162
Left justification, 125
Legato, 74
LEN, 125
Length of file, 127
Light pen, 267
Limiting the size of BASIC's workspace,
    158
LINE, 2, 30, 30, 297
Line buffer, 79
Line feed (on printer), 229
Line graphics, 9
LINE, B-options, 32, 32
LINE, using style with, 180
LINK, 282, 285
Linker, 282, 285
List file, 285, 286
List Manager Program, 131
LOC, 128
LOC (communications), 258
Locate, 9, 32
LOF, 127
LOF (communications), 258
Logical operations on words, 167
LPRINT, 229
LPRINT USING, 229
LSET, 125

Machine language, 281, 299
Machine language subroutine, 2, 158, 299
Macro Assembler, 309
Mailing labels, printing, 230
Mailing list, reading, 119
Medium-resolution graphics mode, 24
Memory, 154
    address, 2, 155, 159
    location, 155
    locations, some useful, 192
    management, 149
    map, 157
MERGE, 147
Merging programs, 147
Mixing text and graphics, 32
MDK$, 127
MKDIR, 322
MKI$, 127
MKS$, 127,

Mnemonic form, 308
MOD, 152
MODE, 327
Modified bubble sort, 143
Monochrome display interface, 28
Moonlight Sonata, 73
Most significant bit, 162
Music, 73
MX-100, 227
MX-80, 227

NAME, 146
Non-convex figure, 50
Non-executable statements, 202, 295
NOT, 167
NUMBERCK routine, 101

Object code, 282, 284
Object module, 285
Octave, 75
Offset, 160, 301, 303
Offset address, 155
ON COM(n), 263
ON ERROR GOTO, 203
ON KEY(n) GOSUB, 82
ON PEN GOSUB, 271
OPEN, 123
OPEN (Communications), 256
OPEN (File), 113
OPENing a sequential file, 112
OR, 168, 173
Order of operations, 152

PAINT, 2, 47, 51, 297
PAINT, using style with, 181
Palette, 27, 32
Parameters (compiler), 286
Parametric equations for an ellipse, 39
Parity, 252
Parity bit, 252
Parity error, 252
Path, 319, 330
    in BASIC 2.00, 343
PAUSE, 335, 336
PEEK, 79, 160, 164, 196, 312
PEN OFF, 269, 271
PEN ON, 268, 271
PEN STOP, 271
PEN(n), 268
Pi, 34, 36
Pie chart, 44, 46
Pixel, 28, 32, 59
Planetary orbit, 39
Planning large programs, 5, 224
PLAY, 74

PLOTSTRING routine, 183
Plotter, 277
Plotting characters, 183
Pointer register, 300
POKE, 79, 160, 312
Poll of light pen, 268
Polygon, 41
POP, 305, 306
Precedence of operations, 152
Prerequisities, 2
PRESET, 28, 173
PRINT, 9, 32, 331
PRINT #, 121, 122
Print head, 228
PRINT USING, 9, 32, 45
Printer buffer, 229
Printer communications, 229
Printer graphics, 236
Printer Not Ready error, 247
Program execution, 301
Program file, 111
Program requirements, 5, 6
Protected format, 147
PSET, 28, 173
PUSH, 305
PUT, 175   (communications), 257
    (graphics), 60, 172

Radian, 34, 35
Radius, 35
RAM, 2, 162
Random access file, 124, 131
Random file buffer, 130
    setting size of, 130
Reading data items from a file, 116
Recalling a graphics image on diskette, 58
Record, 124
Record length, 125, 127
RECOVER, 332
Rectangle, 30
Redirecting input, 342
Redirecting input and output in BASIC, 343
Redirecting output, 341
Redirecting printer output to communications adapter, 328
Register, 299
Regular polygon, 42
Relative coordinates, 25, 52
Relative motion, 54, 55
REM, 336
Removing a directory, 323
RENAME, 326
Rename a file, 146, 326
RENUM, 203

Rest, 75
RESTORE, 332
RET, 307
RGB monitor, 29
Right justification, 125
RMDIR, 323
ROM, 157, 162
Root directory, 318
Rotate a word, 302
RS232-C interface, 2, 249, 277
RSET, 125
Run file, 285

SAVE, A, 147
SAVE, A, 226
Saving a graphics impage on diskette, 58
Saving a program, 146
Saving a screen image on diskette, 61
Scales, 56
SCREEN, 24, 25
Screen coordinates, 63, 64
Screen dump, 243
SCREENIN routine, 96
Segment, 160
    address, 155, 159, 306
    register, 300
Sequential file, 112, 120, 124
    adding data to, 118
Setting communications interface
        parameters, 328
Setting display parameters, 327
Setting width of print line, 327
Severe error, 297
SHIFT, 335, 339
Shift operation, 166
Signed number, 163
Single-precision number, 165, 192
Small Assembler, 310
Sorting, 138, 139
    algorithm, 2
    techniques, 138
Sound, 71, 73
Source Code, 282, 283
Source file, 309
Source index register, 300
Staccato, 74
Stack, 305
    pointer, 300
    segment, 300
STEP, 25, 30
STICK(n), 273
Stop bit, 253
STRIG OFF, 274
STRIG ON, 274

STRIG(n), 274
STRIG(n) OFF, 274
STRIG(n) STOP, 274
String space, 157
STRING$, 13
Strings, sorting, 143
Style (music), 75
Subdirectory, 317
Switching between interfaces, 29

Telephone directory, 128
    program, 115
Tempo, 75
Text mode, 9, 24
TIME, 325
Tokenized format, 147
Top of memory, 157
Trapping communications, 263
TREE, 333
Tree structure, 318
Truncate operation, 166
Two's complement, 163

User-defined key, 80
USR, 304, 306

VAL, 100, 101
Variable passed to a machine language
        subroutine, 303
VARPTR, 161, 196
VER, 333
VERIFY, 333
VIEW, 2, 62, 66, 297
VIEW SCREEN, 64, 66
VOL, 334

WHILE . . . WEND, 295
WIDTH (on printer), 245
WINDOW, 2, 62, 63, 64, 66, 297
WINDOW SCREEN, 63
WRITE #, 114, 120
WRITEing data items to a sequential file,
        114

X-axis, 5, 14
    labels, 6
    title, 6
X-coordinate, 51
XON-XOFF protocol, 260
XOR, 169, 174

Y-axis, 5, 14
Y-coordinate, 51

Documentation for Optional Program Diskette

All the 59 major programs in this book are available on diskette. You may order this diskette at your local bookseller or via the attached order envelope. Using the diskette, you may use the programs in the book without going through the somewhat painful tasks of typing and debugging.

Using the Program Diskette

1. If you are using the Program Diskette for the first time, make a backup copy just as you would for any master diskette.

2. Start your computer, load BASIC (or BASICA) and obtain the BASIC Ok prompt. (Follow the procedure on page 23.) Note that the Program Diskette does not contain DOS or BASIC. You must use your own copies of these programs. Note also that some programs require BASICA rather than BASIC. If in doubt, use BASICA.

3. The programs on the diskette are listed below by program name and page number. To run a program, first insert the Program Diskette. You may use either disk drive. If you insert the Program Diskette into the current drive, type

    `RUN "<program name>"`

    and press ENTER. For example, to run the program BARGEN type

    `RUN "BARGEN"`

    and press ENTER. If you insert your Program Diskette into a drive other than the current drive, you must include a drive designation, as in

    `RUN "B:BARGEN"`

4. When the program is finished, BASIC will redisplay the Ok prompt. You may then rerun the same program by typing RUN and pressing ENTER or you may run another program by giving a command as described in 3.

5. To interrupt a program, simultaneously press Ctrl and Break.

6. Some of the files on diskette are not complete programs, but are subroutines which you may incorporate in your own programs. To save space on the diskette, all files have been saved in standard format.

359

However, in order to use MERGE to incorporate one of these subroutines into a program, it will be first necessary to resave it in ASCII format. For example, to resave NUMERCK in ASCII format, first obtain the BASIC prompt Ok and type

`LOAD "NUMBERCK"`

and press ENTER. When BASIC redisplays the Ok prompt, type

`SAVE "NUMBERCK", A`

and press ENTER. You may find that it is most convenient to resave your file to be merged (in this example NUBMERCK) on your working diskette rather than on the program diskette.

Program Diskette Contents

Name	Pg	Name	Pg	Name	Pg
HORZLINE	13	KEYIN	93	PHI	178
BLINKLNE	14	SCREENIN	99	LOADCHAR	179
AXES	15	NUMBERCK	101	EXPNDCHR	179
BARTXT	22	BARDEF	104	PLOTSTR	184
TOCOLOR	29	DATAINPT	107	CONTROL	200
TOMONO	29	SQUARES	114	INIT	200
ORBIT	39	TELEINPT	115	BARGEN	206
POLYGON1	41	NUMBERS	117	LABELS1	231
POLYGON2	43	TELESRCH	117	LABELS2	231
PIE	46	MAILLBL	118	LABELS3	232
DRAWDISP	54	TELEAPND	119	PRINTER1	241
SAIL1	56	TELERND	130	PRINTER2	241
SAIL2	57	LISTMNGR	133	SCRDUMP	246
GETLTTR	60	BUBBLE1	141	PCTALK	261
MOVLTTR	60	BUBBLE2	142	COLORS	269
EXPNDREC	64	BUBBLE3	143	JOYSTCK1	274
DRAWBAR	69,188	BUBBLE4	144	JOYSTCK2	276
INPUT	72	BINTODEC	150	ML	312
SOUNDART	73	DECTOBIN	153	CREATFIL	313
ARITH	83	CAPITALS	172		

TIME	Specify the current time.	**TIME [hh:mm:ss.xx]**	
TREE	Display the current tree structure of a directory.	**TREE [d:] [/F]**	
TYPE	Display the contents of a file.	**TYPE [d:] [path] file-spec**	
VER	Display the DOS version number.	**VER**	
VERIFY	Enable or disable verification.	**VERIFY [ON OFF]**	
VOL	Display the volume label.	**VOL [d:]**	

71	Disk not ready
72	Disk media error
73	Advanced feature
74	Rename across disks
75	Path/file access error
76	Path not found
-	Unprintable error
-	Incorrect DOS version

PEN(n)	Read light pen coordinates, service routine **n**. (See BASIC MANUAL)	PEN(n)
STICK	Return the x-coordinate (**n**=0 or 1) or y-coordinate (**n**=2 or 3) of joystick A or B.	STICK(n)
STRIG	Enables trapping of joystick buttons.	STRIG ON STRIG OFF
STRIG(n)	Returns the status of joystick buttons.	STRIG(n)
WAIT	Await input from port.	WAIT port,n[,m]

L. ERROR TRAPPING

ERR	Returns the error code of the most recent error.	ERR
ERL	Returns the program line number that generated the most recent error.	ERL
ERROR	Simulates the occurrence of error **n**.	ERROR n
ON ERROR	On error, transfer control to **line**.	ON ERROR GOTO line
RESUME	Clear error condition and transfer control to line after error line (NEXT), to the error line ([0]) or to line.	RESUME [0] RESUME NEXT RESUME line

M. MACHINE LANGUAGE INTERFACE

BLOAD	Load a binary file from diskette into memory beginning at **offset**.	BLOAD filespec [,offset]
BSAVE	Save a memory image beginning at **offset** and continuing for **length** bytes.	BSAVE filespec, offset,length
CALL	Call a machine language subroutine.	CALL numericvariable [(variable [,variable]...)]
DEF SEG	Define the current segment of memory.	DEF SEG [=address]
DEFUSR	Define the starting address of a machine-language subroutine.	DEF USR[digit]= offset
PEEK	Returns the contents of the indicated memory location.	PEEK(address)
POKE	Stores the indicated value in the specified memory location.	POKE address, value
USR	Call user-defined machine language subroutine n with argument **x**.	USR[digit](x)

VARPTR	Return the offset address of the indicated variable or file control block.	VARPTR(variable) VARPTR(#filenumber)

N. MISCELLANEOUS STATEMENTS AND FUNCTIONS

CHAIN	Pass control to another program.	CHAIN [MERGE] filespec [,line] [,ALL] [,DELETE range]]]
COMMON	Specify variables to be passed to a CHAINed program.	COMMON variable [,variable]...
MOTOR	Turn cassette motor on/off.	MOTOR state
ON TIMER	Transfers control after a given period of time.	ON TIMER(n) GOSUB line
REM	Remark. Rest of line ignored.	REM remark ' remark

O. PRINTER

LLIST	List program lines on the printer.	LLIST [line[-line]]
LPRINT	Print constants and values of variables.	LPRINT [list of expressions]
LPRINT USING	Print formatted numerical data.	LPRINT USING x$; list of expressions[;]